Isles of the Dead?

The setting and function of the Bronze Age chambered cairns and cists of the Isles of Scilly

Katharine Sawyer

ARCHAEOPRESS ARCHAEOLOGY

ARCHAEOPRESS PUBLISHING LTD

Gordon House
276 Banbury Road
Oxford OX2 7ED

www.archaeopress.com

ISBN 978 1 78491 113 3
ISBN 978 1 78491 114 0 (e-Pdf)

© Archaeopress and K Sawyer 2015

Printed and bound in Great Britain by
Marston Book Services Ltd, Oxfordshire

This book is available direct from Archaeopress or from our website www.archaeopress.com

The author and publisher gratefully acknowledge the permission granted
to reproduce the copyright material in this book.

Every effort has been made to trace copyright holders and to obtain their permission for the use of copyright material.
The author and publisher apologise for any errors or omissions and would be grateful if notified of any
corrections that should be incorporated in future reprints or editions of this book.

Table of contents

List of illustrations and tables

Unless otherwise stated, all photographs are by the author

Table

Appendix 3

Figure

Summary

The number and density of megalithic chambered cairns in the Isles of Scilly, a small archipelago 45km from Land's End, Cornwall, has been remarked upon since the 18th century. It has been suggested that they were the burial places of people from elsewhere, whose remains were brought to the islands. This has led to Scilly being described as the 'Isles of the Dead'. Other interpretations are that they were shrines to ensure soil fertility or that they were navigational markers.

This study examines the evidence about these structures, generally known as entrance graves, and the associated cist graves, as well as the human remains and artefacts found in them. The research seeks to understand how the entrance graves were used, their dating, their positioning in the islands and any links with megalithic burial chambers in other parts of the British Isles and Brittany.

The findings indicate that the entrance graves were indeed used for burial and that a wide range of grave goods, including prestige items such as faience, glass and pumice, were placed in them. The pottery, in particular, shows the development of a specific island identity. The use of GIS-based mapping to study the setting of the sites confirms the selection of hilltop and upper hillslope locations in the majority of cases.

The dating of these sites, including the first radiocarbon determinations from them, shows a period of use between c2000 and 1250 cal BC, with the cists slightly pre-dating the entrance graves. This coincides with the inundation of a significant area of the islands and suggests that the construction of large numbers of entrance graves may have been a response to this loss of land and a way of 'holding the line' against the depredations of the sea.

The comparison of the Scillonian entrance graves with sites in west Cornwall, south-east Ireland, south-west Scotland, the Channel Islands and Brittany, which have been held to be related, indicates that only in Cornwall are there any real similarities.

Acknowledgements

This book is largely based on the results of PhD research, carried out at the University of Exeter between 2006 and 2013, which would not have been completed without the assistance of a number of people.

Firstly, my supervisor, Professor Anthony Harding, was a source of guidance throughout and my second supervisor, Professor Robert Van de Noort, and mentor, Professor Steve Rippon, were always available with support and encouragement. Thanks must also go to my examiners, Professor Chris Scarre of the University of Durham and Professor Alan Outram, for their advice.

In addition, my gratitude goes to Dr Jacqui Mulville of Cardiff University, who prepared the successful application to ORADS for funding for radiocarbon dating and obtained the bone samples, to Dr Anthony Newton of the University of Edinburgh, for testing the pumice from Nornour and to Yvonne Oates of Cornwall College, for assistance with all things GIS.

In Scilly and Cornwall, I have benefited greatly from discussions with Sarnia Butcher and Henrietta Quinnell and with Charlie Johns and Dr Andy Jones of Cornwall Archaeological Unit, Cornwall Council.

My research in museums and libraries was made easier by the assistance of Jane Marley, Curator of Archaeology and World Cultures at the Royal Cornwall Museum, Angela Broome, Librarian of the Royal Institution of Cornwall's Courtney Library, Clare Jones, Curatorial Assistant at Torquay Museum, Dr Ben Roberts, former Curator of the European Bronze Age, British Museum and, in particular, Amanda Martin, Curator of the Isles of Scilly Museum. Thanks are also due to Amanda for help in deciphering and translating George Bonsor's notebooks.

The Cornwall Heritage Trust and the Aileen Fox Fund provided grants to assist with travel costs and my good friends, Paul and Teri Roberts, offered hospitality. The Isles of Scilly Wildlife Trust cleared the vegetation from a number of sites and members of the St Mary's Boatmen's Association, especially Joe Pender, helped me with trips to the uninhabited islands. My thanks go to all of them.

Many visitors to Scilly, who joined my guided walks to the archaeological sites, challenged and inspired me with their questions and insights. In particular, I thank Steve and Chrissie Jackson, Denise and the late Nick Hart and Martin and Gill Schofield for their friendship and interest.

Last but not least, my heartfelt thanks go to my husband, Chas Wood, for his unfailing love, support and encouragement throughout the six years of my research. This book is dedicated to him and to the memory of my beloved parents, Hal and Bea Sawyer, who first inspired in me a fascination with our ancient past.

Chapter 1

Introduction

1.1 The Isles of Scilly

The Isles of Scilly form a tiny archipelago comprising more than 200 islands and rocks and lying some 45km west-south-west of Land's End, Cornwall; the islands form the most south-westerly part of the British Isles. The location of the islands is shown in figure 1.1 and their layout in figure 1.2.

Geologically, the islands are a granite pluton, one of a chain which includes Dartmoor, Bodmin Moor and the Land's End peninsula, but differing from the others in having little in the way of metallic minerals; the Scilly granite is approximately 290 million years old (Scourse 2006b). The total landmass of the islands is now about 15km² but, over the past 10,000 years, sea levels have risen more than 30m,

inundating large areas of low-lying ground and dividing what was once a single main landmass of more than 90 km² into the present-day cluster of islands (Charman et al. 2012a).

Although Scilly is geographically close to Cornwall, there are significant cultural differences between the two. Because of the small size of the islands and because of their position at the western entrance to the English Channel, as shown in figure 1.1, they have experienced considerable population change, many migrants to the islands coming from much further away than Cornwall.

From the mid 16th to the early 20th centuries the construction of several phases of defensive works in Scilly led to the arrival of significant numbers of soldiers and

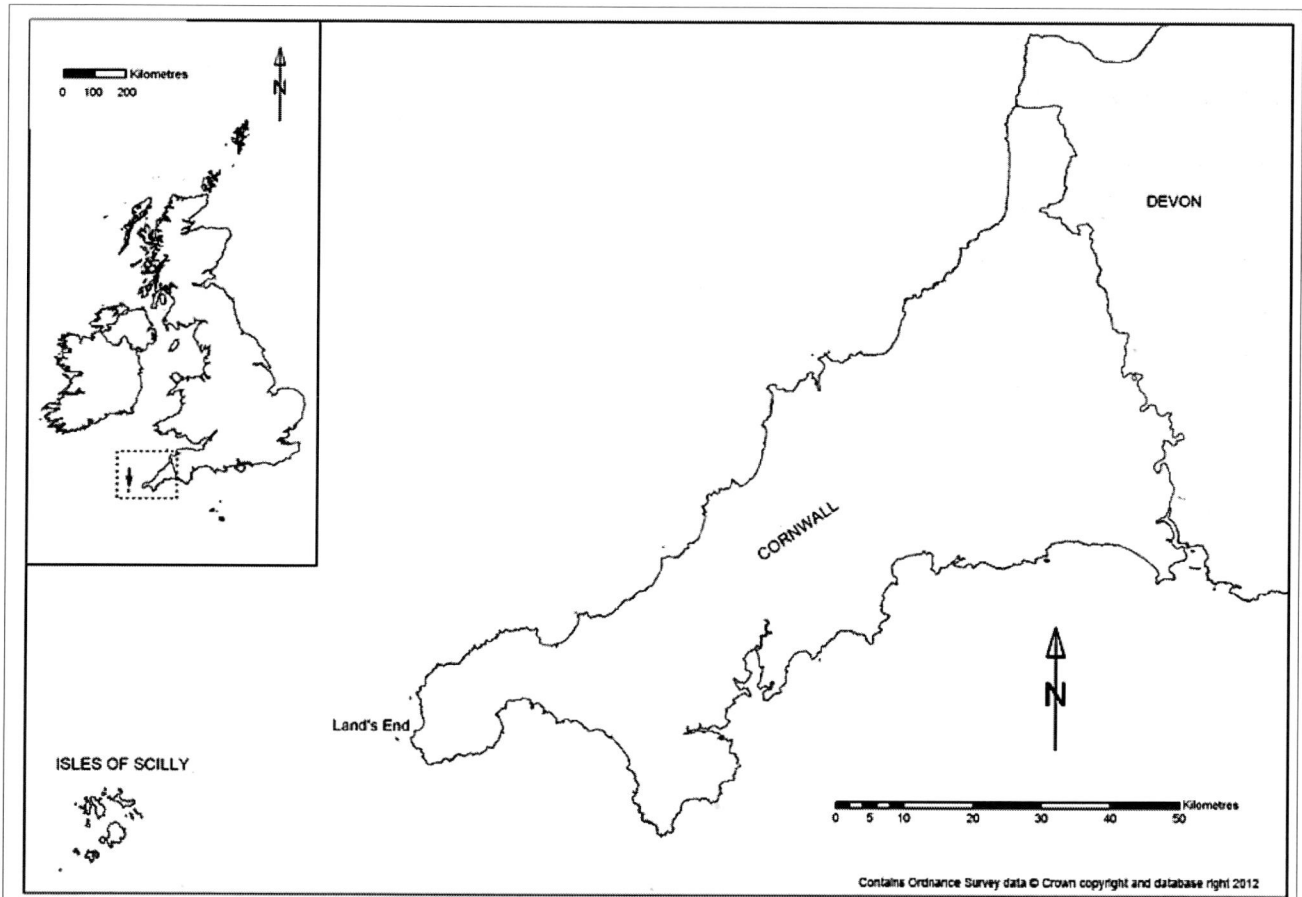

FIGURE 1.1 LOCATION MAP OF THE ISLES OF SCILLY, FROM JOHNS (2012:FIG 2.1)

The Isles of Scilly

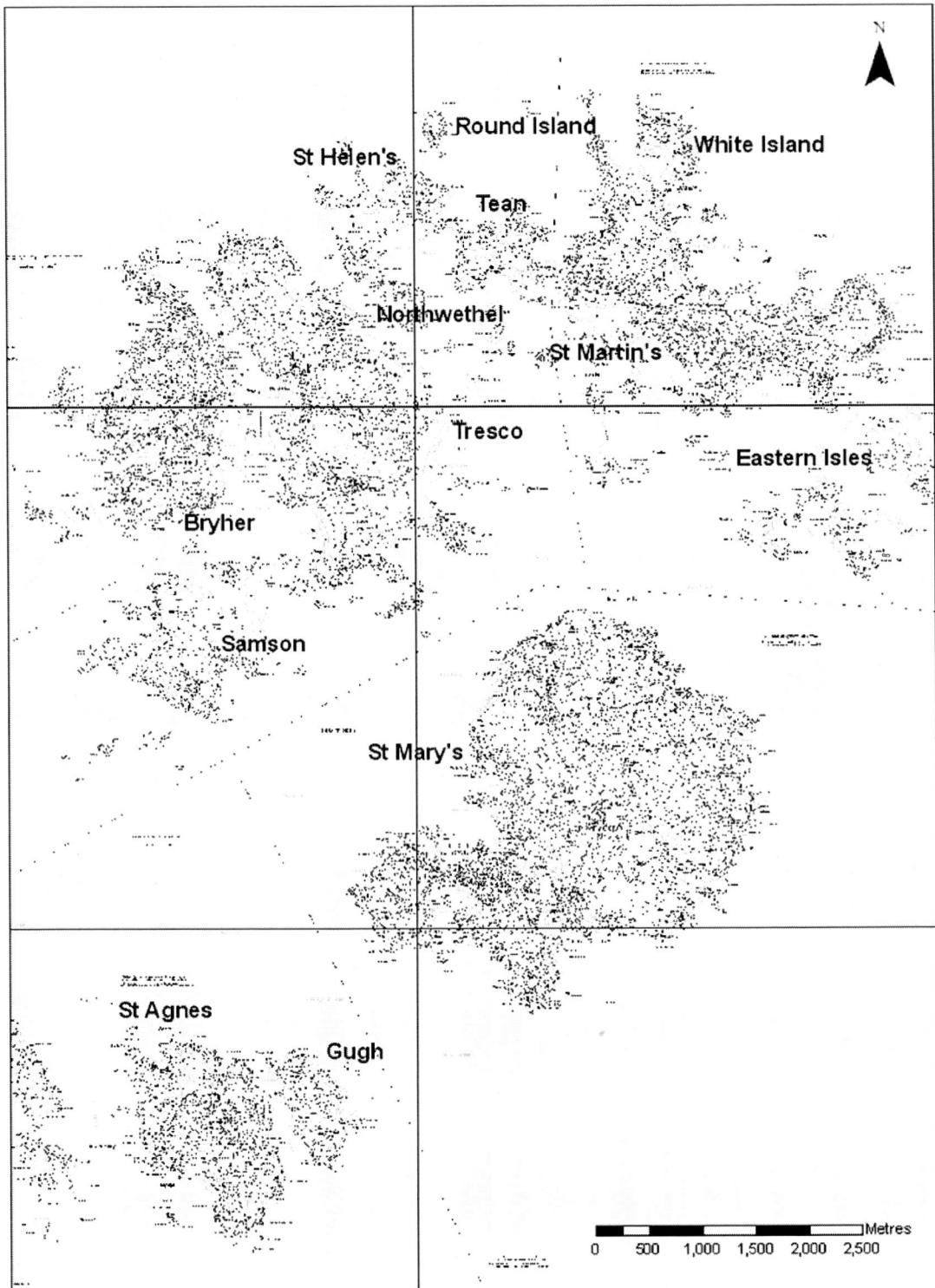

Round Island

White Island

St Helen's

Tean

Northwethel

St Martin's

Tresco

Eastern Isles

Bryher

Samson

St Mary's

St Agnes

Gugh

Metres
0   500   1,000 1,500 2,000 2,500

FIGURE 1.2 MAP OF THE ISLES OF SCILLY, SHOWING THE MAIN
ISLANDS

workmen, some of whom made their home in the islands. Scilly's role as one of the last Royalist strongholds during the Civil War led to an influx of Royalist supporters, many of whom came from distant parts of the country. Although there are many place-names of Cornish derivation in Scilly, it appears that Cornish had died out as a spoken language in the islands by the late 16th century (Thomas 1985:36).

Scilly became part of the Duchy of Cornwall, when it was established by Edward III for his son, the Black Prince, in 1337. The Duchy leased out the entire archipelago for most of the period from 1570 until 1920. The lessees were the Godolphin family and their descendants from 1570 until 1831 followed by Augustus Smith and his heirs from 1834. The lessee was called the Lord Proprietor and had considerable autonomy. Since 1920, the Dorrien-Smith family have leased only Tresco (and, until the early 1980s, the uninhabited islands) and the other islands have been administered directly by the Duchy.

The islands have had their own council since 1891. Prior to that, local administration was undertaken by the Council of Twelve - based on 13th century leaseholder Ralph de Blanchminster's obligation to preserve the peace by using twelve armed men - and then, from 1832, by the Select Vestry. Under the 1888 Local Government Act the Council was granted the power to deal with all aspects of the islands' administration. Thomas Algernon Dorrien-Smith, as Lord Proprietor of the islands, was the first Chairman of the Council and, although the Dorrien-Smiths' hereditary position ended in 1920 with their surrender of the lease for the whole of Scilly, Arthur Dorrien-Smith was Chairman until his death in 1955 (Bennett et al. 1991).

Culturally, many islanders do not regard themselves as Cornish, but as Scillonian and English. There is no discernible interest in Cornish nationalism or in the revival of the Cornish language in Scilly and the flag of St Piran, the patron saint of Cornwall, is rarely flown there.

The islands' position on routes along the western seaways, and more recently as the first landfall following an Atlantic crossing, means that they have provided a base for shelter and reprovisioning of ships for many centuries. The regular arrival of strangers and exotic objects may have been a factor in the development of a strong island identity. Given the distinctiveness of the prehistoric Scillonian pottery, it is possible that this Scillonian identity is of considerable antiquity.

It is likely that, since Scilly was first occupied, its inhabitants have been competent seafarers. The presence of cetacean and seal remains together with a wide range of fish bones, including those from offshore waters, in settlements from the Bronze Age onwards, points to this (Ratcliffe & Straker 1996; Robinson 2007). Whether marine resources formed a significant part of the diet of the Bronze Age settlers has not been established. Stable isotope analysis from several parts of north-western Europe has shown that, whilst Mesolithic populations in coastal and island locations relied heavily on marine foods, terrestrial resources became the main component of the diet from the Neolithic period onwards (Schulting et al. 2004).

Such analysis has not been carried out in Scilly but residues on sherds found at the Neolithic to Iron Age settlement site of Halangy Porth, St Mary's were examined and were found to be 'characteristic of oils and fats of marine fauna' (Evans 1983:37), suggesting that marine resources continued to play a part. Further studies of this kind, as well as stable isotope analysis, would help to provide a clearer picture of the prehistoric diet and economy of the islands.

Industrially, Scilly has been distinct from Cornwall in that it has no mineral resources and consequently mining has never been a part of the economy. Similarly, because of the distance to market, fishing has only ever been small scale, mainly to supply the islands' needs. In the post-mediaeval period, subsistence agriculture was the mainstay of the economy with cash income coming from pilotage and other services to shipping, salvage and kelp burning. From the mid 20th century tourism has formed the major part, currently accounting for about 85% of the islands' income, with flower farming and fishing, particularly for crabs and lobsters, making up most of the balance.

The 2011 census puts the islands' permanent population at about 2,200. In the late 18th and early 19th centuries it was somewhat higher than this and famine was a real threat on the off-islands (the inhabited islands other than St Mary's). Augustus Smith, the Lord Proprietor between 1834 and 1872, introduced various measures, including a change to the system of land inheritance, to encourage islanders to leave and this resulted in a drop in population from about 2,800 in 1840 to about 2,000 by 1900 and a significant improvement in the standard of living of the remaining islanders (Thomas 1985; Bowley 1990).

1.2 Isles of the Dead?

The islands have a wealth of archaeological sites, including more than 230 scheduled monuments and nearly 130 listed buildings (Arbery 2004). Of the prehistoric remains, one of the most striking groups is the megalithic burial chambers, which occur in unusually large numbers in the islands. Indeed, Daniel commented that:

'The Isles of Scilly are, of course, a great exception to our generalizations about the paucity and low density of burial chambers in England and Wales. These islands, with an area of between 4000 and 4500 acres (i.e. between 6 and 7 square miles) have at the present day no less than fifty chamber tombs - between a fifth and a quarter of all the chamber tombs in southern Britain. Yet Scilly is, in point of size, no more than one eight-thousandth part of England and Wales' (1950:29).

In addition, there is a smaller number of cist graves which are often found in close proximity to the megalithic chambers.

The burial chambers of Scilly form one of a number of regional groups of megalithic structures found along the Atlantic façade of Europe, the earliest - in Brittany and Iberia - dating to the mid 5th millennium BC. In the British Isles, these structures first appear in the early 4th millennium BC, a few centuries after the earliest evidence for farming communities, and some continued in use until the second millennium BC (Bradley 2000; Lynch 2004; Scarre 2007).

The large number of burial chambers in Scilly has led to speculation, in popular accounts at least (e.g. Bowley 1990), that the islands were the burial place for people, perhaps tribal leaders, who had not lived there. This has prompted some to describe Scilly as the 'Isles of the Dead'. Similar epithets have been applied to other small islands which have significant numbers of prehistoric tombs.

Pollard (1999) writes about 'Islands of the Dead', particularly in relation to Scotland, and highlights the use of small islands, both in the sea and in freshwater lochs, as burial grounds. Rainbird suggests that the physical separation of islands may have led to them being associated with death, arguing that '[t]he space provided by water acts as a social separation between the living and the dead' (2007:12). He also mentions the many references in classical literature to the dead crossing water in order to reach their final resting place. These associations with the dead led to the belief that certain islands were the home of witches or other malevolent spirits.

In Scilly, as in many other places in western Europe, prehistoric burial sites are more obvious and survive in larger numbers than the contemporary settlement sites. Given the density of distribution of burial chambers in the islands, there is a temptation to regard Scilly as a prehistoric necropolis not only for islanders but also for people from elsewhere, whose remains were taken there for burial. One implication of this is that there would have been comparatively little contemporary occupation of the islands. The research described in this book aims to test this hypothesis using the information available about the burial chambers, their contents, setting, function and relationship with settlements.

1.3 The archaeology of islands

The study of islands has, since the 1970s, developed as a discrete topic within archaeology, some approaches to it being adopted from other disciplines. One source of ideas has been biogeography. Work in this area by MacArthur and Wilson (1967) to identify the principles of island colonisation proposed the distance/area effect, which has been applied subsequently to a number of archaeological studies. This concept outlines the limitations on the colonisation of islands based on their distance from the nearest mainland but taking into account the size of the island. Consequently, large islands closer to mainlands present fewer barriers to colonisation than small islands further away. However, the presence of stepping stone islands was identified as a complicating factor.

MacArthur and Wilson's hypotheses were developed in respect of flora and fauna; when considering human colonisation of islands, Evans (1973) included the concept of locomotion – the ability of people to construct and use boats – in his analysis. The distance/area effect has been applied to a study of the sequence of colonisation of islands in the Mediterranean (Cherry 1981).

Evans' often-quoted analysis described islands as 'laboratories for the study of culture process', arguing that they were closed communities, often with a restricted range of resources available to them. This allowed contacts with the outside world to be observed more readily. Evans suggested that islands were protected from the competitive pressures of mainlands but accepted that, if technology allowed, they could be 'open to cultural stimuli from a wide variety of sources' and that this might include people arriving either deliberately or by chance. He also argued that

'Island communities often display a tendency towards the exaggerated development of some aspect of their culture, which is often connected with the ceremonial' (Evans 1973:518).

More recently, Darvill has reiterated this view, suggesting that 'islands … provide sharply delimited physical spaces that can be used as laboratories for the study of social behaviour and the influence of both internal and external agencies' (Kirch 1986 cited in Darvill 2000). Broodbank, however, rejects much of this 'laboratory' approach, identifying four main objectives for island archaeology: firstly, the focus on archipelagos as the unit of study, secondly, the need for an 'archaeology of the sea', examining the exploitation of the sea, sea-crossings, etc, thirdly, the importance of examining material culture for evidence of social interaction and, finally, the study of pot styles, etc as signifiers of island social practices (Broodbank 2000:33-35).

Rainbird, on the other hand, stresses the diversity of ways in which island communities may perceive themselves, some regarding the sea as isolating them and others seeing it as connecting them (Rainbird 2007). He plays down the significance of islands as areas of land and stresses the importance of the sea surrounding them. Like Broodbank, he proposes an archaeology of the sea but includes islands, seascapes and the coastal parts of larger landmasses in this, in order that the experiences of all seafarers and their maritime exploits can be examined (Rainbird 1999; 2007). In considering Evans' statement about the prevalence of ceremonial sites on islands, Rainbird points out that some mainland areas, for example, Egypt and Mesoamerica, have a wealth of ceremonial sites as well.

Parker Pearson (2004) cites the need to study islands and their people in relation to their outside world and suggests that the connections required within island groups may subsequently have encouraged the development of long-distance trading networks. He describes as 'Easter Island syndrome' the tendency in some islands for 'excessive building schemes ... [to] take over an island population's self-identity' (Parker Pearson 2004:129). He includes Orkney, Arran, the Azores, Malta, Gotland, Öland and Atlantic Scotland – but not Scilly or the Channel Islands – in the list of places where this phenomenon can be seen. The recent work of Rainbird (1999; 2007), Broodbank (2000), Parker Pearson (2004) and Scarre (2002b; 2008; 2011a; 2011d) in relation to the density of burial chambers on islands and to aspects of island identity, will be considered in chapter 9.

1.4 Scilly's prehistoric maritime connections

The nearest mainland to Scilly is west Cornwall and the islands are visible, on a clear day, from the Land's End peninsula. It is likely that the first visitors to, and the first settlers in, the islands came from there. However, the journey between the two involves the crossing of 45km of open ocean with no opportunity for shelter on the way, although it is possible that, in the early prehistoric period, there may have been small stepping stone islands at Wolf Rock and the Seven Stones.

The colonisation of Scilly can be compared with that of other island groups around the British Isles. There is evidence for Mesolithic activity on many offshore islands, including Scilly. Subsequently, the Hebrides, Orkney and the Isle of Man had all been settled by the first half of the fourth millennium BC but in Scilly, which is significantly smaller, the results of pollen analysis indicate some agricultural activity from the early third millennium BC but no permanent settlement until the late third millennium BC (Scaife 1984; Charman et al. 2012b).

The archipelago of St Kilda, some 65km west of the Outer Hebrides (which acted as stepping stone islands to it) appears to have been occupied in the Neolithic. It has been suggested that 'by about 3000BC people had developed a viable way of life [there], and the means of maintaining regular and necessary contact with the outside world.' (Fleming 2005b) Scilly is both closer to its nearest occupied neighbour than is St Kilda and larger than St Kilda. One significant difference between Scilly and St Kilda, however, is the height of the two archipelagos. St Kilda rises to 430m above sea level whereas the highest point in Scilly is just over 50m. This limitation on the visibility of Scilly on the voyage across to it may have been a factor in its relatively late colonisation (Johns et al. 2011).

There have been a number of studies examining the use of the 'western seaways' (the Irish and Celtic Seas) in the prehistoric period (e.g. Case 1969; Bowen 1972; Callaghan & Scarre 2009; Garrow & Sturt 2011). Maritime connections between Brittany, Cornwall, Ireland, western Scotland and the Atlantic islands - Scilly, the Isle of Man, the Hebrides and Orkney - have relevance in relation to the Mesolithic/Neolithic transition as well as to patterns of Bronze Age exchange.

Using computer simulation to examine sailed and paddled voyages between places in the western seaways, Callaghan and Scarre established that paddled vessels could have made the journey from Brittany to Ireland in all seasons of the year with the trip taking between seven and nine days. They add:

'It is open to question whether such direct journeys were intentionally undertaken or whether contact between Brittany and Ireland relied on intermediate stopovers in south-west Britain or the Isles of Scilly' (Callaghan & Scarre 2009:367).

It is likely that, even if a direct voyage was planned, Scilly would have provided a refuge in bad weather or if other difficulties were encountered.

Garrow and Sturt, in reviewing the role of the western seaways in the Mesolithic/Neolithic transition, stress the difficult maritime conditions likely to have been encountered in the North Sea between 5000 and 3000BC as low-lying islands and sand flats were inundated by rising sea levels. In contrast, they say, 'the western seaways represent a clear and open maritime route' which experienced much smaller changes, although they acknowledge that navigation there was not easy (2011:63).

There is limited evidence for Mesolithic presence in Scilly with some flint artefacts from this period (Berridge & Roberts 1986); there is also an indication from the pollen sequence at Higher Moors, St Mary's of possible human disturbance at about 5500 to 5000BC (Scaife 1984). Recent excavation by Garrow and Sturt near Old Quay on St Martin's has uncovered flint and other stone artefacts from both the Mesolithic and Neolithic, Neolithic pottery and possible evidence, in the form of ditches and post-holes, for structures (Garrow & Sturt 2014). Robinson (2007) believes that it is unlikely that the islands were permanently inhabited at this time but suggests that they may have been occupied seasonally for fishing, the collecting of shellfish and the hunting of sea mammals.

Garrow and Sturt argue that there was a 'continuity of practice' in the western seaways from the fifth millennium BC onwards, that this involved regular short-distance sea crossings and that longer voyages, including the one between Scilly and Cornwall, were 'commonly made' (2011:67). If this were the case, Scilly would have been part of a network of maritime connections which included Brittany, Cornwall, Ireland and Scotland.

Imported objects of Neolithic date in Scilly include sherds of Hembury Ware from south-west England and gabbroic pottery from Cornwall, both found at the occupation site of East Porth, Samson. In the later burial chambers, small bronze objects and glass and faience beads have been found. Several pieces of pumice are known from prehistoric sites in Scilly, the only recorded examples of this substance in the British Isles outside Scotland. Whilst it is conceivable that the pumice floated from Iceland, its likely place of origin, to Scilly, the possibility also exists that it was brought to the islands by travellers from further north. The provenance of the bronze, glass and faience is not known but it has been argued that the use of seagoing, sewn-plank boats from the early second millennium BC allowed the development of networks of exchange of prestige goods (Van de Noort 2003).

Later, at the sixth and seventh century AD settlement on Teän, there is evidence for trade with the Mediterranean, not only in the form of imported pottery but also because two of the skeletons found in the Christian cemetery there showed signs of leprosy (Ratcliffe & Johns 2003). By the twelfth century, the monks at the Benedictine priory on Tresco were engaged in long distance trade; the *Orkneyinga-saga* records the plundering of one of their merchant ships.

In summary, whilst it is not possible to be certain about the extent of maritime connections between Scilly and elsewhere in the prehistoric period, it is clear that such connections did exist. Scilly should not, therefore, be regarded as an isolated outpost, unaffected by changes and developments elsewhere but as part of a network of islands and mainlands in the western seaways.

1.5 Outline of work

Although the chambered cairns and cists in Scilly have been written about since the 18th century, there has previously been no systematic study focusing on the structures, their contents, their setting and their affiliations. The first radiocarbon dates from a Scillonian entrance grave have been recently obtained and allow the chronology of the sites to be considered in a wider context. This has not previously been possible because of the lack of mainland comparators for much of the prehistoric pottery from the islands. Whilst non-funerary functions for the entrance graves were proposed by Ashbee (1976) and Thomas (1985), there has been no recent consideration of this aspect. This research aims to address these gaps.

Chapter 2 reviews recent approaches to the study of megalithic burial chambers and considers their application to Scilly. This appraisal is used to guide the approach taken in the research reported here. Chapter 3 provides a critical review of the previous research carried out into the Scillonian entrance graves and cists, including the work of George Bonsor between 1899 and 1902. Bonsor's unpublished notebooks about his visits to Scilly were discovered during the course of this study and the contents have added considerably to our knowledge of several sites.

Chapter 4 outlines the physical characteristics of both the entrance graves and the cists and assesses the numbers of each, both extant and destroyed, as well as reviewing the records of excavation. Chapter 5 examines the contents, including artefacts, human remains and other substances, found in both entrance graves and cists and reviews the significance of the assemblages at two excavated sites.

Chapter 6 addresses the setting of the sites, considering both the likely pattern of destruction and the impact of sea level rise on them and using GIS-based mapping to examine aspects of their distribution. In chapter 7 the function of the sites is discussed and possible reasons for their density in Scilly are reviewed. Chapter 8 considers evidence for the dating of the sites and evaluates the radiocarbon dates from two sites obtained during the course of this research.

Chapter 9 examines the basis for comparisons made between the entrance graves and cists of Scilly and megalithic structures in other parts of the British Isles and Brittany and considers the significance of any similarities; chapter 10 draws together the key outcomes of the research and suggests some future lines of enquiry. Appendix 1 is a catalogue of all 197 sites considered, appendix 2 is a concordance of sites and appendix 3 contains extracts from George Bonsor's notebooks about his visits to Scilly between 1899 and 1902.

1.6 Terminology

A wide variety of terms has been used to describe the monuments under consideration in this work. In the 18th and 19th centuries, descriptions such as 'Giants' Graves', 'Caves', 'Burrows' or 'Barrows', 'Cromlechs' and 'Kist-vaens' were used (Borlase 1756; Troutbeck 1796; Woodley 1822; Smith 1863).

It was not until the early 20th century that two distinct monument types were identified and named. Crawford distinguished between the cist: 'a small box consisting of four stones set in the ground at right-angles to each other and generally covered by a fifth' and the burial-chamber, which 'consists of large … stones; or … a dry wall of small stones' with a roof of 'either a large capstone, or a corbelled vault of small stones' (1928:418).

Hencken (1932:15) expanded this definition by introducing a three-fold classification of burial chambers: passage-graves (chambers approached by a stone built passage), covered galleries (passages with no chamber at the end) and closed chambers (built of large stones but with no entrance). He also refers to cists as a separate category. Childe, however, said that 'A small group of collective tombs in Cornwall, the Scilly Isles and south-eastern Ireland are generally classed as entrance graves' (Childe 1940, quoted in Ashbee 1974:73).

It was Daniel who, building on Montelius's classificatory work, introduced the concept of two distinct movements of megalithic grave builders across western and northern Europe leading to two types of structure: the passage grave and the gallery grave (Daniel 1941). Daniel describes 'entrance graves' as being a form of passage grave which does not have a clear distinction between the passage and the chamber and regards the monuments in Scilly as belonging to this category.

Later, Daniel provided definitions of the terms 'burial chamber' – a burial vault – and 'chamber tomb' – used to denote both the chamber and associated structures such as barrows (1950:3). He goes on to say:

'To my mind all the burial chambers in the Scilly group are to be classed as undifferentiated passage graves or entrance graves, the various forms … representing various degrees in the formal divorce of passage and chamber, from form *(a)* which Hencken actually classifies as a passage grave, to form *(d)*, which might almost be described as a gallery grave' (1950:64).

Piggott describes the chamber and passage in Scillonian chambered tombs as having 'lost any structural distinction' and agrees with Daniel that the sites are 'derivative from the passage grave series' (1954a:264-265).

Ashbee, having reviewed the varying descriptions used by earlier authors, believes that the term 'entrance graves' is a misnomer as 'the entrance … is normally the least prominent and distinctive characteristic of the series' and goes on to suggest that 'Scillonian chamber tombs' should be employed as the descriptive term (1974:74). However, two years later, his article about Bant's Carn was sub-titled 'An Entrance Grave Restored and Reconsidered' (Ashbee 1976).

Although Thomas (1985) uses the term 'entrance-grave' only to describe sites in Cornwall and refers to those in Scilly as 'chambered cairns', the majority of more recent authors have described the Scillonian sites as 'entrance graves'. This is the term used in the Historic Environment Record for Cornwall and Scilly (HES 1987-2005) for both the Cornish and Scillonian sites and it is also employed by other recent authors (e.g. Ratcliffe 1989; Ratcliffe & Johns 2003; Kirk 2004; Robinson 2007).

The definition of 'entrance grave' in the National Monuments Record Thesaurus is 'A form of Neolithic burial monument primarily found in Cornwall and the Scilly Isles. It comprises a round cairn, usually with a retaining wall or kerb, and an entrance leading directly into a chamber.' (English Heritage nd)

Consequently, in this work, the term 'entrance grave' will be used to describe structures consisting of a stone-built chamber with an opening at one end, covered by a mound of earth and stones. A coffin-like stone box, constructed of slabs and covered by one or more capstones, will be referred to as a 'cist'. 'Indeterminate sites' are those badly damaged structures which may be either an entrance grave or a cist. There is also a small number of sites which are similar in size and construction to entrance graves but which have a sealed chamber with no entrance; these are described as 'megalithic cists'. The question of whether the sole or primary purpose of the entrance graves was, in fact, burial will be considered in chapter 7.

1.7 A note on nomenclature

Comment should also be made about the names used to describe the archipelago under consideration. Although, in

the past, 'Scilly Isles', 'Scilly Islands' or 'the Scillies' were used as the normal descriptors, the present day inhabitants prefer that their home is called the 'Isles of Scilly' or just 'Scilly'; these terms will therefore be used.

In Scilly, a natural granite outcrop, termed a 'tor' on Dartmoor and elsewhere, is known as a 'carn'. This word occurs frequently in Scillonian place-names, including those of several of the entrance graves which are located close to one of these features. The similarity between the words 'carn' and 'cairn' has caused much confusion and has led to site names being incorrectly quoted in many references. This has happened particularly in respect of the well-preserved entrance grave site of Bant's Carn on St Mary's, where the nearby carn itself was apparently removed early in the 20th century.

1.8 Radiocarbon dates

In order to ensure consistency and to facilitate comparison, the radiocarbon determinations included in this work have all been calibrated using OxCal 4.2 and the IntCal13 calibration curve (Bronk Ramsey 2013; Reimer et al. 2013). All dates are expressed at the 2 SD (95.4%) confidence level. This means that the calibrated dates in this work may vary significantly from those shown in the publications where they have previously appeared.

Chapter 2

Recent approaches to the study of megaliths and their application to Scilly

2.1 Introduction

This chapter will examine and review the main approaches to the study of megaliths – and megalithic burial chambers in particular – since the 1970s. An assessment will be made of the value of these approaches to the study of the Scillonian entrance graves and cists and this will guide the approach and methods adopted in this volume.

Until the mid 20th century the study of chambered tombs was primarily concerned with their morphology and contents. A considerable amount of work was done in an attempt to construct a typological series, which would provide both an explanation for the spread of megalithic burial structures and a framework of relative chronology for them (e.g. Daniel 1941; 1950; Piggott 1954a). There was an assumption that there had been a movement of people, referred to by Childe as 'megalithic missionaries' (Childe 1958), who had introduced the concept of stone-built tombs to western and northern Europe.

More recently, the availability of radiocarbon dates (and the tree-ring calibration of them) has shown that the development of megalithic architecture occurred at about the same time in many different places; attention has subsequently focused more on regional groups than on similarities across Europe (Lynch 2004). An examination of the broader role of megalithic tombs in the societies which built them has prompted research on topics such as their part in the development of territorial divisions and political structures, the place of megaliths in the landscape and the strategies employed in the acquisition of stone for their construction, as well as aspects of the chambers themselves, such as the use of colour and sound in them.

The development of archaeological theory, with the 'New Archaeology' of the 1960s leading to the 'processual' thinking of the 1970s and 1980s and the more recent 'post-processual' studies, is clearly demonstrated in the approaches which have been taken to the study of megaliths over this period.

These approaches will be considered in roughly chronological order of their publication.

2.2 Megalithic burial chambers as territorial markers

The realisation that the megalithic monuments of western Europe did not have their origins in the Near East or the Mediterranean led researchers to reflect upon the discrepancy between the sophistication of the monuments and the relative simplicity of the material culture of those who had constructed them (Renfrew 1973a). The rise of the 'New Archaeology' in the late 1960s onwards prompted the use of the hypothetico-deductive approach in which an explanation was developed and then tested against the available data.

Renfrew used this approach to examine whether the features of a chiefdom society could be identified in late Neolithic Wessex. He listed twenty attributes of chiefdom societies, including a ranked society, more clearly defined territorial boundaries, frequent ceremonies and rituals, organisation and deployment of labour for agriculture or building and distinctive dress for those of high status (Renfrew 1973b:543). He then developed a model of 'territories' around the long barrows of Wiltshire and Dorset using Thiessen polygons. He went on to consider the manpower required to construct a range of monuments from unchambered long barrows (10,000 man hours or less) to Stonehenge Phase III (over 30 million man-hours). He suggested that there were 'emerging chiefdoms in the early neolithic, [based on the causewayed enclosures], developing to full scale chiefdoms at the time of the henges, and possibly to a single unified chiefdom ... at the time of Silbury Hill or Stonehenge III.' (Renfrew 1973b:554)

Renfrew also applied this model of territories to an examination of the Scottish islands of Rousay and Arran. He argued that there was a coherence to the distribution of megalithic tombs in parts of western Europe and that, given the rejection of an explanation based on diffusion, a set of conditions must therefore have existed in those areas which favoured the construction of such monuments. He suggested that one of the functions of the monuments was as territorial markers and that 'their function as a place of burial, an ancestral resting place, was central to that symbolic expression of territory.' (Renfrew 1976:205)

In this paper, Renfrew argued that some of the societies which built megalithic tombs were small-scale and segmentary without the centralised, hierarchical structure of chiefdoms. He adopted Sahlins' (1961) definition of segmentary societies as being based on a village or similar unit and used ethnographic data to support the proposition that monuments were built as territorial markers. He developed three criteria to test this: firstly, a pattern of spaced, simultaneously functioning sites, secondly, that the resultant territories were related to settlement activities and, thirdly, that there was no hierarchy of places. These criteria were then applied to Rousay and Arran.

On the basis that the scale of monuments was fairly uniform, Renfrew considered that the third criterion had been satisfied in those two locations. He recognised the lack of dating evidence to establish simultaneity of use but argued that territorial spacing implied 'simultaneity of veneration' (Renfrew 1976:211).

Applying Davies's (1946) work on the impact of the geology and environment on settlement in Arran, Renfrew argued that a territorial arrangement could be demonstrated. He examined the locations of the chambered cairns and their associated territories, again using Thiessen polygons. This demonstrated a correlation between the distribution of the cairns and modern arable land and a similar correlation with Neolithic arable land was suggested. Renfrew proposed that the pair of cairns on the east side of Arran and the cluster of three on the west side might have been used successively but conceded that this was speculation.

In the final part of his paper Renfrew considered the effects of population increase on communities on the Atlantic façade. Social stress would have been caused by higher population densities and one response to this was centralisation, as in Neolithic Wessex, which allowed greater efficiency and therefore a greater carrying capacity. Such a centralisation does not appear in Rousay or Arran and Renfrew argued that in these, and other, locations there was instead a resistance to change and a symbolisation of the group and its territorial identity in the construction of territorial markers, such as chambered cairns. The exploitation of marine resources would also have helped to prevent conditions of particular stress, he suggested.

Thomas (1985) has applied Renfrew's work to a study of the distribution of entrance graves in Scilly and has argued that it supports Renfrew's model of a segmentary society. However he accepts that, under this model, a segmentary society with a dispersed settlement pattern would be expected to have dispersed megaliths as well. The clusters of chambered cairns found in Scilly do not correspond with this. Thomas overcomes this difficulty by proposing that the initial distribution of entrance graves was dispersed and that, over time, more structures were added to give a part-nucleated distribution. He accepts that, without a 'most massive excavational and dating programme' of the chambered cairns in Scilly, this cannot be confirmed (Thomas 1985:139). The possible role of Scillonian entrance graves as territorial markers will be discussed in chapter 7.

A more recent study of the distribution of chambered cairns in Arran pointed out that the spatial relationship between the settlement sites and burial sites in Neolithic Arran is unknown (Perry & Davidson 1987). This analysis used more than 2700 sampling points in Arran and thirteen

factors, including geology, distances to a stream and to the coast, altitude and relationship to former (i.e. early 19th century) and present-day arable areas to analyse the distribution of cairns. Simulations were run, based on different weightings of these factors, both for all the cairns and for three typologically-based groups, which, in the absence of absolute dating, were hypothesised to be early, intermediate and late in date.

The results of this analysis indicate that overall the distribution of chambered cairns on Arran was most influenced by agricultural land, but that other factors, including proximity to a stream, a nearby cliff coastline and an altitude of 90m to 150m, also played a part. However, for the early cairns, proximity to a stream and an altitude of 30m to 90m were the most important factors. In this period there was a lack of concern for better agricultural land in the positioning of the burial sites, although it became an increasingly significant factor in the intermediate and late periods. Perry and Davidson suggest that this may be because there was a predominantly Mesolithic economy at the time the first tombs were built followed by significant agricultural activity in the later periods. They argue that the relationship between the tombs and agricultural land leads to the conclusion that 'cairns were linked with particular human groups.' (1987:130)

Applying this type of analysis to Scilly is problematic because of issues of scale. Arran, with an area of 432km² is more than twenty-eight times larger than Scilly and the highest peak in Arran, Goat Fell, has an altitude of 874m whereas in Scilly the highest point is Telegraph Hill on St Mary's at only 51m. There are no streams in Scilly today and no significant cliffs. Of the factors considered by Perry and Davidson, only geology, rockiness, drainage, aspect and slope position are likely to produce any insights into the positioning of chambered cairns in Scilly. Some of these aspects will be addressed in chapter 6.

2.3 Megalithic burial chambers and power relations in prehistoric societies

Post-processual approaches to the study of megaliths have focused on their symbolic meaning. In such studies, the structures are viewed as symbolic expressions of ideological belief and, in some cases, as being used to shape and order society (O'Brien 1999).

An approach which, similar to Perry and Davidson's work outlined in the previous section, makes considerable use of statistical analysis, is also to be found in some of the first papers putting forward the argument that megalithic burial chambers or their contents are indicators of power in prehistoric society. Shanks and Tilley examined Neolithic mortuary practices in southern England and southern Sweden. Adopting a Marxist analysis, they argued that ritual activities served to legitimate the social order, 'serving sectional interests of particular groups.' (Shanks & Tilley 1982:130) In small-scale societies, the elders exercise dominance over junior members by control over the marriage system and they also control ritual information. However, Shanks and Tilley argue, ritual is used to emphasise the solidarity of the group, to deny these systems of dominance and to stress the identity of the community in relation to other social groups. The authority of the elders may also be linked to that of the ancestors.

Following their analysis of the skeletal evidence from a small number of chambered and unchambered barrows in Wessex, the Cotswolds and Scania (southern Sweden), where bones had been found in discrete piles in the graves, they concluded that there was statistically sound evidence supporting the hypothesis that there had been deliberate selection and arrangement of bones at these sites. This included contrasts between articulated and disarticulated bodies at Fussell's Lodge and differentiation between adult and immature remains at both the English and Swedish sites, with a 'distinct clustering of immature parts of the body, compared with the wide spread of the adult ones.' (Shanks & Tilley 1982:146) At some sites there was differentiation between the right and left sides of the body while at others differences in treatment between male and female remains were identified.

Shanks and Tilley argue that the placing and re-arranging of human remains in the tombs followed principles designed to misrepresent the power relations within the communities using them. Therefore, the collective rather than the individual was stressed, the regrouping of disarticulated bones with symmetry between body parts denied the asymmetrical relationships which existed in life and solidarity was emphasised by the bounded nature of the deposits (1982:151-152).

Subsequently, Tilley (1984) examined the megalithic tombs of the Middle Neolithic Funnel Neck Beaker (TRB) tradition in Scania, analysing their distribution, location and orientation. He argued for the close link between ritual and power/knowledge and rejected explanations for the construction of monumental megalithic tombs which related them to the need to control resources, such as land, because of population pressure (e.g. Renfrew 1976). Tilley stressed the importance of place and of sacred places, such as megaliths, in particular and suggested that they may have 'acted as instruments for the creation and maintenance of political and social space.' (Tilley 1984:122)

In his examination of the orientation of the graves he considered, as well, the orientation relationships between neighbouring sites and focused on a group of thirteen sites in the Håslöv/Skegrie area where he identified that a river appeared to provide a division between the sites on either side of it in terms of their orientation. The mounds of those on the west side were oriented in different directions whilst those on the east side were all oriented north-west to south-east. However, Tilley ascertained that there was a pattern in the orientations of the sites on the western side. Analyses of other groups of sites demonstrated that it was only those on the sides of a north-south river which had these similar and patterned orientations.

Tilley went on to look at the mortuary practices at these graves, which included the disarticulation of skeletons and the deposition of large quantities of pottery, as well as axes, flint fragments and amber beads together with the sprinkling of red ochre in some tombs. Some sites, particularly those which are part of clusters, had more than 15,000 sherds (from 1,000 or more vessels) deposited around and outside their entrances. An analysis of the decoration on more than 8,000 sherds from grave and settlement sites was carried out in order to distinguish between bounded and unbounded design forms. Ornamentation techniques, infilling of motifs and vessel shapes were also examined (Tilley 1984:126-135).

From this, Tilley identified a number of parallels between aspects of the treatment of human remains and of pottery at the tombs. He went on to argue that the concept of boundedness at the tombs created an us/them distinction between different groups and, consequently, a solidarity between members of the same group, which served to deflect power differences within the group. The complex pattern of tomb orientations, he suggested, showed tension, but also inter-dependence, between groups. The disarticulation of human bones and the crushing of pottery symbolised an attempt to deny the imbalance of power within the group and to achieve unity.

The monumentality of the tombs suggested that dominant groups were legitimating their claims through a link with the past, Tilley argued, and the pottery deposits were offerings to the gods or the spirit world, with the destruction of highly-decorated vessels perhaps being the basis on which prestige and social power were built (Tilley 1984:140-141). He suggested that, ultimately, this misrepresentation of power relations could not be sustained and this resulted in the end of the TRB tradition and the succeeding, very different, funerary practices of the Battle-Axe/Corded Ware tradition.

Tilley's conclusions can be challenged in a number of ways: the different proportions of bounded and unbounded motifs on pottery sherds at funerary and settlement sites may be linked to the different vessel types used in the two types of location, for example, rather than reinforcing the distinction between different groups. Similarly, other explanations for the orientations of the chambers could be considered, such as astronomical connections or views of nearby natural features. Tilley's extensive statistical analyses confirm the non-random patterning but they do not prove the hypotheses he puts forward. More recent work in this area has concentrated on the layout of tomb interiors and the placing of human remains within them, rather than on pottery motifs or tomb orientation. Thomas looked for evidence of the social relations of the communities which built the Cotswold-Severn tombs by focusing on a study of the burial practices in them (Thomas 1988). He developed an outline chronology for these sites with earlier tombs having lateral chambers and later ones terminal chambers. In examining the distribution of these sites, Thomas concluded that many of the laterally-chambered tombs had been built beyond the settled area of the Cotswolds whilst the terminally-chambered tombs were closer to the settlement areas.

A difference was also identified between the two types of tomb in terms of mortuary practice: many of the laterally-chambered tombs have only fragmentary human remains in them because, Thomas suggested, skeletal material was removed and circulated. Where human remains were found, many of them were disarticulated and bones were sometimes carefully organised with, for example, skulls placed against passage and chamber walls. Articulated and disarticulated skeletons were often grouped together whether or not the chamber was sub-divided by septal slabs or portholes. There is, however, no consistent pattern between the sites as, in some cases, the disarticulated bones were found further into the chambers whereas at others they are closer to the entrance (Thomas 1988:546-549). Thomas also argued that other activities, such as feasting and exchange, took place at these tombs which were, perhaps, constructed in locations which had previously been used for these purposes.

Thomas traced a different pattern in the deposition of bones in the later terminally-chambered Cotswold-Severn tombs. In the transepted tombs, he suggested, bones were removed, but not circulated and re-deposited elsewhere, and the bones were not disarticulated and re-arranged. At both earlier and later sites Thomas noted that bones or skeletons were sometimes placed according to gender and age, particularly the latter. At three sites with transepted terminal chambers (Burn Ground, Notgrove and West Kennet) there is considerable similarity, Thomas argued, in the patterns of deposition according to gender and age whereas in the simple terminal chambers disarticulated skeletons are the norm. From this, Thomas identified 'two different strategies for coping with internal stress and contradiction' (1988:553).

He also argued that there was a deliberate 'antiquation' of the sites, at the laterally-chambered sites, by blocking the tombs and placing material around the revetment walls to make it look like a process of natural slippage and, at the terminally-chambered sites, by building them with revetment walls which appeared to be collapsing. This reflects a legitimising link with the past similar to that suggested by Tilley (1984) in relation to the monumentality of the TRB graves. In conclusion Thomas argued that:

'Within tombs a set of rules appears to have been followed regarding the laying out of corpses, emphasising the divisions of society. This must clearly relate to a growing rigidity within the social fabric, yet these divisions relate to gender and, above all, age categories…. [T]he abiding impression … is of how the past was manipulated and recreated to support social change.' (Thomas 1988:557)

The eventual blocking of megalithic tombs 'interrupted any flow of reciprocity between the living and the dead,

and separated the past from the present', however the use of cairns and forecourts for secondary burials demonstrated their continuing influence (1999:151).

Power can be defined in different ways: it may be regarded as simply authority or social control. Power can also be considered as a 'relational phenomenon, a set of imbricated connections immanent in all social dealings which create knowledge, enable action, facilitate understanding and promote tastes and desires' (Thomas 1999:128). The representation of the dead in mortuary rituals is something that is within the control of the living and which, Thomas argues, tells us more about those who conducted the funerary ritual than about those who were buried. The remains may have been presented in a particular way so that they conformed to accepted norms for a person of that age, sex and position in society. Tombs, he suggests, should be considered as places of transformation rather than graves.

Thomas also suggested that the architecture of megalithic burial chambers was an expression of control as the approach to chamber was channelled and a degree of influence was exercised over the interpretation of space. He argued that 'the restricted space available *inside* monuments indicates activities which were *socially* restricted' (Thomas 1999:48, emphasis in original). Thomas's analysis is valuable as an examination of the uses of megalithic burial chambers, rather than just their typology. His suggestion that they were places for exchange and feasting, as well as burial, and his use of ethnographic analogies all provide a broader perspective than some earlier approaches. However, there is little, other than his assertions about the significance of the articulated and disarticulated bones, to support his argument that there were two different forms of social organisation in the Cotswold-Severn area at the time the tombs were constructed. The uncertainty regarding their dating is another complicating factor.

Thomas does not consider other possible explanations for the arrangement of the bones, nor how the 'ritual classification, rigid definition of social ranks and insistence on the integrity of a genealogical (elite?) line' which he proposes in relation to the tombs with transepted chambers, were established and maintained. Equally, he does not address the issue of whether this form of social organisation can be distinguished in other aspects of the burial or settlement sites, or their material culture, from that of the simple terminal chambers 'where all internal divisions were broken down' (Thomas 1988:553).

The view of the controlling role of tomb architecture is echoed by other authors. For example, Edmonds (1999) considers that relations between the living were ordered by distinctions about who could have access to tomb interiors and forecourts. This state of affairs was legitimated by the link between the funerary monuments and the ancestral past. Edmonds also cites the importance of the arrangement of certain skeletal remains and the values implicit in this and in the masses of disarticulated bones.

The approach used by Tilley and Thomas has been challenged by Brück, who believes that it is based on modern Western concepts of the self as an autonomous subject. This view seems to have informed their idea of the elite who controlled the use of monumental space, she argues, and is contrasted with the passive, manipulated group who followed the routes designated by them (Brück 2001). She suggests that a relational concept of the person, which stresses the self in terms of interpersonal relationships, may be a more appropriate model for considering the Neolithic. This would imply that people did not experience power in the same way in every setting.

Brück argues that the wide variety of activities carried out at monuments would have led to a diversity of interpretations and, consequently, very different experiences of it. She illustrates this with the analogy of an English church and the different actions and experiences an individual would go through there, depending on whether they were alone or with others, attending a wedding or a funeral, arranging flowers or working as a paid cleaner (Brück 2001:658). She concludes that more subtle ways of viewing the social complexities of the Neolithic are required.

None of the approaches set out above has been applied to the study of entrance graves or cists in Scilly. With the exception of a single inhumation burial (now missing) from Obadiah's Barrow (Hencken 1933) and very small quantities of unburnt bone recorded at Bant's Carn and Knackyboy Cairn (Bonsor 1899-1900; O'Neil 1948-1949), the excavated sites there have contained only cremations, usually in urns. There is, therefore, no opportunity to study the articulation or disarticulation of skeletal remains.

There has been little analysis of the cremated remains, many of which also are missing, and, in most cases, the location of each urn was not recorded. This means that it is not possible to examine whether the position of inurned cremations in the chambers is related to gender or age. Thomas, however, considered that single-cell chambers (as all the Scillonian sites are) suggested a 'lack of concern with classification and segmentation' (Thomas 1999:149).

At a number of sites in Scilly, including Bant's Carn and Obadiah's Barrow, deposits of sherds have been found outside the chamber entrance. The motifs on these have not been studied with the degree of rigour employed by Tilley in relation to the sherds from Scania (Tilley 1984) but the general impression is that the pottery found both within and outside entrance graves is the same as that from the contemporary settlements (e.g. Hencken 1932; Dudley 1968a; Ashbee 1974).

Because of the consistency of chamber shape, the general absence of inhumation burials and the lack of information about the position of cremation burials, there is little scope to apply the types of analysis employed by Tilley and Thomas to the chambered cairns of Scilly. A number of concerns about these approaches have already been highlighted and, consequently, they have not been adopted in the research reported here.

2.4 Phenomenology

Phenomenology, developed by philosophers including Heidegger, is the 'study of conscious human experience in everyday life' (Johnson 1999:114). Tilley's *A Phenomenology of Landscape* (1994) was the first major exposition of the application of this approach to the study of landscape archaeology. It has subsequently been followed by studies by a number of other researchers (e.g. Bender et al. 1997; Cummings 2004) and critiqued by others (e.g. Fleming 1999; Brück 2005; Fleming 2005a; 2006). More recently there have been attempts to combine phenomenology with more analytical approaches, particularly GIS (e.g. Chapman 2003; Gillings 2009).

The phenomenological approach to the study of landscape archaeology has focused on the physical experience of moving through monuments and how this affects the perception of them, often described as 'thinking through the body'. Tilley (1994) argues that two-dimensional representations of space, such as maps, cannot convey the significance of past landscapes and that it is necessary for archaeologists to experience them physically by, for example, climbing a hill to a burial chamber and appreciating how its orientation reflects the surrounding escarpments. He suggests that, in this way, it is possible to gain an appreciation of how the builders of these monuments understood and interpreted the landscape and the place of the monuments in it.

Subsequently, other researchers have used similar approaches: Cummings has adopted a phenomenological approach to the examination of the landscape settings of monuments in several areas of the Irish Sea zone and in other parts of Scotland considering, in particular, inter-visibility between mountains and monuments (e.g. Cummings 2002; 2004). In a study of chambered cairns in South Uist (Cummings et al. 2005) it is argued that, in most cases, they are positioned in order to block the view of them from certain directions and to provide views of mountains and peaks from them. In respect of the sites in southern Orkney, the importance of views of the sea is considered a governing factor in their positioning, although it is accepted that it is almost impossible to avoid this (Cummings & Pannett 2005).

One of the criticisms of the application of phenomenology to landscape archaeology is that it has focused on visual perception to the exclusion of the other senses. This has been addressed by Hamilton et al. (2006) who examined sound and smell, as well as colour and the visibility of communication signals, in their study of the areas around Neolithic settlement sites in southern Italy. This is also one of the few projects which has adopted a phenomenological approach to the consideration of sites other than monuments.

Another criticism is that there has been little attention paid to the vegetational cover which existed at the time the sites under consideration were constructed and used. Cummings and Whittle (2003) have examined this in respect of the presence of woodland which may have obscured the view from monuments to distant peaks, for example. They conclude that some sites were in open settings and others in woodland but argue that:

'It seems likely that from sites which were surrounded by trees, the encircling landscape would still have been visible, even if only for part of the year.' (Cummings & Whittle 2003:263)

However, as Fleming (2005a) points out, this would not apply if one was approaching the site from below as then, at all times of the year, it and the surrounding hills would be obscured by tree trunks.

More fundamental criticisms of the phenomenological approach relate to its validity, firstly, in terms of whether contemporary encounters with landscape can ever compare with the experiences of prehistoric people and, secondly, whether the relationships between sites and their surroundings identified by archaeologists had any significance in the past. In respect of the first of these, Brück (2005) draws attention both to the variability of human physical experience (in terms of age, gender, disability, etc) and to the fact that embodied experience is subject to social and cultural influences. She also points out that, whereas Tilley carried out his fieldwork on the Dorset Cursus alone, prehistoric people are likely to have walked along it in the company of others and that this would have significantly affected their experience of it. Consequently, present-day experiences of ancient sites are unlikely to be the same as those of the people who built and used them.

In relation to the second aspect, Brück (2005) and Fleming (1999; 2005a; 2006), amongst others, have argued that a much more rigorous examination, with a larger sample size, is needed to establish whether there is a relationship between the siting of monuments and other landscape features. As Brück says, 'This requires careful distinction between association and causation.' (2005:51) For example, Tilley (1994) has suggested that megalithic sites in south-west Wales were frequently located in close relationship to inland rock outcrops. However, as Fleming points out, such sites are likely to survive better on agriculturally poorer land and also where there are other sources of stone, such as quarries and outcrops, which would have reduced the likelihood of megalithic structures being destroyed for their stone. Consequently, the chances of surviving sites being located close to outcrops is increased (Fleming 1999:120).

Fleming has also challenged the accuracy of some statements made by phenomenologists such as Tilley and Cummings. He draws attention to the flexibility shown by Tilley in his definition of a relationship between a tomb and a rock outcrop; in some cases, this indicates that they are in immediate proximity, in others that there is a distance of a few hundred metres between them and in still others that the outcrop is several kilometres distant.

Likewise, he demonstrates that a significant association is claimed between a megalithic tomb and an outcrop when the outcrop is visible from the tomb and also when it is invisible (Tilley 1994; Cummings & Whittle 2004, quoted in Fleming 2005). Fleming also argues that some of Cummings' field observations are not accurate, citing, for example, her assertion that Cerrig Llwydion is on the top of a hill whereas, in fact, the summit is approximately 100m away and her inclusion of the outcrop 400m from Carreg Samson in her diagram of features around the monument although it cannot be seen from it.

Tilley's and Cummings' study areas are quite small but, in each case, they have identified a variety of different relationships between monuments and the surrounding landscape features. Despite their confident assertions that these relationships are deliberate, it is impossible to be certain that they are not just chance occurrences.

Although Tilley, Bender and others have carried out work in different parts of Cornwall, particularly at Leskernick and elsewhere on Bodmin Moor and in West Penwith (e.g. Tilley 1995; 1996; Bender et al. 1997; Tilley & Bennett 2001), they have not studied the sites of Scilly. Robinson, however, in his study of the prehistoric landscape of Scilly, states that his 'overriding approach to fieldwork was phenomenological, in that research questions and fieldwork strategies evolved from being in and experiencing the island landscape.' (Robinson 2007:26) Robinson criticises other researchers such as Richards (1996) for not taking sufficient note of the role of the sea in the setting of Neolithic monuments on islands and addressed this in his own research by undertaking journeys between the islands by kayak so that he could observe features, both natural and built, from the sea.

Robinson continues the work of Tilley, Bender and others by examining the relationship between monuments and natural features of the landscape. He argues that entrance graves have a coastal distribution in Scilly and suggests that this is related to inter-visibility between sites and over coastal inlets and bays, marking entry and landing points. However, in assuming that the current, largely coastal, distribution of entrance graves is the original one, Robinson does not take account of the sites in the interior of St Mary's known to have been destroyed in the late 19th or early 20th century and the likelihood that many others in agricultural areas have also been lost. The effect of this on the distribution of sites will be considered in chapter 6.

Breen has also adopted a broadly phenomenological approach (without defining it as such) to her study of the relationship between built and natural features in Scilly but has considered whether the prehistoric observer would have made the same distinction between them (Breen 2006). Her work has examined the stone walls, cairns and entrance graves on Shipman Head Down, Bryher, Kittern Hill, Gugh, Chapel Down, St Martin's and Castle Down, Tresco. She records her failure to find a pattern in these different areas and concludes that built and natural features were given equal account so that, for example, a wall could be terminated at either an entrance grave or an outcrop.

In a further study of Shipman Head Down (Breen 2008), she recognises the bias towards the visual in phenomenological studies of landscape and identifies the need for other sensory aspects to be addressed. In her discussion of the function of the stone walls on Shipman Head Down, she argues that there is no evidence that they have been robbed for stone in later periods and rejects an agricultural purpose for them. Her experience of walking along the walls and the need to negotiate cairns and wall junctions led her to notice many gaps in the walls, which were often flanked by cairns. She goes on to consider other aspects of the experience of walking on Shipman Head Down including the impact of the weather and the possibility that prehistoric people walked barefoot.

While this is a thought-provoking piece, adopting a more considered approach than many phenomenological studies, unfortunately Breen does not draw many conclusions from her work other than to state that fields 'structure the movements and experiences of people' (2008b:107).

In the light of the critique of the phenomenological approach to the study of monuments presented above, such an approach will not be adopted in this work. The value of examining the landscape setting of burial monuments is recognised however and the setting of the Scillonian monuments, their inter-visibility and their relationships with natural and built features will be considered, using GIS-based mapping, in chapter 6.

2.5 Colour, light and sound in megalithic chambers

The interest in the use of colour, light and sound in megalithic tombs has, in some cases, been part of an 'archaeology of the senses'. In others, it has been prompted by a consideration of burial chambers as special places, as outlined in section 2.6 below.

One of the first authors to consider the role of colour in megalithic structures was Lynch (1998), whose perspective was mainly aesthetic rather than symbolic. She drew attention to the use of coloured stones at a number of sites, including the importance of quartz at Newgrange and the Clava cairns but commented that at many sites the stones were all of the same, local, material.

A different approach was taken by Jones who examined the use of different rocks in the construction of megalithic graves. He argued that the colours red, black and white have a widespread importance as the components of a symbolic colour system (Jones 1999). In Arran, the use of red sandstone and white schist and granite in the construction of the chambered tombs reflects the island's geology. However, Jones argues, this is not simply a matter of convenience for the builders as the different rocks were used in a structured and patterned way.

Jones also suggests that the architecture and orientation of the tombs in Arran would have created areas of darkness and light inside the tomb which would have emphasised the coloured stones in the façade and entrance. This, he argues, was further enhanced by the deposition of artefacts of black pitchstone and grey and red flint in the tombs. Overall, the construction and location of the tombs served to 'give meaning to the properties and relations of the wider landscape.' (Jones 1999:349) Jones has also argued that, in some individual burials of the Early Bronze Age, coloured grave goods, made of substances such as jet, gold and faience, served to commemorate the personhood of the deceased rather than simply to indicate their status (Jones 2002).

Owoc has examined the use of colour in the mounds surrounding funerary/ritual sites of the Bronze Age in south-west England. Drawing on ethnographic data relating to the importance of colour in ritual, she argues that the use of yellow clay to form mound caps on sites in the St Austell area of Cornwall is linked to the importance of the sun in the alignment of these sites (Owoc 2002).

Darvill has reviewed the use of white stone, in particular quartz, at sites in the Isle of Man and elsewhere in northern and western Britain. Quartz has been widely found in megalithic tombs, both as a component of the structure and as a deposit in the chamber (Darvill 2002). The excavator of the chamber at Achnacree, Argyll commented that the quartz pebbles there 'shone as if illuminated' (Smith 1872, quoted in Darvill 2002), suggesting a possible reason for their inclusion and significance. Darvill argues that quartz is used to symbolise 'the presence or soul of a person.' (2002:85)

In reviewing the role of colour in prehistoric societies, Scarre has traced the use of naturally coloured materials, such as ochre, from the Palaeolithic and suggests that red has a widespread symbolic importance and also that red, white and black are significant in many different cultures (Scarre 2002a). These colours appear in megalithic structures in several parts of western Europe, in some cases requiring certain stones to be transported from a considerable distance. A contrast can also be found at some sites in terms of the brightness of the rocks used, for example, dull schist and bright quartz, as well as their texture and shape. However, Scarre points out that it may not have been the colour of the stones which was important in itself but the fact that this marked them out as being from elsewhere.

There has been little consideration of the use of colour in the Scillonian sites. The islands are composed almost entirely of granite with quartz dykes and tourmaline present within it (Scourse 2006b). The entrance graves and cists all appear to have been constructed of granite and, because quartz occurs in quantity around the islands, its presence in burial chambers may not have been recorded. Only one site, Wingletang Down E, a possible cist grave on St Agnes, has been noted as incorporating quartz in its construction. Whilst the fabric of the funerary urns often contains quartz inclusions, quartz pebbles have not been recorded at any site. However, boulders arranged in a north-south alignment, recorded during archaeological monitoring on Bryher, were found to have concentrations of quartz pebbles around them, suggesting that quartz may have had a special significance in Scilly as elsewhere (Sawyer 2011a).

The presence of mortar has been recorded at entrance graves on St Martin's, St Mary's and Samson and will be discussed in chapter 5. The quantity of mortar surviving from Knackyboy Cairn, St Martin's suggests that 'it may originally have been carried up the sides of the tomb, to form a complete rendering' (O'Neil 1948-1949:49). This mortar is pale grey in colour but it is possible that it was originally painted or decorated in some way and that different colours were thereby incorporated into the chamber.

Examining a related aspect to the use of colour, Bradley (1989) has considered how light and dark within megalithic tombs was influenced by the tomb's design as well as its orientation and how this relates to the location of decorated stones. In Scilly, all the entrance graves have a single rectangular chamber with no divisions within it and no decorated stones have been identified. In most cases, the entrance is slightly narrower than the chamber itself but this does not significantly restrict the light entering the chamber.

An exception is Porth Hellick Down A, St Mary's where there is both a passage and an upright stone blocking more than half of the entrance; this site is also oriented to the north-north-west so the sun only shines into the chamber shortly before sunset on and around the midsummer solstice. Unlike other intact chambers, such as Innisidgen Carn, St Mary's, which are illuminated from the outside, the chamber at Porth Hellick A is almost completely dark most of the time. At a few other Scillonian sites the chamber entrance faces into the hillslope, so that light into the chamber would have been restricted; this can be seen at Works Carn, Bryher, Obadiah's Barrow, Gugh and Lower Innisidgen, St Mary's. From the limited information available about excavated sites, it does not appear that human remains were placed in the darkest parts of the chamber in Scilly, as Bradley suggests would have been the case at some Severn-Cotswold tombs.

Sound in megalithic chambers has received less attention than colour and light but Watson and Keating (1999; 2000) have studied the acoustics of megalithic monuments including the restored passage grave of Camster Round in Caithness. Here it was found that the chamber walls reflected the sound waves, amplifying noises and creating echoes, the sound was transmitted along the passage and could be heard outside the entrance but was much quieter at the edge of the forecourt. Around the perimeter of the cairn, sound could be heard clearly in some places but was indistinct in others (Watson & Keating 1999:328). Other experiments were carried out using vocalisation

and percussion and the possibility of producing infrasonic resonances, which can have both psychological and physiological effects on people, was considered. Watson and Keating suggest that acoustic effects of the chambers would have combined with other aspects to produce a very powerful impact on those present.

However, Brück (2005) points out that all enclosed spaces have an effect on sound waves and that it is not clear whether megalithic tombs and other structures were designed to have particular acoustic properties or whether this was a chance outcome. She compares this with the similar lack of evidence for a link between the siting of monuments and their landscape setting in the work of Tilley, Cummings and others.

There is limited scope, from the present evidence, for examining the use of colour in Scillonian burial chambers. The stones employed in their construction appear all to be local granite and, in the absence of a detailed geological study of them, it is not possible currently to identify the sources of individual stones or to discern any pattern in their use. Equally, there has been little recording of the cairns which cover entrance graves and cists and so no opportunity to examine whether coloured soils were used in them. Given this lack of information, the use of colour and light at Scillonian sites will not be considered further.

2.6 Megaliths in the landscape

It is not only those adopting a phenomenological approach who have examined the landscape setting of megalithic monuments. This aspect has been addressed by several authors who have taken a broader perspective. Some of the most satisfactory explanations of the purpose and function of megalithic burial chambers have been put forward by authors who have not invoked just one model but have suggested that several of the approaches described above - and others - can be put together to produce a more multi-faceted understanding of these structures.

In his study of the wedge tombs of the Mizen peninsula, south-west Ireland, O'Brien argues that megalithic tombs would have had a variety of meanings for the societies which built them (and, indeed, for subsequent generations) and that, therefore, our attempts to find a simple explanation of their 'function' is misguided. He stresses the need to consider not only the secular aspects of the tombs but also their spiritual and ritual importance and he highlights their role as both a 'burial place' and a 'place with burials' (O'Brien 1999:191). He suggests that the building of wedge tombs would have been attended by ritual and ceremony at all stages, including selecting the site, sourcing, transporting and preparing the stones for construction and, finally, building the tomb.

O'Brien discusses the importance of ritual in societies and suggests that it is a way in which fundamental beliefs are confirmed and communicated. Megalithic tombs, as settings where rituals relating to the dead and the otherworld took place, would have had a significant role in this. The sacred space constituted by the tomb and its chamber would have been an important aspect of the landscape. O'Brien outlines many possible functions of the Mizen wedge tombs, including roles as shrines or cenotaphs and as places for offerings, particularly of metal objects.

The wedge tombs of the Mizen peninsula have a number of similarities with the Scillonian entrance graves: they are small structures with a simple form and mode of construction, there is no obvious pattern to suggest a chronological development of tomb architecture and they 'all conform to certain general principles of design and execution, while differing in specific architectural details on an individual level' (O'Brien 1999:195). In addition, most wedge tombs were located near, but not on, good agricultural land and, probably, close to settlements.

Their locations do not indicate that a particular landscape setting was of over-riding concern to their builders. The consistency of chamber shape (in both wedge tombs and entrance graves) and mound shape (in the case of entrance graves) may demonstrate a religious imperative linked, O'Brien argues in the case of wedge tombs, with an opening facing the west to emphasise the contrast between light/life and darkness/death.

Like the entrance graves of Scilly, the Mizen wedge tombs do not have internal divisions nor, in the majority of cases, septal stones or other restrictions at the entrance. However, O'Brien argues that this does not necessarily imply that they were open and accessible in the prehistoric period. The control of space in megalithic chambers, proposed by Tilley, Thomas and others and outlined above, did not rely only on physical barriers but could equally have been achieved by '[s]ocial convention and religious taboo' (O'Brien 1999:198). However, in contrast to many other megalithic tombs, the height of the chamber at many Mizen and Scillonian sites would have meant that access was only possible by crawling in and this would have enhanced the sense of encountering the otherworld.

The evidence for burials at the Mizen sites is limited; although both inhumations and cremations are present, no remains have been uncovered at some sites and, where they are present, there is usually only a small quantity of bone. O'Brien suggests that some of the smaller wedge tombs may have been erected for the burial of a single individual or for a very small number of burials only.

The megalithic tombs of the Mizen peninsula and Scilly are not directly comparable: the entrance graves in Scilly do not have a consistent orientation, as will be outlined in chapter 6, and they include much larger stones than the wedge tombs, suggesting that a larger community was involved in their construction. The Scillonian sites are frequently located prominently on hilltops or the upper part of hillslopes and, unlike the Mizen wedge tombs, monument inter-visibility seems to be an important factor; again this will be discussed in chapter 6.

O'Brien's wide-ranging review of the possible interpretations which can be made from the, often limited, information from megalithic tombs provides a useful contrast to the more restrictive analyses put forward by some of the other authors whose work has been considered earlier in this chapter (e.g. Shanks & Tilley 1982; Tilley 1984; Thomas 1988; Tilley 1994).

In another paper which seeks to challenge the way prehistoric monuments have been viewed by archaeologists, Brophy, in a consideration of the development of typological systems for the chambered tombs of Scotland, stresses the attention paid in this to their architectural aspects, such as the shapes of the chamber and cairn, the length of the passage, etc. He suggests that other aspects may have been more important to the builders of these monuments and includes in these 'the height of the cairn, the landscape setting of the monument, the materials used to build the cairn, its biography, and its usage.' (Brophy 2005:8)

He suggests that we should consider monuments primarily as places. These places were monumentalised and the reasons for this, he suggests, relate much more to the memories and actions associated with the site than they do to its architectural components or radiocarbon date. Like O'Brien, Brophy stresses the importance of the people involved in the building and use of these monuments and encourages an interpretation which takes them into account, rather than focusing on a classification of the monument types.

Scarre has examined landscape setting and materiality in relation to megalithic monuments, particularly in Brittany and the Channel Islands. Of particular relevance to this review is his work in the Molène islands off the north-west coast of Brittany and in Herm in the Channel Islands, both areas with a considerable density of megalithic burial chambers.

Scarre highlights the selection of coastal headlands and islands as locations for passage graves in Brittany and the fact that the low-lying islands of the Molène archipelago have a significantly greater density of megalithic monuments than neighbouring Ouessant, which has high cliffs surrounding it. He cites a number of ethnographic parallels relating to the liminality of coastlines to explain the large number of sites in the Molène islands (Scarre 2002b). Molène and Scilly have both been affected by rising sea levels and it may be that similar factors influenced the building of megalithic tombs in the two archipelagos.

Scarre's recent examination of the megalithic chambers of Herm, where the landmass appears to have increased in size since the prehistoric period due to the deposition of sand, again indicates a coastal setting for the majority of the structures. There is evidence, also, for contemporary settlement in the vicinity, as there is on some of the Molène islands, and no reason to believe that either Herm or Molène was a necropolis (Scarre 2008; 2011c).

FIGURE 2.1 STATUE-MENHIR ON CHAPEL DOWN, ST MARTIN'S

Scarre has also stressed the significance of the quarrying and movement of the large stone blocks used in megalithic burial chambers, citing aspects such as the selection of stones which already had cup-marks in them or which had been brought from some distance away as links to special places in the landscape (Scarre 2011b). Whilst cup-marked stones have been identified in Scilly, none have been noted in entrance graves or cists. However, as many of the chambers are overgrown with bramble and gorse, it is possible that they are present but not currently visible.

As well as the power of place invoked by cup-marked stones, the anthropomorphic form of some of the stones used in megalithic structures has been highlighted by Scarre. In particular, he has drawn attention to the carved face on the capstone at Le Déhus and the statue-menhirs at Câtel and St Martin, all in Guernsey, and suggested that these may be elements in establishing an island identity (Scarre 2011d), a topic which will be touched on in chapter 9.

Whilst no stones with human features have been found in Scillonian burial chambers, a statue-menhir was discovered on Chapel Down, St Martin's in the late 1940s (Lewis 1948:6). Its precise location was not recorded but there are several entrance graves on Chapel Down and it is possible that it was associated with one of them. It is illustrated in figure 2.1. In addition, Lewis recorded finding a shaped stone at Tinkler's Hill E, as outlined in chapter 5.

These more wide-ranging approaches to the study of megaliths, employed by researchers such as O'Brien,

Brophy and Scarre, have provided opportunities to examine different aspects of the structures in their physical and cultural settings. This has facilitated the study of megaliths in relation to contemporary settlement and landscape and the consideration of a variety of roles for them, as places for burial, for offerings and for ceremonies, as providing links with other significant locales, as sites with their own history and, essentially, as special places.

In this work this type of analysis of the Scillonian entrance graves will be attempted. It will examine not only their physical structure and contents but will also consider their relationship with landscape features, with each other and with settlements. A range of possible functions will also be considered.

2.7 Refitting of megaliths

Another aspect of megalithic structures, which has been examined in recent years, is the refitting of the stone blocks used in their construction to their original quarries. This has enabled the order and method of construction of some stone alignments and tombs to be established. This approach, initially used in western France, has developed techniques for distinguishing between the weathered and fresh faces of stone blocks so that the order in which the blocks were removed from an outcrop can be reconstructed. This has enabled the sequence of construction of the Le Manio alignments at Carnac to be proposed (Mens 2008).

Analysis of megalithic graves is more difficult because, in many cases, the stones are hidden by a barrow or cairn. However, Mens has studied the passage grave of Kerbourg in Loire-Atlantique where the cairn has disappeared. Here, he found that the fresh faces of the stones were consistently oriented towards the inside of the chamber, an arrangement which Mens has observed at other sites in western France. He also identified that the capstones had come from the upper part of an outcrop but that the orthostats were from the lower levels.

This suggests that the capstones were stored for a period while the orthostats were quarried and set up. Mens (2011) argues that this arrangement of the stones means that the passage tomb is, effectively, a reconstruction of the natural outcrop. This has resonance with Scarre's work on the use of cup-marked and non-local stones in burial chambers.

Mens' examination of the stones in the circle at Boscawen-Un, Cornwall has shown that, where it is possible to identify the weathered face, it is normally oriented to the interior and at the timber circle (Seahenge) at Holme-next-the-Sea, Norfolk all but one of the trees had their cut sides facing inwards and their bark on the outside of the circle.

In Scilly, Robinson has examined the arrangement of stones in entrance graves and has concluded that, in respect of capstones, they were consistently arranged with the weathered side facing outwards (2007:132-133). Only a small sample is available for inspection as many entrance graves have most of their mounds in place, making a detailed examination impossible. Some information about the orientation of stones in chamber walls and kerbs can be obtained from excavation plans and the results of this will be discussed in chapter 4.

2.8 Conclusions

This chapter has sought to review recent approaches to the study of megaliths, to examine their relevance and usefulness to the study of entrance graves in Scilly and to identify the approaches which will be adopted in the research reported in this work. In the last twenty years, studies of burial chambers have progressed from single explanations for their construction, distribution or use, such as a role as territorial markers or as indicators of power relations, to more complex, multi-faceted interpretations.

Phenomenology has had a significant influence on the study of monuments and, particularly, of megalithic structures. Whilst many researchers would reject the premise that 21st century archaeologists from the developed world can replicate the experiences of prehistoric people in their encounters with these structures, the focus on studying the position and role of monuments in the wider landscape has been a valuable development.

This has led to an appreciation that, whilst most of these structures were probably built initially as graves, they acquired other roles. These structures were community monuments, where significant events in the life of that community took place and, in examining them, it is important to attempt to appreciate their significance to the people who built and used them. O'Brien has highlighted the ceremonial aspect of all phases of their use, from the selection of a location to their construction, then to the deposition of burials in them and the placing of offerings (O'Brien 1999). In attempting to identify one function for them we fail to recognise the wide-ranging significance that they had not only to their builders but to subsequent generations. The long periods of use of these structures indicates their continuing relevance.

In this study, therefore, a broadly based consideration of the entrance graves and cists of the Isles of Scilly will be undertaken. Their physical structure and contents as well as their landscape setting, orientation and inter-visibility will be examined. The origins and functions of the monuments and their significance to the communities that built and used them will also be considered. An analysis of their relationship with settlements will allow their possible role as territorial markers to be addressed and a review of their proximity to natural features will permit aspects of the phenomenological approach to them to be considered. Overall, however, no single theoretical model will be followed.

Chapter 3

Previous research on the entrance graves and cists of Scilly

3.1 Introduction

This chapter will consider the previous authors and researchers who have written about the entrance graves and cists of Scilly and will review the contribution they have made to our current knowledge and understanding of these structures.

The earliest references to the Isles of Scilly are in the writings of the Roman authors, Pliny, Solinus and Sulpicius Severus, between the first and fifth centuries AD (Thomas 1985:2). The islands are also mentioned in two of the Norse sagas, the *Orkneyinga-saga* and the *Heimskringla*.

The first English authors to write about Scilly, as part of works covering a much more extensive area, were William Worcestre, writing in about 1480 (Harvey 1965) and John Leland (Leland 1745), who may have visited Scilly in about 1540 (Bowley 1990). Leland mentions the 13th century castle in Old Town but makes no reference to the prehistoric monuments.

3.2 The 18th and 19th century authors

It was not until the mid-18th century that the first detailed works about Scilly were published. These were aimed to provide a general description of a little-known part of the British Isles and covered both the islands' history and their contemporary appearance, economy, people and customs. In some cases they were intended to impress upon the authorities Scilly's importance to the defence of the country and, in others, particularly those written at the end of the eighteenth and beginning of the nineteenth centuries, one of the main motivations was to draw attention to the extreme poverty of some of the population.

Heath

The earliest account is that of Robert Heath who spent a year in Scilly as an Army officer in 1744. He provides a description of the islands together with directions on sailing to Scilly but, although his title page includes 'Antiquities' as one of the topics to be addressed, his chapter on history does not go back beyond the tenth century. In his preface Heath states that: 'These Islands were first discovered by the Phoenicians and afterwards by the Romans' (1750:3) but he does not mention any sites relating to these supposed occupiers or any others of prehistoric date.

Borlase

William Borlase (1696-1772), the well-known Cornish antiquarian and natural historian, visited Scilly for about a fortnight in May and June 1752 (Pool 1986) and was the first author to record the prehistoric sites. He remarks that there were no 'remains of Phenician, Grecian or Roman art' but that the antiquities were 'of the rudest Druid times'. He lists 'several rude stone pillars; Circles of Stones erect; Kist-vaens without number; Rock-basons; Tolmêns' (Borlase 1753:56).

On St Mary's he identified several 'ancient Sepulchres' which he divides into two categories: 'Caves' and 'Barrows' or 'Burrows', although he does not give details of the construction of Caves and does not use this classification in his subsequent descriptions of the monuments.

He describes the Giant's Cave near Toll's Hill on St Mary's as being four feet six inches wide, thirteen feet eight inches long and three feet eight high, covered with large flat stones and having a tumulus of rubbish on top. He concedes that 'it may admit Giants when they are dead' (1756:14). Barrows/Burrows he describes as having an outer ring of large stones placed on end around a heap of smaller stones, clay and earth in which there is generally a 'cavity of stone work … cover'd with flat stones'(1756:15). He makes the point, however, that there is considerable variation in the sizes of both the Barrows and the cavities.

Borlase records both types of burial site on St Mary's, as well as 'one sepulchral Burrow' on Northwethel. On St Martin's he mentions a stone circle and 'two circular sepulchral Burrows; a third erected on the very summit, had a covered Cave in the middle' and a fourth is referred to nearby. On Bryher again he records 'many small Burrows edged with stone' as well as a very large example containing 'many Kistvaens' and comments: 'This Burrow, you see, was not the Sepulchre of one only, but of many.' (Borlase 1756:23-25) On Samson Borlase found eleven Stone-Burrows on one hilltop and a Stone-Burrow and a Kistvaen on the other, while on the island of Arthur in the Eastern Isles he found three Burrows.

Borlase attributed many of the sites he identified, both in Scilly and in Cornwall, to the Druids and has been subsequently criticised for this (Pool 1986). He regarded natural rock basins as being Druidical as well as describing man-made structures, such as stone circles, as 'places of Druid worship' (Borlase 1756:11). In this he was following the accepted ideas of his time as there was no established chronology for the pre-Roman period.

Borlase undertook the first recorded excavations in Scilly when he opened two barrows on Buzza Hill, St Mary's. In the first he found no bones or urns, just 'some strong unctuous earth which smelt cadaverous' (1756:15). He describes a stone chamber in the middle of the mound with a narrowed entrance at the eastern end and a covering of large flat stones.

The second he describes as being smaller, with a 'small round cell' in the centre of the chamber which had contained different coloured earths (Borlase 1756:15). This chamber was also covered with flat stones. He makes no mention of any artefacts and states that he was unable to find any evidence that urns had ever been found in Scilly. In both these cases, Borlase provided the dimensions of the chambers in his published work as well as scaled drawings of the mounds and chambers (1756:Pl II, figs i and iv).

Borlase also drew attention to the fact that on Samson there were stone walls under the sand banks and some running down the hills and under the sea towards Tresco (1753; 1756). He suggested from this that the islands were once a single land-mass and that the low-lying areas, which had been inundated by sea and sand, were previously cultivated. Having considered the possibilities that either the sea levels had risen or the land had sunk, he concluded that the latter was the more likely explanation.

Although Borlase spent only a short period in the islands he left a valuable record of the sites which he observed, some of which are no longer visible, and of the excavations which he carried out. The following two authors, Troutbeck and Woodley, each spent more than a decade in Scilly and consequently provide greater detail of the monuments.

Troutbeck

The Rev John Troutbeck was the chaplain to the Duke of Leeds, the tenant of Scilly, and lived in the islands between 1780 and 1794. He relied heavily on the earlier authors mentioned above, particularly Heath, in his account of the islands (Troutbeck 1796).

Although not an antiquarian like Borlase, Troutbeck makes several references to the prehistoric sites of Scilly. He too refers to the inundation of the islands and says that the sea was still continually encroaching on the land, to the extent that 'many acres and some houses' had been lost within living memory (Troutbeck 1796:2). He mentions stone circles, which he too regarded as Druid temples, and ancient sepulchres or barrows.

In his descriptions of the barrows, of which he had clearly made careful observations, he stresses that the manner of construction is nearly always the same but that the size of the barrows varies considerably. Like Borlase, he says that the outer ring was composed of large stones and the mound within of smaller stones, clay and earth mixed together. He says that there is generally a cavity inside the mound which is covered with flat stones; in some cases the cavity is scarcely apparent, in others it is made of such large stones that 'they make the principal figure in the whole monument' (Troutbeck 1796:4). In these cases he felt the cavity was so big that it might have contained more than one body.

Troutbeck believed that the barrows must have been the burial places for those of high rank only. He mentions the fact that small stones, burnt clay and earth were found in the area near where the body was deposited; he felt that the natural heat of these would have soon reduced the body to a skeleton. He concludes that the burials were probably those of Phoenicians who had traded with Scilly.

In his catalogue of the barrows, rock basins, 'Druidical temples' and other ancient sites, Troutbeck refers to some barrows, such as one at 'Inazigan Hill', St Mary's (now known as Innisidgen Carn) as containing a 'cave of mason's work' (Troutbeck 1796:99). By this he seems to mean one where the chamber walls were built, at least partially, of coursed drystone or mortared walling rather than large slabs of stone.

On Watch Hill, Bryher Troutbeck records a pit in the ground, measuring four feet long, two feet eight inches wide and two feet deep, surrounded by four flat slabs, the top stones of which had been taken away for house-building. From this brief description no definite conclusions can be drawn but it is likely that these were the remains of a cist grave.

In his description of St Agnes Troutbeck mentions the opening, a few years previously, of a barrow on the north hill of 'The Guew' (now known as Kittern Hill, Gugh). This was done in order 'to gratify their curiosity' by some people from St Agnes. In the barrow they found 'some coarse earthen pots' which they broke accidentally with their shovels and pickaxes. Troutbeck explains that, because of the damage to the pots, their shape was not known but that they appeared to have contained about one gallon each. He states that 'nothing was found therein but some ashes and cinders' and adds that the people of St Agnes could not conceive why a giant's grave should have earthen pots in it (Troutbeck 1796:154-155).

A further mention is made of earthen pots being discovered in a barrow on Great Arthur; again they were so badly broken that their shape and size could not be determined. There is no discussion of or comment on the ashes and cinders; as the cremation of human remains was unknown in eighteenth century England the discoverers of the urns would have no reason to suspect that their contents were human burials.

Woodley

The Rev George Woodley was a minister in the islands in the 1820s and 1830s being the missionary of the Society for

Promoting Christian Knowledge. He again provides detailed records of the prehistoric sites, describing 'cromlechs' as having a large flat stone lying horizontally on others fixed in the ground and 'barrows' as large sepulchral caves covered by a mound of earth (Woodley 1822).

He reports that on Porth Hellick Down, St Mary's:

'I caused a cromlech and a burrow to be opened, to the depth of several feet, but found nothing but a greasy black earth, as if resulting from the decomposition of animal substances' (Woodley 1822:211).

It is clear from Woodley's subsequent description that the chamber had already been disturbed as at least one capstone was missing and the earth had been cleared away from below where it had been. This echoes information given by both Borlase and Troutbeck that stones had been recently removed from the entrance graves for building purposes.

In his later publication Woodley provides a detailed description of Scillonian 'burrows', saying that they are circular but with flat rather than round tops, and adding that they 'do not appear to agree precisely with any of the denominations given to these sepulchral monuments by antiquarian writers'. He goes on to say that they are defined by a ring of large stones, from two to four feet high, 'serving both as fences and as objects to attract attention'. Within this there is a mound of earth and small stones with a chamber 'composed of massy blocks' in the centre. The chamber is covered with two or three large slabs laid cross-wise over it. He ends his description by saying that 'sometimes a cromlech stands at the head of the depository or a small circle of stones skirts the top of the mound' (Woodley 1833:30; Ashbee 1955).

Smith

Augustus Smith (1804-1872) was the Lord Proprietor of Scilly from 1834 until his death in 1872. He had wide-ranging scientific interests and in 1862 excavated a barrow on North Hill, Samson with a visiting group from the Cambrian Archaeological Association. He gave a lecture on their discoveries to the Royal Institution of Cornwall the following year (Smith 1863).

In this he described the cairn of earth and stone which covered a cist containing burnt bone. By this time, the practice of human cremation was known and the significance of this discovery was therefore recognised. However, Smith did not connect it with Troutbeck's (1796) reports of ashes and cinders as he describes the Samson cist as the 'single instance where the burning of the body had been resorted to' (1863:53).

Although Smith reported only bone as having been found in the cist, William Copeland Borlase states that during a subsequent examination of the remains a flint flake was found amongst them (1872:161).

3.3 20th century researchers

From the very beginning of the 20th century detailed archaeological research, including the first modern excavations, took place in Scilly. There was no concerted programme of research, however, and the majority of those who carried out this work were not resident in the islands. Their work was, in some cases, an adjunct to a holiday visit to Scilly and was therefore often *ad hoc* in nature.

Bonsor

George Bonsor (1855-1930), an Anglo-French archaeologist who spent much of his life in Spain, carried out excavations in Scilly between 1899 and 1902 (Bonsor 1899-1900; Bonsor 1901-1902; Ashbee 1980; Maier 1999). Although Ashbee approves of the accuracy of Bonsor's plans and says that his excavations were 'in advance of their time' (1976:11), unfortunately, Bonsor did not publish the results of any of his work in Scilly. His only reference to it is in a non-academic article in which he says: 'Three years of excavation, however, have assured me definitely that today there is no tin to be found in ... Scilly' (1928:17).

Our knowledge of Bonsor's work is based on the study of his unpublished notes and letters (Bonsor 1899-1900; 1900; 1901; 1901-1902; nd c1904) and on the subsequent publication of parts of these by others (Hencken 1932; 1933; Ashbee 1974; 1980; Maier 1999; Robinson 2005).

From these published sources it has been established that Bonsor excavated three of the largest entrance graves in Scilly: Bant's Carn and Porth Hellick 'Great Tomb' (Porth Hellick Down A) on St Mary's and Obadiah's Barrow on Gugh as well as drawing plans of some smaller graves and a section of the midden at Halangy Porth, St Mary's. Maier (1999) records that Bonsor also excavated on Normandy Down, St Mary's in 1902 and Robinson, in his recent research in the British Museum, discovered sherds of pottery found by Bonsor at barrow A there (2005:26). In the course of the research reported here, flints found by Bonsor at a site on Samson (North Hill K) were also discovered to have been donated to the British Museum.

Bonsor's own notes about his visits to Scilly and Maier's detailed examination of them have enabled the following summary of his work there to be compiled. Extracts from Bonsor's notebooks are included in Appendix 3.

Bonsor first went to Scilly in September 1899. He visited the islands in order to establish whether they could be identified as the Cassiterides, the location recorded by Herodotus as being the Phoenicians' source of tin. Bonsor had excavated Phoenician sites in Spain, hence his interest in this topic. He spent about a month in Scilly, visiting and drawing prehistoric sites on many of the islands but carried out no excavations.

However, when he returned in September 1900 he had obtained permission from T A Dorrien-Smith, Augustus

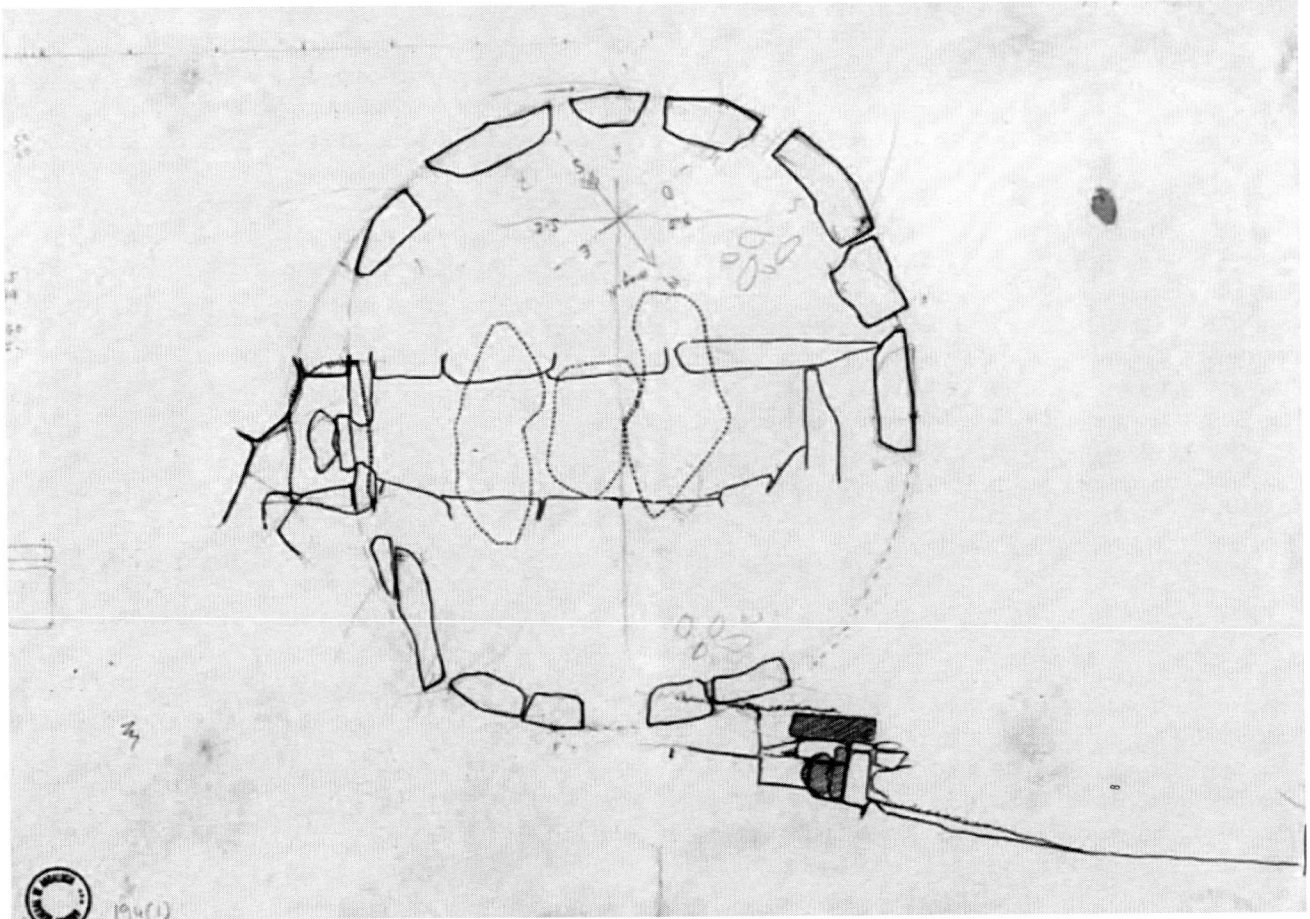

FIGURE 3.1 PLAN OF OBADIAH'S BARROW, GUGH, FROM BONSOR (1901-1902)

Smith's nephew and the then Lord Proprietor, to excavate. Having visited several more sites on other islands, he started work at Bant's Carn on St Mary's, whilst also investigating the nearby settlement site in the cliff-face at Halangy Porth. He believed that the material from the tomb and the huts was of the same period.

Bonsor's main interest was in the settlement site (Maier 1999:155) so he recorded relatively little about his excavation at Bant's Carn although he did draw a plan and sections of the structure. Inside the chamber he found four piles of burnt human bone accompanied by ash, charcoal and numerous fragments of pottery which he said was from funerary urns. The ground outside the entrance to the chamber was covered with broken pottery identical to that in the chamber. Bonsor interpreted this as being the result of a violation of the tomb during which the contents of the urns were tipped out inside the chamber and the urns then smashed. Bonsor believed that this violation had taken place 'many centuries ago' (Bonsor 1900).

Bonsor's next visit to Scilly was in September 1901, when he planned to carry out excavations simultaneously on St Mary's, Gugh and Samson. At Bant's Carn he made further drawings of the site and found more pottery around the chamber entrance. On Gugh, he worked at Obadiah's Barrow, his best recorded excavation. Indeed, it was Bonsor who named this site in honour of Obadiah Hicks

of St Agnes with whom he stayed occasionally whilst undertaking the work (Ashbee 1974). Although part of the chamber had been disturbed, much of it was still untouched (Hencken 1932). According to Bonsor's account, a large quantity of limpet shells had been deposited in the chamber and uncremated bone, both human and animal, had consequently survived in the more alkaline conditions created.

Bonsor's account, which is quoted at length by Hencken, describes the dimensions and contents of the chamber, which included 'parts of the contracted skeleton of a man' and about a dozen funerary urns as well as other artefacts, including bone points and a bronze object. Hencken (1933:22) queries whether it was really a contracted skeleton or just skeletal debris scattered through this layer although Bonsor's notes identify the locations of specific bones (Maier 1999:162-163).

In Bonsor's letter to T A Dorrien-Smith, dated 2 October 1901, he refers to his discovery of the skeleton and says:

'I think this discovery is exceedingly important, it seems at least to indicate that the custom of burial was practised here before cremation' (1901:2).

This is the first recorded identification in Scilly of this sequence of burial rites and, given the scarcity of prehistoric inhumation burials in the islands, because of the acidity of the soil, it is an extremely important observation. Bonsor also mentions that there were over twenty urns, all broken except one. The intact urn he describes as being 'reversed on the ground and covering the ashes which I collected back again into the Urn' (Bonsor 1901:1-2). Bonsor's plan of Obadiah's Barrow is shown in figure 3.1.

At the same time Bonsor was also investigating sites on South Hill, Samson. Here one of his workmen excavated two 'kistvaens' and Bonsor drew a plan of one of them.

Bonsor's final visit to Scilly was in September 1902 when he excavated the 'Great Tomb' on Porth Hellick Down, St Mary's. Here he exposed the capstones of the grave, uncovered the kerb and examined the chamber. The site had already been disturbed and Bonsor found no human remains, only pottery and a piece of pumice stone (Hencken 1932; Ashbee 1980; Maier 1999).

The plan of the site, published by Hencken (1932:21), shows the unusual feature of a large stone slab partially blocking access from the passage to the chamber. Ashbee's version (1974:80) of Bonsor's plan shows an area outside the passage marked 'destroyed surround' although this does not appear in Hencken's version. A contemporary photograph of Bonsor at the site is shown in Appendix 3.

Bonsor was also working nearby, at Normandy Down. Here he examined two mounds in close proximity to each other and found pottery, but no bones, in the chamber and at the entrance of one of them. Bonsor also visited several of the other islands, making lists of sites and plans of their locations. He excavated a further tomb on South Hill, Samson but found nothing in it and two mounds on North Hill, Samson, one of which he interpreted as a hut (North Hill L) and in the other of which (North Hill K) he found two flints, one worked.

He carried out excavations of two mounds of stone and earth on Bryher (but did not give their location) and concluded that they might have been cremation sites (Maier 1999:170). He appears to have investigated three hut sites also, but found no pottery and, finally, excavated the cist on Gweal Hill. Here he found fragments of pottery in the bottom which he said was from a single, undecorated vessel which contained charcoal.

Bonsor's excavations, although frustratingly poorly documented, were the first to provide clear evidence for the use of entrance graves for multiple cremation burials with the urns containing the cremated bones often being placed upside down. He also recorded the occurrence of pottery outside the entrance to chambers as well as identifying an earlier burial rite of inhumation.

In 1926 Bonsor was visited in Spain by Thomas Kendrick, then an Assistant Keeper at the British Museum. Subsequently Bonsor gave some of the artefacts from Obadiah's Barrow, Porth Hellick Down, Normandy Down and Samson to the Museum. His other finds from Scilly, including all the material from Bant's Carn, have never been located but Maier says that they are not at Bonsor's home in Spain, the castle at Mairena del Alcor near Seville (1999:165).

Crawford

O G S Crawford was the Archaeology Officer to the Ordnance Survey when he visited Scilly in 1926 in order to investigate the field boundaries recorded by Borlase (Ashbee 1974). The first article in the first issue of the journal *Antiquity*, which Crawford edited, was about the submerged field boundaries which he had observed on Samson Flats (Crawford 1927).

In the following year he published a paper on stone cists, including descriptions of the example on North Hill, Samson excavated by Smith in 1862 and others elsewhere in the islands (Crawford 1928). In this he drew a useful distinction between burial chambers and cists insisting that, in Britain, cists were not 'degenerate' burial chambers. He stated that:

'These West Country cists are plainly quite different from, and later than, the numerous burial-chambers which occur there, such as those on Normandy Down and Porth Hellick Down, St Mary's. The burial-chambers, or passage-graves, though for the most part not very large, are much bigger and belong to quite a different type. Though of earlier date they belong to the Bronze, not to the Stone Age' (Crawford 1928:421).

He does not, however, explain why he believed that cists were later in date than burial chambers or why he felt that the burial chambers were Bronze Age in date. However the appearance of two articles about Scilly in the first two volumes of *Antiquity*, a national, rather than county, journal can only have helped to spread the word that there were prehistoric sites of great interest in the islands.

Hencken

This increased awareness of Scilly was further assisted by the publication of Hencken's book on *The Archaeology of Cornwall and Scilly* in 1932. Much of this book was based on Hencken's doctoral research, carried out between 1926 and 1929, at the University of Cambridge (Hencken 1929) and it had been Crawford who had first encouraged him to study Cornwall and Scilly (Hencken 1932:viii).

Although the majority of the book is about Cornwall, chapter II, entitled 'Great Stone Monuments', devotes more than 20 pages to the burial chambers of Scilly and appendix B lists 55 chambered barrows and a large cist in the islands. Before commencing his description of the monuments, Hencken assures his readers that Scilly 'is not so difficult of access as might be supposed' and that there are 'comfortable hotels' to be had in Hugh Town. He warns, though, that:

'The steamer trip to Scilly however is nearly always rough, even in summer, and is calculated to impress upon the visitor the seafaring qualities of the mariners of four thousand years ago' (Hencken 1932:20).

As set out in chapter 2 Hencken divides megalithic tombs into three categories: passage-graves, covered galleries and closed chambers. In Scilly, he says, there are only two passage-graves (Porth Hellick 'Great Tomb' and Bant's Carn) and the remainder are all covered galleries. However, he also says that there is a site 'structurally half-way between' the two types on Porth Hellick Down with another, similar one on Northwethel (Hencken 1932:24). He states that the chambered barrows of Scilly are 'really miniature megaliths' (1932:20), pointing out their small size in comparison with sites such as Newgrange and stressing that many of the stones used in their construction are quite small, with large ones employed mainly at the back of the chamber and in the roofing.

Hencken draws extensively on Bonsor's unpublished work and compares the pottery from sites such as Obadiah's Barrow with that from the Breton megaliths. He refers to a small cist being found on St Mary's (but does not give its location) and says that this contained pottery of the same type as that found in the barrows. On this basis, and unlike Crawford, he suggests that the cists were contemporary with the barrows. Hencken concluded that the tombs dated to about 2000BC, adding that 'some were perhaps built a few centuries earlier, and the group may have remained in use for burials for some time afterward' (1932:29).

Although he compares the burial chambers in Scilly with examples in Portugal, Spain and Brittany he concludes that Brittany provides the closest link. This is not only because of its geographical proximity but also because of similarities in chamber structure, burial rite (burned and unburned bones being discovered in chambered tombs in both places) and pottery.

Hencken ends his section on the Scillonian barrows by drawing attention to the large number of them. He compares Scilly with the Channel Isles, islands off Brittany and Scotland as well as those in the southern Baltic, all of which he says have numerous megalithic monuments and all of which he describes as 'obvious place[s] for a sea-borne culture to strike deep root' (Hencken 1932:33).

Hencken's other publication about Scilly is his paper in the *Antiquaries Journal* (1933). In this, he published some of Bonsor's notes and also described his own excavation of a chambered barrow on North Hill, Samson in 1930. This site had already been disturbed and, although he found no human remains, he does record the discovery of flint, pottery and animal bone as well as paving, including the 'upper stone of a saddle quern', in the middle of the chamber (Hencken 1933:27).

Daniel

Just as Hencken was encouraged by Crawford in his study of Scilly so Glyn Daniel cites Hencken as one of his influences in his decision to study the prehistoric megalithic chambers of England and Wales (1982:5). Daniel's book, *The Prehistoric Chamber Tombs of England and Wales,* was based on research which he carried out between 1933 and 1940 and in the course of which he studied all the known and alleged burial chambers in southern Britain (1950:xi). This enabled him to compare the Scillonian examples with the rest of the country and to comment on the similarities and differences.

Daniel defines nine groups of chambered tombs on morphological grounds and the chambers of Scilly (with the similar examples in Penwith, west Cornwall) form one of these groups. In his consideration of the distribution of chambered tombs he highlighted the large number of such structures to be found in Scilly.

Daniel is substantially concerned with the typology of the burial chambers and, from this, with establishing their evolution and relationships. He identifies two types of prehistoric burial chamber in Europe: the passage graves and the gallery graves. He regards the burial chambers of the Scilly group as 'undifferentiated passage graves or entrance graves' with the four forms he defines 'representing various degrees in the formal divorce of passage and chamber' (1950:64).

Daniel's review of the chambered tombs includes a chapter on the finds from them, in which he outlines the discoveries made by Bonsor and Hencken. He also refers to a site on St Martin's which he believes to be a burial chamber but about which he says 'it is impossible to obtain exact information' where burnt flints, pots and pieces of a bronze dagger were found (Daniel 1950:125).

Pursuing his typological approach, Daniel concludes that the Scillonian chambers (and the very similar chambers in Tramore, Co Waterford) represent degenerated true passage graves and that their origins must therefore be sought in a region where there is evidence for passage graves developing into entrance graves. He suggests that this is Brittany or the Channel Islands and favours the former.

Part Two of the book consists of an inventory of sites. Daniel devotes section VIII of this to the tombs of Scilly, providing descriptions and a numbering system (which differs from the one put forward by Hencken) for sites on ten islands. In a footnote he says:

'This account is necessarily short: I hope to publish a full description of the Scilly tombs in due course' (1950:242).

This further publication never appeared but it is interesting to contrast the frequent references to Scilly in *The*

Prehistoric Chamber Tombs of England and Wales with their treatment in more recent publications of a similar scope. Lynch deals with the entrance graves of Cornwall and Scilly in less than half a page with a single reference to Scilly (2004:56) while Scarre (2007) does not mention Scilly at all. Daniel's account, though now dated in much of its approach, remains valuable therefore for the detailed consideration of the Scillonian sites which it provides.

Piggott

In his major work, *Neolithic Cultures of the British Isles*, Stuart Piggott considers what he describes as the Scilly-Tramore group of chambered tombs primarily in connection with their dating. In reviewing the pottery from the sites he stresses that, with the possible exception of a single sherd (now missing) from Bant's Carn, St Mary's, none of the Scillonian pottery 'belongs or is related to any group of Neolithic wares of the British Isles, nor of west France-Iberia' (Piggott 1954a:265). Instead, he says, they show much closer affinities with Cornish pots of the Middle or Late Bronze Age and the associations of the pots with bronze artefacts at two sites in Scilly and the presence of faience beads at Knackyboy, St Martin's provide further support for this dating.

In an earlier article Piggott wrote about the cist grave on Samson excavated by Augustus Smith in 1862. He compared the Samson cist, whose end stones are fitted into grooves cut into the side slabs, with examples in Argyll and proposed an Early Bronze Age date for it. He suggested that these cists are 'stone versions of wooden coffins' (1941:81). Piggott also commented on the likelihood of maritime connections between western Scotland, Co Waterford and Scilly in which Scilly received ideas from the north.

O'Neil

Bryan O'Neil was the Chief Inspector of Ancient Monuments for England and Wales and became a regular visitor to Scilly, where he usually stayed on St Martin's. Much of his archaeological work on the islands was carried out privately during his holidays and most of it has not been published. However, information about two of his excavations, which are relevant to this review, is in the public domain: the preliminary report on the excavation of the entrance grave at Knackyboy Cairn, St Martin's in 1948 (O'Neil 1952) and a short note on work on the burial chamber on Middle Arthur in the Eastern Isles in 1953 (O'Neil 1954).

O'Neil (1952) says that he had been intending to examine settlement sites, in which pottery similar to that from the entrance graves had been found, but was persuaded to work at Knackyboy by the Rev Henry Lewis, the Anglican minister on St Martin's and a keen amateur archaeologist. The chamber at Knackyboy had apparently been badly damaged in about 1912 by islanders obtaining stone for building. However urns and beads had been recovered

and Alexander Gibson, a local antiquarian, had carried out some excavation. O'Neil believed that Knackyboy was the site referred to by Daniel (1950:125) where a 'bronze dagger' had been discovered although he thought (having questioned the alleged finder) that it was more likely to have been a triangular plate from a box.

Following work by Lewis, during which he recovered one hundredweight of pottery, O'Neil continued what was the first excavation of a relatively intact Scillonian chambered tomb since Bonsor's work at Obadiah's Barrow in 1901. O'Neil proceeded to retrieve a further three hundredweight of pottery from Knackyboy which he believed represented the remains of at least 70 urns (1949a:6).

Below the mound an unpolished flint axe or adze was found. Of the urns, eight were standing on the floor of the chamber covered by a layer of ash and cremated bone, in which small pieces of bronze (including a hook and a possible handle) and nine beads were discovered. One of these was a star-shaped faience bead, believed at the time to have originated from nineteenth dynasty Egypt and therefore to date to c1320 to 1200BC. On the basis of this and the range of pottery styles O'Neil concluded that the chamber at Knackyboy had been built shortly before 1200BC and that the tomb had continued in use until c700BC (1952:30). This provided the first chronology for the chambered tombs and was therefore a key step forward in their study.

O'Neil's work at the tomb on Middle Arthur was published as a note in the *Antiquaries Journal*. He examined the site which had been recorded by Hencken as an 'exceedingly small [chambered barrow] in a cairn only 10½ feet in diameter' (1932:26). O'Neil says that the structure is closed at both ends and that it is therefore a cist, not a chamber. He describes it as being triangular or boat-shaped, constructed of orthostats and unique in Scilly (O'Neil 1954).

The site had already been disturbed when O'Neil visited it and he records that only one capstone was in place. However he found sherds of a cinerary urn, including part of the base with cremated bones adhering to it. He says that the pottery is similar in shape to some of the vessels from Knackyboy, which he believed to be of Late Bronze Age date, although not the latest in the series from that site.

O'Neil's sudden and untimely death in 1954 meant that he did not publish a full report on Knackyboy nor pursue the further studies which he had planned (Ashbee 1974).

Ashbee

A further link between researchers on Scillonian chambered tombs is provided by the fact that it was because of O'Neil that Paul Ashbee first visited Scilly in 1949 (Ashbee 1974). Ashbee has published extensively on his work in Scilly and his book *Ancient Scilly* (1974) remains the only overview of the prehistoric and early Mediaeval periods in the islands.

Ashbee devotes chapter 4 of this to 'Chamber Tombs and Barrows' and chapter 5 to 'Stone Cists and Cist-Grave Cemeteries'. Throughout, his book provides detailed information about the sites under consideration but with limited interpretation. Wailes, in his review of the book in *Antiquity*, comments on this but accepts that Ashbee aimed to provide an 'introduction and survey' rather than a critical analysis of cultural process (Wailes 1976).

In relation to chamber tombs Ashbee gives details such as the relative diameters of their mounds, their orientations and the variation in the shape of the chambers as well as plans and sections of many of the sites, which display his skilled draughtsmanship. His chapter on cists includes both those containing cremations and believed to be Bronze Age in date and the larger, later structures dated to the Iron Age and Romano-British period. *Ancient Scilly* therefore provides a valuable synthesis of work prior to 1974, including, in one volume, details of many discoveries and excavations from the mid-18th century onwards.

Ashbee's subsequent publications on Scillonian chambered tombs and cists include his work at Bant's Carn in 1970 when the outer capstone of the chamber was replaced (Ashbee 1976). This entailed resetting one of the jambstones and the original setting was therefore excavated. Pottery sherds from approximately 11 vessels were found beneath the jambstone and in Bonsor's trench; Ashbee says that these were comparable to the vessels from Knackyboy and from contemporary settlement sites in Scilly.

In this article Ashbee also considers the function of Scillonian entrance graves and comments on the apparent association between them and ancient field systems. He refers to the absence of human remains in some of the chambers and the discovery of broken pottery and soil in them and suggests that their primary purpose may not have been as graves. He suggests that the structures should be regarded rather as *fana* or repositories.

Ashbee developed this view further in his 1982 article in which he proposed a Mesolithic origin for the Scillonian entrance graves, linking the distribution of megalithic tombs in Atlantic Europe with the movement of fish and the fishermen following them (Ashbee 1982:5). However, the paucity of Mesolithic and Neolithic sites in Scilly and the absence of radiocarbon dates from the vast majority of the entrance graves and cists make it difficult to adduce evidence to support or challenge these views.

These papers are valuable as representing the first occasion when the rationale for the construction of chambered cairns in Scilly and their function in prehistoric society had been addressed in any detail. The arguments are considered further in chapter 7.

Thomas

Charles Thomas has carried out survey and excavation in Scilly since the 1950s and has published a number of books and articles about the islands. He developed some of Ashbee's work in his key publication on Scilly, *Exploration of a Drowned Landscape* (Thomas 1985). This is a wide-ranging review of many aspects of the islands' archaeology and history and is particularly known for the section on the submergence of Scilly.

Thomas put forward a model of the rate of sea level rise in the islands, based on minimal occupation levels (i.e. the tendency for settlements to be situated at the lowest available level above high spring tides), place names and the more recent data from the Newlyn tide gauge station. He concluded that the sea level rise has been about 2.4mm per year, equating to a rise of 9.6m since 2000BC.

In addition, Thomas examined the process of settlement in Scilly. He discussed the environmental conditions in the islands when they were first permanently occupied and the impact of early agriculture on them. In particular, he applied Renfrew's work on the indicators of a segmentary society to Scilly (Renfrew 1976; Renfrew 1979 cited in Thomas 1985) and, in his chapter on 'Tombs, Temples and Territorial Markers', he considered the function of the chambered cairns and cists. His work in this area will be discussed in chapter 7.

3.4 Recent work

Cornwall Archaeological Unit and Historic Environment Service, Cornwall Council

In recent years, much of the archaeological investigation in Scilly has been carried out as part of monitoring or rescue excavation in advance of development or because of coastal erosion. Because Scilly does not have its own archaeological service, most of this work has been done by archaeologists based in Cornwall.

From the mid-1980s, Jeanette Ratcliffe took lead responsibility for this work and her publications have documented the monitoring carried out when the runway at St Mary's Airport was extended, when mains electricity was installed on the off-islands and when telecommunications trenching was dug on St Martin's (Ratcliffe & Sharpe 1990a; Ratcliffe 1991; 1997).

Further studies assessed the archaeological resource of Scilly and made recommendations for its study, protection and interpretation, provided a detailed record of a number of important sites, including some being affected by coastal erosion and presented an environmental assessment of cliff-face and inter-tidal sites, as well as a model for sea level rise (Ratcliffe 1989; Ratcliffe & Sharpe 1990b; Ratcliffe 1993; Ratcliffe & Straker 1996). During the course of this work, the cist at Borough Farm, Tresco was recorded and the cliff-face sites at Porth Conger and Porth Killier were monitored (Ratcliffe 1991:125-128).

More recently Ratcliffe's work has been continued by Charlie Johns and the archaeology of Scilly has benefited from the input of a number of other academics and specialists (e.g. Johns 2002-03; Ratcliffe & Johns 2003; Mulville 2007; Taylor & Johns 2009-2010; Johns 2011; 2012). This has helped highlight the importance of Scilly's archaeological heritage mainly on a regional scale, although a recent article, which includes a comparison of Scillonian entrance graves with those in Cornwall, has been published in a national journal (Jones & Thomas 2010).

Robinson

The most substantial piece of research in recent years in Scilly has been that carried out by Gary Robinson for his doctoral thesis at University College, London and subsequently published (Robinson 2005; 2007). Robinson examined the prehistoric landscape and seascape of Scilly, assessing the islands' environment and proposing a chronological framework for Scillonian prehistory. He also studied the distribution and architecture of prehistoric settlement and the landscape setting of a range of monuments, including entrance graves, cairns and standing stones, as well as exploring the role of imported artefacts and island identity.

Robinson's work has provided a wealth of new information and interpretation, partly informed by his use of a sea kayak to study the islands. His thorough analysis of the pottery sequences at the settlement site of Nornour and the Knackyboy Cairn entrance grave has been particularly valuable in helping to establish a more detailed chronology at these sites.

3.5 Conclusions

Scilly has had the benefit of more than 250 years of antiquarian and archaeological recording and occasional excavation. For much of the first half of the 20th century, the megalithic burial chambers and other sites there featured in detail in works reviewing all or most of the British Isles and were discussed in articles published in national journals. More recently, however, they have received little, if any, attention in such syntheses. There were major publications about the islands by Ashbee and Thomas in the second half of the 20th century but very little on a similar scale since then.

Much of the archaeological work carried out in Scilly has been on an *ad hoc* basis. Only in the late 1980s and early 1990s was there a planned programme of monitoring, recording and, where necessary, excavation in the islands. Happily, Scilly's archaeological resource is now becoming better known and appreciated and researchers from a number of institutions are working together to record what is known and to identify the priorities for future work.

Chapter 4

The physical characteristics of the Scillonian entrance graves and cists

4.1 Introduction

This chapter will review and assess the recorded information about the physical structure of the entrance graves and cists in Scilly and the results of visits to the sites carried out during this research. It will not touch on their contents, which will be covered in the following chapter. The setting, interpretation and chronology of these sites will be considered in subsequent chapters.

Following an outline of the data sources used, a brief summary of the basic structure of entrance graves and cists will be provided first. An assessment of the numbers of each type of site and of the excavations carried out will then be given, followed by a more detailed description of the various elements of each type.

4.2 Data sources

The main source of information used is the Cornwall and Scilly Historic Environment Record (HER), which is compiled and maintained by the Strategic Historic Environment Service, Cornwall Council (HES 1987-2005). In addition, the listings of sites in Hencken (1932), Daniel (1950), Ashbee (1974) and Russell (1980) have been examined, as have other local sources of information such as 'The Scillonian' magazine.

The HER was initially searched for all references to 'entrance grave', 'cist' and 'chamber' and the list thus obtained then checked to ensure that other details, including date, were relevant. On this basis the Iron Age/Romano-British period Porthcressa-type cist graves were excluded from consideration and a total of 151 sites identified.

Subsequently, in the course of other work, information about a further possible cist grave was obtained. When the details of the HER entry were checked it was discovered that the word 'cist' was not used but that the mound was described as having an 'internal structure'. The HER was then searched again for all references to 'structure', 'cairn', 'barrow' and 'tumulus' and an additional 41 sites identified. Two further sites, a cremation urn found in a natural cleft in a rock and a barrow with no visible chamber excavated by Bonsor, were later identified and included. This gives a total of 194 sites recorded in the HER which have been considered.

Three sites, which do not currently have full entries in the HER, have also been included to give a grand total

of 197 sites considered. One of these is a cist grave on Par Beach, St Martin's, which was excavated by O'Neil in 1949 (O'Neil 1949b; O'Neil 1949c). This is referred to in the HER entry for the Romano-British cist cemetery on Par Beach *(PRN 7148)* but does not have its own entry. The other two sites are recent discoveries: the probable cist found during coastal monitoring work at Porth Killier, St Agnes in 1996 (Ratcliffe et al. forthcoming) and the probable cist found during archaeological recording of a development site at Dolphin Town, Tresco in 2003 (Taylor & Johns 2009-2010). These have been numbered with the PRN for their respective sites. Appendix 1 sets out details of all 197 sites.

The entries in the HER are, in many cases, made up of information from several sources including visits to the sites by Ordnance Survey fieldworkers, archaeological staff from Cornwall Council and English Heritage and references in published works. In many cases the information from different sources is contradictory.

Each record in the HER has a Permanent Record Number (PRN) and these are shown in the catalogue in Appendix 1. Throughout this book, sites will be identified by the site name used in the HER; the PRN will be included only if it is necessary, there being duplication of site names in a few cases. The PRNs are used in preference to the numbering systems adopted by Hencken (1932) and Daniel (1950) as they provide a complete, consistent and up-to-date coverage of all the sites under consideration. The HER entries also include an eight figure Ordnance Survey grid reference, making it straightforward in most cases to match the entry with the site on the ground, something which it is not always possible to do with certainty with the other numbering systems referred to above. A concordance of sites is provided in Appendix 2.

As far as is possible the extant sites have been visited and the details contained in the HER checked. This has revealed some further inconsistencies. In some cases the site is currently inaccessible because of the growth of gorse, bramble, bracken or other vegetation and so a field examination has not been possible.

The situation is further complicated by the large number of kerbed and unkerbed mounds and cairns in Scilly, some of which are built around natural rocks. Where there is a damaged mound, with evidence of disturbance by digging, it is impossible to be certain whether it once contained a chamber of any kind. As Russell says:

'Barrows are by far the most numerous kind of prehistoric monument remaining in Scilly. Of the 530 listed here, possibly 85-90 are entrance graves: the exact number cannot be ascertained since several possible examples are too decayed for certainty.' (1980:5).

It is also possible that undamaged mounds cover cists, or even entrance graves, which reveal no trace on the surface. Russell goes on to say: 'These mounds might reveal internal structures if excavated though they could only be small'.

It has been necessary, in these cases, to form a judgement based on an assessment of the HER entry, together with, where appropriate, an examination of both the physical remains and any documentary records. This has led to some sites being classified, for the purposes of this study, as 'probable' or 'possible' entrance graves or cists. In deciding whether a damaged site should be included, consideration has been given to the location and size of any pits dug into the mound. If it appeared that there was a pit which was fairly central to the mound and thus might indicate the former presence of a structure, disturbed either as a result of antiquarian excavation or to obtain the stone for building purposes, the site has been included. If the damage was peripheral to the mound or seemed to be as the result of another factor, for example, burrowing by rabbits or erosion, the site was not included.

When allocating a particular mound to one of the three categories of possible cist, possible entrance grave or possible entrance grave or cist, regard was given to the size and shape of the pit. For example, a mound on Wingletang Down, St Agnes (PRN 7016.05) is described in the HER as having a hollow in it which 'measures 1.5m x 0.8m, and is 0.2m deep'. This site has been classified as a possible cist as the hollow appears too small to have accommodated an entrance grave and a surrounding robber pit or excavation trench. Information about, or observation of, any large stones on the surface of a damaged mound was also used to help determine whether a structure might once have existed in it. As the guidance notes to the HER say: 'Archaeological interpretation is an art rather than a science' (HES 2004).

The information in this chapter is therefore based on a critical review of the HER data supplemented by information in other published sources and by field visits.

4.3 Basic structure

Entrance graves

Scillonian entrance graves are generally regarded as a distinctive type within the range of megalithic tomb types found in the British Isles. Lynch, for example, identifies

twelve groupings, of which 'Entrance graves (Britain and Ireland)', occurring in Scilly, west Cornwall and south-east Ireland, is one (2004:36). Daniel recognises nine groups in England and Wales including the 'Scilly Group' which he describes as 'consisting of the entrance graves and similar chamber tombs in the Isles of Scilly and Penwith' (1950:52).

The distinguishing features of the Scillonian tombs, according to Daniel, are that they have round barrows, that each barrow has only one chamber, that the barrows are small and that the chamber always extends from the edge to at least the centre of the barrow and sometimes across almost the entire diameter (Daniel 1950:61). The chambers are all a single rectangular or, occasionally, boat-shaped space; there is no trace of side chambers at any of the sites.

Typically most of the stones used to construct the chamber walls are quite small, but elsewhere large boulders or orthostats are employed and, at the majority of sites, the end stones and capstones are sizeable. Often natural earth-fast rocks are included in the walls or the mound surrounding the chamber. No evidence of rock carving has been identified at any entrance grave site in Scilly.

Around the mound there is usually a kerb of stones and several sites show evidence for inner and outer kerbs; this can be seen clearly at Bant's Carn, St Mary's. In only two cases, Bant's Carn and Porth Hellick Down A, St Mary's, is there clearly a passage leading to the chamber entrance, although one was recorded by Bonsor (1901-1902) at Obadiah's Barrow, Gugh and at Porth Hellick Down E, St Mary's there is a short narrower section inside the entrance to the chamber . The absence of passages at most sites may, of course, be a matter of survival rather than original design. In some cases, the chambers and their mounds appear to mimic the natural stone outcrops found around the islands. Clefts in these rocks, such as the one at Yellow Rock Carn mentioned earlier, may have been earlier locations for burial.

A typical, well-preserved entrance grave is Innisidgen Carn A, St Mary's, shown in figure 4.1, with its massive capstones and kerb of large stones surrounding the mound.

Cists

There are two types of prehistoric cist grave which occur in Scilly: only the earlier type will be considered in this work. These consist of a 'rectangular box-like structure formed by four upright slabs, sometimes with a single stone capstone' (Russell 1980:5). They are underground structures, with the capstone typically being just below ground level.

The later type, the Porthcressa-type cist graves which date to the late Iron Age and Romano-British period (c100BC to 200AD), are larger and usually oval in shape, being constructed of drystone walling and covered with two or more capstones (Ashbee 1974; Johns 2002-03).

FIGURE 4.1 ENTRANCE GRAVE: INNISIDGEN CARN A, ST MARY'S

FIGURE 4.2 CIST: NORTH HILL H, SAMSON

In some cases the earlier cists were covered by a cairn of stones, such as the example at North Hill H, Samson which is shown in figure 4.2. Others, when found, were covered only by soil as with the structure at Carn Morval Down, St Mary's discovered in c1899 (Ashbee 1953, 1974).

4.4 Numbers

Establishing the number of known entrance graves and cists in Scilly is no straightforward matter. As mentioned above, a total of 197 sites has been identified; of these 56

are regarded as entrance graves, 21 are probable entrance graves and 13 possible entrance graves. There are 16 cists (including one site where several such structures were recorded), 11 probable cists and 34 possible cists. In addition, there are 7 sites which are either an entrance grave or a cist and a further 34 which fall into the category 'entrance grave or cist - possible'.

One of the sites in the category 'entrance grave or cist' is a well-preserved but atypical structure and is described in section 4.8 below; there are also several damaged or overgrown sites in this category where it is not possible to be sure of the form of the original structure. Those included in the final category are badly damaged sites, usually mounds, where both the existence and the form of an internal structure are uncertain.

There are also five sites which have been classified as 'other'; three of these (Arden Craig, St Mary's, Carrion Rock, St Martin's and Giant's Grave, St Mary's) are recorded in the HER as 'entrance grave' and one (Northwethel) as 'chambered tomb'. The mound at Arden Craig is believed to be a bulb dump, there is no entrance grave at Carrion (or Carron) Rock and the location appears to have been confused with the nearby site of Cruther's Neck; Giant's Grave is almost certainly a duplication of Innisidgen Carn A and Northwethel is a natural rock feature. The final site (Yellow Rock Carn) is recorded as a 'findspot' in the HER, where a funerary urn was found in a natural cleft in the rock. It is not clear from either the record of this discovery (Lewis 1948) or the photograph of it whether there were cremated remains in the urn.

Of the total of 197 sites, ten appear to have been destroyed and in another 20 cases the condition of the structure is unknown. There are a variety of reasons for this: for example, the cist recorded (and photographed in about 1908) at Town Lane, St Mary's is now covered by tarmac, that on Watch Hill, Bryher is known only from a documentary record in Troutbeck (1796) and the cist at North Hill W, Samson recorded by Russell (1980) could not be located by the Cornwall Council archaeologist who visited in 1988, nor, due to the cover of heather, during the research reported here. The numbers of sites are summarised in Table 4.1.

4.5 Excavations

There is documentary evidence of excavation at thirty-six of the sites included in the HER but in only twenty-two of these cases does the HER entry mention that excavation has taken place. The earliest recorded excavation was of two cairns on Buzza Hill, St Mary's (PRN 7578.02 and 7578.03) by William Borlase in 1752 (Borlase 1756). George Woodley excavated two sites on Porth Hellick Down in the 1820s (Woodley 1822:211-212); it is not certain which these were, though Russell suggests Porth Hellick Down C and E (Russell 1980). Augustus Smith excavated a cist at North Hill H, Samson in 1862 (Smith 1863) and, in 1876, W M Gluyas investigated an apparent entrance grave near Old Town, St Mary's (PRN 7559) a site for which the HER does not have a location (Cornish 1878).

Three sites are recorded as having been excavated by George Bonsor between 1899 and 1902: Bant's Carn, St Mary's, Porth Hellick Down A, St Mary's and Obadiah's Barrow, Gugh. Ashbee carried out further work at Bant's Carn in 1970 (Ashbee 1976). Although both Maier (1999) and Robinson (2005) found evidence that Bonsor had also worked at Normandy Down A, St Mary's, this is not yet reflected in the HER entry which does, however, say that the site is 'much disturbed by excavation' (HES 1987-2005). Bonsor's notebooks (1899-1900; 1901-1902) also provide details of his work at South Hill A and C (PRN 7081.01 and 7081.02C) and North Hill K and L, all on Samson, Gweal Hill C, Bryher and Buzza Hill A and Normandy Down B, both on St Mary's although, again, none of this is recorded in the HER.

In the late 19th or early 20th century Alexander Gibson photographed in situ a funerary urn which had been found in a natural cleft in the rock near Yellow Rock Carn, St Martin's (Lewis 1948). Gibson also excavated at Carn Morval Down (PRN 7496) and Cruther's Neck (Bonsor 1901-1902) and in about 1912 he started work at Knackyboy Cairn, St Martin's where work has subsequently been continued by Lewis between 1944 and 1947, O'Neil in 1948 and Mulville in 2006 (Lewis 1948; O'Neil 1952; Mulville 2007).

In 1929 or 1932 Alec Gray cleared a 'small covered gallery' at Halangy Down, St Mary's (Gray 1972:29) and in 1930 Hencken excavated the previously disturbed entrance grave of North Hill E, Samson (Hencken 1933). Ashbee records that during the winter of 1938-1939 J Treneary examined a cist at Content Farm, St Mary's which Ashbee himself and O'Neil re-excavated in 1950 (Ashbee 1953; 1974). W F Grimes excavated an entrance grave at Salakee Down A, St Mary's (PRN 7537.01) in 1942 in advance of its destruction by the construction work for St Mary's airfield (Grimes 1960) In 1944 Lewis 're-opened' a pit between the two boulders at Barnacle Rock, St Martin's (Lewis 1945:46). Between 1944 and 1947 he cleared Cruther's Hill B and excavated at Pernagie Carn and Tinkler's Hill E (Lewis 1948).

Since then the majority of recorded excavations of entrance graves or cists are those carried out by O'Neil. Apart from his work at Knackyboy Cairn mentioned above he also excavated in 1949 at Par Beach, St Martin's (referred to in PRN 7148) where a small cist was uncovered (O'Neil 1949c) and in 1950 at the entrance grave of Tinkler's Hill A, St Martin's. His final work relevant to this review was carried out in 1952 at the cairn and cist at Hill Bennigates, St Martin's (Beagrie 1989) and in 1953 at Middle Arthur B, Eastern Isles where the unusual closed triangular chamber was investigated (O'Neil 1954).

In 1964 Minett-Smith carried out an excavation at a settlement site at Little Bay, St Martin's where a stone-lined cist was uncovered inside one of the round huts. Further work was done at the site by Butcher in 1974 and Neal in 1980 (Neal 1983). Finally, a probable cist at Porth Killier was excavated by Ratcliffe in 1996 (Ratcliffe et al. forthcoming) and one at Dolphin Town was uncovered by

Type of site	Total number in HER	Extant	Destroyed	Unknown
Entrance grave	56	52	3	1
Probable entrance grave	21	19	2	
Possible entrance grave	13	10	2	1
Cist	16	5	2	9
Probable cist	11	10		1
Possible cist	34	29		5
Entrance grave or cist	7	7		
Possible entrance grave or cist	34	32	1	1
Other	5	3		2
Totals	197	167	10	20

TABLE 4.1 NUMBERS OF ENTRANCE GRAVES AND CISTS

FIGURE 4.3 INTERIOR OF KITTERN HILL A, GUGH,
SHOWING COURSED DRYSTONE WALLING

FIGURE 4.4 CRUTHER'S HILL B, ST MARTIN'S, SHOWING
CHAMBER WALLS CONSTRUCTED OF ORTHOSTAT

Taylor during monitoring work in 2003 (Taylor & Johns 2009-2010).

At the vast majority of the funerary sites excavated it appears that only the chamber was examined and the surrounding mound was only excavated insofar as this was necessary to give access to the structure within it. In all, just over 18% of the sites identified in the HER have been excavated.

4.6 Details of construction – Entrance graves

Chamber walling

Within the group of Scillonian entrance graves a wide variety of construction types can be found. At many sites the side walls of the chamber are built of undressed, coursed, drystone walling, the stones of which are typically about 300mm by 150mm by 150mm, although sometimes much larger. An example of this type of walling can be seen at Kittern Hill A, Gugh, illustrated in figure 4.3. Some sites include what appear to be roughly dressed stones in their walling.

There are also records of mortared walling, for example Borlase reports that one of the chambers which he excavated on Buzza Hill, St Mary's (PRN 7578) in 1752 had walls constructed of 'masonry and mortar' (1756:15). Hencken says that Crawford pointed out to him 'a kind of rough mortar surviving in places between the stones' at Innisidgen Carn A, St Mary's (1932:24); the site has subsequently been consolidated by English Heritage so this feature is no longer visible. The same author recorded a 'coarse yellow sandy mortar' between the stones of the chamber of North Hill E, Samson when he excavated there in 1930 (1933:25).

O'Neil refers to 'a granite clay paste, which lacks lime, but otherwise resembles mortar' in the walling on the south side of the chamber at Knackyboy Cairn (1952:23) and elsewhere mentions a 'considerable spread' of it within the chamber (1948-1949:99). This suggests that the chamber walls may have been covered with mortar and the possibility

exists that this might have been decorated. It may well be that a closer examination or excavation of other chambers would reveal the presence of such mortar elsewhere.

At other sites, such as Cruther's Hill B, St Martin's, shown in figure 4.4, the chamber walls are constructed of much larger stones with smaller ones filling the spaces between them and some chambers, such as that at Innisidgen Carn A, contain a combination of both types of walling. The use of small 'trig' stones to level the top of the chamber walls has also been noted at a few sites and at Salakee Down A, St Mary's (PRN 7537.01) small stones were found as wedges underneath some of the orthostats forming the chamber walls and kerb (Grimes 1960).

At a number of sites natural bedrock has been incorporated into the chamber walls. Indeed so extensive is the use of bedrock at South Hill C, Samson that Daniel says that the site (Samson 12 in his numeration) 'might almost be described as a rock-cut tomb' as 'It consists of a rock-cut pit across the top of which megaliths have been laid to form the roof of the chamber' (1950:46). More typically, an earthfast boulder forms much of one wall of the chamber at Cruther's Hill B, shown in figure 4.4, and at Porth Hellick Down C, St Mary's a natural outcrop makes up a significant part of the cairn and one side of the chamber.

In all cases where the state of preservation of the chamber permits an examination to be made, the distal end wall is constructed exclusively or mainly of a single large stone; this feature can also be seen in figure 4.4. At a few sites where the side walls are of coursed drystone walling there is evidence for corbelling of the walls with each course being slightly built out over the one below, thus narrowing the width of the chamber towards the top. This feature can be seen, for example, at Bant's Carn, St Mary's and North Hill E. At Kittern Hill A it is suggested in the HER entry that there is a possible sill around the top of the chamber walls.

Although the chambers are generally described as being rectangular, many of them are in fact coffin-shaped, being wider in the middle than at either end. This can be seen, for example, at North Hill E where one sidewall of the chamber is straight and the other convex and at Bant's Carn where the chamber is 1.6m wide in the middle and 1.2m wide at each end. In contrast, the entrance grave of Northwethel A has a chamber which is 1.2m wide at the distal end but tapers to only 0.5m at the entrance.

Excavation reports do not record the positioning of weathered and fresh faces of the stones forming the chamber, although Bonsor's plan of Bant's Carn shows that the majority of the slabs forming the base of the chamber walls have flat sides facing into the chamber and rounded sides facing outwards (Hencken 1933:fig 5). This may indicate the same arrangement as noted by Mens in the chamber at Kerbourg, where the fresh faces were oriented to the interior of the chamber (Mens 2008). However, the kerbstones around the mound have their flat sides facing outwards.

At Salakee Down A, the stones of the chamber, which was badly damaged when excavated, also appear to have their flat sides facing inwards. The kerbstones around the northern side of the mound have their rounded side facing outwards whilst those on the southern side have the flat side facing out (Grimes 1960:fig 69). Some of these smaller stones may be from the inner part of the outcrop and thus have two unweathered faces. Clearly more work needs to be done to establish whether the pattern identified by Mens in France applies in Scilly and what the implications of this might be, both for the method of construction of the entrance graves and for their symbolism.

Capstones

At those entrance graves where the capstones survive they are the largest stones used in the structure and most chambers appear to have been originally roofed with between four and six capstones.

Capstones are typically rectangular slabs, the four at Bant's Carn average 2.2m long, 1.1m wide and 0.25m deep. At both Bant's Carn and South Hill C, Samson, where the capstones are not covered by the mound, the one above the entrance to the chamber has a very irregular appearance due to weathering and it is possible that they were selected for this reason.

At most sites with capstones in place, only these large slabs survive. However, at Bant's Carn and Great Arthur C smaller stones can be seen wedged between the slabs, indicating how the chamber roof may have been sealed before the mound was constructed over it.

Chamber floors

At a small number of sites there is evidence for a paved or natural stone floor to the chamber. This is only obvious where a site has been excavated or where the floor is exposed by erosion, generally when the capstones have been removed. At many sites the floor is covered with earth and/or vegetation and so this feature, if it were present, would not be visible. Examples of stone floors are known at North Hill E, Samson where traces of paving including the upper stone of a saddle quern were found (Hencken 1933) and at Cruther's Hill B, St Martin's which has a natural rock floor.

Hollows in the chamber floor have been noted at a small number of sites. During the excavation of one of the entrance graves on Buzza Hill (PRN 7578.03) in 1752 'a small round cell dug deeper than the rest' was recorded in the floor of the chamber. This was found to contain 'some earths of different colours from the natural one, but nothing decisive' (Borlase 1756:15).

At Obadiah's Barrow, Gugh Bonsor found part of a skeleton, apparently in a pit which was 'surrounded by soil pounded hard' (Hencken 1929 Volume I:79). At Knackyboy Cairn, St Martin's, an area of stone paving at the inner end of the chamber covered a fill of dark soil and another hollow in the chamber floor was found to contain layers of charcoal and granite sand (O'Neil 1952). Dark or 'blackish' soil has been recorded at other excavated sites including Obadiah's Barrow, Gugh and Bant's Carn, St Mary's and Bonsor's manuscript notes of his visit to Gugh in 1900 refer to barrows containing charcoal and blackish sand (Hencken 1929).

Passages

Passages leading to the chamber entrance survive at a very small number of sites, the only two currently visible and obvious examples being Bant's Carn and Porth Hellick Down A, both on St Mary's, the latter shown in figure 4.5. However, the plan of Obadiah's Barrow, Gugh (Bonsor 1901-1902) also depicts a passage, which is no longer visible, and Porth Hellick Down E, St Mary's appears to have a short passage, described by Hencken as 'scarcely more than a narrowing prolongation of the chamber' (1929 Volume I:71). It has been suggested that the badly damaged site of Salakee Down A, St Mary's (PRN 7537.01) may also have had a passage (Grimes 1960).

At Porth Hellick Down A and Bant's Carn the orientation of the passage differs from that of the chamber by some 20 or 30 degrees, whilst Bonsor's plan of Obadiah's Barrow, included at figure 3.1, shows the passage orientation there to be almost 90 degrees different from that of the chamber. Porth Hellick Down A has been described as being 'fairly complete except for the roofing stones of the passage' (Hencken 1932:20) but, in fact, there is no evidence at any site to indicate whether or not the passages were originally roofed.

Those entrance graves which have passages display a narrowed entrance to the chamber, most clearly shown at Porth Hellick Down A, St Mary's, where a stone obstructs more than half the entrance, as illustrated in figure 4.5. This narrowing can also be seen at Bant's Carn, St Mary's and Obadiah's Barrow, Gugh. Hencken says that it has probably been destroyed at Innisidgen Carn A, St Mary's,

FIGURE 4.5 PORTH HELLICK DOWN A, ST MARY'S, SHOWING
PASSAGE AND NARROWED ENTRANCE

FIGURE 4.6 OBADIAH'S BARROW, GUGH, LOOKING TOWARDS
ENTRANCE FROM CHAMBER INTERIOR, SHOWING BLOCKING STONE

which does not have a passage, where 'the entrance has been interfered with' (1929 Volume I:78). Both Hencken and Ashbee comment on the similarities in design between Bant's Carn and Innisidgen Carn A with Ashbee suggesting that the latter originally had a passage and that it might be 'the work of the same tomb architect who built Bant's Carn' (1974:304).

At Obadiah's Barrow, where the entrance has not been disturbed, a large stone is still in situ completely blocking access to the chamber from the passage. It is placed beneath the capstone which covers the entrance and between the portal stones and is shown in figure 4.6. It is likely that such blocking stones were used to prevent disturbance to the interior of the chamber, both between burials and when the chamber ceased to be used.

Mounds

Scillonian entrance graves are surrounded by roughly circular mounds, which may serve to support the chamber as well as to enhance the size of the structure. As mentioned

above, the mounds are small in comparison with those found in other parts of western Europe and, in many cases, the chamber takes up a significant proportion of the volume of the mound, again in contrast with sites elsewhere.

Several of the best-preserved examples of entrance graves are now English Heritage guardianship sites and the mounds of others have been restored. In these cases turf has been used to cover the mounds, in order to protect the structures from erosion. Elsewhere mounds have become covered with vegetation. These all serve to give the impression that the mounds are of earth whereas early photographs of them make it clear that they are composed largely of stones, described in many of the HER entries as being 'grapefruit sized'. The pale granite in Scilly would have made these cairns particularly obvious against the surrounding vegetation.

The cairn is normally completely or partially defined by a kerb of stones which may act as a retaining wall and which, in some cases, includes natural bedrock. At many sites the kerb is now found just inside the perimeter of the cairn as material has eroded from the cairn to lie outside it. At the majority of sites the kerb, although sometimes constructed of large boulders, consists of separate stones rather than a continuous line of them. However, at monuments such as Bant's Carn, St Mary's the kerb is a substantial structure of coursed walling around the cairn, as shown in figure 4.7.

A number of sites, including Bant's Carn, have both inner and outer kerbs, the inner one being typically within the cairn and the outer one around its perimeter. At Bant's Carn the outer kerb is separated from the cairn by a raised 'collar'. However, early 20th century photographs of Bant's Carn, such as that included by Hencken (1929 Volume I Figure 23A), show the inner kerb on the south side of the entrance (that is to the left of it in figure 4.7) almost completely obscured by the cairn outside it and earth built up against the stones forming the north side of the passage.

It may be therefore that the cairn at Bant's Carn originally extended as far as the outer kerb. This would make the position of the passage analogous to that at Porth Hellick Down A, St Mary's, extending from the outer edge of the cairn to the chamber entrance, rather being completely outside the cairn as it currently appears at Bant's Carn. However, Ashbee (1974) says that Porth Hellick Down A originally had a 'collar' outside the cairn which was destroyed during Ministry of Works restoration and that Innisidgen Carn A, St Mary's still has one, although it is masked by the grassed area around the cairn.

It has been suggested that the presence of two kerbs at sites such as Bant's Carn and Knackyboy Cairn, St Martin's indicates that there was a later enlargement of the cairn. O'Neil argues that this may have been done at Knackyboy in order to accommodate satellite burials (1948-1949:92-94). However, the radiocarbon dates recently obtained from Knackyboy and reported in chapter 8 indicate that the satellite burials were contemporary with, rather than

FIGURE 4.7 BANT'S CARN, ST MARY'S, SHOWING INNER KERB
AROUND CAIRN AND REMAINS OF OUTER KERB

later than, the use of the chamber. This may indicate that both kerbs are part of the original structure.

There is evidence for satellite burials at only three sites. At Knackyboy Cairn two urns, protected by stones and containing cremations, were found close to an inner kerb within the cairn (O'Neil 1952; Robinson 2005). The HER entry for Kittern Hill N, Gugh states that there are two distinct depressions on the top of the mound. However, a closer examination suggests the presence of two possible cists within the cairn, one towards the western edge, the other on the southern side, as well as evidence for a substantially destroyed structure in the centre. Finally, at Shipman Head Down N, another badly damaged site, there is evidence for a number of cists around the perimeter of the mound, as well as a central hollow. In the majority of excavations of entrance graves only the chamber has been examined and it may be that satellite burials exist at other sites.

Dimensions

In most cases the HER entries include measurements of the chamber and cairn and the figures quoted below have been taken from this source. These data, which are for the 52 extant sites confidently defined as entrance graves, indicate that the chambers range between 2.0m and 7.0m in length, between 1.3m and 2.0m in width at the midpoint and between 0.3m and 1.5m in height.

It must be remembered however, when considering the heights of the chambers, that many of them are now partly filled with soil and decayed vegetation and that, if this were removed, they would be higher than these measurements suggest. Sites which have been cleared and are maintained, such as Bant's Carn, St Mary's and Obadiah's Barrow, Gugh have chambers which are, respectively, 1.5m and 1.1m in height.

There is a much greater variation in recorded mound size and, undoubtedly, some of the mounds have been subject to considerable erosion and/or damage by antiquarian

or other digging. The range of diameters recorded is from 6.0m to 22.9m and mound heights vary between 0.3m and 2.5m. Whilst the majority of the mounds are approximately circular there are some which are oval in shape. Whether this was their original form or whether it is due to subsequent damage of some kind it is now impossible to tell.

Although smaller chambers are typically covered by smaller mounds there is no consistent relationship between the two. For example, the chamber of North Hill A, Samson is only 2.0m long by 1.2m wide but is surrounded by a mound measuring 12.0m by 10.0m. Conversely, at Works Carn, Bryher a chamber measuring 6.5m by 1.3m has a covering cairn of 11.0m by 9.0m. The cairn has an almost complete kerb of stones suggesting that it retains its original dimensions.

Orientation

The HER records the orientation of 72 entrance graves (including sites defined, for the purpose of this study, as probable and possible entrance graves). There is, however, confusion in the way the orientation is described; for example, in some cases where a chamber is said to have a 'SE-NW' orientation the entrance is at the south-east end and in others it is at the north-west end.

Of the sites examined, the majority have an entrance facing between north and east. A significant minority, however, face between south-west and north-north-west with at least one site facing almost due north: Porth Hellick Down E which is oriented to 352°. The orientations of the chambers will be considered further in chapter 6.

4.7 Details of construction – Cists

Walling and capstones

In comparison with entrance graves cists are a much more homogenous group. Extant examples are also much less numerous: as table 4.1 shows there are only five extant cists and a further ten probable sites.

The site at North Hill H, Samson, shown in figure 4.2, is a visible example in good condition and it consists of a rectangular box made of four granite slabs. The slabs forming the longer sides have grooves in them, into which the shorter slabs were fitted to form the ends of the cist. Clay mortar had been used in these joints as well as between the uprights and the single slab which formed the lid (Smith 1863). This use of mortar echoes that at several of the entrance graves, as outlined above.

At two photographed but no longer visible sites, Town Lane, St Mary's (PRN 7517) and Content Farm, St Mary's, again each wall is constructed of a single stone slab but the extant examples at Gweal Hill C, Bryher, Shipman Head Down, Bryher (PRN 7404.02) and Cruther's Hill D, St Martin's all incorporate natural bedrock on one side.

Typically cists, such as North Hill H and Content Farm, seem to have a single capstone (Ashbee 1953) but an unlocated site on St Mary's (PRN 7246) is described in the HER as having had five capstones. Recorded capstones are either a rough rectangle, as at North Hill H and Carn Morval Down, St Mary's (PRN 7496) or approximately circular, as at Content Farm.

Cist floors

Details of the cist floor are recorded at North Hill H, Samson which had a 'pavement' of three flat but irregularly shaped stones with their joints filled with clay mortar (Smith 1863:53), at Par Beach, which was paved with stone and clay (O'Neil 1949c) and at Content Farm, St Mary's where the side walls were resting directly on the subsoil with, apparently, no stones in the base of the cist (Ashbee 1953).

Mounds

Some cists were covered with substantial mounds: that at North Hill H, Samson has a cairn 22.5m by 17.5m in diameter and still 2.2m high. It is larger than the mounds surrounding the adjacent entrance graves. Similarly, the mound around the excavated cist at Hill Bennigates, St Martin's is 15.5m by 13.5m in diameter and 1.1m high.

Elsewhere, at Content Farm it was recorded that the cist, when discovered in 1938, 'might have been covered by a small cairn' (Ashbee 1974:129). Many of the sites classified as possible cists, where there are signs of antiquarian excavation or stone robbing, have small cairns; examples include Wingletang Down E, St Agnes where the cairn is 7.0m by 6.0m in diameter and 0.4m high and Castle Down J, Tresco whose cairn measures 6.0m in diameter and 0.6m in height.

Other recorded sites, such as those at Town Lane (PRN 7517) and Carn Morval Down, both on St Mary's, however, have revealed no trace of a mound.

Dimensions

Those sites classified as cists or probable cists vary in length between 0.9m and 2.0m, in width between 0.3m and 1.2m and in height between 0.1m and 0.6m. Again, as with the entrance graves, the present recorded height of cists is misleading as many are partly silted up. North Hill H, Samson, which is regularly cleared, is 0.5m high. It can be seen therefore that the cists are, in general, significantly smaller than the entrance graves and there is very little overlap in dimensions of the two types of structure.

Orientation

The HER entries record the orientations of the long axis of a number of cists. As these structures do not have entrances the problem of inconsistency, mentioned above in section 4.6. in relation to entrance graves, does not apply. The majority of cists are oriented N-S although there are a few examples each of NW-SE, NE-SW and E-W orientations. This will be considered further in chapter 6.

4.8 Atypical structures

As Brophy (2005) has pointed out, there are always sites which do not fit conveniently into the categories we devise. In Scilly, there is an excavated site classified as being either an entrance grave or a cist, not because a poor state of preservation does not permit a definite conclusion but because it displays features of both types of structure.

Middle Arthur B has the dimensions of a small entrance grave, measuring 2.4m long and 1.2m wide and is surrounded by an orthostatic kerb enclosing an area of only 4.0m by 3.4m but now with no trace of stones or earth which might have formed the body of a cairn or barrow. It is constructed mainly of orthostats of up to 1.0m in height. This site is unique in Scilly in being triangular or boat-shaped.

It was excavated by O'Neil (1954) who regarded it as a cist but Daniel (1950) and Ashbee (1974) treat it as an entrance grave. The HER entry says that the southern end may be formed by a displaced coverstone (HES 1987-2005), although this was not suggested by O'Neil. The site, which is now very overgrown, is shown in figure 4.8.

Another similar example is to be found at Buzza Hill A, St Mary's, shown in figure 4.9, which is a substantial structure with a chamber measuring 2.5m long and 1.5m wide, constructed of large stones and surrounded by a cairn some 12.0m in diameter. It has the appearance of a typical entrance grave but has a closed chamber. Some authors regard the site as a massive cist (Ashbee 1974), others describe it as a 'chamber or cist' (Russell 1980:26) while Daniel treats it as an entrance grave (1950:247).

The HER entry suggests that the stone sealing the north-east end (the foreground in figure 4.9) may be a fallen capstone but says that the site 'could not be discounted as a cist rather than a chamber' (HES 1987-2005). Bonsor's notes reveal that he cleared the chamber at this site in October 1901 and confirm that the stone at the north-east end is a fallen capstone (Bonsor 1901-1902).

These examples illustrate the difficulty in classifying some sites, even when they have been excavated and draw attention to the fact that there is considerable variation between the structures. Although Middle Arthur B has a closed chamber it is very different from other cist sites in Scilly and is best described as a 'megalithic cist'.

4.9 Boulder walls

In several areas, where there is a number of entrance graves or cists in close proximity, boulder walls can be seen to link their mounds. Hencken says Bonsor recorded two or three barrows being joined by an 'alignement' on Kittern Hill, Gugh where five entrance graves, cists and indeterminate sites (Kittern Hill B, C, J, L and N) are now recorded as being crossed or connected by boulder walls. A wall crosses at least two of the mounds but another one is built against it.

Hencken also quotes Bonsor as recording on Samson that a 'dilapidated field-wall pursues a winding course among the barrows on North Hill' (1929 Volume I:87). Despite the growth of heather and gorse on the hilltop this can still be seen joining two of the entrance graves (North Hill E and J) and leading away from another (North Hill M).

On Great Arthur, a boulder wall runs along the crest of the hill linking an entrance grave (Great Arthur C) two probable entrance graves (Great Arthur A and B) and two ring cairns. There are two possible cist grave sites on Shipman Head Down, Bryher (PRN 7413.13 and 7413.19) where the HER entries record an ancient wall being built across both mounds.

It appears, therefore, that on both Kittern Hill and Shipman Head Down the walls post-date at least some of the mounds. The possible function of these boulder walls will be considered further in chapter 7.

FIGURE 4.9 BUZZA HILL A, ST MARY'S, SHOWING APPARENTLY CLOSED CHAMBER

4.10 Conclusions

It will be seen from the foregoing that there is variation amongst both the entrance graves and the cists in Scilly in terms of their shape, size, method of construction, orientation and other aspects. Despite these differences of detail, it is clear that, with a very few exceptions, they form part of coherent classes of sites, that is, the overall similarities are greater than the differences.

Although entrance graves and cists differ considerably from each other, they are found close together in groupings of sites and, in some cases, are linked by boulder walls. Similarity of construction is also seen in the use of paved floors and mortar in some sites of both types. The burials and accompanying objects found in entrance graves and cists, which will be considered in the next chapter, illustrate further links between them.

Chapter 5

The contents of the Scillonian entrance graves and cists

5.1 Introduction

This chapter will provide a description and analysis of the artefacts, human remains and other substances which have been recorded as being found in Scillonian entrance graves and cists. Each type of find will be discussed in turn; the significance of the assemblages from two sites, Obadiah's Barrow, Gugh and Knackyboy Cairn, St Martin's, will then be considered.

Finds have been recorded at a total of 40 sites, just over 20% of the total database under consideration. There are recorded excavations at 36 sites, of which 28 yielded finds of some kind. In addition, there are finds from another 12 sites which have not been excavated; most of these are chance discoveries, some made by visitors to the site, others by workmen.

5.2 Data sources

The Historic Environment Record (HES 1987-2005) was examined for information about artefacts, human remains and other finds recorded from the sites under consideration. In addition, excavation reports, excavators' site notes and letters, contemporary sources, such as newspaper reports, and records of chance finds were checked and the accessions registers of those museums known to hold material from entrance graves and cists in Scilly were searched. Visits were then made to the Isles of Scilly Museum, St Mary's, the Royal Cornwall Museum, Truro, the Torquay Museum and the British Museum, London.

In some cases, it proved possible to link artefacts in a museum's collection to a specific site; for example, the two flints from Samson donated to the British Museum by Bonsor match the record (Bonsor 1901-1902; Maier 1999) of his excavation and discoveries at North Hill K, Samson in 1902.

In other cases, objects recorded in a museum's accessions register cannot now be located; this is the case, for example, for the contents of North Hill H, Samson accessioned by the Royal Cornwall Museum in 1864. In the past, the objects from Scilly given by Bonsor to the British Museum and those found by Hodson at an unnamed site on St Mary's and donated to the Torquay Museum have been in this category (Ashbee 1974; HES 1987-2005), happily, these have now been re-located.

The table below summarises the information obtained from all these sources. It sets out the sites with recorded finds and indicates the excavator or finder (discoveries made without excavation are shown in italics), the year of excavation or discovery, what was found and, where it is known or suspected, the museum at which all or some of the finds were deposited.

5.3 Pottery

Vessels and sherds

The most numerous discovery, both in terms of the number of sites at which it has been found and the number of items discovered, is pottery. This has been found at 31 of the 40 sites which have produced finds. Of the nine sites where pottery was not found, three are cists (one in the inter-tidal area), five are entrance graves and one is an indeterminate structure. Finds from these sites without pottery include human remains, ashes, mortar, flints and an apparently carved stone, as well as 'unctuous', 'greasy' or coloured earth, which was found at four of the entrance grave sites. Possible interpretations of this will be discussed in section 5.10 below.

In the vast majority of cases the pottery finds are of small sherds; complete vessels survive only from Obadiah's Barrow and Knackyboy Cairn while vessels from Knackyboy Cairn and Salakee Down A have been reconstructed. One of the intact vessels from Knackyboy is shown in figure 5.1 and the only intact urn from Obadiah's Barrow in figure 5.2.

Where the shape and size of the vessel can be determined from the sherds, in most cases they appear to be biconical urns between approximately 140mm and 270mm high, made of a granitic fabric which usually has quartz and mica inclusions and which is typically between 8mm and 15mm thick. It varies in colour from almost black to grey, buff and light orange. Often the upper part of the vessel, between the rim and the widest part, is decorated with impressed, incised or stamped decoration while the lower part is plain (Hencken 1932; Patchett 1944). Many of the sherds have carbonisation, sometimes quite extensive, on the outside.

The base of the urns is flat and the rim is usually plain, sometimes with a slight bevel and sometimes slightly

FIGURE 5.1 INTACT UNDECORATED VESSEL FROM KNACKYBOY
CAIRN (ISLES OF SCILLY MUSEUM RN 6052),

FIGURE 5.2 INTACT URN FROM OBADIAH'S BARROW,
SHOWING CORD-IMPRESSED DECORATION ON UPPER PART
(ISLES OF SCILLY MUSEUM RN 1078)

Site	PRN	Excavator/ *Finder*	Date	Type of structure	Human remains	Pottery	Other finds	Museum (see note1)
Bant's Carn	7443	Bonsor Ashbee	1900-01 1970	Entrance grave	✓	✓	Flint, quern rubber, limpet shells	
Barnacle Rock	7175	Lewis	1944	Entrance grave or cist		✓	Flint	
Buzza Hill	7578.02	Borlase	1752	Entrance grave			'Unctuous earth'	
Buzza Hill	7578.03	Borlase	1752	Entrance grave			Coloured earths	
Carn Morval Down	7496	Gibson	Late 19th century	Cist			'Ashes'	
Carn of Works	7057	*Not known*		Entrance grave		✓		
Content Farm	7519	Treneary O'Neil & Ashbee	1939 1950	Cist		✓		RCM
Cruther's Neck/ Carrion Rock (see note 2)	7169/ 7170	Gibson	Late 19th century	Entrance grave	✓	✓	Bronze dagger, limpet shells	IoS
Great Hill B	7110.02	*O'Neil*	1953	Entrance grave		✓		RCM
Great Stitch	7451.02	*Gray*	1920s/ 1930s	Entrance grave		✓	Flint	RCM
Gweal Hill C	7384.02	Bonsor	1902	Cist		✓	Charcoal	
Halangy Down	7446	Gray	1929	Entrance grave		✓	Flint, pig jawbone	RCM
Hill Bennigates	7138.01/ 02	O'Neil	1952	Cist		✓	Flint	RCM
Kittern Hill A	7030.01	*Davey*	1984	Entrance grave		✓		
Knackyboy Cairn	7162.01 7164.01/ 02	Gibson Lewis O'Neil Mulville	1912 1947 1948 2006	Entrance grave	✓	✓	Flint, animal bone point, faience and glass beads, stone disk, bronze objects, mortar/daub objects, ?gold object, ?agate bead	IoS RCM
Little Arthur C/D/E (see note 3)	7225	*Gibson*	1898	Entrance grave		✓		IoS
Lower Newford	7498	*Recorded by Borlase*	1753-1758	Cist	✓	✓		
Middle Arthur B	7224.01	O'Neil	1953	Entrance grave or cist	✓	✓	Flint	RCM
Normandy Down A	7236.01	Bonsor	1902	Entrance grave		✓		BM
North Hill E	7068.05/.06	Hencken	1930	Entrance grave		✓	Flint, pebbles, quern rubber, hammer-stone, animal bone, ?faience beads	RCM
North Hill H	7068.09	Smith	1862	Cist	✓		Flint	RCM
North Hill K	7068.13	Bonsor	1902	Entrance grave			Flint	BM

Site	PRN	Excavator/ Finder	Date	Type of structure	Human remains	Pottery	Other finds	Museum (see note1)
Obadiah's Barrow	7031	Bonsor *Samuels* *Greeves*	1901 1965 2006	Entrance grave	✓	✓	Animal bone and horn points, bronze awl, hammer-stone, limpet shells	BM IoS
Old Town	7545.01	*Recorded by McKenzie*	1964	Cist	✓	✓		IoS
Old Town	7559	Gluyas	1876	Entrance grave		✓	'Greasy matter', 'stones'	
Oliver's Battery	7348.03	*O'Neil* *Tangye*	1954 1984 1985	Entrance grave or cist		✓	Flint, burnt bone (?human or animal)	RCM
Par Beach	(7148)	O'Neil	1949	Cist			Mortar	RCM
Pendrathen	7485.02	*Crawford*	1926	Cists		✓		
Peninnis Head	7422	*Not known*	1812	Entrance grave or cist	✓	✓	2 bronze armlets, agate bead, stone spindle whorl	RCM
Pernagie Carn	7187	Lewis *O'Neil*	c1947 1947	Entrance grave		✓	Clay balls, charcoal	IoS
Porth Hellick Down A	7528.01	Bonsor	1902	Entrance grave		✓	Pumice pendant	BM
Porth Hellick Down C (see note 4)	7528.03	Woodley	1820s	Entrance grave			'Greasy black earth'	
Porth Hellick Down E (see note 4)	7528.05	Woodley	1820s	Entrance grave			'Greasy black earth'	
Porth Killier	7029	Ratcliffe	1996	Cist		✓	Clay, mortar/socket stone	IoS (not yet deposited in 2012)
St Mary's	7246	Hodson	1927	Cist		✓	Flint	Torquay (transferred to IoS 2010)
Salakee Down A	7537.01	Grimes	1942	Entrance grave		✓		RCM
South Hill A	7081.01	*Not known*	1978	Entrance grave		✓		
Tinkler's Hill E	7190.05	Lewis	Between 1944 and 1947	Entrance grave or cist			'Stone with rough carving on it'	
Top Rock Hill E	7198.04	*Not known*	?1890	Entrance grave or cist		✓		
Yellow Rock Carn	7163	Gibson	Late 19th century	Natural cleft in rock	?	✓		IoS?

NOTES: 1. BM = BRITISH MUSEUM, IoS = ISLES OF SCILLY MUSEUM, RCM = ROYAL CORNWALL MUSEUM; SOME ARCHIVES COULD NOT BE TRACED IN 2006-2013
2. CRUTHER'S NECK/CARRION ROCK: SEE 4.5 BELOW
3. LITTLE ARTHUR C/D/E: THE POTTERY WAS RECORDED BY GIBSON AS BEING FROM 'THE GRAVE ON TOP OF LITTLE ARTHUR'
4. PORTH HELLICK DOWN C AND E: RUSSELL (1980) SUGGESTS THAT THESE WERE THE SITES EXCAVATED BY WOODLEY

TABLE 5.1 DETAILS OF FINDS FROM ENTRANCE GRAVES AND CISTS

everted. Occasionally there is impressed decoration, usually small holes, in the top of the rim. Lugs, either horizontally pierced (some with trumpet ends) or unperforated, occur frequently and are positioned at or immediately below the shoulder of the vessel.

Typically, Scillonian urns have two lugs, although the example found by Grimes at Salakee Down A has been reconstructed with four lugs. However, Helen O'Neil's note with the urn, dated 1 March 1955, says 'It is highly improbable that it had four lugs and the pot must therefore be treated with great caution and not used as a type. After handling the sherds of over 100 urns found by us during 1948-1954, not a single urn had such a feature.' (RCM 1956,4)

Two sherds from Porth Hellick Down A with cord-impressed decoration in a herringbone pattern are shown in figure 5.3, the left-hand sherd shows the remains of a small lug on the shoulder of the vessel. The decoration on these sherds suggests that they may be Trevisker Ware (H Quinnell, pers. comm.) and, if so, this is the only known example of this Cornish pottery in Scilly.

Otherwise, the pottery from the entrance graves and cists in Scilly shows little similarity to the contemporary wares from Cornwall where Food Vessels, Collared Urns, Biconical Urns and Trevisker Ware, many vessels including gabbroic fabric originating from the Lizard, are typical. Indeed, O'Neil says that at Knackyboy he found

> 'upwards of four hundredweight of pottery. Yet it is not possible to date it by analogy, because there seem to be no close parallels for the pottery either in the British Isles or elsewhere' (1948-1949:96).

Early Scillonian pottery is regarded as being different from mainland forms until the Late Bronze Age, with no gabbroic ware occurring in the islands during the Bronze Age (H Quinnell, pers. comm.). Because of this, there is little published information on Scillonian pottery, for example, Gibson does not mention Scillonian urns in his summary of regional urns but his description of biconical urns as 'large urn-shaped pot[s] with a marked carination at the top of a truncated body after which the pot narrows to a rim' (Gibson 1986:46) applies to many of the vessels from Scilly.

Parker Pearson treats Scillonian urns as a separate category in his review of Bronze Age pottery in south-western Britain. He suggests that, as both thin section petrological analysis and visual inspection of pottery from settlement and funerary sites in Scilly shows a granitic origin, it is likely that the fabrics are derived locally. His microscopic examination of pottery from Knackyboy Cairn and the settlement site at English Island Carn, St Martin's showed inclusions of mica, quartz, feldspar and granite, all of which occur in Scilly. He also stresses that the decoration of Scillonian pottery is different from Trevisker Ware and concludes that 'the group is best considered as a separate regional ceramic style' (Parker Pearson 1990:20)

FIGURE 5.3 SHERDS OF DECORATED WARE FROM PORTH HELLICK DOWN A (BRITISH MUSEUM 1926, 1112.3)

Only one example of an urn of non-local fabric is mentioned in the literature about Scilly and this is a Collared Urn with greenstone inclusions referred to simply as being from Normandy Down, St Mary's (Parker Pearson 1995). It has not been possible to trace this pot during the course of this research although Robinson (2007:140) states that it was wrongly attributed by Parker Pearson to Normandy Down and in fact comes from the cliff face at Pendrathen.

Robinson's reference suggests that the pot is the one found by Samuels in 1974 and described by him as a 'coarse storage vessel' found in a clay-lined pit (Samuels 1975:117). However, Samuels' illustration shows that only the lower part of the pot survives, from which it is not possible to identify it as a Collared Urn. There is, therefore, uncertainty about the identification of this vessel. If it is the one found by Samuels it appears from his description that it is not from an entrance grave or cist.

In general, the pottery from the entrance graves and cists is of the same type as that from the contemporary settlements (Gray 1972; Ashbee 1974; Butcher 1978). Ashbee and Butcher both make the point that, even within a single pot, the fabric can vary considerably, making it very difficult to match sherds to a vessel.

The majority of the pottery found in the entrance graves and cists is from biconical urns, however, one sherd, referred to as being discovered by Bonsor at Bant's Carn, has been described as being from a Neolithic vessel. This interpretation appears to have been made initially by Hencken, who, working from Bonsor's notes and drawings, says of the sherds found by Bonsor just outside the chamber entrance: 'The most important of these is part of a bowl evidently with a round base like the usual neolithic pottery of Britain' (Hencken 1932:24).

Hencken refers to an illustration of some of the sherds found at Bant's Carn, from which it appears that the sherd from the round-based bowl is that shown in the centre of the upper row (Hencken 1932:fig 10). This illustration

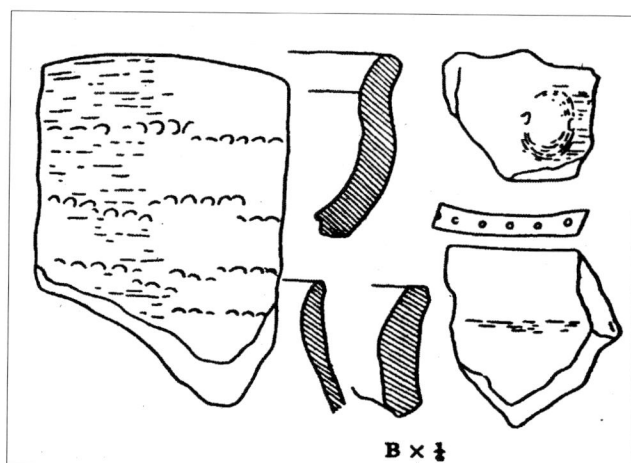

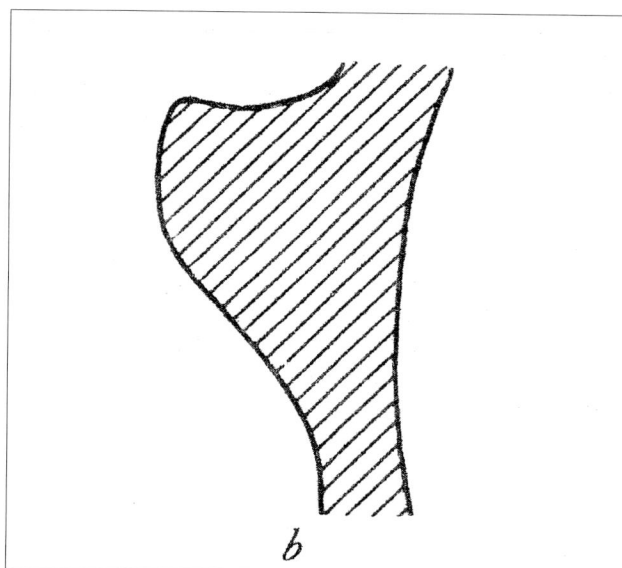

FIGURE 5.5 'LEDGE HANDLE' FROM NORTH HILL E, FROM HENCKEN (1933:FIG 12B)(BY PERMISSION OF THE SOCIETY OF ANTIQUARIES OF LONDON)

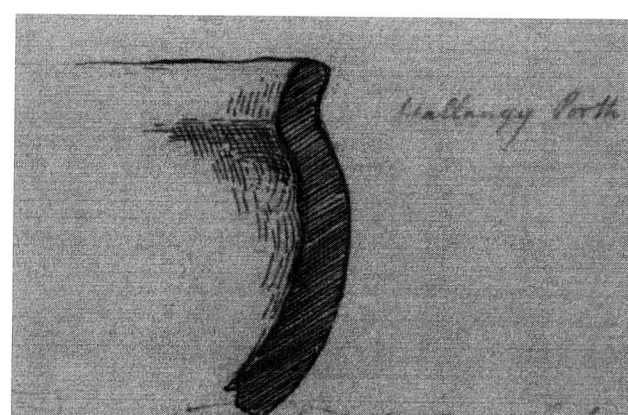

FIGURE 5.4 ILLUSTRATIONS OF SHERD FROM 'NEOLITHIC BOWL WITH ROUND BASE' FROM (ABOVE) HENCKEN (1932:FIG 10) AND (BELOW) BONSOR (1899-1900:150)

appears to be a composite of several drawings taken from Bonsor's notes. That of the sherd in question seems to be a copy of one in the notes of his 1900 excavations where it is labelled 'Hallangy Porth' (Bonsor 1899-1900:150). These two illustrations are shown in figure 5.4.

If this is indeed the same sherd then, regardless of whether or not it is from a round-based bowl, it is not relevant to a consideration of the date or use of Bant's Carn as it is from the neighbouring settlement site where structures and artefacts from the Neolithic, Bronze Age and Iron Age have been uncovered. The argument for it not being from Bant's Carn, or not being from a round-based bowl, is supported by the fact that in all Bonsor's references to the shape of vessels he found at Bant's Carn he says that they had flat bases (Bonsor 1899-1900; Maier 1999).

Hencken's interpretation of this sherd has been followed by many authors (Ashbee 1974; Thomas 1985; Kirk 2004) although the pottery found by Bonsor at Bant's Carn has not been examined by any other researcher, even Hencken stating that he had been unable to locate it (1933:14).

Hencken also refers to a possible Neolithic sherd in the report of his excavation of North Hill E, Samson. Here he found, just outside the entrance to the chamber, a large number of sherds, some of which formed part of the side

of a vessel. Hencken describes this as being 'of the bulging or shouldered kind common in the Scillonian tombs' but says that it had a 'ledge handle' at the bulge which was similar to those found at the Neolithic site of Abingdon (1933:27). His illustration of this 'ledge handle' is shown in figure 5.5.

It has not been possible to locate the finds from this excavation but, from the drawing, it seems likely that this is an unperforated lug, a common feature on Scillonian urns, and very similar to that shown in the illustration of an urn from Knackyboy in figure 5.1. The rest of Hencken's description of the vessel points to it being a typical biconical funerary urn and there is no reason to suppose that it is Neolithic in date.

The only site where a significant amount of pottery has been discovered, enabling changing vessel shapes and decoration to be traced through time, is Knackyboy Cairn and the ceramics from this site will now be considered in detail. There was a complex sequence of deposits at Knackyboy which it is now not possible to determine with certainty, because of the disturbance to the site by local men in 1912 and the removal by Rev Lewis of more than a hundredweight of pottery, without any apparent record of its location or stratigraphic position.

O'Neil had not intended to work at Knackyboy in 1948 but when he saw 'before him in section across the chamber a stratigraphic sequence of squashed urns such as must have fallen to the lot of few English archaeologists of this century' (O'Neil 1952:22) he decided to continue Lewis's work. He recorded the position of 18 urns, 16 in the chamber and two in the cairn and these are depicted in his plan, redrawn by Ashbee (1974), which is shown in figure 5.6.

O'Neil identified the earliest urns as numbers I, II, III, IV, V, VI, VII and XVI, the majority of which were grouped on the floor at the distal end of the chamber with number

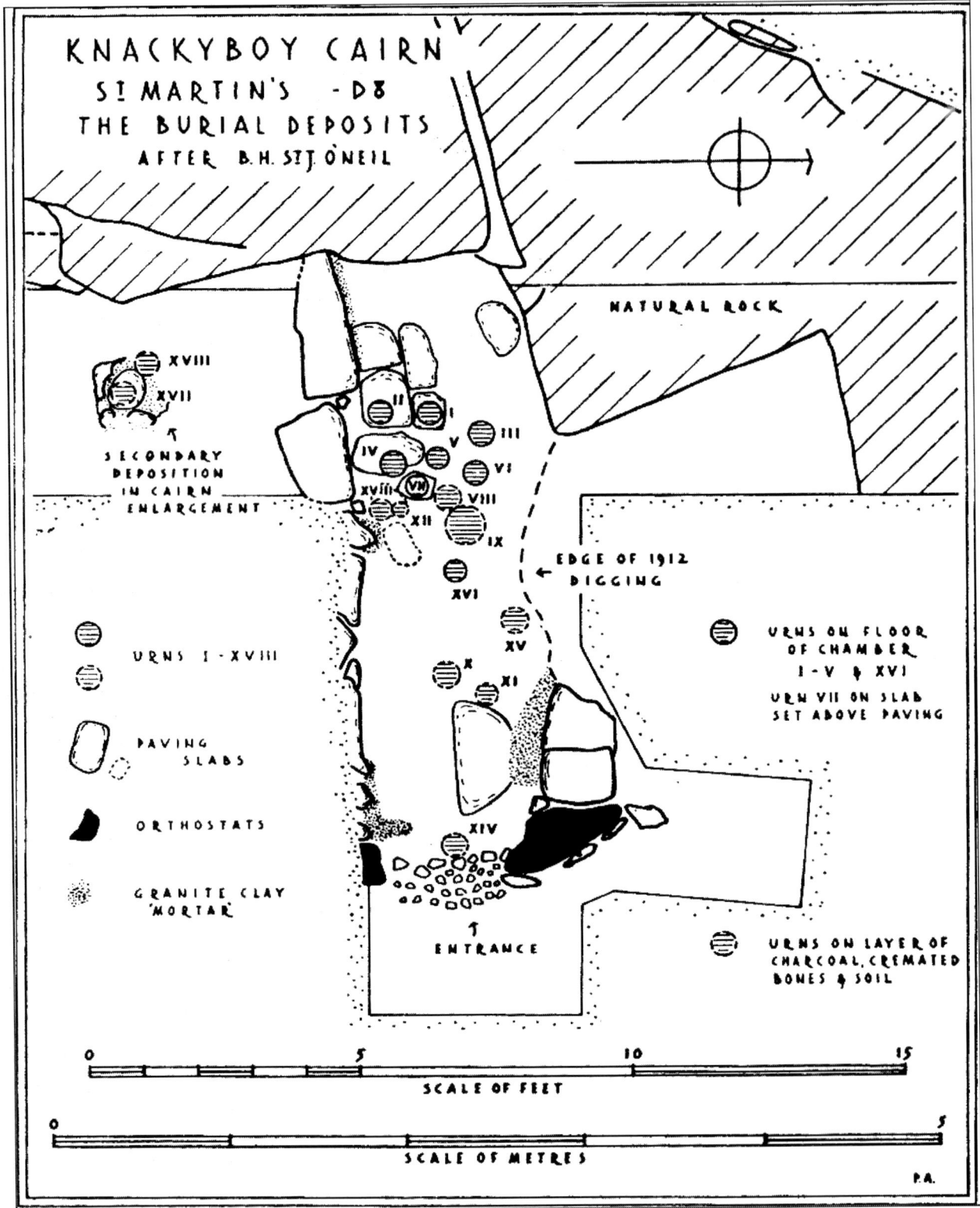

Figure 5.6 Plan of Knackyboy Cairn from Ashbee (1974:fig 18)

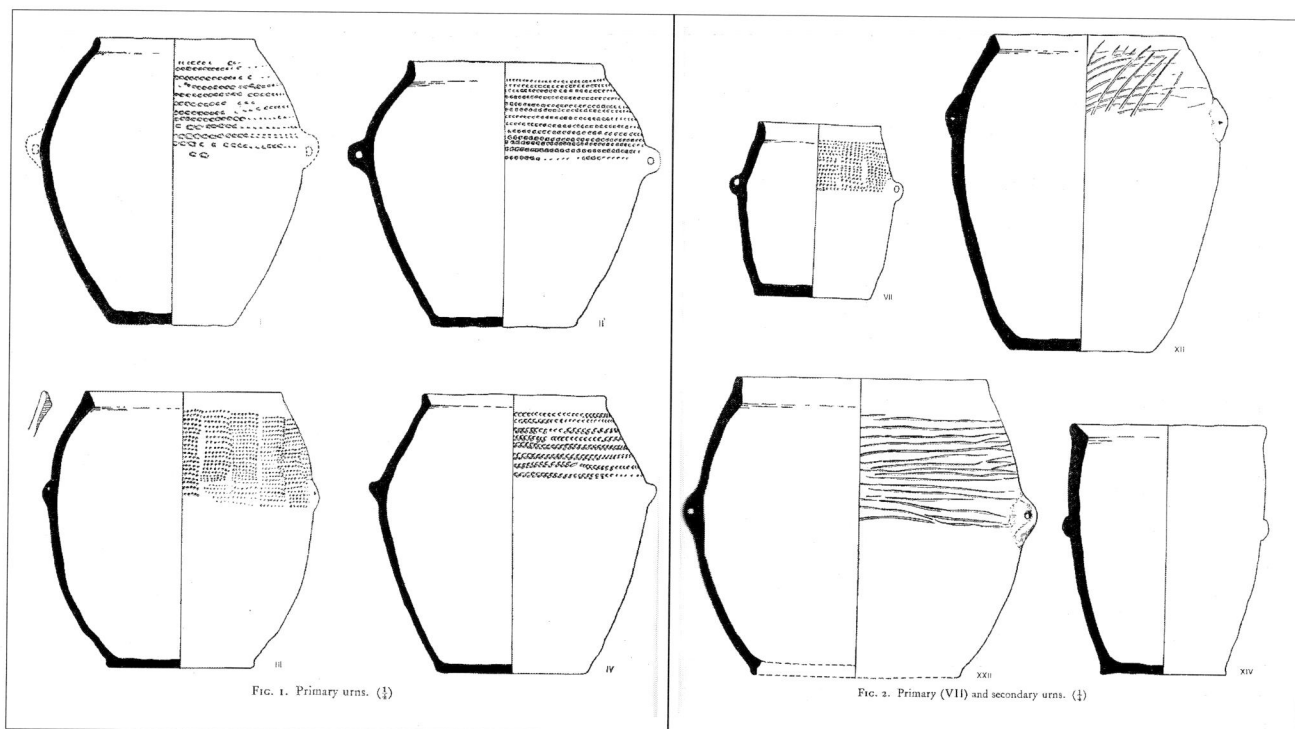

FIG. 1. Primary urns. (⅓)

FIG. 2. Primary (VII) and secondary urns. (⅓)

FIGURE 5.7 URNS I, II, III AND IV (UPPER IMAGE) AND VII, XII, XIV AND XXII (LOWER IMAGE) FROM KNACKYBOY CAIRN (ROYAL CORNWALL MUSEUM 1950.40), FROM O'NEIL (1952:FIGS 1 AND 2) (BY PERMISSION OF THE SOCIETY OF ANTIQUARIES OF LONDON)

VII standing on a flat stone slightly above the level of the others and number XVI being in the centre of the chamber.

Urn IX was later in date, having been placed above urn XVI, and urn VIII was later still. Urn XIII post-dated number XII, which in turn was above urn VII. Urns X and XI also post-dated the earliest group as, like numbers IX and XII, they had been placed on top of the layer of ashes and bones which surrounds the earliest vessels. Urn XV was at the same level as urn XIV, the last urn to be deposited in the chamber, which was placed just inside the entrance in the centre of the threshold. Urns XVII and XVIII were found close together in the cairn (O'Neil 1948-1949; 1952).

O'Neil's illustrations of primary urns I, II, III, IV and VII and secondary urns XII, XIV and XXII (the last is not mentioned in his published text nor shown in his plan or sections) are shown in figure 5.7. From these illustrations it will be noted that the earlier urns (numbers I, II, III, IV and VII) have a clearly biconical shape and impressed decoration. The later ones have straighter sides and either have incised decoration (Urn XII and XXII) or are plain (Urn XIV). Unfortunately, the upper part of several of these later vessels does not survive so their shape and decoration cannot be determined.

There has been some debate as to how the impressed decoration was applied. O'Neil states that his wife carried out experiments which established that only linen thread 'twisted or in stitches' produced the same effect as seen on the Knackyboy urns (O'Neil 1952:25). More recent work has shown that a variety of different twisted cords was used to form the impressions as well as loops, knots and other embroidery (Manske et al. 2004). However, Bonsor believed that the decoration on the urns from Bant's Carn, which appears from his illustrations to be very similar to that at Knackyboy, had been made with a punch (Bonsor 1899-1900). It is possible that a knotted string was used instead.

Eleven samples of cremated human bone from within or close to urns III, VI, VII, XIV, XV, XVI, XVII and XVIII were submitted for radiocarbon dating. The results are outlined and discussed in chapter 8.

At a number of sites it has been recorded that all or some of the pots had been deliberately broken. Bonsor notes this at Bant's Carn, where fragments were found both in the chamber and outside the entrance and where there were no intact urns (Bonsor 1899-1900). At Obadiah's Barrow he recorded fragments of pottery outside the chamber entrance (Hencken 1933). More recently Quinnell has suggested that the sherds found in the Porth Killier cist had been deliberately smashed before deposition (Quinnell forthcoming).

The placing of deliberately broken sherds outside the chamber entrance suggests ritual or ceremonial activities there, perhaps at a time when the entrance was sealed. Sherds have been found in this location at Bant's Carn, Obadiah's Barrow, Knackyboy Cairn and North Hill E.

Clay balls

These have been recorded at only one site, Pernagie Carn, by Lewis who says that he found 'a large amount of imported clay …, some of it made up into balls, and some bearing a distinct impress suggestive of daub on ancient huts' (1948:9). It is not clear from this whether by 'imported' he meant brought to the site, or brought to the islands, from elsewhere. In the course of this research, the clay balls could not be located in any museum collection and their exact provenance is also uncertain. It is possible that they are the same as or similar to the clay mortar/daub described below.

Clay mortar/daub

This is recorded among the finds from two sites, Knackyboy Cairn and Par Beach, both excavated by O'Neil. From Knackyboy, there is a pale grey-buff, perforated lump of mortar in two pieces about 120mm in length and a lump of grey mortar or daub, smoothed on one side and measuring 85mm by 60mm by 12mm, described in a note by O'Neil as a 'libation stand' (RCM 1950.40). From Par Beach, there are large pieces of a pale grey fine clay mortar (RCM 1955.38.10).

As described in Chapter 4, mortared walling has been recorded at some sites, both entrance graves and cists, including Knackyboy Cairn as well as Innisidgen Carn and North Hill E and the finds outlined above may well be connected with this practice. It is clear from O'Neil's unpublished notes and report that the 'libation stand' from Knackyboy is made of the same mortar which was found on all the *in situ* walling at the site (O'Neil 1948-1949).

5.4 Flint and other stone

Flint

Flint has been found at twelve sites, including both entrance graves and cists, making it the second most common discovery after pottery. Flint occurs in Scilly as glacial moraine, deposited during the late Devensian period (c20,000BP) (Scourse 2006a), and can be found on the ground surface around the northern border of the islands, as flakes and as nodules up to the size of a grapefruit. This glacially-deposited flint is believed to originate from the area now covered by St George's Channel (J Scourse, pers. comm.) and is typically light to mid-grey in colour.

The largest and most significant flint object discovered at an entrance grave or cist is the flaked handaxe or adze found by O'Neil at Knackyboy Cairn in 1948. The colour of the flint is typical of the glacial moraine and, as O'Neil comments, it might well be a local artefact. He records that it was 'under a portion of the original barrow material' (O'Neil 1952:22), a description that has led Robinson to state that:

> 'The intentional placement of this artefact immediately on the ancient land surface prior to the construction of the monument suggests that it represents a foundation deposit associated with the monument's construction.' (Robinson 2007:54)

The significance of this discovery for the dating of Knackyboy Cairn will be considered further in chapter 8. Small flint flakes were also found at this site and similar flakes have been discovered at Halangy Down, Hill Bennigates and Middle Arthur B; at the last site some of the flints had been burnt.

At two sites, flint of a different colour and possibly, therefore, a different provenance, has been discovered. Some of the small flint flakes from Hill Bennigates are dark brown in colour and the larger flint flake, recorded at Torquay Museum only as being from 'a cist in St Mary's Isle, Scilly' (and now transferred to the Isles of Scilly Museum) is of a similar colour.

Because of the availability of glacial flint, prehistoric flint implements are widely found in Scilly, both at known sites and on beaches and downland. The majority of them are scrapers, whilst arrowheads, flakes and blades are also well-represented in the collections of the Isles of Scilly Museum. Large objects, like the Knackyboy axe, are very uncommon and this may be due to the size of flint nodules available in the islands.

Granite

Objects of granite have been definitely recorded from only two sites: North Hill E, where a hammer-stone and a quern rubber were discovered and Porth Killier, where a mortar or socket stone was found. Obadiah's Barrow yielded a hammer-stone, Bant's Carn a quern rubber and Tinkler's Hill E a 'stone with rough carving on it' (Lewis 1948:7) and it is probable that these were made of granite also, although neither of the excavators specify this. With the exception of the stone from Porth Killier, these finds cannot now be located.

Hencken, who excavated at North Hill E in 1930, describes the hammer-stone as being 'a smooth pebble of fine-grained granite, 3½ in. long by 1½ in. wide, with its rounded end roughened as if by pounding.' It was found inside the chamber. The quern rubber was found amongst paving in the middle of the chamber and is described as being '12 in. long, 8¼ in. wide and 2½ in. thick, and one surface, which is slightly convex, is remarkably and unnaturally smooth.' (Hencken 1933:27)

Bonsor discovered a hammer-stone whilst excavating at Obadiah's Barrow in 1901. No description of this object is given other than that it was '[a] pebble which had served as a hammer' (Hencken 1933:23). It was apparently found in the centre of the chamber close to human bones and fragments of pottery (Hencken 1933; Maier 1999). Bonsor does not record the discovery of a quern rubber at Bant's Carn (Maier 1999) but Hencken, who had access to Bonsor's original notes and plans, says that he found a 'muller' there; no further information is given (Hencken 1929).

The stone found at Tinkler's Hill E, a site which was badly damaged before Lewis's excavation there, is described by him as having been found at a depth of about 300mm. His comments about it make it clear that some who saw it thought it was modern. He records that he left it on the surface at the site. There is no trace of it there now but a shaped stone was found in Middle Town, St Martin's in 2012 when a wall was rebuilt. It is impossible now either to establish whether it is the stone found by Lewis or to date it.

Pumice

At Porth Hellick Down A, Bonsor found a small piece of pumice, perforated at one end, which he described as a pendant (Maier 1999). It was discovered in the entrance to the chamber, together with some sherds of pottery. The pumice is dark-brown in colour with a fine texture. It measures a maximum of 38mm long and 34mm wide and weighs 12g. It has a small circular perforation at one end and rounded edges but one side is flat, as though the pendant had been cut from a larger piece of pumice. It is illustrated in figure 5.8.

Pumice is an unusual discovery in the British Isles and is clearly not of local origin. Indeed Hencken stated that it was 'obviously a foreign import' (1932:21); however, as pumice floats, it is possible for it to arrive in Britain through natural agencies, rather than through human intervention.

Pumice has been found at four other sites in Scilly, though not published in detail. At the Bronze Age settlement site at Little Bay, St Martin's, Neal and Butcher found a single piece of grey pumice (RCM 1993,36.4) measuring 46mm by 34mm (Neal 1983). Neal also found a fragment of pumice at the multi-period site at East Porth, Samson (Neal forthcoming). A piece of pumice, described by its finder, Alec Gray, as being a 'surface find, locality unknown, but not far from Bant's Carn, St Mary's' was located at the Royal Cornwall Museum (RCM 2005,47.3) during the current research. It is roughly circular, of brown pumice about 16mm in diameter and has an off-centre hole through it.

Two pieces of brown-grey pumice (IoS Museum RN 362 and 363) were found by Dudley during her excavations at the prehistoric settlement and Romano-British shrine site on Nornour, Eastern Isles (Dudley 1968a). One is circular, 40mm in diameter, the other is semi-circular, 33mm in diameter, and has the slight trace of a central hole through it. These two pieces of pumice from Nornour were submitted to Dr Anthony Newton of Edinburgh University for examination and analysis.

The larger of the two (RN 362) was found at site IIIa 'midden with small hut', which is shown on the published site plan as 'Bronze Age Hut'. It has not proved possible to trace the small finds record for this site in the archive but the site notes record a midden with limpet shells and animal bone covering a small hut; there were some Romano-British finds from the upper level. The excavation report

FIGURE 5.8 PUMICE PENDANT FROM PORTH HELLICK DOWN A (BRITISH MUSEUM, 1926, 1112.9)

says that the site 'produced little but Bronze Age and Iron Age sherds and some pumice stone' (Dudley 1968a:18). It seems reasonable to assume that RN362 came from the prehistoric levels but it is not possible to be more specific as to its date.

The smaller piece (RN 363) is from Dudley's site II (the more easterly of the two joined huts with Roman artefacts) and was found in September 1962. Its find spot is not far from that of RN362. It is not mentioned in the excavation report but it is recorded in Dudley's small finds notebook for site II as find 24 and is described as a 'crucible' (i.e. one of the very small pots now generally regarded as votive offering jars). No provenance or level is indicated in the notebook. Other finds from this site include prehistoric artefacts and Roman brooches both before and after the pumice in the sequence of small finds numbers. This piece, therefore, could be from either a prehistoric or Romano-British context.

As there was no Roman occupation or administration of Scilly, the large number of Roman brooches and other jewellery, Roman coins, 'Dea Nutrix' and 'pseudo-Venus' figurines found at Nornour are now regarded as being offerings at a shrine and as having been deposited by visitors to the islands (Butcher 2000-2001). The brooches are of both British and Continental types and are believed to represent offerings by travellers from the Roman world, sailing between mainland Britain and continental Europe. If RN 363 is from the Romano-British period, then it may have been brought to Scilly by people visiting from far afield and not represent material that has arrived through natural processes.

Following his analysis Dr Newton reports that the two pieces of pumice from Nornour are silicic pumice and both originate from the Katla Volcano System in southern Iceland. This produced eruptions of silicic, as opposed to the more usual basaltic, pumice in c3000BC, c1950BC, c1400BC, c1200BC and c400AD (Larsen et al. 2001) but, without further analysis, it is not possible to say from which eruption the Nornour pumice originated (A Newton, pers. comm.).

Enquiries in Scilly have led to the conclusion that pumice occurs in the islands very infrequently and an Icelandic source for pumice there is unexpected given the prevailing west to east winds and currents in the Atlantic (Binns 1967). Layard, writing about the archaeology of Scilly, comments in a footnote, that he had been told that:

'after the Mount Pelee disaster in the West Indies some 30 years ago [in Martinique in 1902], quantities of pumice stone were washed around these shores and that the same occurred, in less degree, about 12 years ago.' (1933:122 fn)

Elsewhere in the British Isles pumice has been recorded from Scotland, where it has been found at over 140 archaeological sites, both on the mainland and on the islands of Shetland, Orkney and the Hebrides, in contexts dating from the Mesolithic to Modern periods (Newton 2004). Worked pumice, including pendants, has been found in the Hebrides at Clettraval and Unival, both in North Uist and at Camas Daraich, Skye, in Shetland at Stanydale, West Mainland and in Orkney at Quoyness, Sanday and Taversoe Tuick, Rousay (Henshall 1972; Clarke et al. 1985; Davidson & Henshall 1989; Wickham-Jones 2004).

In particular, the pendant from Taversoe Tuick, which was found with 35 shale disk beads and which is dated to c2400BC, is very similar to that from Porth Hellick Down A. Whilst pumice may have had a utilitarian function as an abrasive material, the discovery of small, pierced pieces, particularly in association with beads as at Taversoe Tuick, suggests that it was also worn as a pendant. It may be that it was regarded as a charm or amulet as a result of its property of floating on water.

Geochemical analysis of samples from Scotland has demonstrated that most of this pumice also comes from eruptions of the Katla volcano in Iceland (Newton 2004). Its occurrence at coastal sites suggests that it has arrived there through natural processes although it is possible that it was traded. The absence of pumice from coastal sites between northern Scotland and Scilly is difficult to explain but may be due to a lack of publication of such discoveries.

Other stone

The only other worked stone objects clearly recorded as having been found in a Scillonian entrance grave or cist are the agate bead and stone spindle-whorl discovered at Peninnis Head and what appears to be an unfinished spindle-whorl from Knackyboy Cairn. In addition, a bead and a small perforated stone were apparently also found at Knackyboy.

The Peninnis Head finds were made in 1812 (Douch 1962) and the objects were given to the Royal Cornwall Museum

in 1852 by Augustus Smith, the Lord Proprietor of the islands. Human remains, pottery and two bronze armlets, which will be discussed in section 5.5 below, were also discovered.

The records of the RCM show that the bead and the spindle-whorl were missing in 1942 and they have not been re-found subsequently. The bead was described in 1852 as 'a large Bead of agate, finely polished', though the size and colour were not given, and the spindle-whorl as a 'flat perforated disc of stone, diameter about 1¾ in.' (Penrose 1942). The Isles of Scilly Museum has a number of unprovenanced, and therefore undated, agate beads in its collection and stone spindle-whorls are known from prehistoric settlement sites on the islands, including Nornour (Butcher 1978).

There is considerable doubt surrounding the discovery of the objects from Peninnis Head: they are recorded in the *West Briton* newspaper of 30 October 1812 as having been found by 'some workmen, employed in removing the foundation stones of a very ancient building which was on a piece of waste ground' (Douch 1962:97). This is the only site in Scilly at which bronze armlets have been found and the only entrance grave site, apart from the records from Knackyboy discussed below, which has yielded either an agate bead or a spindle-whorl. These objects must therefore be treated with caution and it would be unwise to draw any definite conclusions from them.

In the course of the study reported here, a small flat piece of pink-brown stone (apparently sandstone), measuring 58mm by 44mm, was found at the Royal Cornwall Museum inside Urn IV from Knackyboy Cairn. It is recorded in the Museum's accessions register but is not mentioned in the preliminary excavation report nor in O'Neil's manuscript notes about the site (O'Neil 1948-1949; O'Neil 1952). It has circular depressions, probably made by drilling, near the centre of each side and appears to be an unfinished spindle-whorl.

The other possible finds of stone from Knackyboy Cairn are more uncertain: Lewis obtained an account of the discovery of a 'small perforated, flat stone, about the size of a small coin' and a 'salmon pink bead' when questioning two local men (Leggo Ashford and Fred Stephens) who had opened the chamber in 1912, when quarrying for stone (Lewis 1949). As Lewis did not speak to them until almost forty years later, their recollection of what they found and of what became of their discoveries is necessarily limited.

One interpretation of the perforated stone is that it was a spindle-whorl, although it would seem to be very small for this. Another possibility is that it was a quoit-shaped faience bead and this will be considered further in section 5.6 below.

The pink bead may have been of carnelian, a type of agate, as Lewis suggests. 'It was certainly not amber', he concluded (Lewis nd-b). In other notes, Lewis reports that he was told that the pink bead was 'cylindrical with rounded corners. Perforated longitudinally ... Very smooth. Looks glassy.' (Lewis nd-a).

As mentioned above, a number of agate beads are in the collection of the Isles of Scilly Museum and some of them are salmon pink in colour. Ashbee (1996) found a longitudinally perforated carnelian bead during excavations at the Iron Age to Early Mediaeval settlement of Halangy Down, St Mary's and there are also records of similar carnelian beads from Cornwall in the database of the Portable Antiquities Scheme (e.g. Tyacke 2010). There is, however, uncertainty about the dating of all these objects.

5.5 Metalwork

Prehistoric bronze is rare in Scilly (Ashbee 1974; Ratcliffe & Johns 2003) but much of what has been found comes from funerary contexts, with four sites, three of them entrance graves and the other an indeterminate site, yielding bronze objects. By far the largest and best preserved of these are the two bronze armlets, referred to above, from Peninnis Head.

The armlets, which are almost identical, have a 100mm external diameter and are made of a solid rod of bronze, roughly circular in cross-section but with squared corners and slightly splayed at the ends. They weigh 350g and 344.2g. A single, smaller armlet was identified in the database of the Portable Antiquities Scheme (Richardson 2005). This weighs only 80.5g and has a rounded cross-section which expands into squarish terminals. It was found, by a metal detectorist, in Thanet, Kent and may be Bronze Age in date.

Otherwise, it is hard to find any parallel for these armlets although Ashbee (1960:114) suggests that they might be local versions of the massive ingot torcs known from elsewhere in the Early Bronze Age. However, as mentioned above, the precise location of the site in which these armlets were discovered is not known and it is possible that it was not an entrance grave.

Finds from more secure contexts are the bronze awl from Obadiah's Barrow and the bronze objects from Knackyboy Cairn. Unfortunately, these are all in very poor condition, limiting the opportunity for determining their form and function and thus making comparisons difficult.

The awl was found by Bonsor in 1901 but he appears to have recorded little about the precise location of its discovery (Maier 1999). Hencken (1933) reproduced Bonsor's plan of Obadiah's Barrow, which shows it in the centre of the chamber, close to fragments of urn and ashes. The awl, which is 37mm long and 3mm wide, is square in cross-section and has one pointed end. Hencken says that it was analysed at the British Museum and found to be 'bronze very poor in tin' (1933:23).

The bronze objects found at Knackyboy Cairn by O'Neil in 1948 comprise four small fragments. O'Neil described them as 'a hook, and perhaps a handle from a brass-bound wooden box or bucket' (1952:30) but Ashbee suggests that the hook could be from an earring and the handle a bracelet end. This difference of interpretation is indicative of the state of preservation of these objects. The bronze fragments were found in a layer of ashes, containing pieces of charcoal and cremated bone with a small amount of soil, in the chamber.

Lewis, in his investigations into what was found at Knackyboy when it was opened early in the 20th century, records the discovery by local men of 'bits of bronze (green)' and a 'figurine' (bronzy colour but not green)' (Lewis 1949). In another note the latter is described as follows:

> 'About 3 inches long – Head, face, figure, and feet distinctly shown. Arms held down, and as if hands folded in front. Legs separated by incision only. Outline on both sides. A sort of bronze colour, but NOT GREEN. More like an old penny. ... Thickness of figure was not much more than that of a coin. Found inside an urn.' (Lewis nd-a, emphasis in original)

Unfortunately the 'figurine' was broken and then lost and it is difficult to identify possible parallels for it from this description. It may be that what are described as features by the finders were simply the products of corrosion.

The fact that it is recorded as having been found inside an urn would presumably preclude it being a later intrusion to the grave. Its different appearance from the other bronze objects found by the local men may be due to different environmental conditions or may indicate that it was of a different metal, the only likely alternative being gold. Whatever the interpretation, it provides further evidence for the deposition of metal artefacts with the cremation burials at this site.

It is also recorded that Alexander Gibson, a local antiquarian, removed artefacts, including pieces of bronze, from Knackyboy at this time (Lewis 1949). In his diary of his work in Scilly in 1901, Bonsor recorded a visit to John Gibson, the father of Alexander Gibson. Here he was told of the discovery of a 'kistvaen' at Cruther's Neck where, amongst urn fragments and burnt bones, a bronze point had been found (Bonsor 1901-1902:232-233). The fragments of this are now in the Isles of Scilly Museum and consist of three joining pieces of corroded bronze approximately 15mm wide and 60mm long in total. They appear to be a small dagger or knife. The object is shown in figure 5.9.

There has been much speculation amongst subsequent researchers, who have not had access to Bonsor's diaries, about the provenance of this object. Hencken (1932) refers to the find being made on St Martin's but does not give an exact location. Daniel said that it had been 'impossible to obtain exact information about it' (1950:125) but O'Neil concluded that it had come from Knackyboy, that it was now lost, but that it was likely to have been 'a small

FIGURE 5.9 BRONZE 'DAGGER' FROM CRUTHER'S NECK, ST MARTIN'S (ISLES
OF SCILLY MUSEUM RN 1214)

triangular plate off a box' (1952:21 fn 4).

Ashbee (1974) refers to a bronze dagger, said to have been found at Carrion (or Carron) Rock, being given to the Isles of Scilly Museum. However, the Historic Environment Record (HES 1987-2005) entry (*PRN 7169*) says that there is no barrow in the vicinity. There is a mound at Cruther's Neck (*PRN 7170*), the HER entry for which says that it has a trench cut across it (which has been revealed by recent clearance), and which is in the exact location described by Bonsor; it is therefore very likely that this the site where the fragments were found.

The loss or poor state of preservation of most of the bronze artefacts from Scillonian entrance graves and the doubts about the well-preserved ones mean that, unfortunately, they can add little to our knowledge of their origins or connections.

5.6 Faience and glass beads

Faience and glass beads have been found at only one site, Knackyboy Cairn. O'Neil found nine beads there, some complete, some broken and some in fragments. The report on them indicates that eight of them are of glass and only one of faience (Stone 1952). The faience bead is a six-rayed star bead with a maximum diameter of 20mm and a weight of 1.28g. Stone notes that the tips of all the points are worn or broken, suggesting that the bead was not new when it was buried.

The vast majority of faience beads found in Britain and Ireland have been discovered in burial sites and most have been associated with a burial rite of cremation. Pottery found with the beads has been mostly funerary urns or 'accessory' vessels. Faience beads have also often been found in association with 'special' grave goods, such as beads of other precious materials including amber and jet, bronze articles and V-perforated buttons. Sheridan and Shortland argue that this, together with the rarity of the beads themselves, is an 'indicator of special status' (2004:270). The Knackyboy bead is therefore typical of

this general pattern, having been discovered in association with eight glass beads (with the possibility that all nine beads came from the same necklace) and bronze objects.

The commonest form of faience bead found in Britain and Ireland, accounting for about 75% of all discoveries, is the segmented bead, with a concentration in Wessex. Star-shaped beads, like the one from Knackyboy, are the second commonest and occur in a variety of forms. They have a scattered distribution in south-west and central England with a greater number of examples from Scotland and a handful from Ireland. Quoit-shaped beads and pendants are less common and have a generally similar distribution to star-shaped beads (Sheridan & Shortland 2004).

When the Knackyboy beads were found in 1948 they were believed to have been manufactured in Egypt (Beck & Stone 1935) and the presumed date of this (c1320-1200BC) was used by O'Neil to date the grave at Knackyboy (1952:30). Subsequent work has shown significant differences in the chemical composition of faience beads from Egypt, Mycenae, Central and Western Europe, suggesting different centres of manufacture including one or more in the British Isles (Stone & Thomas 1956; Newton & Renfrew 1970; Harding 1971; Aspinall et al. 1972; Harding & Warren 1973; Sheridan & Shortland 2004). The beads from the British Isles are distinguished from other faience beads by their high tin content.

Radiocarbon dates from sites in Britain and Ireland with discoveries of faience span the period from about 1900BC to 1450BC (Sheridan & Shortland 2004:265), considerably earlier than the date suggested by O'Neil. The faience bead from Knackyboy was found in 'the dark brown soil very close to the base of Urn XVI' (O'Neil 1952:24). It cannot therefore be definitely associated with an urn or its contents, although it should be noted that one of the glass beads was found in Urn XVI.

Urn XVI was one of eight urns found, upright, on the floor of the chamber, surrounded and partly covered by a thick deposit consisting of charcoal, cremated bones and some soil. Several of the beads as well as the pieces of bronze were found in this layer, suggesting that they may originally have been deposited together. The significance of the faience bead for the dating of Knackyboy Cairn will be considered in chapter 8.

The other eight beads from Knackyboy are of glass, being turquoise, blue or green in colour and oblate in shape with a central perforation. In addition to the one bead found in an urn, four more were discovered in the ashes and cremated bone around the urns, whilst the other three were unstratified. At least three of the glass beads show signs of having been subjected to intense heat, presumably on the funeral pyre (Stone 1952).

Glass beads are much rarer in the British Bronze Age than those of faience. Analysis of the glass beads from Knackyboy showed them to be of high magnesium glass, similar to examples from the Isle of Lewis, Tayside, Galloway, Dorset, Wiltshire, Oxfordshire, and Co Down (Henderson 1988; 1989). Even if a 13th or 12th century BC date for Knackyboy is accepted, the beads there were in a context several centuries older than many of these sites.

Newton and Renfrew state that the glass beads from Scilly form a separate group, in terms of their chemical composition, and 'can at present be presumed to be of local manufacture' (1970:205). However, Henderson (1988) suggests that it is likely that high magnesium glass, either in raw form or as finished artefacts, derived from the Near East or the Mediterranean.

Although the one faience and eight glass beads are the only ones mentioned by O'Neil and the only ones which can currently be traced, it has been suggested that other beads were found at the site. One of the men who opened the chamber in 1912, and reported to Lewis that he had found a salmon pink bead, a perforated stone, 'bits of bronze' and the 'figurine' all described above, also recalled finding blue beads, one, at least, at the bottom of an urn (Lewis 1949).

The pink and blue beads were described as being 'very beautiful and of very fine workmanship … both were more or less opaque, and with a very fine polish. Well perforated, and with the colour right through them.' (Lewis nd-b). Lewis concluded that the blue bead was probably similar to those found in 1948. The beads found in 1912 and described to Lewis had all been lost by the time Knackyboy Cairn was excavated by O'Neil in 1948 and it is difficult to know what reliance to place on the recollections of their finders some forty years later. The salmon pink bead might have been made of carnelian, as discussed above, or of glass, like the blue beads: a red glass bead was found in a barrow at Wilsford, Wiltshire (Guido et al. 1984).

As suggested above, it is possible that the object described by the men as a perforated stone was a quoit-shaped faience bead. Faience can be mistaken for stone, especially if it has lost its glaze: for example, the faience bead from Harristown, Co Waterford was described in the excavation report as being of red sandstone (Hawkes 1941).

Lewis refers to items in Alexander Gibson's collection which may have come from Knackyboy; apparently quoting Gibson's description he says that one is 'A very rare bead. It is of clay about the size of a sixpence but thicker. British Museum says it is part of a necklace of a Prehistoric Belle. They have the only other known specimen.' (Lewis 1949) This could be the same or another quoit-shaped faience bead. A further possible record of faience can be found in Hencken's report on his excavation at the previously disturbed site of North Hill E in which he refers to '[t]wo small fragments of some fused sandy substance' discovered inside the chamber (Hencken 1933).

The technologies required for the production of bronze, faience and glass have many elements in common and similar raw materials, such as fine grained sand (widely found in Scilly), are desirable for faience and glass (Henderson 1978). It is likely either that both the faience and glass beads were produced in Scilly or that both were imported. The relative absence of bronze objects in Scilly suggests that there was probably not a local bronze industry and makes the latter case the more likely.

5.7 Animal bone

Both worked and unworked animal bone has been found in Scillonian entrance graves, though none is reported from cists. Worked bone points were discovered at Obadiah's Barrow and Knackyboy Cairn, a pig jawbone at Halangy Down and 'a small part of the humerus of some animal' at North Hill E (Hencken 1933:28).

Three worked points were found at Obadiah's Barrow, two of which were recorded by Bonsor as being of bone and the third as being of horn (Maier 1999). However, the one described by Bonsor as horn may, in fact, be antler. It is 45mm long and the bone points measure 72mm and 77mm in length. All three show longitudinal groove marks where they have been sharpened. The horn or antler point was found amongst human ashes and the bone points were in a deposit of limpet shells in the grave, perhaps suggesting that they were used to remove limpets from their shells. The horn or antler point is illustrated in figure 5.10 and Bonsor's sketch of the two bone points is shown at figure 5.11.

The bone point from Knackyboy Cairn is very similar to the two from Obadiah's Barrow. It measures 70mm in length and again has longitudinal grooves. It is not mentioned in O'Neil's (1952) preliminary report on his excavation (the only one ever published because of his untimely death) nor in his unpublished papers (1948-1949) nor by the other commentators on the site (Lewis 1948; Ashbee 1974). Consequently, no information is available as to where in the chamber or cairn it was found. It was discovered during the research reported here, in the Royal Cornwall Museum, where it had been archived with the human remains from the site.

Three similar bone points, described as punches, gouges or awls, were found at the settlement site on Nornour in contexts dating to the mid-second millennium BC onwards and were identified by Turk as being made from seal and sheep bones (Butcher 1978:96).

The pig jawbone, recorded by Gray from Halangy Down, was described by him as being 'probably, but not certainly part of the grave's original contents' (1972:29); no further information is given. Hencken says that the animal humerus at North Hill E was found '9 ft. in from entrance in middle of chamber' together with several pottery sherds (1933:28). Both Halangy Down and North Hill E had been badly disturbed and it is clear that material from both sites had been removed before their excavation. It is therefore impossible to say whether other animal bones

FIGURE 5.10 HORN OR ANTLER POINT FROM OBADIAH'S BARROW (BRITISH MUSEUM, 1926, 1112.11)

had originally been deposited in these entrance graves. It is also possible that the animal bones at both sites are later intrusions; rabbit bones were also found at North Hill E.

5.8 Shells

Limpet shell middens are a common feature of settlement sites of all periods in Scilly but few references have been made to the presence of shells in burial sites. However, a close reading of Bonsor's reports about the entrance graves of Bant's Carn, Cruther's Neck and Obadiah's Barrow (Bonsor 1899-1900; Bonsor 1901-1902; Maier 1999) shows that limpet shells were found at all three. At Obadiah's Barrow there were considerable quantities of them, forming a layer more than 300mm deep inside the chamber.

Bonsor believed that the shells at Obadiah's Barrow were not part of the original deposits but had been introduced at a later date, through the gap between two of the capstones, when the chamber had been used as a rubbish dump. Much smaller quantities of shells were apparently found by him at Bant's Carn but no explanation for their presence was offered.

Limpet shells have also been recorded in megalithic burial chambers in the Channel Islands. At Robert's Cross, Herm, limpet shells were found, together with pottery, animal bones and a complete human skull, in a parallel-sided chamber 4.5m long (Scarre 2008). On Jersey, at Les Monts Grantez, a number of inhumation burials was covered with limpet shells, animal bones and teeth and colourful sea pebbles and a 1m thick layer of limpet shells was discovered in the chamber at Le Déhus on Guernsey. A layer of limpet shells and pebbles was found separating two phases of inhumation burials at La Varde, Guernsey (Johnston 1981). Limpet shells have also been found with burials at Barclodiad y Gawres, Anglesey and Midhowe, Rousay. Cunliffe has suggested that these occurrences may be 'a tantalising hint' that the Mesolithic tradition of burying the dead in coastal shell middens was 'being symbolically acknowledged' (2001:558).

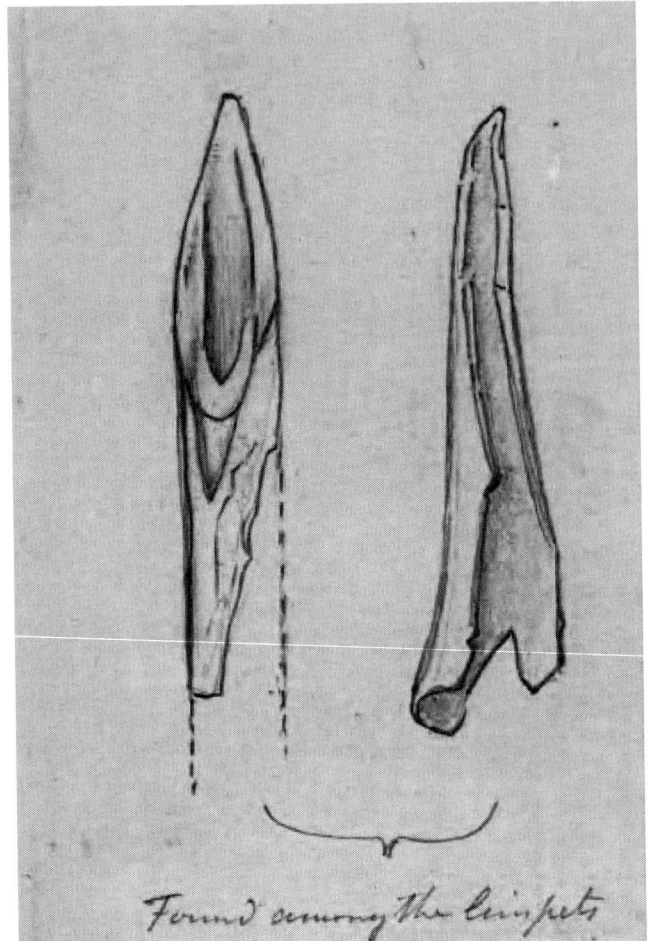

FIGURE 5.11 BONE POINTS FROM OBADIAH'S BARROW, FROM BONSOR (1901-1902:219)

5.9 Human remains

Human remains have been recorded at nine sites: four entrance graves, three cists and two indeterminate sites. In addition, there is one site where no precise information is available but where the record suggests that human remains may possibly have been present as Lewis writes of a 'funerary urn' (1948:8) being found in the rock cleft at Yellow Rock Carn, St Martin's. There are also references in earlier writings to 'ashes and cinders' being found in chambers on Gugh (Troutbeck 1796:155).

At only one site, Obadiah's Barrow, is there a record of articulated bones. Here Bonsor discovered, in different parts of the chamber, several vertebrae, the bones of the forearm and, elsewhere, those of the foot, ankle and lower leg; also in the chamber were other parts of the skeleton. He believed that all the bones were from a single, male skeleton which had been a contracted inhumation burial. These remains were in a layer of hard, blackish soil, with no other finds, on top of which urns, containing cremated human bones, had been placed (Hencken 1933; Maier 1999).

It appears that the inhumed bones survived in identifiable condition at Obadiah's Barrow because of the presence of limpet shells in the grave, as mentioned above. These, being alkaline, reduce the acidity of the soil and assist bone preservation, as can be observed in many of the middens associated with prehistoric settlement sites in Scilly (Dudley 1968a; Butcher 1978; Ashbee 1996).

Bonsor calculated, on the basis of the fragments, that there had been twelve urns in the chamber, although he said in a letter to T A Dorrien-Smith that there were more than twenty urns (Bonsor 1901; Hencken 1933; Maier 1999). Bonsor was clear that the inhumation pre-dated the cremation burials, confirming this in the letter to Dorrien-Smith.

Of the cremated remains at Obadiah's Barrow, Bonsor commented that they had not been burnt naked because he had noticed traces of oxidised copper on some of the skull bones (Maier 1999:165). A similar phenomenon is recorded by Cummings and Fowler on some of the cremated bones from Bargrennan White Cairn (2007:41).

Only one of the urns at Obadiah's Barrow was intact when found and the bones from it were examined in 2011 by Priscilla Ferreira Ulguim, then a Master's student at the University of Exeter whose work was supervised by Professor Chris Knüsel. She reports that they are those of a premature baby and that they had been cremated at a temperature of between 300°C and 800°C (Ulguim 2011). A sample of the bone was submitted for radiocarbon dating but, unfortunately, it was not possible to obtain a result.

Ulguim also examined the cremation from an intact urn discovered at Knackyboy Cairn (illustrated in figure 4.1). This is not one of those recorded by O'Neil and so was probably collected by Lewis. It contained a single individual, probably adult, whose remains had been cremated at below 300°C. Ulguim suggests the bone surface modifications may indicate that dry bones were cremated (2011:18).

At Bant's Carn, Bonsor found four heaps of ash containing burnt bones and charcoal at the distal end of the chamber, together with fragments of pottery. As mentioned above, pottery sherds were also discovered outside the chamber entrance and Bonsor interpreted this as a violation of the tomb when the urn contents were tipped on to the floor of the chamber and the urns broken (Bonsor 1899-1900; Maier 1999). He states in a letter that this happened 'many centuries ago' (Bonsor 1900). No other burials were found in the chamber.

At Knackyboy Cairn, however, a thick deposit of ashes, described as being charcoal, cremated bone and a little soil and practically the same as the cremations themselves, was found around the lowest level, of eight urns, in the chamber. O'Neil's unpublished report of the excavation says:

'Over 80 rims were recovered during the excavation, and, allowing for disturbances, ancient and modern, which may have scattered some urns, it seems likely

that the tomb once held about 100 or more cremations.' (O'Neil 1948-1949)

This is based on the assumption that each urn contained the remains of one individual, which is borne out by Ulguim's findings but may not apply in all cases. There is also a passing reference in O'Neil's unpublished report on Knackyboy Cairn to a 'few unburnt pieces of human bone, including a piece of skull' being found in the dark soil between the urns in the lowest layer (1948-1949:9), although O'Neil said that there was no evidence for a primary inhumation burial in the chamber. At Bant's Carn Bonsor also recorded the discovery of unburnt bone (1899-1900:140).

The initial discoverers of the chamber at Knackyboy Cairn told Lewis that one of the urns they examined, in which they found a blue bead, had 'a cover of something like parchment, bound round the neck like a jam-pot with some sort of cord, which perished at a touch.' (Lewis 1949). Unfortunately, partly due to the damage they caused, nothing like this survived for Lewis or O'Neil to find.

Only two of the cists, from which human remains have been recorded, were sufficiently intact when discovered for a picture of the number of individuals buried in them to be established. At Lower Newford (called 'Newfort' by Borlase) a single urn containing human bones was discovered (Borlase 1758) and at North Hill H, Smith found the remains of a single individual, apparently accompanied only by a flint flake (Smith 1863).

Many of the cremated remains, such as the fragments surviving from the cist at Old Town, have been incompletely cremated, by modern standards, and quite substantial pieces of bone still survive. One of the bone samples from Knackyboy Cairn which was submitted for radiocarbon dating was found to be charred, rather than cremated.

5.10 Greasy and black earth

At several sites where no human remains have been found, greasy or coloured earth has been recorded. The earliest example of this is at Borlase's excavation of two entrance graves on Buzza Hill in 1752. In one, he says, he found 'neither Bone nor Urn, but some strong unctuous earth which smelt cadaverous' and, in the other, different coloured earths in a pit in the centre of the chamber (Borlase 1769:220). He goes on to say that, in some barrows, there are no urns but round or square pits instead, which contain black greasy earth. He interprets this as being the result of moisture from the surrounding earth consuming the bones.

Woodley also writes of finding 'greasy black earth' during his excavation of sites on Porth Hellick Down. He describes it as 'resulting from the decomposition of animal substances' (Woodley 1822:211). In the barrow at Old Town, excavated in 1876, it was reported that 'No bones were found, but at the bottom of one urn there was a small quantity of greasy matter.' (Cornish 1878)

It seems likely that these deposits represent the remains of inhumed, or incompletely cremated, human remains which have decayed in the acidic soil of Scilly. The discovery of this substance at four entrance graves which yielded no pottery suggests that these may well have been completely decomposed inhumation burials. The presence of 'greasy matter' in a funerary urn strongly points to this being an incomplete cremation.

Robinson draws attention to the environmental data from Scilly which suggests that there may not have been sufficient trees on the islands to provide fuel for the large number of cremations present and that, as an alternative, gorse and seaweed, perhaps supplemented with marine mammal oil, may have been used. This, he suggests, might produce pyre material that was black and oily (2007:106).

Some authors have argued that the presence of black earth, containing pottery sherds, ashes, charcoal, animal bone, etc., points to a non-funerary use of the chambers (e.g. Ashbee 1976). Thomas (1985) states that it is the deliberate deposition of occupational material. Kirk also follows this line of argument, saying that entrance graves 'primarily contain midden debris' (2004:239). However, O'Neil, in his description of the black earth which surrounded the lowest layer of urns at Knackyboy Cairn, says that it was 'practically the same as that of the actual cremations' (1952:23). This tends to support the argument that these deposits derive from funerary deposits. The arguments relating to the use of the entrance graves will be considered further in chapter 7.

5.11 Obadiah's Barrow and Knackyboy Cairn assemblages

Obadiah's Barrow, excavated in 1901, and Knackyboy Cairn, at which the main excavation took place in 1948, are two entrance grave sites which were relatively undisturbed when they were excavated. They are also among the most recently examined graves and they have the most complete records. The assemblages from these two sites are therefore of particular interest.

Both these sites provided evidence for multiple burials: one inhumation and up to twenty cremations at Obadiah's Barrow and up to 100 cremations (and possibly some inhumations) at Knackyboy. As it has been suggested that the primary purpose of Scillonian entrance graves was not burial (Ashbee 1976; Thomas 1985), it is important to recognise the numbers of individuals known to have been interred at some sites.

There is evidence at both Knackyboy and Obadiah's Barrow for a variety of artefacts, in addition to the funerary urns, being placed in the chamber. Bronze objects and animal bone points occur at both sites, as well as faience and glass beads and flint tools at Knackyboy and a hammer-stone at Obadiah's Barrow. These discoveries should be borne in

mind when considering the much more limited range of finds from other, usually more disturbed, sites.

The presence of high status objects (made of bronze, faience and glass) at these sites is significant and the pumice pendant from Porth Hellick Down A should also be considered in this context. Sheridan and Shortland suggest that exotic materials, such as were used for beads and pendants in necklaces, might have been regarded not only as prestige items but also as being made of magical substances and therefore having special powers which could protect the deceased (2004:276).

In addition, both sites show successive phases of use: at Obadiah's Barrow an initial inhumation burial was succeeded by a number of cremation burials (Maier 1999). At Knackyboy a complex stratigraphy was uncovered which included a flint handaxe under the cairn, a number of funerary urns surrounded by charcoal, cremated bone and soil in the chamber and then further urns with cremations, both in the chamber and as satellite burials in the cairn (O'Neil 1952). There is also evidence for unburnt bone.

In contrast, Bant's Carn, a site which appears to have been undisturbed when it was excavated in 1900, yielded only four cremation burials which had been tipped on to the ground in the chamber and the urns smashed. There is the possibility of at least one inhumation burial here as well. Bant's Carn has one of the largest entrance grave chambers in the islands and, in comparison with Knackyboy and Obadiah's Barrow, a very small number of burials. The apparent desecration of the site may indicate inter- or intra-community conflict or may suggest that it had become, for some reason, an unpropitious place for burial.

5.12 Summary

This chapter has described the artefacts and other finds from the entrance graves and cists and has sought to demonstrate the wide range of objects discovered. It is clear that, despite the fact that many sites had been damaged prior to excavation, the majority of them have yielded some finds; objects have been recovered from other sites by workmen or visitors.

Significant quantities of pottery were found at sites such as Knackyboy and these provide valuable data about ceramic traditions in the islands, both in terms of the use of local clay and of the decoration on the vessels. The chapter has also shown that some of the best-preserved sites provide evidence for the burial of a significant number of individuals and for the presence of high status grave goods. Finds of bronze, faience, glass and possibly other prestige items indicate that some of the islands' residents had access to such imports. However, 'everyday' items, such as quern rubbers, hammer-stones and animal bone points, were also found in the graves.

If the suggestion that greasy or coloured earth represents the remains of inhumation or incomplete cremation burials is accepted, it would increase by five the number of sites at which human remains have been found. There are a further three sites which have yielded ashes or charcoal. If this too is regarded as an indication of cremation, a total of seventeen sites would then show evidence for burials.

Chapter 6

The setting of the Scillonian entrance graves and cists

6.1 Introduction

This chapter will examine the geographical setting of the entrance graves and cists in Scilly, paying attention to aspects such as their clustering, inter-visibility and orientation as well as their proximity to contemporary settlements and natural features. To assist in this analysis, use has been made of geographical information systems (GIS) software (ESRI ArcGIS version 9.3).

The base mapping used for this was the raster dataset for Scilly, supplied by EDINA. Data about both the bedrock and the superficial geology of the islands was added to this, as layers, as was the altitude information to allow contours to be displayed. In addition, the marine mapping of the islands was used to permit an examination of sea level rise. Information about the sites under consideration, including geographic location, type (entrance grave, cist or indeterminate) and status (extant, destroyed or unknown) was also exported into ArcGIS. Data about settlements was added in the same way and buffers of 50m, 100m, 150m and 200m were set up around each settlement site so that their proximity to burial sites could be assessed.

This has enabled a detailed examination of the islands and the site locations to be carried out and for new insights into the distribution of the sites to be obtained.

Before any detailed analysis can be undertaken, two issues must be considered: firstly, how far the present distribution of sites is representative of their original distribution and density and, secondly, the impact of rising sea levels on the landmass of the islands and the survival of sites. Following this, the distribution of the sites and other aspects of their setting will be examined. Possible explanations for this distribution, and for the density of sites in Scilly, will be considered in chapter 7.

6.2 Survival of sites

Establishing the original distribution of entrance graves and cists in Scilly, as elsewhere, is fraught with difficulty. On the one hand, it could be argued that, given that the present density is greater than anywhere else in the British Isles, it is likely that a significant proportion has survived. On the other hand, there is documentary evidence for the destruction of sites in the late 19th and 20th centuries (e.g. Layard 1933; Grimes 1960) and it is probable that earlier such destruction was not recorded.

Sprockhoff's (1938) analysis of the density of megalithic tombs on the Baltic island of Rügen indicated that, although more than 80% of the tombs were destroyed between 1829 and 1929, the distribution remained similar. This considerable level of destruction took place even though Rügen had no intensive agriculture or industrial development. Scilly has also had a small-scale agricultural economy and no industrial development. Unlike the Channel Islands and Lundy, it has not experienced commercial quarrying of granite and this is undoubtedly a factor in the preservation of megalithic sites there.

O'Brien (1999) has argued that the preservation of such monuments is affected by changing ritual beliefs, land-sea practices and population variability. In Scilly, as elsewhere, the chambered cairns were known as 'Giants' Graves' in the post-mediaeval period and this belief may have afforded them some protection. Borlase records that a violent storm occurred the evening after his excavation of two sites on Buzza Hill, St Mary's in June 1752 and the following day he was informed that the opinion in the islands was that 'the Giants were offended, and had really raised that storm.' (Borlase 1756:33)

Agricultural improvement, including clearance, field wall building and cultivation, is also a factor affecting the survival of sites. In Scilly, the change from subsistence agriculture to the growing of narcissus at the end of the 19th century led to the division of fields into narrow bulb strips. The stone for the building of at least some of these new walls is likely to have been obtained from megalithic burial chambers and their cairns. In addition, Layard recorded in the 1930s that two megalithic tombs were 'demolished about 30 years ago when breaking ground for pasture at Helvear' (1933:133).

Place names can also provide clues as to the whereabouts of destroyed sites. In Scilly, the place name 'Borough' is found on both St Mary's and Tresco. Layard records, when writing about sites on St Mary's, that 'one of the largest barrows on the island, now destroyed, gave its name to Borough Farm, near Watermill.' (Layard 1933:133) No entrance graves have been recorded in the vicinity of Borough Farm, Tresco but a cist was found there by workmen in 1985 (Ratcliffe 1991). It is possible that this was once covered by a barrow or cairn.

The map in figure 6.1 shows all the recorded sites, including entrance graves, cists and indeterminate sites

Status of sites

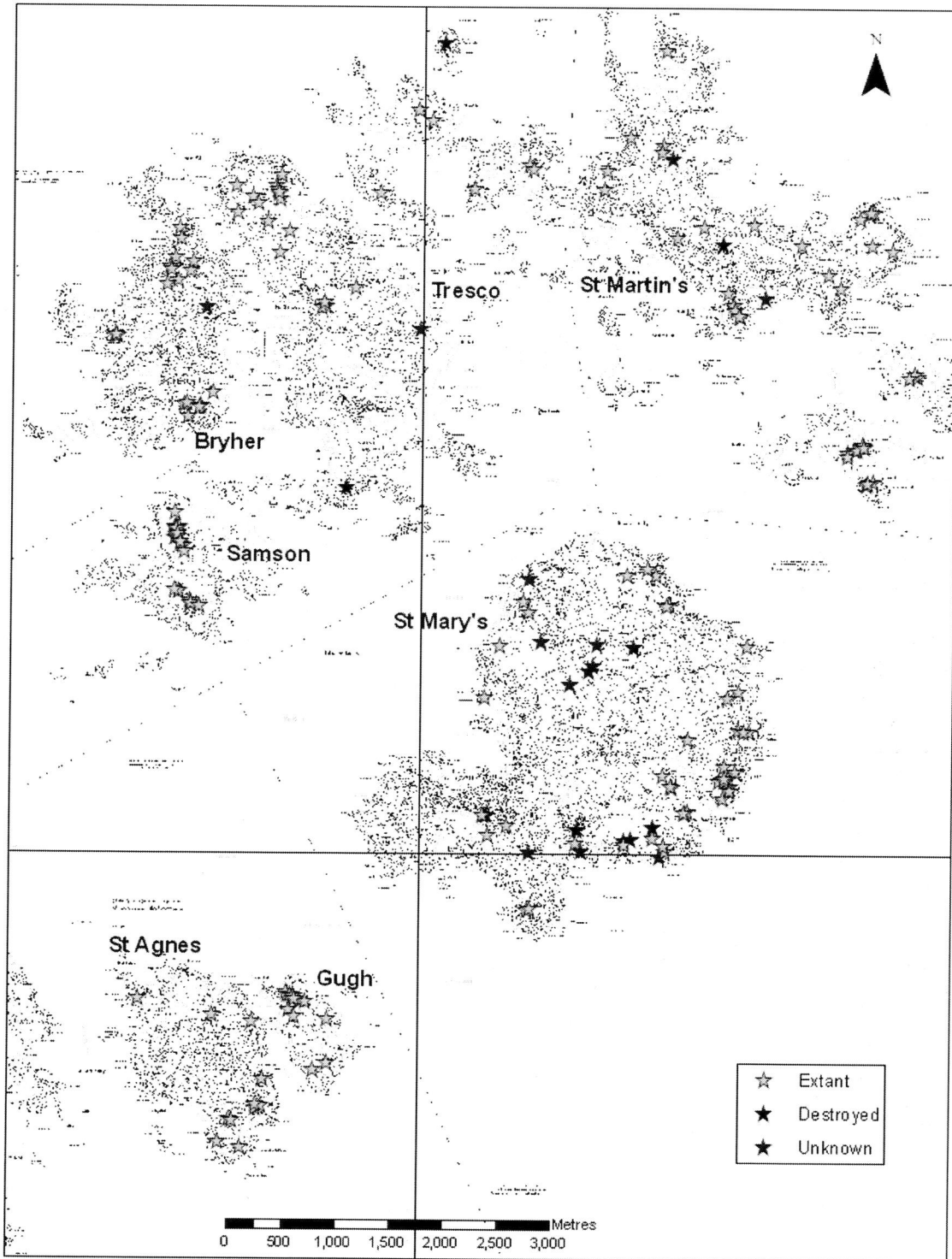

FIGURE 6.1 DISTRIBUTION MAP OF RECORDED ENTRANCE GRAVES, CISTS AND INDETERMINATE SITES IN SCILLY, SHOWING THEIR PRESENT STATUS

(i.e. those which are either an entrance grave or a cist), for which an accurate location is known and indicates their current status. Those whose status is shown as 'unknown' include sites for which there is documentary evidence only and which have not been traced; it is likely that many of these have been destroyed.

It will be noted that the surviving sites have a predominantly coastal distribution on the larger, still inhabited islands (St Mary's, St Martin's, Tresco, Bryher and St Agnes) and that, on St Mary's in particular, many of the sites which have been destroyed or whose status is unknown are in the centre of the island. On the larger of the now uninhabited islands, such as Samson and Gugh, the sites are found in clusters on the hilltops and it may be that similar concentrations of sites once existed elsewhere in the islands.

There are no extant or recorded sites on the south-western promontory of St Mary's. This area, now known as The Garrison, has been the centre of defence for the islands since the late 16th century and has a wealth of military structures. It is highly likely that prehistoric sites were destroyed in the course of the construction of the castle, gun batteries and other fortifications there.

There is, therefore, a strong correlation between the survival of sites and subsequent land use, in that agricultural areas now have few extant sites compared with coastal headlands and heathland. Even with this limited data it appears that Scilly differs from Rügen in that, in the former, there has been differential destruction of sites and their distribution has been affected accordingly. This must be borne in mind when considering the setting of the surviving sites

6.3 Sea level rise

The impact of sea level rise in Scilly has been debated since the mid 18th century when Borlase recorded 'Hedges of stone … running many feet under the level of the Sea' and concluded that some of the islands 'were once one continued tract of Land, divided into Fields, and cultivated even in those low parts which are now over-run with the Sea and Sand.' (Borlase 1756:63) Subsequent studies of sea level rise in Scilly have been carried out by Crawford (1927), Thomas (1985) and Ratcliffe and Straker (1996).

Most recently, the Lyonesse Project has sought to 'reconstruct the evolution of the physical environment of Scilly during the Holocene, the progressive occupation of this changing coastal landscape by early peoples and their response to marine inundation and changing marine resource availability' (Camidge et al. 2010:15). This work is based primarily on the examination and radiocarbon dating of submerged and inter-tidal peat deposits and the optically stimulated luminescence (OSL) dating of sand deposits in the inter-tidal zone.

Sea level curves have been produced by Thomas (1985) and by Ratcliffe and Straker (1996). There is also a more recent sea level curve for Scilly based on work on glacial isostatic adjustment (Bradley et al. 2009, quoted in Johns 2011). The curve produced by Bradley et al. shows a faster rate of sea level rise in the earlier post-glacial period with the rate slowing more recently, whereas those produced by Thomas and by Ratcliffe and Straker are both straight lines. The radiocarbon and OSL dates obtained during the Lyonesse Project correspond very closely with Bradley et al.'s curve and, together, these data provide the most reliable information about the rate of sea level rise. It is this curve which will be used in the following analysis.

Of particular importance to the study of the distribution of entrance graves and cists is the need to establish the sea level in the second millennium BC. The findings of the Lyonesse Project suggest that at 2000BC it was approximately 5.0m lower than the present day level. Further, it appears that there was a significant sea level rise between 2500BC, when it was about 6.0m lower than today, and 1500BC, when it was some 4.0m lower. Because of the topography of the islands, large areas of land, especially low-lying agricultural land, could have been inundated at high spring tides during this period as a result of this rise in sea levels.

This is summarised in the Project's final report as follows:

> 'The Early Bronze Age (2500-1500 BC) sees the most rapid loss of land and the development of the greatest extent of inter-tidal area at any time in the history of Scilly. The loss of land during the period was equivalent to losing almost the entire modern area of the islands. Changes of this magnitude would clearly have been perceptible over a single human lifespan and would have been part of the backdrop against which cultural development took place.' (Johns 2012:17)

This rise in sea level resulted in the division of the northern part of the archipelago into two main islands (now Bryher/Tresco and St Martin's) and their separation from St Mary's, with the loss of large areas of sheltered land between them and the consequent impact on, and loss of, settlements. There is, however, little change to the eastern and southern coasts of St Mary's, to the northern coasts of Bryher and Tresco or to much of the coastline of St Agnes and Gugh.

The marine map of Scilly in figure 6.2 shows Chart Datum, which equates to the lowest astronomical tide (LAT) and is 2.91m below Ordnance Datum, and the 5m and 10m marine contours. The dark blue and green areas therefore broadly represent the land lost since c2000BC and the dark blue area approximates to the area lost between c2000BC and c1000BC. The map also shows the positions of all entrance graves, cists and indeterminate sites, whether extant, destroyed or of unknown status.

The presence of coastal cordons, which might have formed outside or between the islands, would have had an effect on the inundation of the central area. If these cordons were of a sufficient height they would have prevented

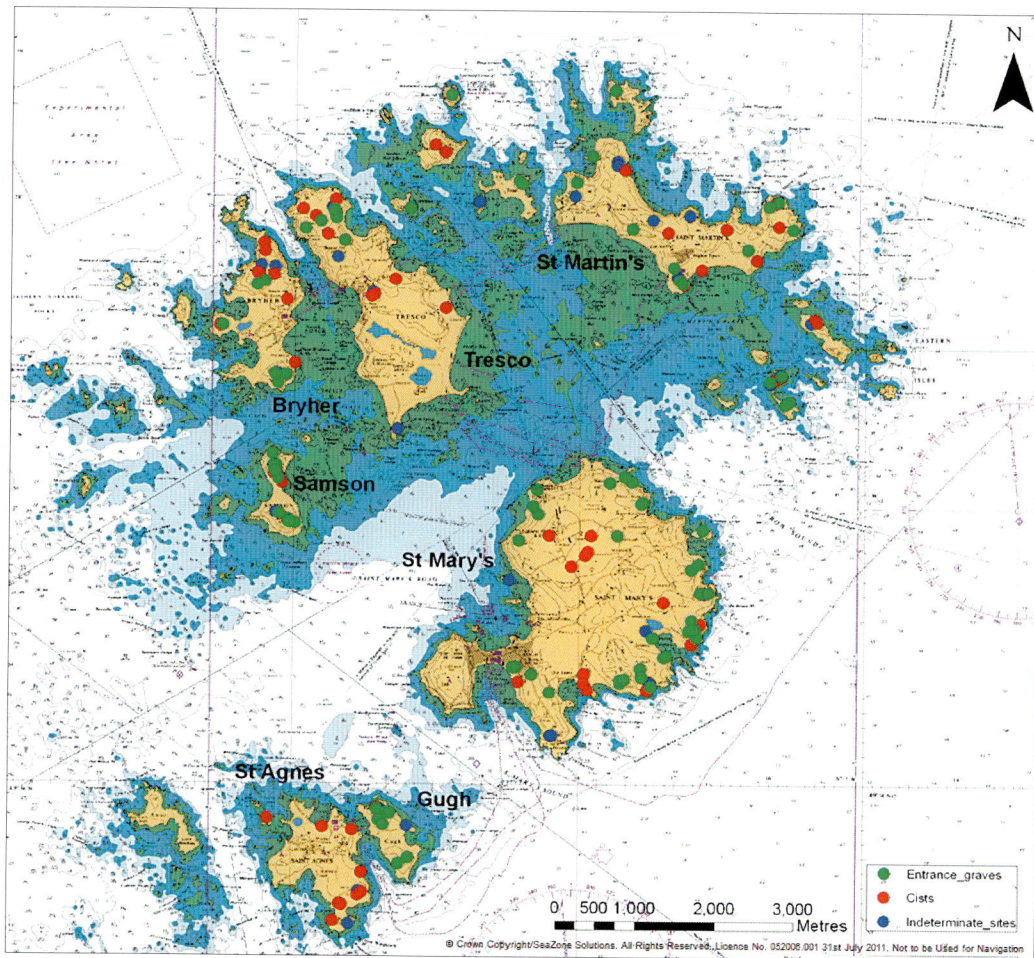

FIGURE 6.2 MARINE MAP OF SCILLY SHOWING CHART DATUM (DARK GREEN), 5M (DARK BLUE) AND 10M (PALE BLUE) MARINE CONTOURS AND LOCATIONS OF SITES

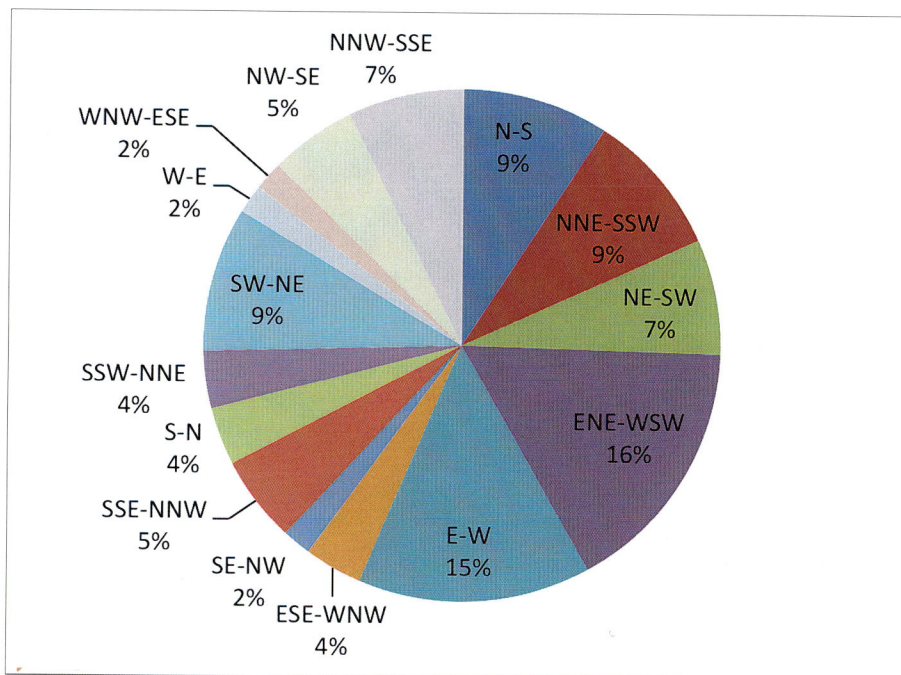

FIGURE 6.11 ORIENTATIONS OF ENTRANCE GRAVES (BASED ON 55 SITES)

the flooding of land by the sea even though this land lay below the level of high tide. Cordons between St Mary's, Tresco and St Martin's might have protected all or part of the central area of land and its inundation may not have occurred until later. However, the work of the Lyonesse Project has demonstrated the presence of pollen indicating saltmarsh in peat deposits, dating to the Early Bronze Age, from the area between the islands. It appears, therefore, that part at least of this area was regularly inundated at that time (Charman et al. 2012b).

If coastal cordons were breached by a storm surge, large areas of land may suddenly have been flooded by the sea. Heath (1750) described the surge which occurred in 1744 when the isthmus, on which Hugh Town, St Mary's is situated, was breached by the sea. Thomas (1985) discusses the storm surges of 1962 and 1974 and also refers to the existence of causeways in Scilly. These are now submerged but may have been used as routes between the islands in the past; it is likely that they were coastal cordons, some of which may have been built up artificially in order to prolong their use.

No trace has been found of any entrance graves in the inter-tidal zone and only two cist graves have been identified there. However, a number of submerged settlement sites and boulder walls have been found, particularly in the areas between Tresco, Bryher and Samson and between Tresco and St Martin's where, it will be noted, the sea is still very shallow. This suggests that the entrance graves, in particular, were positioned at some distance above sea level when they were constructed. A similar phenomenon is seen in Brittany, described by Giot as 'La loi des sommets relatifs', which means that sites were situated in the most elevated location within their local setting (Giot 1987:191; quoted in Scarre 2002b).

Another aspect of sea level rise to be considered is its impact on the superficial geology of the islands. Whilst the bedrock is mapped as almost entirely granite (Scourse 2006b), this is covered in places by later deposits, as illustrated in figure 6.3. It will be noted that large areas of St Martin's and Tresco, in particular, are covered with blown sand. The date of the deposition of this is not known; samples have been taken for OSL dating but the results are not yet available. However, work close to Knackyboy Cairn, St Martin's revealed that up to 2.2m of blown sand overlay the old land surface (Mulville 2007) and, nearby, excavations for the construction of a holiday chalet uncovered only blown sand to a depth of 1.5m (Sawyer 2011b).

The rise in sea levels, discussed above, would have led to the formation of sand dunes in the areas between the islands before they were inundated. As the prevailing wind is from the south-west, sand is likely to have been blown and deposited on to land to the north-east of the areas being inundated, leading to the large areas of blown sand now covering the south of Tresco and much of St Martin's. These almost certainly post-date the construction of the entrance graves and cists.

There are a few recorded sites which are located at the edges of the areas of blown sand but only one which is within it, Trelawney, in the centre of St Martin's, a cist grave which is reported to have been destroyed during agricultural work in 1969. It is likely that there are other, as yet undiscovered, sites covered by these blown sand deposits.

6.4 Distribution of sites

Entrance graves

It will be seen from the map in figure 6.4 that the present distribution of entrance graves includes several concentrations of sites, the largest of which are on Samson, Gugh and the south-eastern side of St Mary's. Ashbee calculated that more than half of the extant entrance graves are concentrated in these areas (Ashbee 1974:74). This study suggests that 40 of the 90 definite, probable and possible entrance graves are located there.

Samson, which today is less than 0.4km² in area, has 15 entrance graves (as well as five cists and three indeterminate sites). The entrance graves are concentrated on the two hilltops of North Hill and South Hill where they have a mainly linear distribution. Today the highest point on North Hill is 35m above sea level and that on South Hill is 42m. On North Hill, the ten graves follow the north-south ridge of the hill, with some sites on the upper part of the slopes to both the west and the east of the ridge and single outliers at the northern and southern ends of the hill. With the exception of the outliers, the sites cluster on the highest part of the hill. On South Hill, there is a line of three graves on the rocky ridge in the south-east with two outliers, one on the eastern slope of the hill at a lower elevation and the other to the north-west on a more rounded hilltop.

The sites on Gugh, which is connected by a sandbar to the still inhabited island of St Agnes, have suffered more damage than those on Samson and the original form of several of them is less certain. On Kittern Hill, which forms the northern part of Gugh, there are five entrance graves, one cist and four indeterminate sites, the majority of which have a linear arrangement along the ridge of the hill; in the southern part of Gugh there are two entrance graves. Again the majority of the sites are located on the hilltops but two sites, one on Kittern Hill, the other in the south of Gugh, are located on the upper part of the western hillslopes.

On both North Hill and Kittern Hill boulder walls connect several of the sites; this also occurs on Great Arthur in the Eastern Isles and on Shipman Head Down, Bryher where the walls cross the cairns. The possible function of these walls will be considered in chapter 7.

The distribution on the south-eastern coast of St Mary's differs from those on Samson and Gugh. Several groups of up to seven entrance graves, with some cists and

Sites and superficial geology

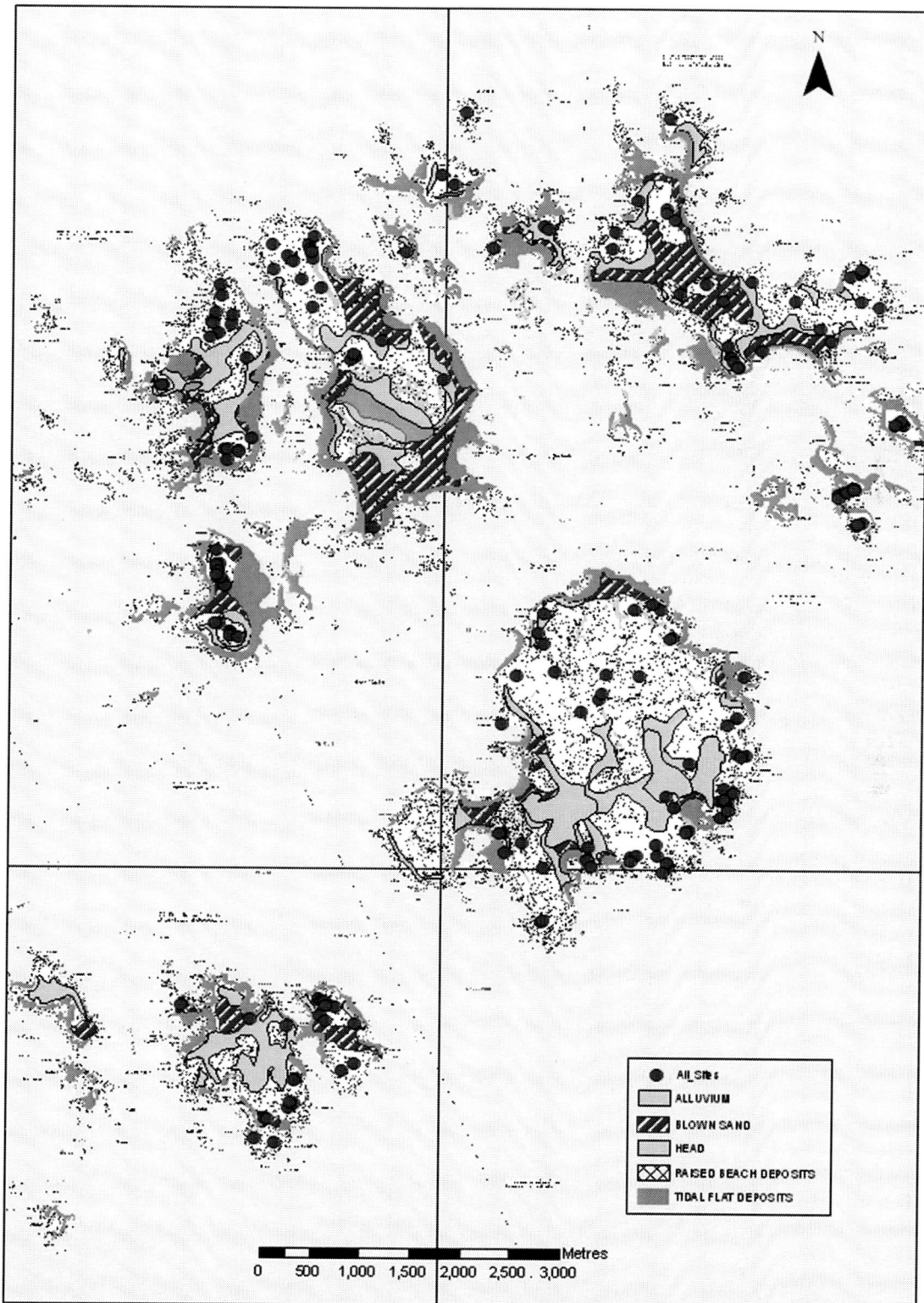

FIGURE 6.3 MAP OF ALL SITES (ENTRANCE GRAVES, CISTS AND INDETERMINATE SITES) SHOWING RELATIONSHIP WITH SUPERFICIAL GEOLOGY

Distribution of entrance graves

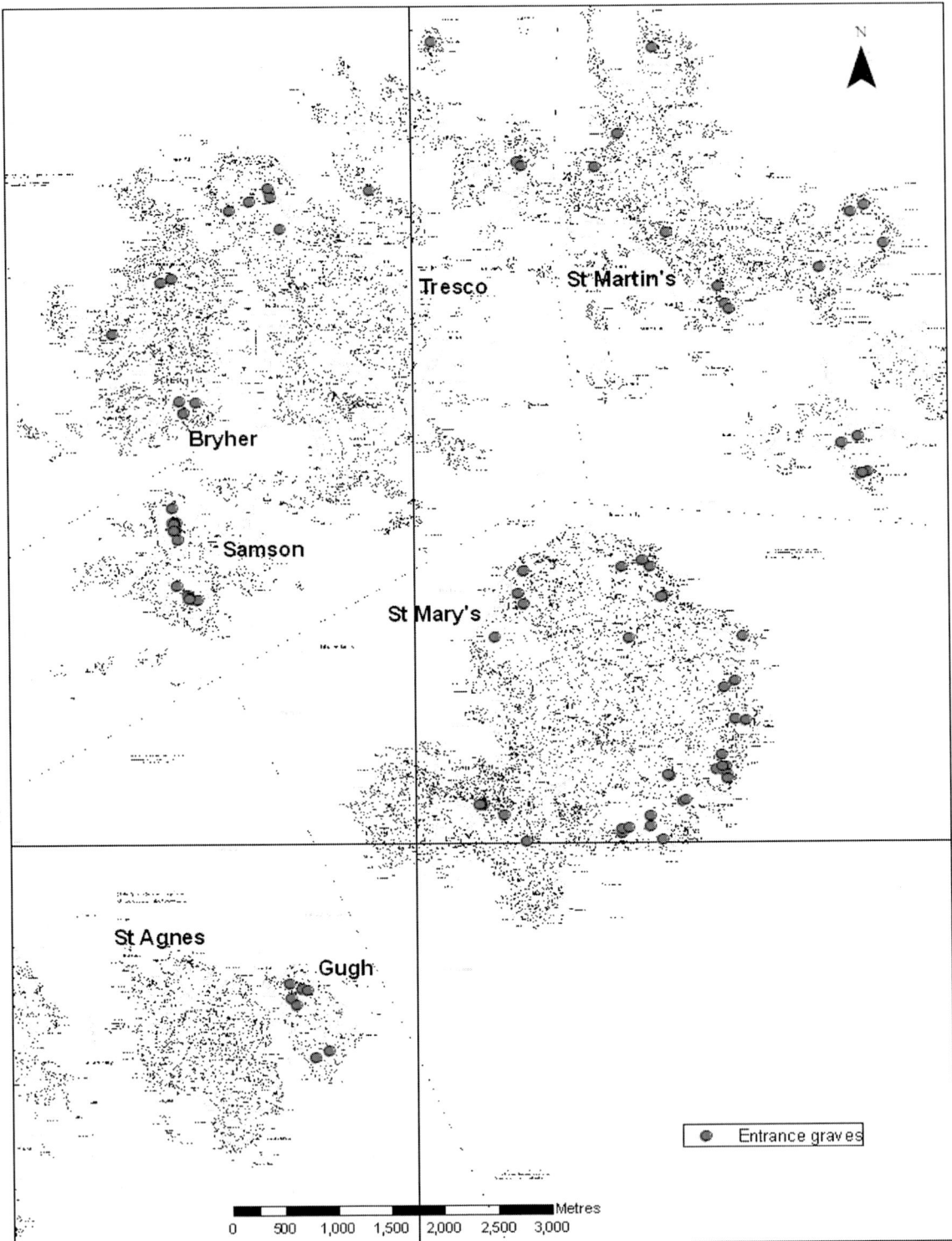

Tresco

St Martin's

Bryher

Samson

St Mary's

St Agnes

Gugh

● Entrance graves

Metres

0   500 1,000 1,500   2,000   2,500   3,000

©Crown copyright/database right 2012. An Ordnance Survey/EDINA supplied service.

FIGURE 6.4 DISTRIBUTION OF RECORDED ENTRANCE GRAVES (INCLUDING PROBABLE AND POSSIBLE SITES)

indeterminate sites, are found along this coastline. In most cases they are in discrete clusters of sites, on the highest part of the plateaux between the small bays, but still less than 100m from the coast. The layout of the sites is influenced by the topography; there are few hill ridges in this area to facilitate a linear arrangement of sites.

Elsewhere in Scilly, the present distribution of entrance graves is typically of two or three sites positioned close together, usually less than 100m apart and often considerably closer than this. In some places, for example, Cruther's Hill, St Martin's, Buzza Hill, St Mary's and Tregarthen Hill, Tresco, they are sited along the ridge of a hill, as they are on North Hill, Samson. Entrance graves also frequently occur in pairs, one above the other on a hillslope; examples of this arrangement are found at Innisidgen and Halangy on St Mary's and on Great Hill, Teän. Single sites are uncommon and may indicate a sole survivor from an earlier pair or group of graves.

Robinson has argued that the positioning of entrance graves in Scilly 'mark[s] out movement on the sea and in particular approach and entry into the archipelago.' (2007:114) He suggests that many of the entrance graves were positioned to mark the main access routes into the islands when approaching from the north-east, the safest route. However, in reaching this conclusion, he considered only the extant sites, which are unlikely to be representative of the original distribution, as has been set out above.

Although his interpretation may explain the positioning of some coastal sites, it does not account for the locations of all of them, for example, those on the northern and western sides of Bryher, where the waters are very treacherous. It is also not certain at what distance from the islands the entrance graves would have become visible, not only because of their size but also because of the positioning of many of them on hilltops. The author's experience of travelling by boat around the eastern and southern coasts of St Mary's, at a distance of approximately 200m from land, is that most of the entrance graves are not visible.

Cists

The map in figure 6.5 shows the distribution of all recorded cist and indeterminate sites. A comparison with figure 6.4 shows that, in many cases, cists and indeterminate sites are concentrated in the same areas as entrance graves. The clusters of sites on Samson, Gugh and St Mary's include both entrance graves and cists, as well as those whose form cannot be determined. However, cists are also found in areas where there are few or no entrance graves, such as St Agnes, the north of Bryher, parts of St Martin's and Tresco and the centre of St Mary's.

The distributions on St Agnes, Bryher, St Martin's and Tresco are mainly on exposed heathland, where there are other, apparently unchambered, cairns. In many cases, these cists have been defined as possible sites, identified as such because there are hollows, approximating to the

size and shape of a cist, dug into the cairns, sometimes with stone slabs associated with them. They are typically covered by very small cairns.

On St Mary's, on the other hand, several of the cists are on land which has been used for agriculture over recent centuries. Many of these structures were intact when recorded and four sites (with a possible fifth, whose location is not known) are located within 500m of each other on the high ground in the north-west of St Mary's. None of these sites is recorded as having a covering mound but, because of their locations on or near agricultural land, it is likely that, if they had existed, any mounds would have been removed long ago.

The majority of cists, like entrance graves, are on hilltops. However, as mentioned above, there are two cist sites now in the inter-tidal zone. One of these, at Par Beach on St Martin's, is associated with contemporary settlement. Three other cist graves, on St Agnes, Tresco and St Martin's, which are also located close to or within settlements, are at an altitude of less than 5m above sea level. The relationship between burial sites and settlements will be considered further below.

Relationship between entrance graves and cists

As mentioned above, the main clusters of burial sites contain both entrance graves and cists, as well as sites whose precise form cannot now be established. Their close proximity suggests that they are contemporary. Figure 6.6, which combines the data set out in figures 6.4 and 6.5, shows the distribution of all these sites.

In all the major clusters of sites, on Samson, Gugh and St Mary's, the majority of the structures are entrance graves. However, on North Hill, Samson, it is a cist which occupies the highest point of the hill at 35m above sea level. This site, North Hill H, was excavated in 1862 and was found to contain the cremated remains of a single individual, described by the excavator as probably a man aged about 50 (Smith 1863). The cist is very carefully constructed with the side slabs having grooves into which the end slabs are fitted. It also has mortared joints and a paved floor. The cist is oriented N-S, the same as the ridge of the hill. The covering mound, now measuring about 21.5m by 17.5m diameter and 2.2m high, is by far the largest on North Hill.

It is tempting, therefore, to see this single burial as being of a high status individual, in contrast to what were probably multiple burials in the neighbouring entrance graves, although no human remains survive from any of the other sites on North Hill. However, the individual buried in North Hill H was accompanied only by a flint flake.

On Kittern Hill, Gugh, the highest points, at 34m and 32m above sea level, are both occupied by burial structures. That at 34m (Kittern Hill L) is a badly damaged entrance grave but the structure at 32m (Kittern Hill B) is a probable cist, damaged partly by the positioning of a trig point within it.

Distribution of cists and indeterminate sites

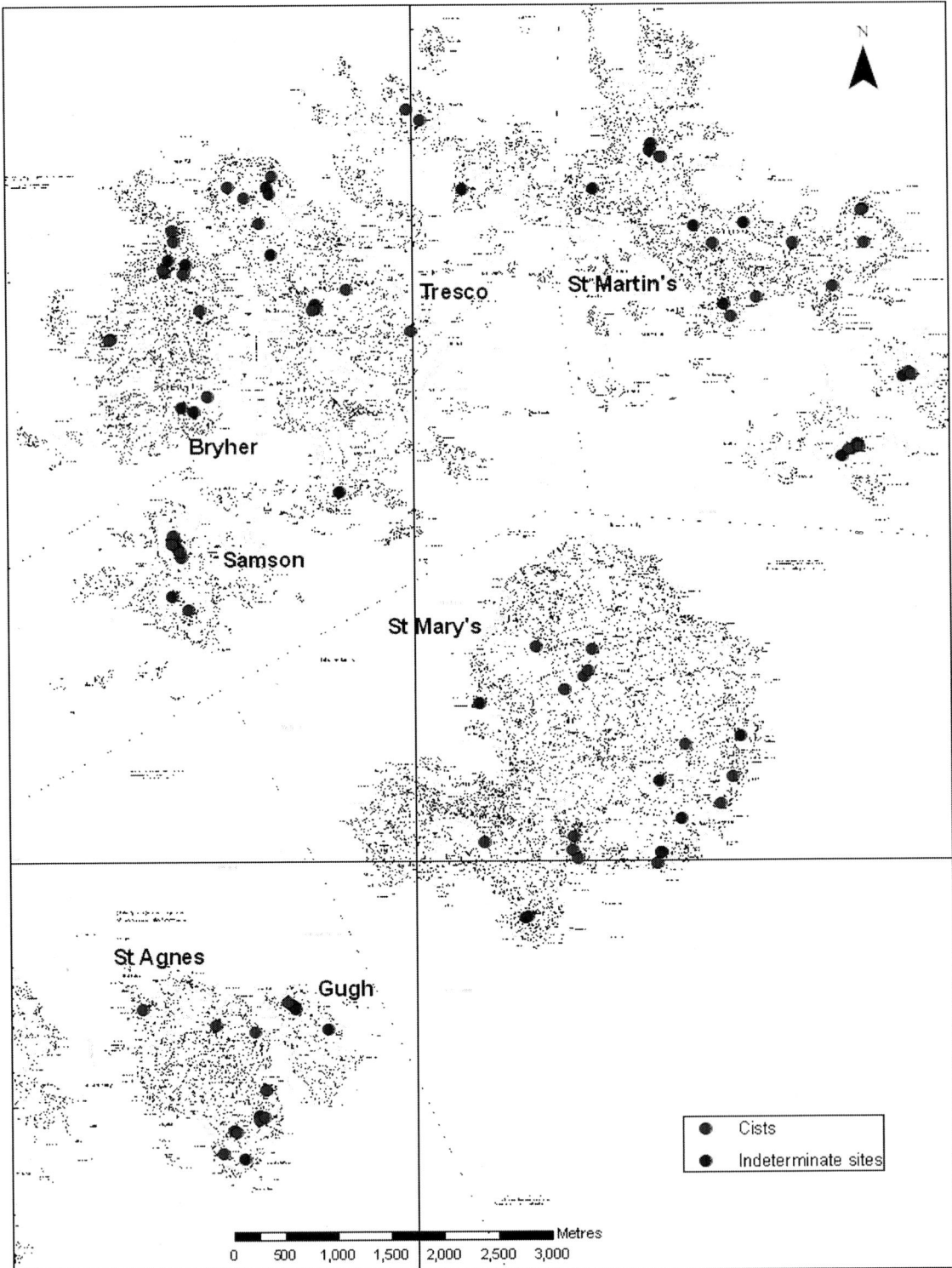

FIGURE 6.5 DISTRIBUTION OF RECORDED CISTS AND INDETERMINATE SITES (INCLUDING PROBABLE AND POSSIBLE SITES)

Distribution of all sites

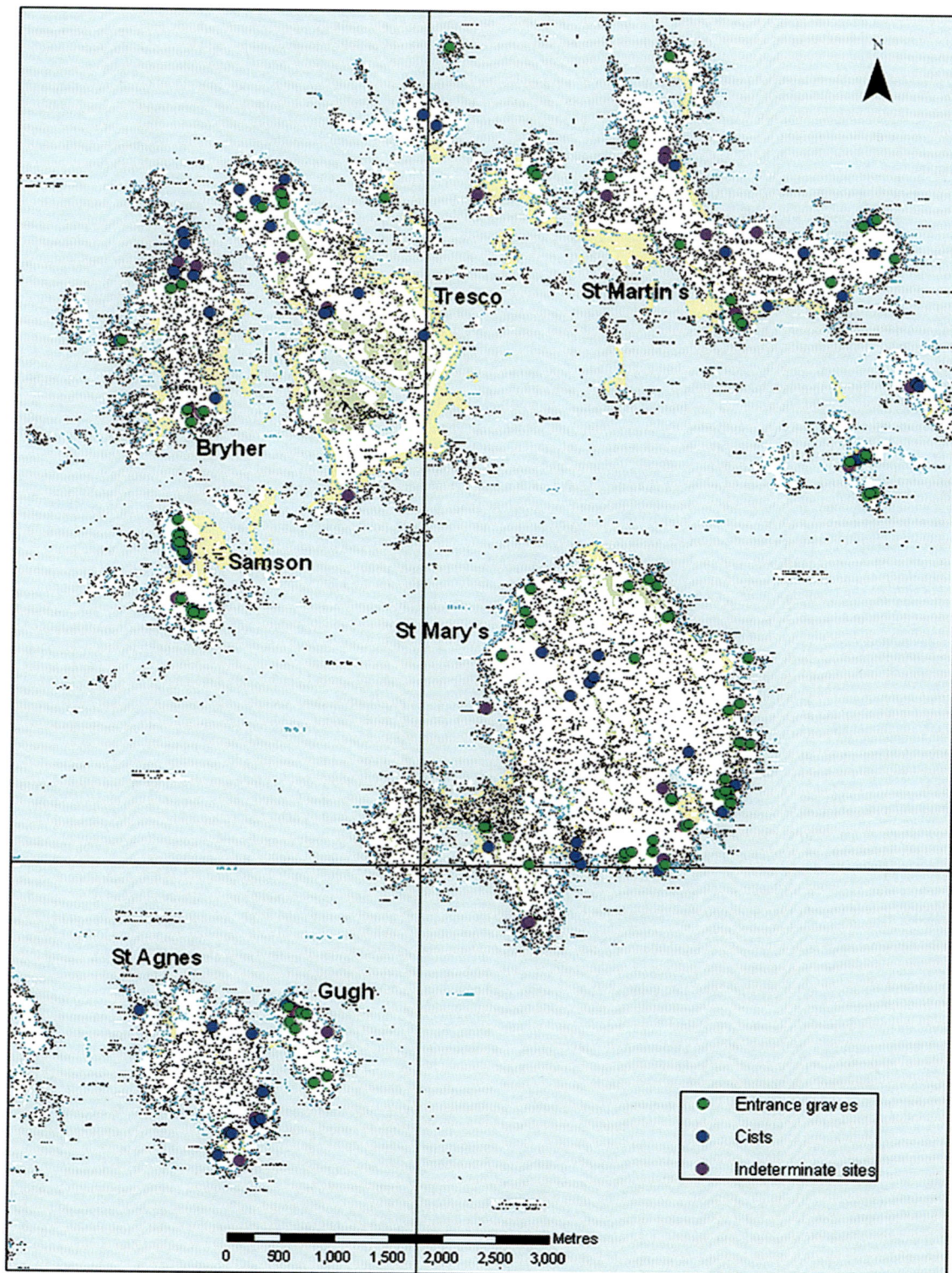

FIGURE 6.6 DISTRIBUTION OF RECORDED ENTRANCE GRAVES, CISTS AND INDETERMINATE SITES (INCLUDING PROBABLE AND POSSIBLE SITES)

Both have substantial mounds around them. Unfortunately, there is no record of the excavation of either of these sites and no finds from them.

Distribution: a summary

As the preceding overview has indicated, the distribution patterns of the entrance graves and the cists are complex. In many cases, both types of structure are found in the same areas, particularly in the main clusters of sites on Samson, Gugh and St Mary's. However, there are also places where one type does not occur: there are no entrance graves on St Agnes, for example. It is also clear that, whilst locations on hilltops or upper hillslopes were the norm, some sites were positioned much closer to sea level.

On North Hill, Samson and Kittern Hill, Gugh, the distribution of sites appears planned, with a burial structure occupying the highest point of the hill and others ranged along the ridge on either side. Elsewhere, as on Porth Hellick Down, St Mary's, there appears to be a less structured arrangement (although the sites here appear to follow the ridge of the hill when viewed from the hilltop to the south-west). This may be simply because of the differing topography but it is possible that other factors, such as status or family relationships, were involved in the location of entrance graves and cists.

6.5 Inter-visibility of sites

One of the results – and probably one of the purposes – of positioning burial structures on hilltops and ridges is to enhance their visibility from the surrounding area. Examination of the inter-visibility of cairns, and the views from them to other significant landscape features, has formed an important part of their recent study (e.g. Cummings 2004; Jones 2005). As would be expected because of the small scale of the islands, there is considerable inter-visibility between entrance graves, as well as those cists with substantial mounds, in Scilly.

Robinson (2007) has examined this aspect of the entrance graves and his diagram of inter-visibility is shown in figure 6.7. The sites shown include both those on hilltops and those on hillslopes. Whilst the former are clearly visible, even in their present often eroded condition, the latter are much more difficult to see.

From Bant's Carn (on the north-west coast of St Mary's), several of the sites on North Hill, Samson are clearly visible as mounds along the ridge of the hill. However, Bant's Carn, which is located on the upper part of the hillslope and whose cairn still survives to a height of more than 2m, is not particularly obvious from Samson as it blends into the surrounding slope. It can, however, be clearly viewed from below.

Robinson argues that the entrance grave on Buzza Hill, St Mary's has been located so that it has 'views across St Mary's Road [sic] towards Gugh, but only limited views

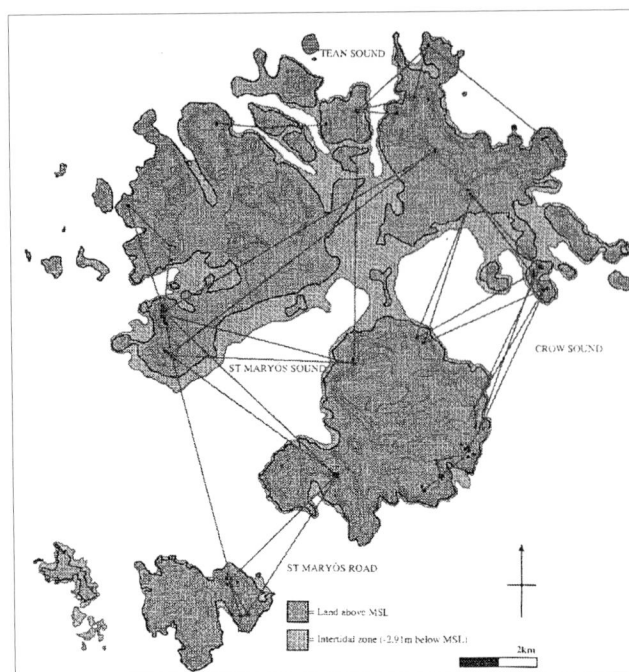

FIGURE 6.7 INTER-VISIBILITY BETWEEN SCILLONIAN ENTRANCE GRAVES (LINES BETWEEN MONUMENTS DENOTE INTER-VISIBILITY), FROM ROBINSON (2007:FIG 7.12)

in other directions' (2007:111). (The plan transposes the names of St Mary's Road, which is between St Mary's and Samson, and St Mary's Sound, between St Mary's and Gugh.) However, as is shown in figure 6.8, there are clear views from this site not only to the south-west across St Mary's Sound to Gugh, but also to the north-west to Samson, Bryher and Tresco.

Sites on hillslopes would have been visible from settlements and agricultural land below them whereas those on hilltops could be viewed from many places around the archipelago, but not from the lower parts of the hills on which they were situated. In all studies of inter-visibility it is necessary to take account of the vegetational cover likely to have existed when the burial structures were built (Cummings & Whittle 2003).

A palynological study of the islands' prehistoric environment, based on samples from the peats at Higher Moors and Lower Moors, St Mary's, demonstrated the presence of mixed deciduous woodland, scrub and sedges in Scilly during the second half of the sixth millennium BC. This was followed by a reduction in the arboreal and an increase in the herbaceous content, with the appearance of cereal pollen, weeds and plants indicative of disturbed habitats by the mid second millennium BC (Scaife 1984). Subsequent work has confirmed this transition from woodland to a predominantly grassland environment and Ratcliffe and Straker (1996) suggest that this may indicate a pastoral economy.

During the Lyonesse Project, peat samples dated to c3000BC to 1500BC were taken from the inter-tidal zones of Par Beach, St Martin's and Porth Mellon, St Mary's.

FIGURE 6.8 VIEWS FROM BUZZA HILL A, LOOKING
(ABOVE) SOUTH-WEST TO THE GARRISON AND GUGH
AND (BELOW) NORTH-WEST TO SAMSON, BRYHER AND TRESCO

These again show a decline in woodland with pollen representative of open disturbed grassland and some indications of maritime species (Charman et al. 2012b). Overall, therefore, these studies indicate a reducing amount of deciduous woodland during the prehistoric period and suggest that, in the first half of the second millennia BC, there were some areas of woodland but that much of the islands was grassland or other open ground. It is unlikely that the hilltops and upper hillslopes had tree cover because of their exposure to the wind.

Issues of inter-visibility are complex and subtle, as is illustrated in figures 6.9 and 6.10. These show the sites visible from two substantial entrance graves on St Mary's, Bant's Carn and Porth Hellick A. Bant's Carn is positioned on a north-west facing hillslope at a height of about 25m above sea level and commands wide-ranging views across the northern part of the archipelago. As will be seen from the first map, there are views from it to at least nine other sites or groups of sites. (A single line is shown to a group of sites and the inter-visibilities between the other sites are not shown, for clarity.) Several of these other sites are at some distance, the furthest being about 5.5km away. As mentioned above, sites on hilltops are more obvious from Bant's Carn than it is from them, however, it is still visible from all of them.

Porth Hellick A, on the other hand, is on the south-eastern side of St Mary's, on a rounded hilltop and again at a height of about 25m above sea level; it is approximately 200m from the coast. Because of its different location, being on the outer edge of the archipelago, there are views to only five sites or groups of sites from it, one of them being some of the other structures on Porth Hellick Down, and the distances involved are much shorter, the furthest visible site being about 1.0km away.

The locations of and inter-visibility between the sites in the northern part of Scilly, surrounding the area which was steadily being inundated by the sea, may well be significant. It is possible that these visual links between the sites may have been regarded as a way of protecting the land. In contrast, the coastline around Porth Hellick Down was not affected by the rising sea levels.

6.6 Orientation

Much has been written about the orientation of megalithic burial chambers. In some types of structure there is a consistent orientation, for example, wedge tombs are nearly always oriented to the west or south-west (O'Brien 1999). In Scilly, however, both the entrance graves and the cists have a wide range of orientations and the situation is complicated by the fact that many of the sites are badly damaged and so identifying the original orientation is not easy.

Additionally, where documentary evidence is relied upon to establish the orientation, there is no consistent system used to indicate the orientation of the chamber entrance. In some documents an orientation described as SE-NW means that the entrance was at the SE end, in others that it was at the NW end.

Table 6.1 sets out the orientations of all sites in Scilly at which it is possible to establish a clear orientation, either from examination in the field or from documentary sources. For entrance graves, the orientation of the entrance is shown first and those sites at which it is not possible to identify the entrance end have been excluded. For cists and indeterminate sites, the direction closest to north is shown first. Of the total of 192 entrance graves, cists and indeterminate sites in Scilly it has been possible confidently to identify the orientation at 87 sites.

These results differ significantly from the picture presented by Ashbee, whose analysis indicated that the most frequent orientation of entrance grave chambers in Scilly was to the east. He suggested that 13 of the 39 (33%) entrance graves he recorded were oriented in this way (Ashbee 1974:fig 7 and Appendix 1).

Where it has been possible to reconcile Ashbee's findings with those from this study, it has been found that, whilst there is agreement at four sites, four others described by Ashbee as having an E-W orientation have been measured as ENE-WSW, one as NNE-SSW and one as SSW-

Visibility of sites from Bant's Carn

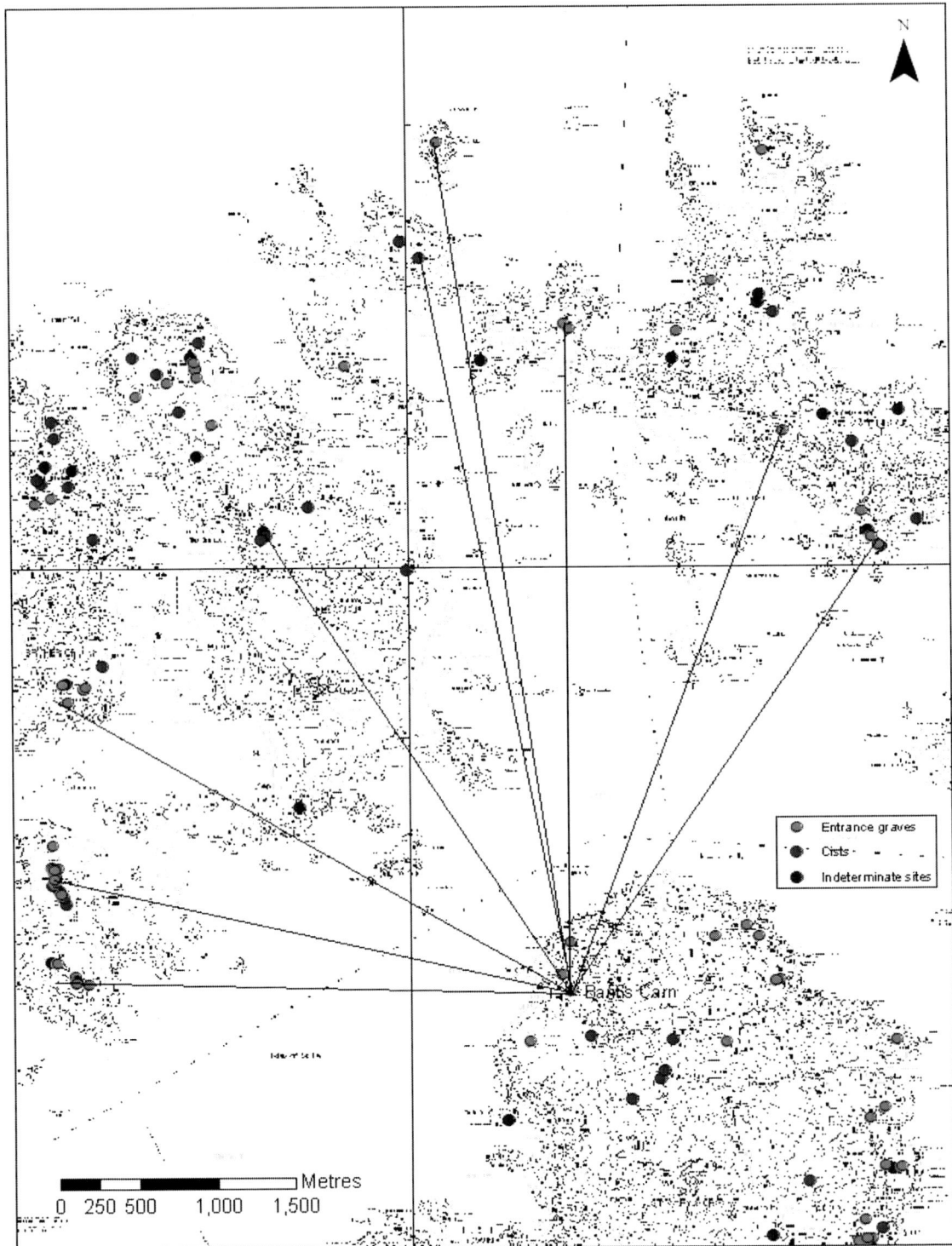

©Crown copyright/database right 2012. An Ordnance Survey/EDINA supplied service.

FIGURE 6.9 VISIBILITY OF OTHER SITES FROM BANT'S CARN (LINES BETWEEN MONUMENTS DENOTE INTER-VISIBILITY)

Visibility of sites from Porth Hellick Down A

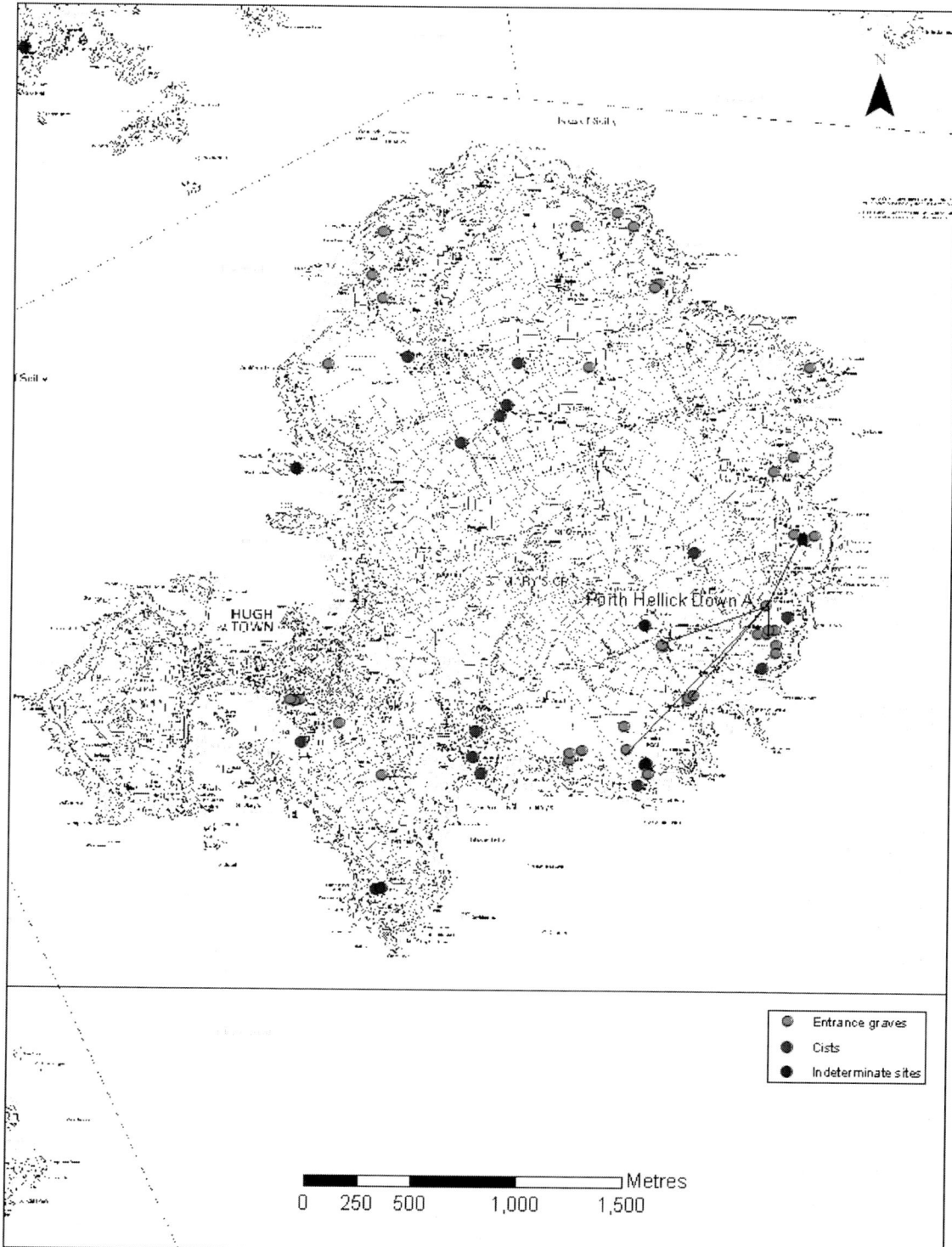

FIGURE 6.10 VISIBILITY OF OTHER SITES FROM PORTH HELLICK DOWN A (LINES BETWEEN MONUMENTS DENOTE INTER-VISIBILITY)

Orientation	Number of sites	Number of entrance graves	Number of cists	Number of indeter- minate sites
N-S	10	5	5	0
NNE-SSW	8	5	2	1
NE-SW	12	4	4	4
ENE-WSW	9	9	0	0
E-W	15	8	3	4
ESE-WNW	2	2	0	0
SE-NW	1	1	-	-
SSE-NNW	3	3	-	-
S-N	2	2	-	-
SSW-NNE	2	2	-	-
SW-NE	5	5	-	-
WSW-ENE	0	0	-	-
W-E	1	1	-	-
WNW-ESE	1	1	-	-
NW-SE	12	3	6	3
NNW-SSE	4	4	0	0
Totals	87	55	20	12

TABLE 6.1 ORIENTATIONS OF ENTRANCE GRAVES, CISTS AND INDETERMINATE SITES

NNE. Whilst the recording of this last (Lower Innisidgen B) as E-W appears to be an error by Ashbee, the slight discrepancy at many of the other sites illustrates the difficulty of taking accurate readings from damaged sites.

If the orientations of the Scillonian entrance graves were connected with the movements of the sun, an interest in the rising sun between the midsummer solstice and the autumn equinox and the setting sun throughout the year is indicated (although neither of these account for the N-S orientations). However, another, probably more influential, factor in the orientations is the relationship of the chamber entrance to the surrounding topography.

At a number of sites which are positioned on a hillslope, such as Lower Innisidgen B, Obadiah's Barrow and Works Carn, the entrance is oriented towards the hill, rather than facing out. This means that at Lower Innisidgen B it faces to the SSW, at Obadiah's Barrow it faces to the ESE and at Works Carn it faces to the NNE. However, this arrangement of the chamber does not occur at other sites which are in a similar location. So, at Bant's Carn the chamber entrance faces to the ENE along the hillslope contour and at North Hill E it faces directly out from the hillslope towards the E. It is clear that there is no readily discernible pattern in the placing of the chamber entrance.

Similarly, entrance graves which are built along narrow rocky ridges, such as those on South Hill, Samson, are usually positioned with their long axes along the ridge and their entrances facing in the same direction, in this case to either the S or SSE. On wider ridges, like Cruther's Hill, St Martin's, the chambers may be aligned at right angles to the ridge but again they are usually all oriented in approximately the same direction, between NE and E on this occasion.

FIGURE 6.12 KNACKYBOY CAIRN, SHOWING LARGE NATURAL OUTCROP INCORPORATED IN MOUND

In groups of tombs on plateaux, there may be a variety of alignments. Of the six measurable entrance graves on Porth Hellick Down, St Mary's, two are oriented N-S, one ENE-WSW, one SW-NE and two NNW-SSE. Porth Hellick Down D, which is oriented ENE-WSW is less than 50m from Porth Hellick Down E, which is oriented N-S. A similar spread of alignments is seen on North Hill, Samson, which has a wider ridge, where again the proximity of the sites to each other does not seem to have led to consistent orientations.

In a significant number of cases, natural rock is incorporated into the mounds surrounding entrance graves or used to form one wall of the chamber. The remains of the Knackyboy Cairn entrance grave are shown in figure 6.12. At this site the built chamber has been completely removed but the large natural outcrop which formed part of the cairn, as well as the end wall and part of one side wall of the chamber, is still apparent. It would seem that the use of outcrops in this way may have been another factor influencing the orientation of the chamber, just as the availability of building stone may have affected the location of the entrance graves.

Although Ashbee recorded the orientations of the entrance graves, he did not offer any analysis or interpretation of them. Robinson, however, has argued that 'the chambers of entrance graves were consistently visually oriented away from the sea' (2007:112). He goes on to suggest that this may be connected with taboos relating to the power and destructiveness of the sea but that the importance of the sea to the islanders was referenced by incorporating it as a backdrop to the monuments.

However, he shows, for example, the graves on the ridge of South Hill, Samson (*PRN 7081.01 and 7081.02*) as being oriented to the north (Robinson 2007:fig 7.14) whereas the orientation measured in the course of this research was 149.5° (i.e. SSE) meaning that the entrances face towards the sea. Ashbee also records the sites as being oriented to the SSE (1974:309). In practice, it is impossible to locate structures on most hills in Scilly without them having a view of the sea. Whilst many chamber entrances do not

FIGURE 6.13 WORKS CARN ENTRANCE GRAVE, SHOWING LOCATION ON HILLSLOPE CARN (VISIBLE BEHIND CHAMBER)

FIGURE 6.14 NATURAL GRANITE OUTCROP OF INNISIDGEN CARN, SHOWING (CENTRE) POSSIBLE REMOVAL OF ROCK

face towards the nearest coastline, they are not consistently oriented away from the sea. It is also important to remember the impact of sea level rise on the relationship between the entrance graves and the sea.

In summary, therefore, there is no straightforward explanation available for these orientations. It seems likely that a variety of factors, including local topography, the availability of natural rock, the orientations of neighbouring structures and other influences not now accessible to us, affected both the choice of site and the orientation of the chamber.

6.7 Relationship with natural features

A distinctive aspect of the Scillonian sites is the widespread use of rock outcrops to form part of the chamber walling or the mound of both entrance graves and cists. This may have simply been a way of reducing the work needed to build the structure, but it could be interpreted as a way of referencing the importance of the rock by binding the structure to it. There has been little examination of the rocks which have been incorporated in this way; they may have been selected because of their location on an appropriate hilltop but there may be other factors, such as their colour, which were important.

As well as incorporating natural rock into mounds and chambers, the builders of the entrance graves, it has been suggested, positioned them close to natural features, particularly rock outcrops (Robinson 2007). As outlined in chapter 1, the bedrock in Scilly is granite and, in many places, both around the coast and inland, this has been subject to erosion and weathering which has resulted in exposed rock stacks, known in Scilly as carns. These occur as horizontal and vertical formations and as hillslope outcrops (Scourse 2006c).

In some cases, the chambers and their mounds seem to mimic outcrops. Clefts in these rocks, such as the one at Yellow Rock Carn, where a funerary urn was found, may have been used as locations for burial. There is also a small number of sites in Scilly, such as Samson Hill D and

Tregarthen Hill A and B, where kerbstones or rocks have been positioned around a natural outcrop, similar to the tor cairns found on Dartmoor and Bodmin Moor. It appears that there is no clear dividing line between 'natural' and 'built' structures.

In attempting to quantify the relationship between entrance graves and carns it is necessary to consider both what constitutes a carn and what constitutes a relationship. Robinson, who refers to carns as 'tors', argues that 'entrance graves were consistently located in close proximity to tors.' (2007:115) His plan of Porth Hellick Down includes, as 'tors', both coastal outcrops of up to about 20m in height and inland rocks measuring as little as approximately 2.5m by 1.5m by 1.5m (2007:fig 7.15).

Similarly, his list of entrance graves with a relationship with carns includes both those which are described as 'immediately adjacent' to a carn and those 250m away from one (Robinson 2007:Appendix T). Given the scale of Scilly, where the largest island now measures only 4km by 2.5km, 250m is a significant distance. Robinson's consideration of the relationship between entrance graves and natural rock outcrops in Scilly, indicates a similar flexibility of definition to that shown by Tilley (1994) and referred to in chapter 2.

There are some relatively low-lying, coastal entrance graves situated very close to a carn. For example, the site at Works Carn, Bryher, shown in figure 6.13, is positioned on a hillslope carn at an altitude of 25m on the southern slope of Samson Hill, which rises to 42m.

The well-preserved entrance grave of Innisidgen Carn A, St Mary's, is located less than 20m from the coastal outcrop of the same name and is at an altitude of 15m above sea level. At this site, it appears that rock has been taken from the carn, shown in figure 6.14, perhaps for the building of the entrance grave. Although not all entrance graves are located near carns, the proximity of many of them can be explained by the usual location of both features on high ground and along the coast. There

Burial sites and settlements

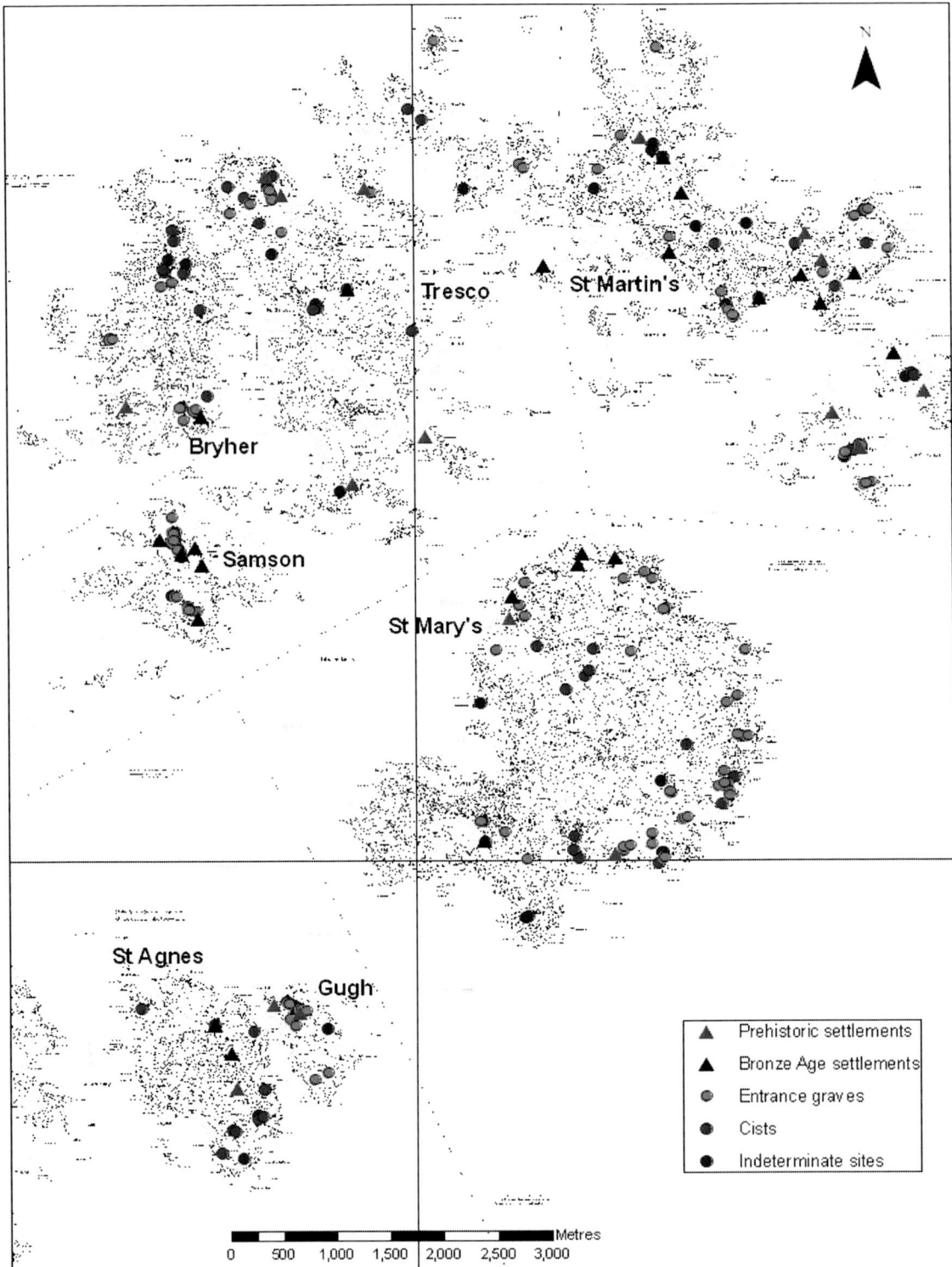

Tresco

St Martin's

Bryher

Samson

St Mary's

St Agnes

Gugh

▲ Prehistoric settlements
▲ Bronze Age settlements
● Entrance graves
● Cists
● Indeterminate sites

Metres

0   500   1,000 1,500 2,000 2,500 3,000

©Crown copyright/database right 2012. An Ordnance Survey/EDINA supplied service.

FIGURE 6.15 DISTRIBUTION OF BURIAL SITES AND SETTLEMENTS

are many substantial carns, for example, in the north of Bryher, the south of St Agnes and on White Island, where there are no neighbouring entrance graves. However, the practice of incorporating natural rock in chambers and cairns led to their frequent juxtaposition.

6.8 Relationship with settlements

The relationship between burial structures and settlements is easier to quantify and the map in figure 6.15 shows the settlement sites recorded in the HER, together with the burial sites already indicated in figure 6.6. Many of the settlement sites have not been excavated and, consequently, have no precise dating. The sites included are classified in the HER as either Bronze Age or prehistoric; it is likely that not all of them are contemporary with the entrance graves and cists but it is not possible to determine this at present. It is clear however that there is considerable evidence for settlement in the islands.

Many of the settlement sites are now in coastal locations, several having been exposed by coastal erosion or during sea defence works. There is a lack of precision in the grid references for some of the settlements recorded in the HER. However, it does not appear that entrance graves and settlements occur within less than 100m of each other. The situation is different for cists, four cist graves having been found within or very close to settlements, at Par Beach and Little Bay, St Martin's, Porth Killier, St Agnes and Dolphin Town, Tresco.

Par Beach has a wealth of prehistoric and Romano-British sites in its inter-tidal zone. Several of these were excavated by O'Neil between 1949 and 1951 but not published (Beagrie 1989); the earliest house was associated with Bronze Age pottery but its relationship with the cist is not clear.

Little Bay was also excavated by O'Neil but has been subsequently examined by Minett-Smith, Butcher and Neal (Neal 1983). The site is now covered by sand dunes and has been exposed intermittently, following storms, since the late 19th century. A stone-lined cist was found on the west side of the interior of a circular hut. Unfortunately, the excavation report provides very little information about it and it is not clear whether the cist represents an earlier use of the area or whether it is contemporary with the settlement.

The other two sites, Porth Killier and Dolphin Town, have been examined more recently. The probable cist at Porth Killier was uncovered during archaeological recording in 1996 in advance of sea defence work. There are three huts, with associated middens; the cist is covered by a cairn and contained pottery, clay and a mortar or socket stone, but no human remains. At this site the cist appears to pre-date the settlement (Johns 2011; Ratcliffe et al. forthcoming).

At Dolphin Town, monitoring was carried out in 2003 in advance of development and the probable cist site,

which is covered by a small cairn, was uncovered but not excavated. It was found at a distance of approximately 20m from four Middle Bronze Age huts and again appears to pre-date these structures (Taylor & Johns 2009-2010). The existence of cairns covering the cists at the last two sites suggests that their presence would have been known to those living in the neighbouring settlements.

6.9 Conclusions

The use of GIS to examine the distribution of Scillonian entrance graves and cists has been valuable in highlighting their present, predominantly coastal setting. The inclusion of destroyed sites in the database for analysis facilitated the recognition that many of them are in areas, particularly the inland parts of St Mary's, where there are no extant sites and which have been used for agriculture for at least the last two hundred years. The impact of superficial geology on the observable distribution has also been demonstrated. It seems that the absence of sites over a large area of St Martin's can be explained by the presence of blown sand there. It is clear, however, that there is no simple explanation for the distribution of the sites nor for the patterning of their orientations.

Most striking, though, is the connection between the location of some of the sites and the inundation of a large area of land in the north of the archipelago. The groupings of entrance graves and cists and the lines of sight between them, illustrated for Bant's Carn in figure 6.9, may indicate a pre-occupation with protecting this area. However, elsewhere in the islands, where the impact of the inundation was much less, clusters of entrance graves and cists were also built around the coast and on hilltops. These aspects will be considered further in chapter 7.

Chapter 7

The function of the Scillonian sites

7.1 Introduction

This chapter will examine the arguments put forward for the function of the chambered cairns and cists of Scilly. Although the term 'entrance grave' has generally been used to describe the Scillonian chambered cairns in recent decades, some authors (Ashbee 1976; 1982; Thomas 1985) have suggested that the primary function of these structures was not as a place of burial. The evidence for other functions will be discussed and consideration will be given to possible reasons for the number and density of megalithic burial chambers in Scilly.

7.2 Historical interpretations of function

The traditional view of the chambered cairns of the islands, in common with those of many other parts of western Europe, was that they were 'Giants' Graves' (Borlase 1756). Borlase himself described them as 'Sepulchres' and subsequent authors (Troutbeck 1796; Woodley 1822) also regarded their purpose as being sepulchral. There is no debate in the writings of these authors about other possible purposes for the structures; the only considerations are about the numbers of individuals buried in them and their rank in society. Woodley suggested that the larger chambers might have been family vaults.

Amongst the early 20th century researchers of Scilly, Bonsor describes the chambered cairns as 'tombs' and his discoveries of human remains at both Bant's Carn and Obadiah's Barrow would have reinforced this interpretation. Sites, such as Porth Hellick Down A and Normandy Down A, where he found no human remains, are likewise described in this way (Bonsor 1901-1902).

Hencken also regarded the structures as places of burial, indeed, the first section of his chapter on 'Great Stone Monuments' (Hencken 1932:Ch II) is titled 'Chambered Tombs' and they are subsequently referred to as 'graves', 'tombs' and 'burial-chambers'. Again, Hencken speculates that that the chambers may have been family vaults, saying that 'Perhaps, … the more ostentatious families built the largest mausoleums while the rest were content with less elaborate monuments' (1932:20). Hencken believed that these tombs must have had a religious significance, suggesting that 'Only an extraordinary veneration of the dead or a compelling fear of them could have driven people to undertake these monumental labours.' (Hencken

1929:Vol I, 54). Hencken did not consider any other possible function for the structures but he did comment on the large number of them in Scilly. He dismissed the idea that their builders might have come to the islands in search of tin (because

of the paucity of tin there) and suggested instead that the most probable reason was that Scilly was a natural stopping place for vessels travelling between Brittany and the shores of the Irish Sea, including western and northern Scotland, chambered cairns being found also in all those areas (Hencken 1929:Vol I, 65). Elsewhere he said that 'it is hard to understand how such an island, which could scarcely have supported much of a population, came to have upon it such a profusion of burials'. He went on to consider early historical references to the sanctity of remote islands and to wonder whether this was prompted by the ruined burial chambers found in places like Scilly (1932:33).

Daniel also regarded chambered cairns as having a funerary purpose: he wrote confidently that 'Excavation has shown that they were burial vaults used collectively over a long period' (Daniel 1947) and the title of his book, *The Prehistoric Chamber Tombs of England and Wales*, confirms the approach he took (Daniel 1950). In this he considered the distribution, construction, morphology, ritual, finds, origins and dating of the structures but did not discuss their function which he took, on the basis of the discovery of human bones in many of them, to be obvious. In relation to Scilly, Daniel also commented on the number of sites. He speculated as to whether it was an island cemetery or whether the concentration could be explained by the fact that the tradition of building such tombs continued longer in Scilly than elsewhere (Daniel 1947).

In the first half of the 20th century the function of the chambered cairns of Scilly was therefore regarded, without challenge, as the burial of human remains. Any further discussion was focussed solely on providing an explanation for the large number of such structures to be found in the islands, although this received relatively limited attention. As outlined above, possible answers included the presence of visitors from elsewhere in the Irish Sea zone where chambered cairns also occurred and a longer timeframe for their construction in Scilly than in other locations. Overall, however, there was little comment on the great concentration of such sites in Scilly.

FIGURE 7.1 POSSIBLE LYNCHET TO THE EAST OF BANT'S CARN

7.3 Entrance graves as *fana*

The first challenge to the concept of the Scillonian chambered cairns as having a solely funerary purpose came from Ashbee. In 1970 he worked at Bant's Carn, St Mary's when the outermost capstone, which by local tradition had been removed in about 1910, was replaced. (In fact, a letter from Bonsor to T A Dorrien-Smith, the Lord Proprietor of Scilly, shows that the capstone had already been dislodged by 1900 (Bonsor 1901-1902)). Ashbee published the results of his excavation of the jambstone setting and surrounding area (Ashbee 1976) and, in the same article, considered the function of Scillonian entrance graves.

In this, Ashbee argued that a 'considerable number' of the entrance graves were 'intimately associated' with ancient field systems (1976:22). On Kittern Hill, Gugh, on North Hill, Samson and on Great Arthur, he said, entrance graves and cairns were linked by stone walls which were part of wider field systems. The site on Old Man of Teän was within a wall system, he argued, and the entrance grave at Bant's Carn was joined to a lynchet. Ashbee compared these sites to others in Ireland, Wessex and Orkney where there were similar associations between chambered tombs and stone agricultural walls.

As discussed in chapter 4, there are several locations in Scilly where boulder walls are found in close association with entrance graves, cists and cairns. There has been limited study of these features, although Breen (2006; 2008) has examined the relationship between the walls and other built and natural features. In many cases the walls are overgrown with vegetation making a detailed analysis impossible. However, it is not at all certain that they are all field boundaries as in several places, including North Hill, Samson and Great Arthur, the boulder wall appears to be a purely linear feature, rather than part of an enclosure.

Ashbee asserted that the wall linking entrance graves on North Hill, Samson 'is clearly part of the extensive system lying largely submerged on Samson Flats' (1976:21) but this is, in practice, far from clear. Samson Flats lie some 35m in altitude below the summit of North Hill with no evidence for a field system on the hillslope between them, other than three post-mediaeval walled fields close to the coastline, shown on the Driver survey of 1831 (Teague Cowan 1991).

Unlike the top of North Hill, the Flats are a sheltered area suitable for agriculture. The summit of North Hill is exposed to the full force of westerly winds from the Atlantic and is an unlikely location even for pasture land. Here a single boulder wall is apparent, running just below the ridge of North Hill and linking several of the chambered cairns. It forms the eastern boundary of the group of entrance graves and cists on the hilltop. The HER entry *(PRN 7069)*, however, suggests that the wall post-dates them (HES 1987-2005).

Fowler and Thomas, in their examination of boulder walls in Scilly, noted the presence of two small enclosures to the west of the wall along the ridge of North Hill, Samson which they describe as 'clearly not part of a field-system as normally understood'. They suggested that the function of the wall may have been to link, rather than to divide, as it connects not only the enclosures but also six of the cairns on the hilltop (Fowler & Thomas 1979:187).

On Great Arthur the boulder wall runs along the top of the hill, linking five entrance graves and cairns. Here, however, there is evidence for a field system on the sheltered slopes below (HES 1987-2005: *PRN 7222*) although not all the walls are contemporary. The wall on the ridge is again in a very exposed position and it is difficult to envisage agricultural activity in this area. On Shipman Head Down, Bryher where a proportion of the walls do form part of enclosures, they cross, and therefore post-date, at least some of the cairns. The same is true on Kittern Hill, Gugh where the Scheduled Monument Record states:

'The slighting of underlying cairns to provide prominent slabs for the field system walling is important not only in clarifying the sequence of land use but also the shift in respect for such funerary monuments during the Bronze Age' (English Heritage 1996).

At Bant's Carn, it is unclear what the bank feature, identified by Ashbee as a lynchet and shown in figure 7.1, actually is. There was quarrying for granite nearby in the late 19th century (Ashbee 1996) and some of the earthworks in the area relate to this. To the east of the Bant's Carn entrance grave there are a number of stone-splitting sites on the downhill slope of the bank and it is possible that the feature was entirely formed by quarrying activity and not by early agriculture. This interpretation is strengthened by the fact that the slope above the bank is very gentle, as can be seen on the right of the photograph, and it is therefore difficult to envisage a lynchet of this size forming here by the Early Bronze Age. Even if it is a lynchet, it is not clear that it pre-dates the construction of the entrance grave.

It can be argued, therefore, that where the boulder walls are contemporary with the cairns, they were not agricultural in function but instead may have had a role either in delineating a separate area for the construction of entrance graves or in marking a route between entrance graves, perhaps for processional or ceremonial purposes.

Ashbee noted the absence of human remains in some of the chambers in Scilly and the discovery of broken pottery and soil in them. He compared this with the earthen deposits found in some Scottish chambers, English long barrows and causewayed enclosures and suggested that Neolithic farmers formed a link between occupation debris and fertile soil. (The actual composition of the black or greasy

soil found in some entrance graves will be discussed later in this chapter in section 7.5.) From this he concluded that the primary purpose of the Scillonian sites (and, indeed, all earthen and stone-built long barrows) may not have been as graves. Instead, he suggested that we should:

'regard them as cult structures, as repositories rather than as *tombs*, each containing a foundation deposit, rather than burials in the long accepted sense, conceived and constructed as a response to soil impoverishment and loss of fertility' (Ashbee 1976:21, emphasis in original).

This, he said, provided an explanation for the presence of both entrance graves and cists in Scilly as it was the cists which were the burial sites. A similar argument has been made in respect of Orkney, where it has been argued that the chambered cairns were originally built as temples and were re-used for burials, either of an elite or of the 'unacceptable dead' such as murder victims (Barber 2000). In the Orcadian case Barber suggested that the number of burials found in chambered cairns does not represent the total population of the islands and that, therefore, they cannot have been the main burial structures of the Neolithic population.

Ashbee argued that early agriculture in Scilly would have caused the destruction of the original vegetation and this, in turn, would have led to soil degradation and the expansion of sand dunes. *Fana* (that is, shrines or repositories) were established to counter this. The position of these *fana* – the entrance graves – in close proximity to field systems indicates their function, he suggested.

As not all Scillonian entrance graves are associated with field boundaries, Ashbee suggested that those sites which are not, may have been *fana* for the perpetuation of pasture or for some other purpose. However, as outlined above, the evidence for the purpose and contemporaneity of the boulder walls connecting entrance graves and cists does not seem sufficiently secure to form the basis of an hypothesis about the role of entrance graves as repositories to secure soil fertility.

As there is variation in the size of the entrance graves, an alternative explanation, put forward by Ashbee in the same article, is that there was a segmentary society leading to a division of the land and that on each of the main land masses was a founder *fanum* which was substantially larger than the others. He identified these as the sites now known as Normandy Down B for St Mary's, Knackyboy Cairn for St Martin's, Tregarthen Hill D for Tresco and Carn of Works for Gugh. For Bryher and Samson, which he treated as being joined, he named a site on Bryher 'on the summit of the hill just to the northeast of Top Rock Carn' (1976:23). The present author has been unable to identify this location as Top Rock Carn is on St Martin's. However, the mound of Shipman Head Down N, which is on the summit of the hill just to the northeast of Puckie's Carn on Bryher, is one of the largest in Scilly and it seems likely that this is the site which Ashbee is referring to.

THE FUNCTION OF THE SCILLONIAN SITES

In selecting these sites, Ashbee took account of the size of the mound, not that of the chamber. Whilst they all have substantial mounds, they are not the five largest sites in Scilly. If one considers chamber length, rather than mound diameter, then a very different hierarchy of sites is suggested, none of which is in close proximity to the site with the largest mound on the same island.

Ashbee considered, however, that the range of size of *fana* in Scilly was not great, suggesting that 'the components of the segmentary society emerge as broadly equal, one to another.' He did not consider contemporary settlement evidence in this but concluded that there were 'disparate communities each with its *fana*', although he felt that the fact that the two largest structures were on St Mary's and Gugh might be of significance, as they were on the two main landmasses at that time (Ashbee 1976:23). It is uncertain whether a population constructing megalithic chambers and their surrounding cairns would build large structures first and smaller ones later. It could equally be argued that the largest structures represent the culmination of the sequence of building. Without secure dates from range of sites, it is not possible to resolve this.

In developing his argument for the interpretation of entrance graves as *fana*, Ashbee went on to suggest that cists were the burial sites for these communities and that the burial rite was, therefore, single cremation. The mound covering the cist grave at North Hill H on Samson measures 21.5m by 17.5m in diameter and is one of the largest in Scilly but, although Ashbee referred to this site, he did not comment on the significance of the cairn size. The cist at Hill Bennigates on St Martin's also has a substantial cairn and Bonsor recorded that there were seven cists in the mound of Shipman Head Down N (cited by Ashbee as a founder *fanum*) (Maier 1999). Separating entrance graves and cists may therefore not be as straightforward as Ashbee suggested.

Ashbee developed his view of the sites as repositories rather than graves in a later article in which he proposed a Mesolithic origin for the Scillonian entrance graves (Ashbee 1982:5). In this he linked the distribution of megalithic tombs in Atlantic Europe to the movement of fish and the fishermen following them. He pointed out that the transition between Mesolithic and Neolithic economies was a gradual one and that elements of a Mesolithic economy, such as the exploitation of fish, shellfish, seabirds, marine mammals and deer, continued in Scilly for a considerable period.

Ashbee went on to suggest three stages in the sitings and associations of Scillonian chambered cairns: the first, he said, were built by Mesolithic peoples, on hilltops, 'in relation to the links with distant places maintained by fishing voyages', in the second phase, lines or groups of chambered cairns were linked by walls 'because of the intrinsic qualities invested in them by the island communities' and in the third stage, the cairns were built on field systems because of the loss of soil fertility (1982:14).

He then drew a distinction between the entrance graves in different parts of Scilly. Those on the eastern side of Scilly (particularly on St Mary's) which are in clusters near the coast were, he argued, Mesolithic navigational markers relating to the first stage. Those on western side (for example, on Samson and Gugh), which have a linear arrangement, date to the second stage and are linked with the processes of clearance and enclosure. The third stage is represented by sites such as Bant's Carn, Innisidgen Carn A, Obadiah's Barrow and Knackyboy Cairn which, he suggested, are all built on lynchets and are linked to a decline in soil fertility.

As has been outlined in chapter 6, many of the entrance graves on the eastern side of St Mary's are not visible from the sea. The sequence set out above is not compatible with what had been put forward by Ashbee in 1976. For example, in that paper it was argued that Knackyboy Cairn, having one of the largest cairns, was a founder *fanum*; in the 1982 paper it is included in the third and final stage of monument construction. Given the absence of reliable dating for any entrance grave site other than Knackyboy, it is impossible to know whether the chronology proposed in either of these hypotheses is correct.

In the later paper, Ashbee accepted that the walls linking some cairns post-date the cairns themselves. However, the difficulty of determining whether cairns have a linear or nucleated arrangement is illustrated by Ashbee's plan of Kittern Hill, Gugh. In this, there is a linear arrangement of seven cairns in the central part of the hill Immediately to the south of the north-western end of this line, however, is a cluster of five sites (Ashbee 1982:fig 8).

It is hard to reconcile the similarities in chamber construction between sites such as Porth Hellick A and Bant's Carn with an argument that they were built several millennia apart. In addition, the complete lack of Mesolithic finds or features from any entrance grave or its vicinity (and, indeed, their paucity in Scilly generally) casts doubt on an interpretation of the entrance graves as having their origins in this period.

7.4 Entrance graves as territorial markers

Thomas, having carefully examined the process of prehistoric settlement in the islands, went on to consider the chambered cairns and cists. He too argued that burial in Scilly at this time was in cists and that 'it is by no means certain that all or most of [the entrance graves] were originally constructed to serve as tombs' (1985:95).

Thomas based his arguments for the early settlement of Scilly on Renfrew's work in relation to Arran and Rousay, in which he outlined the indicators of a segmentary society (Renfrew 1976; Renfrew 1979 cited in Thomas 1985); this analysis has been discussed in chapter 2. Thomas suggested that these indicators can be seen in Scilly and identified five 'founder' sites with their associated cairns. He described the five chambered cairns identified by Ashbee as 'founder' cairns and linked these to five 'founder' settlements. The settlements appeared to have been selected because of their proximity to the cairns rather than because of any evidence suggesting that they are the earliest sites.

Thomas proposed that, within the first few centuries of occupation, the inhabitants would have faced a potential crisis as population numbers outgrew the resources available on such a restricted landmass. He shared Ashbee's view that the chambered cairns might not have been constructed primarily as tombs and suggested that they may initially have been territorial markers which could also have functioned as temples.

Although Thomas said that, over an extended period of time, the spread of settlements and chambered cairns would have complemented each other, he accepted that there would have been considerable variation within this process. Suggesting that the role of chambered cairns was as markers, Thomas had to accept that it is difficult to reconcile the clusters of these cairns in Scilly with a dispersed settlement pattern.

In particular, the density of distribution of entrance graves in Scilly makes it difficult to accept that individual megalithic monuments were associated with particular settlements. Work carried out in 1988 concluded that there were 387 extant cairns, 21 extant cists and 79 extant entrance graves in the islands, which today have an area of about 15km² (Ratcliffe 1989).

The distribution of entrance graves and settlements in Scilly is shown in figure 6.15 with settlements separated into those recorded in the HER as being of Bronze Age date and those simply recorded as prehistoric. In the absence of more accurate dating for the majority of these sites it is impossible to say which were contemporary with the entrance graves.

It will be seen that many of the known settlement sites cluster around the present-day coastline. The distribution of inland sites is much more sparse; this may be because many Bronze Age settlements were located close to the coast for the easier exploitation of coastal and maritime resources, because inland sites have been destroyed by more recent agriculture or because they have not been uncovered.

There is no convincing evidence for the development of chiefdoms in prehistoric Scilly, either in the form of hierarchies of place or in the material culture, and it also seems that, if entrance graves were territorial markers, they were not linked on a one-to-one basis with settlements.

Like Ashbee, Thomas went on to suggest that the main burial sites of the early prehistoric population were the cists and proposed that the cairn fields known in areas such as Shipman Head Down, Bryher and Wingletang Down, St Agnes were cemeteries where 'the mounds ought to reveal

(at best) slab-built cists, or (at least) token depositions in little pits, with cremated remains and occasional coarse pots' (Thomas 1985:133). There has been no controlled excavation of these cairns and it is therefore uncertain whether they are funerary sites or not. It is possible that they are the result of agricultural clearance, although it seems unlikely that some of these areas would have been suitable for agriculture.

Thomas supported his argument that the chambered cairns were not primarily burial places by citing the fact that there was no trace of burial in some chambers and that several contained sherds, charcoal, ash and/or black soil which he interpreted as midden material. He suggested that this was deposited in the chambers as sympathetic magic to improve soil fertility.

Another argument for a relationship between the entrance graves and soil fertility, put forward by Ratcliffe and Johns, is the presence of a saddle quern on a chamber floor (Ratcliffe & Johns 2003). This was found by Hencken at North Hill E and was described by him as the upper stone of a saddle quern (Hencken 1933:27). It formed part of the paving of the chamber floor and, from the illustration, appears to be an oval, flat stone which could be simply a water-smoothed beach stone. Hencken (1929) also recorded that Bonsor found a 'muller', the upper stone of a saddle quern, at Bant's Carn; no other information is given and it is not mentioned in Bonsor's own notes.

Thomas admitted that much of his argument was 'hypothetical and speculative' (1985:145) but believed that it provides an explanation for the joint occurrence of chambered cairns, cist burials and cairn fields. His detailed consideration of the process of the early settlement of the islands and the impact of agriculture on the environment is extremely valuable in identifying the challenges the first settlers would have faced and their possible responses.

The arguments of both Ashbee and Thomas that early agriculture led to soil degradation in Scilly is not reflected in the work of other authors (e.g. Ratcliffe & Straker 1996; Robinson 2007). The pollen evidence from a number of sites points to a landscape in which the post-glacial deciduous woodland was cleared for agriculture from the Late Neolithic onwards. During the Bronze Age and later periods there is a largely treeless environment with evidence for agriculture at some locations (Ratcliffe & Straker 1996).

Ratcliffe and Straker also reviewed the evidence from plant macrofossils, animal bones and shells to draw a picture of the economy and diet of prehistoric Scillonians. Their work in analysing the bone and shell assemblages from a large number of sites, ranging from the Bronze Age to the Early Mediaeval period, shows the exploitation of many different species.

From Bronze Age settlement sites, such as Porth Killier (St Agnes), Nornour, Halangy Porth (St Mary's) and English

Island Carn (St Martin's) there is evidence for sheep/goat, cattle, pig, horse, deer, seal, dolphin and whale, more than a dozen species of fish, nine species of mollusc and two dozen species of land and sea birds. Naked and hulled barley, emmer, oats and celtic or horse bean have also been identified at these sites, together with a wide range of wild plants. This indicates a mixed land/sea subsistence economy including raising domestic animals and growing crops, as well as hunting wild land and sea mammals and birds, fishing and gathering wild food.

Thomas argued that there would have been a rapid population growth in Scilly following the initial settlement of farming communities there. This would soon have led to a shortage of suitable land and the problem might have been compounded by 'sand-blows, desiccation, soil-exhaustion' (Thomas 1985:118). He admitted, however, that there is no evidence for mass depopulation in the prehistoric period. Ratcliffe and Straker's work demonstrates that agriculture was only one part of the Scillonian subsistence economy during the Bronze Age.

Rainbird, writing about Pacific islands, makes the point that soil erosion should not necessarily be seen as detrimental to island environments. The change in vegetation on hillslopes might lead to soil erosion but, when this is washed to the bottom of the slopes, it could increase the area of suitable agricultural land and improve its fertility (Rainbird 2002). Some authors have suggested that this might have been a deliberate process (Spriggs 1985 quoted in Rainbird 2002).

It is hard to reconcile the image, suggested by both Ashbee and Thomas, of islands in crisis because of population growth and soil degradation, with the construction of significant numbers of megalithic chambers and their surrounding cairns. Populations threatened with starvation, or at least with restricted food supplies, might be expected to reduce their energy output rather than to expend the considerable number of hours of physical labour required to build such monuments. Thomas's interpretation also assumes that the population in Scilly was completely island-based by this time and does not allow for the possibility that there was regular movement of people between Scilly and the mainland.

7.5 Entrance graves as burial chambers

Much of the argument for alternative, i.e. non-burial, functions for Scillonian entrance graves has been based on the paucity of human remains found in those structures. It is important, therefore, to assess what has been discovered and how representative these finds are of the totality of the sites.

As has been set out in chapter 4, there is documentary evidence for excavation at 36 of the 197 entrance graves, cists and indeterminate sites, recorded in the Historic Environment Record for Scilly, which form the database for this research. Of these, a total of 21 excavations have

been carried out at entrance graves with a further five taking place at indeterminate sites. Human remains have been found at only four entrance graves (Bant's Carn, Cruther's Neck, Knackyboy Cairn and Obadiah's Barrow) and one indeterminate site (Middle Arthur B). There is also an early 19th century record of human bones being found at a structure of uncertain form at Peninnis Head (Douch 1962) .

Nine cist sites have been excavated and human remains discovered at only one (North Hill H). In addition, cremated bone was found in a cist at Old Town, destroyed by builders in 1964 (Mackenzie 1965) and there is an 18th century record of the discovery of human remains in a cist at Lower Newford (Borlase 1758).

Human remains have, therefore, been found in 19% of excavated entrance graves, 33% of excavated or opened indeterminate sites and 27% of excavated or opened cists. While these sample sizes are too small for any firm conclusions to be drawn, they do indicate that human remains have been found in approximately the same percentage of examined entrance graves, cists and indeterminate sites.

It is important to bear in mind the condition of these monuments when they were excavated. Of the entrance graves where human bone has been found, Bant's Carn, Obadiah's Barrow, Knackyboy Cairn, and, from the limited information available, Cruther's Neck were all intact or had suffered relatively little disturbance when excavated. Bant's Carn contained evidence for four burials (Bonsor 1899-1900), Obadiah's Barrow for about 20 (Bonsor 1901) and Knackyboy for 100 or more (O'Neil 1948-1949). It appears that there were at least three at Cruther's Neck (Bonsor 1901-1902). At Middle Arthur B, all but one of the capstones had been removed before O'Neil excavated there and he found only sherds of pottery, some of which fortuitously had cremated bone adhering to them (O'Neil 1954).

Other entrance graves had also clearly been disturbed before excavation took place and finds from them have been limited. For example, at North Hill E, Hencken records:

> 'This soil [which had blown into the chamber] had been so turned over by countless generations of rabbits that any stratigraphy had been completely upset. Rabbit bones, parts of an iron vessel obviously modern, fourteen discharged shotgun cartridges, and half-decayed vegetable matter were found at all levels.' (Hencken 1933:26)

He goes on to say that '[t]here was no trace of human remains, either inhumed or cremated, but in the disturbed state of the tomb this means little.' (1933:27) Despite this assessment by the excavator, Ashbee insisted that, if burial deposits had been placed in the chamber, 'a few scraps would have survived' (1974:107).

Although Ashbee and Thomas both proposed that it was cists that were used for burial in Early Bronze Age Scilly, there was no trace of human remains at half of the cist sites which have been excavated or otherwise recorded, even though most of them were apparently undisturbed when discovered. Ashbee and O'Neil examined the cist at Content Farm in 1950 and found pottery in it but no trace of a burial. Ashbee suggested that it, and a very similar cist at Carn Morval Down examined in about 1899, might have contained child inhumations which would have disappeared in the acidic soil (Ashbee 1953). He does not mention the possibility that a similar explanation could be given for the absence of human remains at excavated entrance graves.

There is only one definite record of an inhumation burial from this period in Scilly: that found by Bonsor at Obadiah's Barrow (Bonsor 1901-1902; Hencken 1933). Here, as described in chapter 5, the bone seems to have survived because of the presence of limpet shells in the chamber. Bonsor also recorded a fragment of unburnt bone at Bant's Carn (1899-1900) and O'Neil mentioned the presence of a few pieces of it at Knackyboy Cairn but said that there was no evidence for a primary inhumation burial there (1948-1949). At other sites, there are records of greasy black earth, ashes and charcoal. If these discoveries are included as evidence of human burial, the percentage of sites with burials increases to 48% for entrance graves and 45% for cists.

A tradition has developed, in the literature about these sites, of describing this greasy earth as midden material, although this was not put forward as an explanation by any of the excavators of the sites. None of this substance has been retained and no recent researcher has had the opportunity to examine it. The hypothesis appears to have its origin in Ashbee's article about the restoration of Bant's Carn in which he first put forward his argument that the Scillonian entrance graves were *fana* rather than burial places (Ashbee 1976). As mentioned above, he drew a parallel between the soil and pottery sherds found in the entrance graves and similar finds from elsewhere in England and Scotland but did not go so far as to suggest that the entrance grave material was from middens.

However, Thomas, referring to Ashbee's article, stated that:

> '… we can suspect that reports of sherds (as opposed, in the main, to complete pots), charcoal and ash, other than cremations, animal-bone remains, small objects of stone, small pebbles, and what has variously been reported as blackish soil, soil and ashes … all add up to the same thing. This is the deliberate deposition of occupational debris.' (1985:135)

In practice, there is no evidence for the deposition of 'charcoal and ash, other than cremations' and the animal bone remains consist of sharpened bone and horn or antler points (the pig jawbone from Halangy Down is undated

and, like the rabbit bones from North Hill E, may well be modern). The small stone objects include beads, a pendant and spindle-whorls, all objects likely to have been placed with burials as grave goods.

Kirk, again referencing Ashbee's article, says that 'Entrance graves primarily contain midden debris – dark organic earth, ash, charcoal and abraded sherds.' (Kirk 2004:239) He illustrates this with O'Neil's drawing of the section of Knackyboy Cairn which marks 'ashes' and 'black soil'. However, O'Neil made it clear that the black soil was almost the same as the actual cremations and not, therefore, midden material (O'Neil 1952).

Given the friable nature of the majority of the prehistoric pottery in Scilly, it is to be expected that most of it will be found in sherds. At both Obadiah's Barrow and Knackyboy Cairn, there are records of urns being crushed by others placed on top of them (O'Neil 1952; Maier 1999). However, O'Neil does refer to a dark soil containing abraded sherds which had been used to level the floor of the chamber at Knackyboy Cairn, before any burials were placed there, and he believed that the soil had come from 'a nearby habitation site' (O'Neil 1948-1949:102). This is, however, a different 'soil' from that found around the lowest level of urns.

As mentioned above, greasy and/or black earth has been recorded at a number of sites elsewhere in the British Isles. For example, during work at the chambered cairn in the centre of the stone circle at Callanish, Lewis in 1857, a black greasy layer was found inside the chamber. More recently, 'black earth' has been found outside the tomb passage during excavations there and has been interpreted as 'remains of cleared-out burials' whilst the 1857 discovery may be the 'residue of decomposition' (Ashmore 2002).

However, this and the material from Scillonian sites do not appear to be analogous to the remains found in the hearth in the central chamber at Barclodiad y Gawres, Anglesey. There, in 'wet sticky grey earth and ashes with lumps of charcoal' was a deposit of stone chips, oyster and limpet shells and animal bones (Powell & Daniel 1956:16). These last were identified as being fragments of fish, amphibian, reptile and mammal bones and interpreted as being from a 'stew' which had been poured as a libation on to the fire (Pumphrey 1956).

Robinson also refers to Ashbee's and Thomas's arguments but, whilst accepting the presence of soil and ash as 'intentional and significant', says that finds of non-local stone, such as pumice, 'can reasonably be interpreted as 'grave goods'' (Robinson 2007:106).

The evidence from excavated, or otherwise opened, entrance graves and cists does not, therefore, point to a clear division of function between the two types of site. Both provide evidence for human burial at some locations, but not at others. All the entrance graves which were undisturbed when excavated have yielded human remains. At the majority of excavated entrance graves, only the chamber was examined and it is therefore possible that evidence for cremations would have been discovered had a wider area been uncovered. As set out above, it is also possible that some of these sites contained inhumation burials which had decayed completely or which did not leave a sufficient trace for their presence to be detected.

There is a similar paucity of human remains in megalithic chambers elsewhere in north-western Europe. In Brittany, for example, 'the acid soils have almost everywhere destroyed the remains of the dead' (Burl 1985:13); bone has survived only at a few sites where burial took place in sand. In Herm, human bones have been discovered at some structures on Le Petit Monceau and Le Grand Monceau; in the majority of cases these are sites where limpet shells have also been deposited in the chamber, assisting the preservation of bone. However, other sites have yielded finds such as pottery and shells, but no human remains (Johnston 1981).

Whilst it is argued here that entrance graves were used for burial, it is not suggested that this was their sole function. The occurrence of pottery sherds outside the entrance to the chamber at, for example, Bant's Carn (Bonsor 1899-1900; Ashbee 1976), Obadiah's Barrow (Bonsor 1901-1902), North Hill E (Hencken 1933) and Knackyboy Cairn (O'Neil 1948-1949) suggests a deliberate deposition of urns in this position. It is not possible to say whether these were deposited as complete vessels, perhaps containing offerings of some kind, or as sherds. In either case, it suggests that the entrance graves may also have had a function as shrines or temples of some kind.

The parallel is often drawn between megalithic burial chambers and Mediaeval parish churches (e.g. Thomas 1985), in that, it is argued, both types of structures were intended to be prominent markers, were used for regular worship and contained the burials of a select few. Establishing, in respect of prehistoric sites, whether these were their functions is fraught with difficulty.

7.6 The number and density of entrance graves in Scilly

One of the most striking aspects of Scillonian entrance graves is the density of their distribution, which, in common with some other islands in north-western Europe, such as Arran and the Channel Islands, is significantly higher than that found on the nearest mainland. Densities of 0.04 sites per km² in Arran, 0.27 per km² in Rousay, 0.47 per km² in the Channel Islands (with 8.0 per km² in Herm) and 5.4 per km² in Scilly have been calculated (Perry & Davidson 1987; Scarre 2011a; Scarre 2011d) suggesting that, across the archipelago, the density of megalithic burial chambers is greater in Scilly than anywhere else in the British Isles. With the exception of the suggestions by Hencken and Daniel, outlined in section 7.2 above, there has been little consideration of the possible reasons for this high density of sites.

The impact of rising sea levels on the landmass of Scilly has been examined in chapter 6. The recent work of the Lyonesse Project (Camidge et al. 2010; Johns 2012) suggests that the sea would have started to encroach upon the central low-lying area between the present day islands of St Mary's, Tresco and St Martin's in the Early Bronze Age, somewhat earlier than had been postulated by Thomas (1985). The amount of sea level rise in the prehistoric period was, however, greater than that suggested by Ratcliffe and Straker (1996).

It appears from the models produced by the Lyonesse Project that the area of land between St Mary's, Tresco and St Martin's became part of the inter-tidal zone at high spring tides before 2000BC. It is suggested that, at first, it would have been inundated only occasionally and that the land would have continued to be used for grazing as well as hunting (Johns & Mulville 2012). In time the frequency of inundation would have increased. This would have entailed not only the gradual degradation, and then loss, of large areas of agricultural land but also the division of what had been a single landmass into at least three separate islands. The impact of this on the islands' population may have resulted in the building of megalithic structures in an attempt to control or manage the sea's encroachment.

This close chronological relationship between the construction of large numbers of entrance graves and cists in Scilly and the inundation of substantial areas of low-lying land, leading to the sub-division of the main landmass, is significant. As the sea began to inundate agricultural land and settlements the graves, on the higher ground, remained untouched. It may be that this led to the building of further entrance graves as a way of attempting to protect the islands. The lack of precise dating for the majority of sites and, therefore, the absence of a sequence for them means that we are unable to assess whether the concentrations of sites on Samson, Gugh and St Mary's were built earlier than, later than, or at the same time as, the more scattered sites.

It could be argued that the entrance graves were constructed, mainly on high ground and overlooking the sea, as these were safe places in which to keep the remains of the ancestors or the more recent dead. The structures could equally be regarded as standing sentinel over the sea and protecting the land from further inundation.

Woodman has suggested that the building of megalithic burial chambers may have been a response to stress; he mentions 'land pressure, population pressure, environmental deterioration' as possibilities and goes on to say:

> '[I]t is possible that large concentrations ... could reflect the convergence of a series of social and environmental stress factors which were particular to that region ... Their prevalence in a particular area may even be a product of very short episodes of time.' (Woodman 1992:306)

It can be seen that these stress factors would have applied to Scilly at the time of the building of the entrance graves.

The close grouping of sites along the south-eastern coast of St Mary's may also be significant given that there was no loss of land in this part of the islands. Similarly, the area of inundation around much of Kittern Hill, Gugh was small. However, from the evidence currently available, we do not know whether these sites pre-date the beginnings of the inundation of the central area. If they do, it may be that their presence was seen as having defended this stretch of coastline and, therefore, groups of sites were built elsewhere.

The incorporation of natural rock in many of the chambers and cairns may have been seen as a way of tying the island to the structure, or *vice versa*, again in order to protect the land from the sea. Equally, the lines of sight between burial chambers in the northern part of the islands may also have been a way of defending the land from further inundation.

The inundation was a slow process, lasting throughout the second millennium BC and, indeed, continuing to the present day. The building, or certainly the use, of entrance graves seems to have continued until at least the 13th century BC. The Lyonesse Project found that the rate of inundation declined after c1500BC and it is possible that this was a factor in the ending of their use in Scilly (Charman et al. 2012a:173).

The construction of so many entrance graves may have been a result of the continuing threat from the sea but the concept of 'islandness', a term coined by Frieman (2008) and considered further in chapter 9, may also have been a factor. This is the tendency of island populations to develop a specific island identity and to cling to traditional ways of doing things as a way of maintaining this, even when they are aware that they are done differently elsewhere (Broodbank 2000; Parker Pearson 2004). Entrance graves may have been part of 'islandness' in Bronze Age Scilly.

7.7 Conclusions

This chapter has examined a number of different theories about the function and use of entrance graves and cists. It has been argued that the evidence to support interpretations of them as *fana* or as territorial markers does not stand up to scrutiny. The palaeoenvironmental record does not suggest that Scilly experienced a period of agricultural crisis, due to soil exhaustion, during the Bronze Age. Indeed, it shows the exploitation of a wide range of species, both domesticated and wild.

It has been concluded that the most likely explanation for the entrance graves and cists is that they were built as burial chambers, perhaps, in the case of the entrance graves, initially for inhumation burials. As sea levels rose during the second millennium BC, it is possible that these structures became linked in the minds of the islanders with the protection of the land and that this led to large numbers of them being constructed, often in dense clusters. It is likely that they had a function as shrines as well as funerary monuments at this time.

The use, if not the construction, of entrance graves continued until about the 13th century BC by which time the rate of sea level rise had slowed and it is possible that the cairnfields, now to be found in areas such as Shipman Head Down and Wingletang Down, took over as the islands' cemeteries.

Chapter 8

Dating the entrance graves and cists

8.1 Introduction

This chapter will examine the evidence for dating the entrance graves and cists of the Isles of Scilly. Until eleven radiocarbon dates were obtained in 2012, from human bone found at the entrance grave at Knackyboy Cairn, St Martin's and the cist at Old Town, St Mary's, there were only two, as yet unpublished, absolute dates from these burial structures, both from the probable cist at Porth Killier, St Agnes.

The discovery, by Bonsor, of a bronze awl at Obadiah's Barrow in 1901 (Bonsor 1901-1902) had indicated that that site at least had been in use in the Bronze Age. Early attempts to date the construction and use of the structures were based on the comparison of material objects, particularly pottery and faience, from the graves in Scilly with similar discoveries elsewhere. In the case of pottery, this has been very difficult because of the lack of mainland comparators. A small number of radiocarbon dates from settlement sites in Scilly, with similar pottery to that found in the graves, is available and has also provided a basis for dating the entrance graves and cists.

The value of the bronze objects from Obadiah's Barrow and elsewhere for dating those sites and O'Neil's (1952) arguments for the dating of Knackyboy Cairn, based on the faience bead found there, will be examined first. Consideration will then be given to Scillonian chronologies based on pottery, particularly the sequences from the settlement site on Nornour and Knackyboy Cairn entrance grave. The radiocarbon dates from both burial and settlement sites will then be discussed and comparisons made with dates from burial sites in Cornwall, Ireland, south-west Scotland, the Channel Islands and Brittany. All radiocarbon determinations have been calibrated using OxCal 4.2 and the IntCal13 calibration curve (Bronk Ramsey 2013; Reimer et al. 2013) and are expressed at the 2 SD (95.4%) confidence level.

8.2 Dating from bronze and faience

Hencken used Bonsor's discovery of a copper or bronze point at Obadiah's Barrow as one of the factors which led him to suggest that the Scillonian entrance graves dated to about 2000BC, though with a period of use both before and after this date (Hencken 1932:29).

Although Daniel identified this as 'the only bronze object found with the original burials in any burial chamber in the

British Isles' (1947:117), its discovery seems to have gone unremarked by other researchers at that time. However, the object is badly corroded and it is impossible to discern any detail on it. Typological comparison with other bronze points, to assist with dating, is therefore very difficult.

The next attempt at dating the entrance graves of Scilly was by O'Neil, following his excavation of Knackyboy Cairn in 1948. As has been set out in chapter 5, a considerable assemblage of artefacts, as well as large quantities of mainly cremated human bone, was found at this site. The artefacts included several small pieces of bronze, including possible rivets and a handle, eight glass beads and a single faience bead (O'Neil 1948-1949; 1952). Again, because of the poor state of preservation and small size of the pieces of bronze, little attention seems to have been paid to them.

O'Neil did, however, use the discovery of the star-shaped faience bead to date the site. He suggested that this was likely to have been an import from XIXth Dynasty Egypt and therefore to have been manufactured between c1320 and 1200BC. He argued that, allowing for its journey to Britain and for the fact that it was in a worn state when deposited, it was likely to have been placed in the grave by c1200BC. Because it was found in what O'Neil described as 'a thick deposit of ashes i.e. tiny pieces of charcoal, cremated bones, etc., with a little soil' within the chamber, it was not possible to associate the bead with a particular urn and, therefore, to establish whether it was a primary or secondary deposition (O'Neil 1952:23). Despite this uncertainty, O'Neil concluded that the tomb had been built around 1200BC. However, he drew attention to the fact that 'the making of Knackyboy Cairn is far removed in date from the period usually associated with the erection of chambered tombs in the British Isles', noting that Knackyboy is not a megalithic structure but has walls built of coursed small stones (O'Neil 1952:24-25).

More recent work on faience has established that it is likely that the faience beads found in Bronze Age contexts in the British Isles are not of Mediterranean manufacture. British beads have a higher tin content than those found elsewhere in the Near East and Europe and there is considerable variability in their composition, suggesting manufacture in small batches (Sheridan & Shortland 2004). Twenty-five radiocarbon dates relating to the use of faience in Britain and Ireland were collated by Sheridan and Shortland and these indicate a range between the 19th and mid 15th centuries cal BC. Two of the sites quoted are in the south-west of England: Trelowthas, Cornwall with a date of 1883-1631 cal BC (AA-29734; 3435±50 BP) and Shaugh Moor, Devon with a date of 1955-1510 cal BC (HAR-2220; 3430±90 BP).

The faience bead at Knackyboy was found, close to the base of Urn XVI, in the layer of charcoal, cremated bone and soil which surrounded the earlier urns. Two of the recently obtained radiocarbon dates are associated with it: one, from the cremation in Urn XVI, is 1500-1323 cal BC (OxA-26365; 3157±29 BP), the other, from bone in the layer of charcoal and soil between Urns VI and VII, is 1498-1310 cal BC (OxA-26366; 3145±29 BP). These dates compare well with each other but are somewhat later than the dates from Cornwall and Devon mentioned above and at the very end of the date range quoted by Sheridan and Shortland.

8.3 Dating from pottery

The use of pottery in the dating of Scillonian entrance graves has been complicated by two factors: the lack of mainland comparators for the majority of the ceramic material and the view that (now missing) Neolithic sherds had been found at Bant's Carn, St Mary's and North Hill E, Samson. This latter aspect has been discussed in chapter 5 and it was concluded there that the sherd generally attributed to Bant's Carn is, in fact, from the nearby settlement site at Halangy Porth and that there is no reason to believe that the North Hill sherd is Neolithic.

Sherds of pottery from Porth Hellick Down A, St Mary's have been identified as probably Trevisker Ware (H Quinnell, pers. comm.). In Cornwall, this is found throughout the second millennium BC (Jones & Quinnell 2011) and a radiocarbon date of 1612-1436 cal BC (GrA-22371; 3240±40 BP) was obtained from the Trevisker Urn found, in association with faience beads and other objects, at Amesbury, Wiltshire (Sheridan & Shortland 2004; Sheridan 2008). Apart from these sherds, there is no pottery, from either an entrance grave or a cist in Scilly, with obvious similarity to either mainland or continental wares.

Work in the islands has, therefore, concentrated on the examination of pottery from non-burial contexts, from which there are a few radiocarbon dates, and its comparison with the wares from entrance graves and cists. Much of this analysis has been carried out, in relation to the Bronze Age and Iron Age settlement on the island of Nornour in the Eastern Isles, by Robinson (2007). The site was excavated in the 1960s by Dudley (1968a) and subsequently, between 1969 and 1973, by Butcher (1978; 2000-2001). There are no radiocarbon dates and, unfortunately, no record of the stratigraphy from Dudley's work but Butcher produced a detailed study of the sequence of construction with five radiocarbon dates, four of which relate to the Bronze Age and Iron Age use of the site.

Two of the earlier radiocarbon dates from Nornour were obtained from combined charcoal samples, a practice commonly used in the past but now regarded as likely to produce unreliable dates (Ashmore 1999). A further one was taken from a sample which had been wet for several months and Clark raises the possibility that fungal growth might have occurred, thus making the sample appear too recent (Clark 1978). In addition, the earliest result (HAR-239; 3260±280 BP) has a very large margin of error, producing a calibrated date of 2287-848 cal BC and thus encompassing a wide range of possible datings.

Robinson's detailed work on the Nornour pottery, which comprises 4,522 sherds, built on Butcher's analysis and sought to link pottery fabrics and styles to the building sequence. Robinson identified four main fabric groups, three of local granitic origin and a fourth of non-local quartz fabric, only one sherd of which was found in the sample analysed. Only 10% of the sherds are diagnostic as to vessel type and Robinson followed Butcher's division of these into fourteen types from Bronze Age and Iron Age vessels.

Of particular relevance to the consideration of the dating of entrance graves and cists in Scilly is the discovery of pottery at Nornour with impressed decoration, similar to that found at entrance graves such as Knackyboy and Obadiah's Barrow. Robinson identified four sherds of comb-impressed and two of cord-impressed ware, all of which were found in the earliest phases of the settlement, in contexts associated with the construction or abandonment of houses, rather than their occupation. He argues that this suggests that 'their inclusion within the Nornour assemblage might have resulted from the unintentional incorporation of residual material from earlier occupation' or that they might have been intentional foundation deposits. He goes on to propose that they may have originally been associated with a 'previously unrecognised Late Neolithic/Early Bronze Age occupation at Nornour' (Robinson 2007:61-62). On this basis, and using evidence from Knackyboy Cairn which will be considered below, he puts forward a date of 3000 to 1800 cal BC for this impressed pottery.

Robinson also carried out an examination of the pottery sequence at Knackyboy and the results of this are shown in figure 8.1. He suggests that the earliest event in the construction of Knackyboy Cairn was the deposition (or accidental loss) of a flaked flint axe or adze on the ground surface under the cairn (event 1 in figure 8.1). This object is a very unusual discovery in Scilly and is, consequently, difficult to date. O'Neil, who found it, described it as 'not closely dateable [sic]' (1948-1949:94); both Thomas (1985) and, more recently, Johns (2011) have regarded it as being Neolithic. Robinson says that 'through analogy with other similar axes from the mainland [the axe] dates to between 4000-3000 cal BC.' (2007:55)

Following the construction of the chamber, the next event (number 3 in figure 8.1) in the history of Knackyboy was, Robinson proposes, 'a deposit of black soil, contain[ing] a number of coarse and gritty pottery sherds' (2007:54). He suggests that O'Neil's description of this pottery sets it

Event 9: A bucket shaped urn is placed as satellite burial within the cairn of the entrance grave.

Event 8: The chamber is intentionally sealed with rubble soil, and a single bucket shaped urn.

Event 7: The final layer within the monument's chamber comprised of a series of bucket shaped urns that through analogy with mainland Britain date to *c*1400-1100 cal BC.

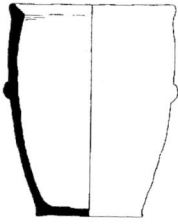

c.1400-1100 cal BC

Event 6: A series of plain and incised globular vessels placed directly on top of underlying layer

Event 5: A thick layer of ash and cremated bone placed directly on top of underlying layers. This layer was not found beneath the primary vessels. This layer contained metalwork and faience beads datable through analogy to c2200-1800 cal BC

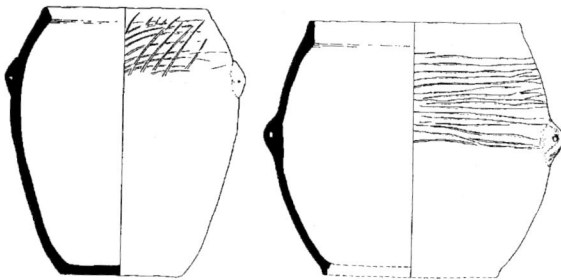

c.2200-1800 cal BC

Event 4: A series of comb impressed and cord impressed vessels placed directly upon paving within monument chamber

Event 3: Paving laid within the monument's chamber sealing underlying layers

Event 3: Deposit of black soil containing pottery sherds found within the monument's chamber

Event 2: Construction of Knackyboy Cairn

Event 1: Flaked flint axe placed on the ancient land surface prior to the construction of Knackyboy Cairn

c.3000 cal BC

10cm

FIGURE 8.1 CONSTRUCTIONAL AND DEPOSITIONAL SEQUENCE FOR KNACKYBOY CAIRN (ALL ARTEFACTS DRAWN TO SAME SCALE), FROM ROBINSON (2007:FIG 5.1)

apart from the urns found in the chamber and that it might be Hembury Ware. Robinson quotes, as his source for this, O'Neil's unpublished notebooks.

In the course of this study these notebooks have been examined in detail and all the notes relating to Knackyboy Cairn have been transcribed. No reference has been found to this pottery being coarse and gritty; instead O'Neil says:

> 'In this dark soil some fifty potsherds were found. All resemble in ware the earliest of the urns which were found in situ in the centre of the chamber.' (O'Neil 1948-1949:98)

In his published account of the excavation also he describes the sherds as 'of kinds which can be closely paralleled amongst the cinerary urns found in the tomb.' (O'Neil 1952:23) Robinson argues that his identification of this pottery as Hembury Ware is strengthened by finds of the same ware at Bant's Carn and North Hill E; this interpretation is referred to above and has been rejected.

Robinson goes on to say that the first burials in the chamber at Knackyboy, which were cremations in comb- and cord-impressed urns (event 4 in figure 8.1), took place between the deposition of the flint axe and the placing of the layer of ashes, containing bronze implements and the faience bead (event 5), around the urns. He dates the bronze and faience to 2200 to 1600 cal BC (although, in the diagram of the sequence, the range is shown as c2200-1800 cal BC) and, consequently, proposes a date of c3000-2000 cal BC for the pottery. The dates suggested by Robinson for the bronze and faience are somewhat earlier than those arrived at by Sheridan and Shortland in their examination of the dating of faience in the British Isles, outlined above.

Robinson accepts that the dating he proposes for impressed pottery in Scilly is earlier than previous interpretations. He supports his argument for this dating with the radiocarbon date from the settlement site at Little Bay, St Martin's. Here, charcoal from a hearth, which sealed a pit containing impressed ware, provided a date of 2127-1535 cal BC (HAR-4324; 3490±100 BP) (Neal 1983). Robinson uses the earliest part of the wide range of dates provided by this determination to support his argument for the dating of impressed ware.

The stratigraphically later urns in the chamber at Knackyboy are described by Robinson as 'globular' and 'bucket-shaped' (events 6, 7 and 8 in figure 8.1) and he believes that they are comparable with the Deverel-Rimbury series in southern Britain and can, therefore, be dated to c1600 to 1200 cal BC (although the dates c1400-1100 cal BC are shown in the diagram) (Robinson 2007:55). This relationship with Deverel-Rimbury is supported by Johns (2011) although Quinnell cautions that it still has to be clarified (Quinnell forthcoming).

From this analysis, Robinson goes on to develop a chronology for Scillonian prehistory. In respect of the entrance graves, he suggests that, although an Earlier Neolithic origin is possible (on the basis of the supposed Hembury ware), it is more likely that the majority date to the Late Neolithic and that some, including Knackyboy, continued in use until c1200 cal BC. As far as cists are concerned, he notes the lack of datable evidence in Scilly and relies on analogies with Cornwall, quoting the example of Watch Hill, St Stephen-in-Brannel which provided a radiocarbon date of 1964-1620 cal BC (HAR-654; 3470±70 BP). Jones's recent re-evaluation of this site, with further AMS radiocarbon dates being obtained, has confirmed the use of the monument between c2000 cal BC and the 17th century cal BC, with the burial dating to 2016-1700 cal BC (WK12940; 3532±48 BP) (Jones 2005:34-36).

Robinson suggests that entrance graves are likely to be earlier than cists (and cairns) in Scilly, mainly on the basis of the transition from communal to single burial seen in the British Late Neolithic. He accepts, however, that 'this transition is blurred on the islands by the continued use of at least some entrance graves into the second millennium BC' (Robinson 2007:67).

There are a number of uncertainties in Robinson's argument that the impressed pottery found in Scillonian entrance graves dates to 2200 to 1800 cal BC, one being the dating of the flint axe found under the cairn at Knackyboy. Even if this artefact does date to the period 4000-3000 cal BC, which itself is unproven, the date of deposition is unknown. The object may have been an heirloom, which was curated for some time before being placed as a foundation deposit. The scarcity of large flint objects in Scilly makes it impossible to draw any parallels.

Further, as has been argued above, the identification of the sherds below the paving at Knackyboy as Hembury Ware is probably mistaken. Whilst Hembury Ware has been found at Neolithic sites in Scilly such as East Porth, Samson (Johns 2011), there is no reliable evidence for it occurring in entrance graves. In addition, it is suggested that Robinson's arguments for the dating of the impressed pottery at Nornour are unconvincing, given the lack of precision of the radiocarbon dates from the site and the need to rely upon 'previously unrecognised … occupation' to explain his proposed Late Neolithic date for it.

Robinson's analysis, however, demonstrates the contemporaneity of impressed ware with the early use of Knackyboy Cairn, which, coupled with the radiocarbon date from Little Bay, suggests a date in the first half of the second millennium cal BC. The lack of precise dating for the deposition of the flint axe (and, indeed, its manufacture) and the large margin of error around the earliest Nornour radiocarbon date mean that these elements do not provide any further refinement of this date range.

8.4 Radiocarbon dates from Scillonian burial and settlement sites

During the course of this research, human bone samples from Knackyboy Cairn and Obadiah's Barrow entrance graves and the cist at Old Town were submitted for AMS radiocarbon dating. A total of eleven samples from Knackyboy and one each from Obadiah's Barrow and Old Town cist were obtained and were dated by the Oxford Radiocarbon Accelerator Dating Service (ORADS).

The bone from Knackyboy Cairn, St Martin's was excavated in 1948 by O'Neil and the excavation archive was deposited at the Royal Cornwall Museum, Truro in 1950 (accession number 1950,40). In many cases, the original notes about provenance, in O'Neil's handwriting, remain with the bone samples. There is a complex sequence at Knackyboy, which had been subject to considerable disturbance before O'Neil's excavation.

Samples 1, 3 and 4 are from urns placed on the paving slabs in the base of the chamber, these form the primary (or earliest surviving) deposition in the chamber. Samples 2 and 5 are from the layer of charcoal, bone and soil around these urns; whilst this layer is depositionally later than the urns, the origin of this material is unknown. O'Neil suggested that it 'looked like a secondary filling of material taken from old cremations and put in to level up the area'

(1948-1949:11). If this is the case, the human remains in it may pre-date those in the urns.

Sample 7 is from a secondary deposition, on top of the layer of charcoal, etc. mentioned above, and sample 8 is from the last urn to be deposited inside the chamber, found just inside the entrance. Samples 9 and 11 are associated with a satellite burial in the mound surrounding the chamber and sample 10 is from a nearby, but later, burial in the mound. These must have been deposited after the construction of the chamber and mound had been completed but there is no stratigraphic evidence to indicate their relationship with the burials in the chamber.

Sample 13 is from a single burial in a cist, found and destroyed during building in Old Town, St Mary's in 1964. The bone and associated pottery were deposited in the Isles of Scilly Museum (accession number RN904) and were examined by Thomas in 1965. He identified the site as being a cist 'of normal Scillonian type' and the pottery sherds as being from a biconical urn, of which only the lower part survived (Thomas 1965). Sample 12, from which, unfortunately, it was not possible to obtain a date, was from the only intact urn in Obadiah's Barrow, Gugh, excavated by Bonsor in 1901.

The results from Knackyboy and Old Town are shown in table 8.1. All but one of the samples were cremated bone,

Ref No	Sample No	Location	Material	Event (Robinson, 2007)	Activity	Associated artefacts	Date (BP)	Calibrated date (cal BC)
Knackyboy Cairn entrance grave								
OxA-26474	1	Urn III	Charred bone	4	Primary use of chamber	Impressed ware	3837±38	2459-2154
OxA-26363	2	Centre of chamber near Urn VI	Cremated bone	4	Primary use of chamber		3319±29	1683-1520
OxA-26364	3	Urn VI	Cremated bone	4	Primary use of chamber	Impressed ware	3365±28	1743-1564
OxA-26365	4	Urn XVI	Cremated bone	4	Primary use of chamber	Impressed ware, glass bead	3157±29	1500-1323
OxA-26366	5	Layer of ash between Urns VI and VII	Cremated bone	5	Primary use of chamber	Bronze, faience and glass beads	3145±29	1498-1310
OxA-26368	7	Urn XV	Cremated bone	7	Secondary use of chamber	Incomplete urn	3215±28	1596-1425
OxA-26369	8	Urn XIV	Cremated bone	8	Final use of chamber	Undecorated ware	3066±28	1412-1260
OxA-26370	9	Under Urn XVII	Cremated bone	9	Satellite burial in mound, first phase	Incomplete urn	3276±29	1626-1466
OxA-26371	10	Under Urn XVIII	Cremated bone	9	Satellite burial in mound, second phase		3146±29	1498-1311
OxA-26372	11	Urn XVII	Cremated bone	9	Satellite burial in mound, first phase	Incomplete urn	3386±29	1747-1621
Old Town cist								
OxA-26373	13	Urn	Cremated bone	n/a	Single burial	Incomplete urn	3492±28	1893-1702

TABLE 8.1 RADIOCARBON DATES FROM KNACKYBOY CAIRN ENTRANCE GRAVE AND OLD TOWN CIST

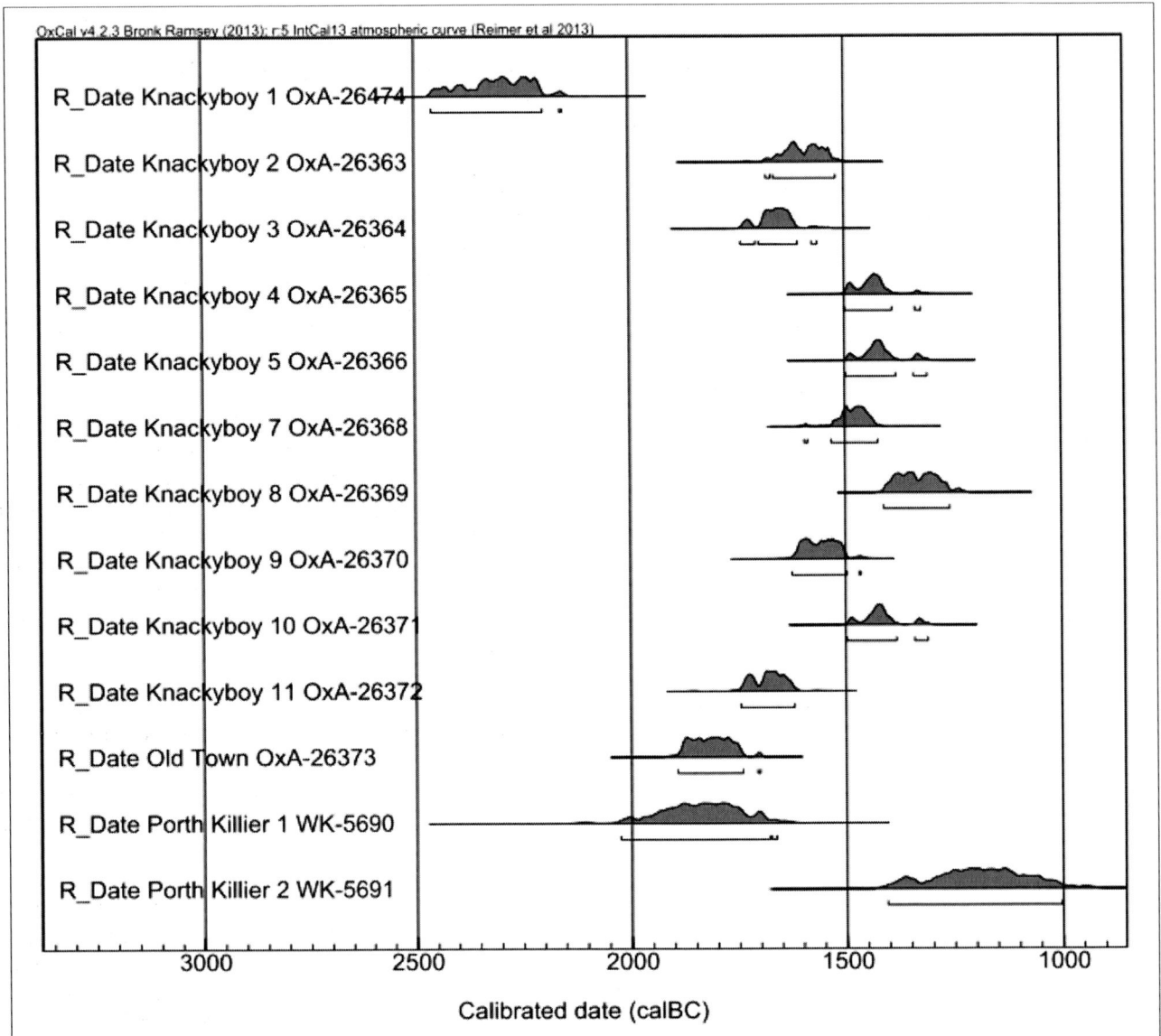

Figure 8.2 Calibrated radiocarbon dates from Porth Killier and Old Town cists and Knackyboy Cairn entrance grave

the exception, sample 1 (OxA-26474) was charred bone. ORADS have indicated that the dating of burnt bone can be problematic because of the difficulty of assessing the accuracy of a determination, although the high carbon content of this sample was a positive. However the result, which is somewhat earlier than the other dates obtained, needs to be treated with some caution. These dates and the two from Porth Killier cist are also shown graphically in figure 8.2.

This illustrates that the date from the Old Town cist is earlier than all but sample 1 from Knackyboy and, with the earlier of the two radiocarbon dates from the cist at Porth Killier, suggests that the use of these structures may have slightly pre-dated that of the entrance graves, although overlapping with them. The Porth Killier dates are 2026-1665 cal BC (WK-5690; 3512±70 BP) from the base of the cist infill and 1406-1004 cal BC (WK-5691; 2973±73 BP) from higher up in the infill (Ratcliffe et al. forthcoming).

The interpretation of this site is not straightforward as there is probable Neolithic pottery in the infill also (Quinnell forthcoming).

Two of the radiocarbon dates obtained for the use of impressed ware at Knackyboy (samples 3 and 4) are substantially later than those proposed by Robinson (2007). There are no samples available to date the urns with incised decoration of Robinson's event 6 (in figure 8.1) but the chronology for the final use of the chamber, associated with bucket-shaped urns, accords well with his model. The satellite burials appear to be broadly contemporary with the use of the chamber, rather than later.

As there are only seven determinations in total from the chamber at Knackyboy and only one date each for two of the phases, there are insufficient dates for satisfactory Bayesian modelling. However, it is possible to identify three phases within the dates obtained from the chamber:

a primary use (samples 1 to 5), a secondary use (sample 7) and a final use (sample 8).

These phases are based on the information recorded by O'Neil during his excavation of the site in 1948 (O'Neil 1948-1949; 1952). As set out above, samples 1, 3 and 4 are from cremated remains found inside urns (numbers III, VI and XVI) placed on the floor at the distal end of the chamber. All three urns are of impressed ware and are very similar in shape and size.

Samples 2 and 5 come from the material (charcoal, bone and soil) surrounding these urns. From the information available there is uncertainty about the origin of this material and thus its chronological relationship with the urns. It is likely that there are two separate phases represented by samples 1 to 5 but it is not currently possible to distinguish them with certainty.

The secondary phase is based on sample 7, which is from urn XV, found on top of the layer of charcoal, bone and soil. Only the base of this urn survives so it is not possible to establish its type. Stratigraphically, however, it is later than the primary phase. The final phase is represented by sample 8 from urn XIV, an undecorated vessel which had been placed in the centre of the threshold of the chamber. O'Neil's notes confirm that this was the final deposition in the chamber as the blocking of the entrance was intact when the chamber was excavated (O'Neil 1948-1949:123).

However, the possibility cannot be ruled out that the construction of Knackyboy took place well before the 18th century cal BC and that earlier, perhaps inhumation, burials were removed before the impressed urns and their cremation burials were deposited there. Sample 1 may relate to an earlier burial which had been replaced in the chamber following its re-dedication, as suggested by O'Neil (1948-1949). Against this, it can be argued that there is little evidence for permanent settlement in Scilly before c2000 cal BC (Johns 2011) and that, given their homogeneity, the entrance graves in the islands are likely to have been constructed by a resident population.

There is a small number of radiocarbon dates from early settlement sites in Scilly; these include Little Bay, St Martin's, which yielded dates of 2127-1535 cal BC (HAR-4324; 3490±100 BP) and 1742-1133 cal BC (HAR-1715; 3190±110 BP) (Neal 1983) and Porthcressa, St Mary's with dates of 1634-1426 cal BC (GU-5413; 3250±50 BP) and 1603-1284 cal BC (OxA-4701; 3165±55 BP) (Ratcliffe & Straker 1996). At Porth Killier, St Agnes and Dolphin Town, Tresco there are cists which appear to pre-date the settlements. The date from charred seeds in the base of a midden in a house at Porth Killier was 1611-1282 cal BC (OxA-3648; 3170±65 BP) (Ratcliffe & Straker 1996) and at Dolphin Town a date of 1416-1133 cal BC (Wk-19092; 3045±42 BP) was obtained from residue in a potsherd found in one of the houses (Taylor & Johns 2009-10).

8.5 Conclusions

The evidence from some of the artefacts found in Scillonian entrance graves, particularly small bronze objects and a faience bead, pointed to a use of these structures during the second millennium BC. This has been borne out by the results of radiocarbon dating of bone samples from Knackyboy Cairn, which indicate that the chamber and mound were used for burials within a maximum date range of between c1750 and 1250 cal BC. Interestingly, the satellite burials in the mound, which had been regarded as a secondary use of the site (O'Neil 1948-1949; Robinson 2007) are contemporary with those in the chamber.

It is unfortunate that the dating of sample 1 from Knackyboy (OxA-26474) is less certain, due to the fact that the bone was charred rather than cremated, as it is up to 700 years earlier than the earliest other determination. If the date is reliable, it is possible that the bone was re-interred following a re-dedication of the site. There are records of inhumed bone being found at Bant's Carn and Obadiah's Barrow, as well as Knackyboy Cairn but, unfortunately, it has not been possible to trace any of these remains during the course of this research.

The possibility exists, therefore, that at least some of the Scillonian entrance graves have their origins in the mid third millennium BC when they were used for inhumation burials. The use of Knackyboy for cremation burials appears to have started soon after c1750BC and continued for some 400 to 500 years.

The earliest use of the cists appears to be slightly before that of the entrance graves: the date from Old Town and the earlier one from Porth Killier both pre-date all but sample 1 from Knackyboy by at least 200 years. This reflects the situation in Cornwall where the dates from the

Watch Hill cist are slightly earlier than those from the Bosiliack entrance grave, as will be outlined in the following chapter. The date from the Tregiffian entrance grave, which is from charcoal rather than bone, is however more comparable to Watch Hill.

The conclusions outlined above, in relation to the radiocarbon dates, are based on a very small number of dates from only three sites in Scilly and so extreme caution must be exercised. However, a consistent picture, of a period of use of Scillonian entrance graves and cists for cremation burials starting in the early second millennium BC and continuing for up to 700 years, is provided by radiocarbon dates obtained from both burial and settlement sites in Scilly and by the dates associated with artefacts such as faience beads from mainland sites.

Chapter 9

Comparisons with chambered cairns and cists elsewhere in the British Isles and in Brittany

9.1 Introduction

This chapter will consider the comparisons which have been made between Scillonian entrance graves and cists and similar sites elsewhere in Britain, Ireland and Brittany and will review what kind of connections these similarities might indicate.

Terminology

The history of the terminology used to describe the entrance graves and cists of Scilly has already been considered in chapter 1. Before examining comparable structures elsewhere, it is necessary to clarify the terms used to describe megalithic chambers and cists over a wider area. This is a subject on which a great deal has been written, particularly in an attempt to determine the typological relationships of different forms.

Chambered cairns have typically been divided into three main forms: the portal dolmen, the passage grave and the gallery grave, the last of these is now generally referred to as the chambered long mound (e.g. Daniel 1970; Bradley 2007; Scarre 2007). Portal dolmens have a single chamber constructed of three or more massive upright stones, roofed with a huge capstone; they do not usually have covering mounds. Passage graves have a narrower passage leading to a circular or rectangular chamber and are covered by round mounds; chambered long mounds have rectangular chambers of the same width throughout and, as the name suggests, are covered by long mounds.

These categories have been further sub-divided into regional types, often using local terms such as *dolmen*, *quoit*, *anta* and *allée couverte*. The proliferation of names led Giot (quoted in Daniel 1969) and then Daniel himself (1970) to call for a simplification of the terminology employed. Daniel outlined the following division:

> 'Apart from regional varieties, there are in western Europe three main varieties of megalithic tomb: the single chamber (polygonal, rectangular, or rectangular with a portal), the chamber-and-passage, and the long tomb.' (Daniel 1970:267)

In practice, however, the situation is not so straightforward; the apparently separate categories of passage grave and chambered long mound form a continuum, with sites such as the Scillonian entrance graves having round mounds but, in the majority of cases, no difference in width or height throughout the rectangular chamber. In these cases a separate passage cannot be distinguished. Such structures are sometimes described as undifferentiated or V-shaped passage graves (Daniel 1963). Some authors (e.g. Lynch 2004) treat them as a distinct group.

These differences in interpretation have been summarised by MacWhite (1956, quoted in Daniel 1963) who said that 'megalithic tombs …have been the subjects of complicated typologies in which it is difficult to distinguish between differentiations which are observer-imposed and those which are real or inherent in the material itself'.

The term 'cist' has been subject to less scrutiny as the structures show less variability in form. The definition from the National Monuments Record Monument Type Thesaurus is:

> 'Generally rectangular structure normally used for burial purposes, and formed from stone slabs set on edge, and covered by one or more horizontal slabs or capstones. Cists may be built on the surface or sunk into the ground.' (English Heritage nd)

However, structures similar in size and structure to entrance graves, but with a closed chamber, are also referred to as cists (O'Neil 1954; Weatherhill 1981).

In the review below, the term 'entrance grave' is used to describe megalithic structures where there is no distinction between the passage and the chamber, the term 'cist' to describe the slab-built stone boxes. The description 'megalithic cist' is applied to structures which are generally similar to entrance graves but which have a closed chamber.

Areas considered

In geographical terms the closest area to Scilly is Cornwall and a small group of entrance graves there has been regarded as being of the same type as the Scillonian examples (Barnatt 1982; Mercer 1986; Rowe 2005) although Ashbee describes the Cornish (and other) examples as only 'approximating' to the Scillonian ones (1974:74).

Comparisons have also been drawn with five graves in the Tramore area of County Waterford, Ireland (Powell 1941b), with the Bargrennan White Cairn in south-west Scotland (Piggott & Powell 1948-49) and, more generally, with sites in the Channel Isles and Brittany (e.g. Mercer 1986). Scillonian cists also have comparanda in other parts of the British Isles, in particular, a link has been made with Scotland (Piggott 1941). Each of these will be considered in turn.

Comparisons, not of the morphology of the tombs but of the density of their distribution, will be made with other island groups, notably the Molène archipelago in Brittany and the Channel Islands. Finally, the significance of these similarities will be considered.

9.2 Penwith

Penwith, the most south-westerly part of Cornwall, is the nearest landmass to Scilly, lying 45km to the east-north-east of the islands, so it is not surprising to find similar structures there. Unlike Tramore, considered in the next section, where a group of five sites has consistently been considered to be similar to those in Scilly, different authors have drawn comparisons with a variety of Cornish sites. This is largely because there has been much more analysis of them by a greater number of researchers but also because there appears to be much greater structural variation in Penwith than in Tramore.

The Cornwall Historic Environment Record (HER) lists fourteen entrance graves: Ballowall (also known as Carn Gluze), St Just parish *(PRN 29786)*, Bosavern Ros, St Just parish *(PRN 29799.01)*, Bosiliack, Madron parish *(PRN 30467)*, Brane, Sancreed parish *(PRN 28666)*, Chapel Carn Brea, St Just parish *(PRN 16073.03)*, Mayon Cliff, Sennen parish *(PRN 16006)*, Pennance, Zennor parish *(PRN 4200)*, Pordenack, Sennen parish *(PRN 28411.10)*, Rosemergy, Morvah parish *(PRN 30677)*, Tol Creeg, Madron parish *(PRN 31503)*, two structures at Treen, Zennor parish *(PRNs 30726.10 and 30726.30)*, Tregeseal, St Just parish *(PRN 29757)* and Tregiffian, St Buryan parish *(PRN 28192)*. The locations of these sites reveal a mainly coastal distribution and, with the exception of Treen, one of individual sites.

The majority of authors (e.g. Hencken 1932; Barnatt 1982) include most or all of these sites in their list of Cornish entrance graves but Daniel listed only four: Brane, Pennance and the two at Treen. He regarded Tregiffian as 'two small cists juxtaposed' (Daniel 1950:59) and treated Ballowall, Bosavern Ros, Chapel Carn Brea and Tregeseal as 'doubtful' (1950:240), whilst stating elsewhere that they 'may trace part of their ancestry to this [Scilly] group' (1950:61,fn3).

Mercer, however, believes that twelve sites can be attributed to the group: of those included in the Cornwall HER, he omits Ballowall (which he classifies as a 'chambered tomb'), Mayon Cliff and Pordenack but

adds Trendrine Hill, Zennor parish *(PRN 31257)* (Mercer 1986). Weatherhill (1981) divides the sites in Penwith into two categories: Penwith chamber tombs (described by other authors as portal dolmens or quoits) and Scillonian chamber tombs. In the latter group he includes Ballowall, Brane, Chapel Carn Brea, Pennance, Treen, Tregeseal, Tregiffian and Tregiffian Vean, St Just parish *(PRN 28469)*.

In discussing entrance graves Barnatt states that 'clear traces of only six chambers survive', although he illustrates seven: Ballowall, Brane, Pennance, two at Treen, Tregeseal and Tregiffian (1982:48-9). In his catalogue of destroyed chambered tombs he includes Bosavern Ros, Chapel Carn Brea, Tol Creeg, Treworrian, St Buryan parish *(PRN 28805)* and Truthwall Common, St Just parish *(PRN 16127)*, (the last two being listed simply as barrows in the HER) but states that Tregiffian Vean and Trewavas Head, Breage parish *(PRN 29250)* are mistaken interpretations. Trewavas Head, which is well to the east of all the other sites considered in this section and now falls in Kerrier district rather than Penwith, is mentioned by Daniel in his list of doubtful sites and is described by him as 'either a large cist or (more probably) a ruined entrance grave of Scilly type' (1950:240). It too is described in the HER as a barrow.

It is clear from this brief survey that there is considerable uncertainty about the classification of a number of these sites. This is partly due to the fact that many structures have been subject to severe damage, often through the excavations of William Copeland Borlase in the late 19th century, and some have been completely destroyed. In Penwith, though not in Scilly, entrance graves sometimes occur as one element in a composite monument and this further complicates the picture.

For example, at Ballowall there is a central domed structure which contains cists and a pit, surrounded by an outer cairn which also contains cists. An entrance grave is built into the exterior of the outer cairn. The site was excavated by W C Borlase in 1878; he then built a new retaining wall which has changed the appearance of the cairn significantly, making it very difficult to interpret the sequence of construction. It is possible that the entrance grave formed the first phase and that its mound was later incorporated into the larger monument. Alternatively, it may be the latest feature, being built into the perimeter of an existing cairn (Barnatt 1982).

At Chapel Carn Brea, Borlase found a cairn with three concentric walls, the innermost of which contained a drystone-walled chamber (apparently of an entrance grave) partly sunk in a pit. A stone-lined cist was found nearby and there was another cist higher in the cairn. Subsequently a mediaeval chapel and a Second World War shelter and observation post have been built on the cairn. Again, the damage to the site and the lack of recent excavation make interpretation very difficult.

There has been only one recent excavation of a Penwith entrance grave, that of Bosiliack in 1984 by Thomas

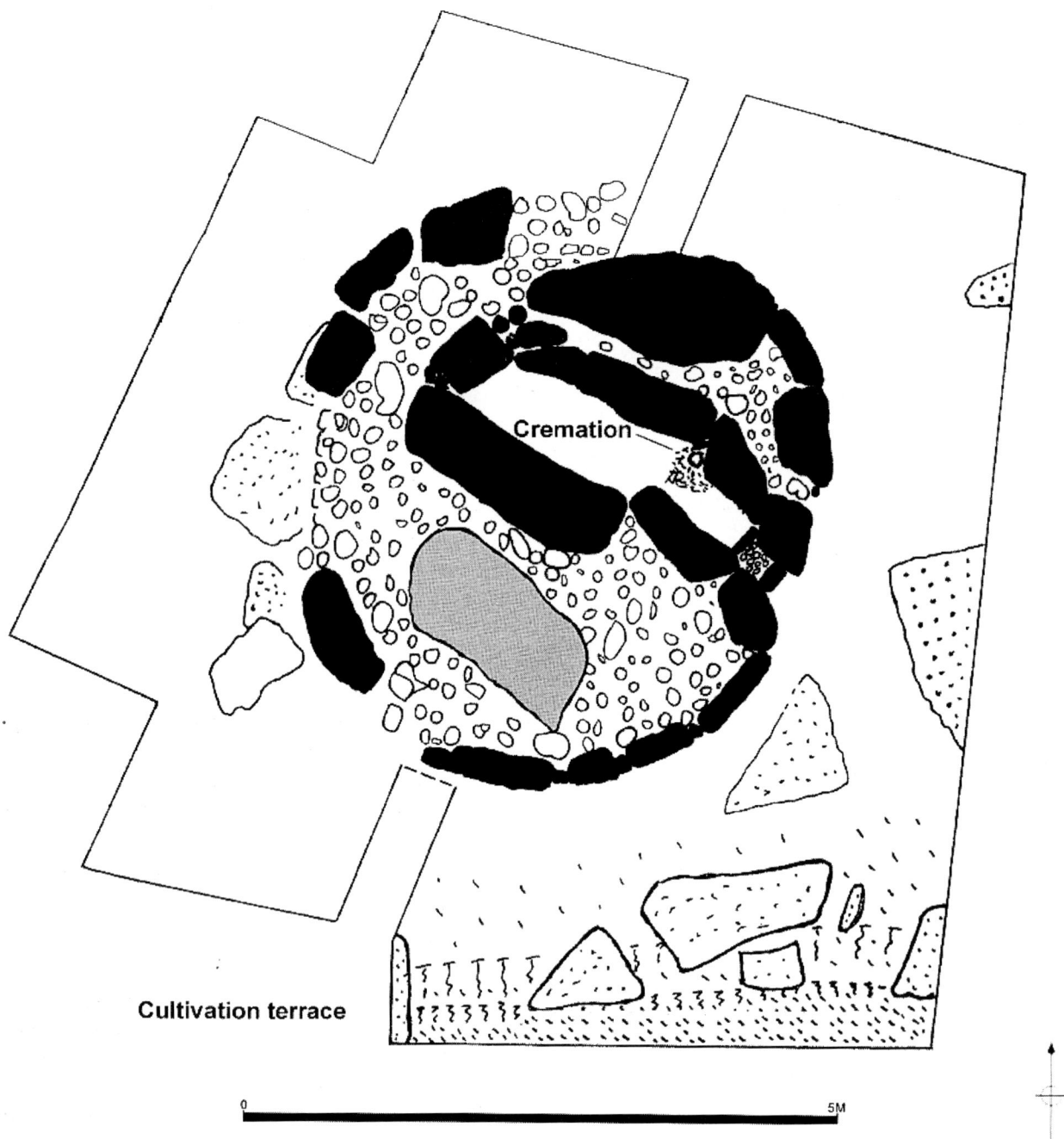

FIGURE 9.1 PLAN OF BOSILIACK , FROM JONES AND THOMAS (2010:FIG 2) (DARK SHADING INDICATES IN SITU CHAMBER AND KERBSTONES, DISPLACED CAPSTONE SHADED GREY, IN SITU BOULDERS STIPPLED)

(Thomas 1984; Jones & Thomas 2010). This site is described as consisting of a chamber, measuring about 3m in length but only 0.6m wide, with an even narrower, slightly offset, entrance. It is built of large orthostatic granite slabs and is oriented SE-NW with the entrance to the SE. No capstones survive *in situ* but one lies on the top of the cairn, which measures about 5m in diameter and is surrounded by a kerb of granite slabs of up to 1m in height.

Cremated human bone, believed to be from a single individual, was found in the chamber together with charcoal, pebbles and sherds from three plain vessels. Calibrated radiocarbon dates of 1686-1511 cal BC (SUERC-15589; 3320±35BP) and 1665-1502 cal BC

(SUERC-15590; 3305±35BP) have been obtained from the bone (Jones & Thomas 2010:275).

The plan of the structure is shown in figure 9.1 and the site is illustrated in figure 9.2.

Although Jones and Thomas describe only a chamber at this site, it will be noted from the plan that there is a differentiation between chamber and passage, with the passage being narrower and having a different orientation to the chamber. Indeed they refer to 'the short 1.2m length at the south-eastern entrance end' as being particularly narrow and as being 'slightly off-set to the south-east of the main body of the chamber.' (Jones & Thomas 2010:273)

FIGURE 9.2 BOSILIACK, SHOWING ENTRANCE TO CHAMBER
AND KERB AROUND CAIRN

Bosiliack shows only limited features in common with typical Scillonian entrance graves: the shape and dimensions of the chamber, the sizes of the cairn and of its surrounding kerbstones are all hard to parallel in Scilly. In a Scillonian context, these aspects can be most closely matched at two atypical structures. Middle Arthur B, the plan of which is shown in figure 9.3, was excavated by O'Neil, who regarded it as a cist rather than an entrance grave (O'Neil 1954); indeed, prior to its excavation, Bosiliack was identified as a cist by Russell (1971). North Hill L, excavated by Bonsor in 1902 and regarded by him as a hut, also has a small chamber and massive kerb (Bonsor 1901-1902).

Mayon Cliff, a much more damaged site but one showing considerable similarities with Bosiliack, has also been regarded by some authors as a cist (Russell 1971; Weatherhill 1981). In all these cases, the definition of 'cist' appears to be that of the 'megalithic cist', outlined above; sites such as Bosiliack, Mayon Cliff and Middle Arthur B are very different from the typical underground, rectangular, slab-built Scillonian cists described in chapter 4.

At two Cornish sites, underground, slab-built cists or slab-covered pits have been found inside or close to the chamber of an entrance grave. At Tregiffian, the barrow was badly damaged by road-builders in the 1840s and was then opened by W C Borlase in 1868. He found the remains of a kerb and a chamber with a small, slab-covered pit at its southern end. This pit was lined with shell sand and contained bone and ashes, pebbles and flint (Borlase 1872). Although the 'cist' and tumulus at Tregiffian were identified and described before 1916 (Henderson 1917), the site is referred to by Hencken (1932) only in his inventory and is not mentioned at all by Daniel (1950).

Tregiffian was next examined by Dudley in the 1960s but not fully published. In a note she recorded a megalithic passage (which is oriented roughly S-N at 192.5°) surrounded by a setting of large granite slabs about 1m high. The stones blocking the entrance, one of which is cup-marked, had been displaced by Borlase. Below the chamber floor she found two further pits, an oval one with charcoal, stone and cremated bone and a round one with an undamaged urn containing a cremation (Dudley 1968b).

Further work, carried out by ApSimon in 1972, established that the existing polygonal kerb is a reconstruction of an original circular kerb and that the chamber was blocked when the kerb was remodelled (ApSimon 1972). If this is the case, it appears to be a conversion from an entrance grave to a megalithic cist, a process which may have occurred at other sites. The charcoal found by Dudley provided the only other radiocarbon date so far obtained from a Cornish entrance grave and this is calibrated to 1958-1660 cal BC (BM-935; 3489±59BP) (Jones & Thomas 2010:275).

At Tregeseal, which was excavated by W C Borlase in 1879, part of a chamber survives with two capstones in place. The chamber is oriented NW-SE but it is not clear at which end the entrance was, as the structure is now in the centre of a low oval mound and, when examined in 2010, was very overgrown. A cist, which contained a Trevisker urn with a cremation, was recorded at the NW end of the chamber. The plan of the site is shown at figure 9.4.

Barnatt (1982) regards Tregeseal as being a two-phase monument, like Tregiffian, and argues that the cist belongs to the second phase when the mound was also enlarged,

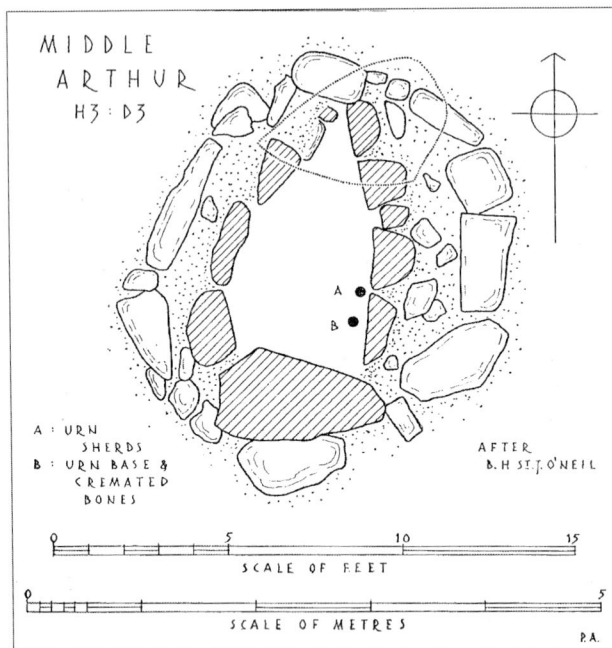

FIGURE 9.3 PLAN OF MIDDLE ARTHUR B,
FROM ASHBEE (1974:FIG 15)

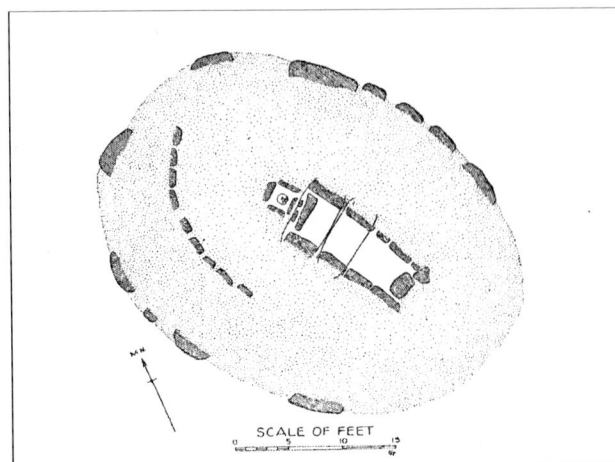

FIGURE 9.4 PLAN OF TREGESEAL, SHOWING CIST AT NW END, FROM HENCKEN
(1932:FIG 14)

thus blocking the entrance to the chamber. However, Quinnell says 'it does seem clear that the cist shared part of the roof of the entrance grave' and therefore treats it as contemporary with the rest of the structure (Quinnell 2010:282). Both Tregiffian and Tregeseal may therefore represent further examples of composite monuments like Ballowall and Chapel Carn Brea.

Of the four Cornish sites identified by Daniel (1950) as being entrance graves, three, Brane, Pennance and Treen South, are well-preserved but have no recorded excavation and no finds and one, Treen North, is in a damaged state and again has no recorded excavation or finds. It is therefore not possible to compare the material culture or the burial rite with those known from Scilly.

The site at Brane shows some features in common with a miniature Scillonian entrance grave, but this may be due to the removal of stones at one end of the chamber. In dimensions it is much more similar to a megalithic cist and its location on agricultural land in a valley bottom is not typical of entrance graves in Scilly.

In the HER it is recorded under two numbers: PRN 28666 being an entrance grave and PRN 28666.10 a cist. The 19th century accounts of it describe it as a cist in a barrow (e.g. Borlase 1872). It appears that part of the mound has subsequently been removed to expose the chamber. The site has, apparently been the subject of a recent, unrecorded restoration as the HER entry for 1990 says that there had been 'extensive erosion' resulting in a 'tumble of earth and stones' (HES 1987-2005). When visited in February 2010 it was in good condition. The site is illustrated in figure 9.5. Its similarities to both Bosiliack and Middle Arthur B are obvious.

The plan of the site at Brane shows the narrowing of the chamber towards the entrance, as seen at Bosiliack. It is now impossible to tell whether Brane had an entrance, like Bosiliack, or whether the chamber was closed, as at Middle Arthur. When considering sites such as these, it is apparent that there is a continuum between entrance graves and megalithic cists.

As well as differences in the structure of the chamber and cairn between Scilly and Penwith, the Cornish sites are also distinct in the fact that, with the exception of the two structures at Treen (where there are also two other, possibly chambered, barrows), they occur singly, whereas the vast majority of Scillonian sites occur in groups of two to more than a dozen. The southern entrance grave at Treen (the better preserved of the two) shows the greatest similarity with the sites in Scilly, being of typical dimensions and mode of construction. The chamber is oriented NNW-SSE (to 335°) with the entrance at the northern end. The illustrations in figure 9.6 show the significant differences between this site and Bosiliack.

Treen North, of which only 0.9m of the distal end of the chamber survives, is unlike Scillonian entrance graves in that it is built entirely of drystone walling. All the sites in Scilly have one or two large slabs forming the distal end. Pennance, which is also in a low-lying situation on agricultural land, is more similar in size to a typical Scillonian entrance grave but again has a massive kerb like Bosiliack and Brane.

The majority of the Penwith entrance graves show differences of detail from the Scillonian examples. Tol Creeg was destroyed in 1963, just before which it was the subject of a hasty rescue excavation. There had already been significant

FIGURE 9.5 BRANE, SHOWING ENTRANCE TO CHAMBER AND
KERB AROUND CAIRN

damage and, although an empty cist was found in the upper part of the barrow, little of the primary chamber remained. A plan of the site, originally drawn in 1870, shows that the chamber extends only about half way across the barrow, again an atypical feature for a Scillonian entrance grave.

The Penwith sites are located in a variety of landscape settings. Chapel Carn Brea is on a prominent hilltop and Bosiliack is on the upper part of a hillslope in open moorland whilst Ballowall and Mayon Cliff are on coastal cliff tops. Tregeseal and the two sites at Treen are on slopes at the edge of moorland but Pennance, Tregiffian and Brane are all on agricultural land. This contrasts with the strong preference for hilltops and the upper part of hillslopes for the construction of entrance graves in Scilly.

Finds have been made at only six of the Penwith sites: Ballowall, Bosiliack, Chapel Carn Brea, Tol Creeg, Tregeseal and Tregiffian. All the sites except Bosiliack and Tol Creeg were excavated by W C Borlase in the 1860s and 1870s and Tregiffian has been subsequently examined by Dudley and by ApSimon, as described above. At all these sites, pottery has been discovered, with cremated human remains also being found at all except Tol Creeg.

Quinnell, in discussing the pottery from Bosiliack, describes the shape of it as 'very much that which occurs in entrance graves on the Isles of Scilly … but lack[ing] the distinctive decoration found in the Isles' (Quinnell 2010:279). She stresses, however, that the pottery forms at the other Cornish entrance graves show considerable variation and none match Bosiliack closely. For example, Trevisker Ware was found at both Ballowall and Tregeseal and a Collared Urn/Enlarged Food Vessel at Tregiffian. Other finds include beach pebbles, flints and whetstones.

Although several authors (e.g. Barnatt 1982; Jones & Thomas 2010) suggest that the Penwith entrance graves form a homogenous group with clear similarities to the structures in Scilly, it is argued that the position is more complex. The Penwith sites fall into at least three

FIGURE 9.6 EXTERIOR AND INTERIOR OF TREEN SOUTH

categories: the first being 'megalithic cists', small, closed or almost closed structures of large orthostatic stones, such as Bosiliack, Brane and Mayon Cliff and the second being those where an entrance grave forms part of a composite structure, as at Ballowall and Chapel Carn Brea, and where identifying its position in the sequence of construction is now impossible. Only the third category, which includes sites such as Pennance, Treen North and South, Tregeseal and Tregiffian, show significant similarities to the majority of Scillonian entrance graves and, of these, only Treen South would not look out of place in Scilly.

As outlined above, there are currently only three radiocarbon dates from entrance graves in Penwith, two of which are from cremated bone from the probably single burial found at Bosiliack and one from charcoal associated with the Collared Urn/Enlarged Food Vessel at Tregiffian (Jones & Thomas 2010:284). The Bosiliack dates compare well with the earlier Knackyboy dates, although, as mentioned above, the form of the structure at Bosiliack is very different from the usual Scillonian entrance grave. However, the Tregiffian date is slightly earlier.

As Jones and Thomas point out, the radiocarbon determinations from Bosiliack and Tregiffian cannot be used to date the construction of those sites. However, they state that there is no evidence of reworking at Bosiliack and conclude that it was likely to have been used for a short period of time. Their assessment of the artefacts from other Penwith entrance graves leads them to conclude that they are likely to be Early Bronze Age in date and they reach a similar conclusion in relation to the Scillonian sites. This has been borne out by the radiocarbon dates subsequently obtained from Knackyboy.

9.3 Tramore

Tramore, a coastal area of County Waterford in south-east Ireland, is about 225km to the north-north-west of Scilly across the Celtic Sea and St George's Channel. The link between Scilly and Tramore was first proposed by Powell (1941b). He identified five sites in this area – named by him as Harristown, Carriglong, Munmahagoe, Matthewstown and Carrigavantry – which he described as 'quite unlike other megalithic monuments in southern Ireland' but as having a likeness with the Scillonian sites (1941b:142). He drew attention to the fact that portal dolmens, such as Knockeen and Gaulstown, also occurred in Tramore and that these had parallels at sites like Zennor in Penwith.

Powell's excavation of the Carriglong site and Hawkes' work at Harristown were both carried out in 1939 and published two years later (Hawkes 1941; Powell 1941a). The structure at Carriglong is described as a 'round cairn, retained by a kerb of large slabs, and enclosing a long V-shaped megalithic chamber whose entrance was on the north-eastern edge of the cairn.' (Powell 1941a:56)

The area enclosed by the kerb was approximately 8.5m in diameter and the kerbstones averaged 1.1m in length and 1.2m in height. The chamber was found to be 5.2m long,

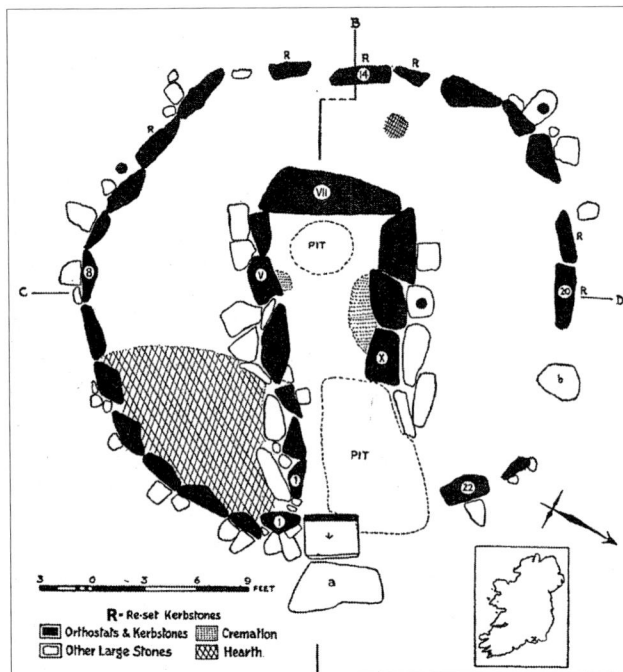

FIGURE 9.7 PLAN OF CARRIGLONG, CO WATERFORD, FROM POWELL (1941A:FIG 2)

FIGURE 9.8 CARRIGLONG, CO WATERFORD

0.9m wide at the entrance and 1.8m wide at the distal end and constructed of orthostats. The sidestones increase in height towards the distal end. All but one of the capstones were missing. The cairn was of stone and earth and large blocks of stone had been positioned close to the outer faces of the chamber orthostats. The site is on a hillslope with extensive views. Powell's plan of Carriglong is shown in figure 9.7. The site had been disturbed prior to excavation with a large pit being dug inside the chamber, which had destroyed part of one side wall. This had also dislodged a rectangular slab, which Powell interpreted as a septal stone, from the chamber entrance.

Flecks of charcoal, cremated bone, three flint scrapers and eighteen small potsherds were found inside the chamber. The pottery is described as being too small to indicate the vessel shape but of a fine paste with small particles of stone and some sherds were decorated with rows of impressions made with a 'cog-toothed implement' (Powell 1941a:60). It has subsequently been identified as a probable Food Vessel (Herity 1974:180). The site, which was somewhat overgrown when visited in 2010, is illustrated in figure 9.8.

Hawkes' excavation at Harristown revealed a roughly circular cairn some 15.2m in diameter with a kerb of 9.1m in diameter within it. The kerb, described by Hawkes as a 'megalithic circle' (1941:183), was formed of stones up to 1m in height. The chamber, which opened towards the east, was 6.1m in length and 1.1m wide except at the western (i.e. distal) end where it widened to 1.4m. The chamber also increased in height towards the western end. As at Carriglong, the orthostats of the chamber were supported on their outer faces by large blocks of stone. Only one of the original five capstones was in place but two others were still on site. Harristown is located just below the summit on a hilltop with very wide-ranging views of the surrounding area. The plan of the structure is shown in figure 9.9.

The plan indicates that about 0.9m inside the entrance was a sillstone, which rested on the floor of the chamber

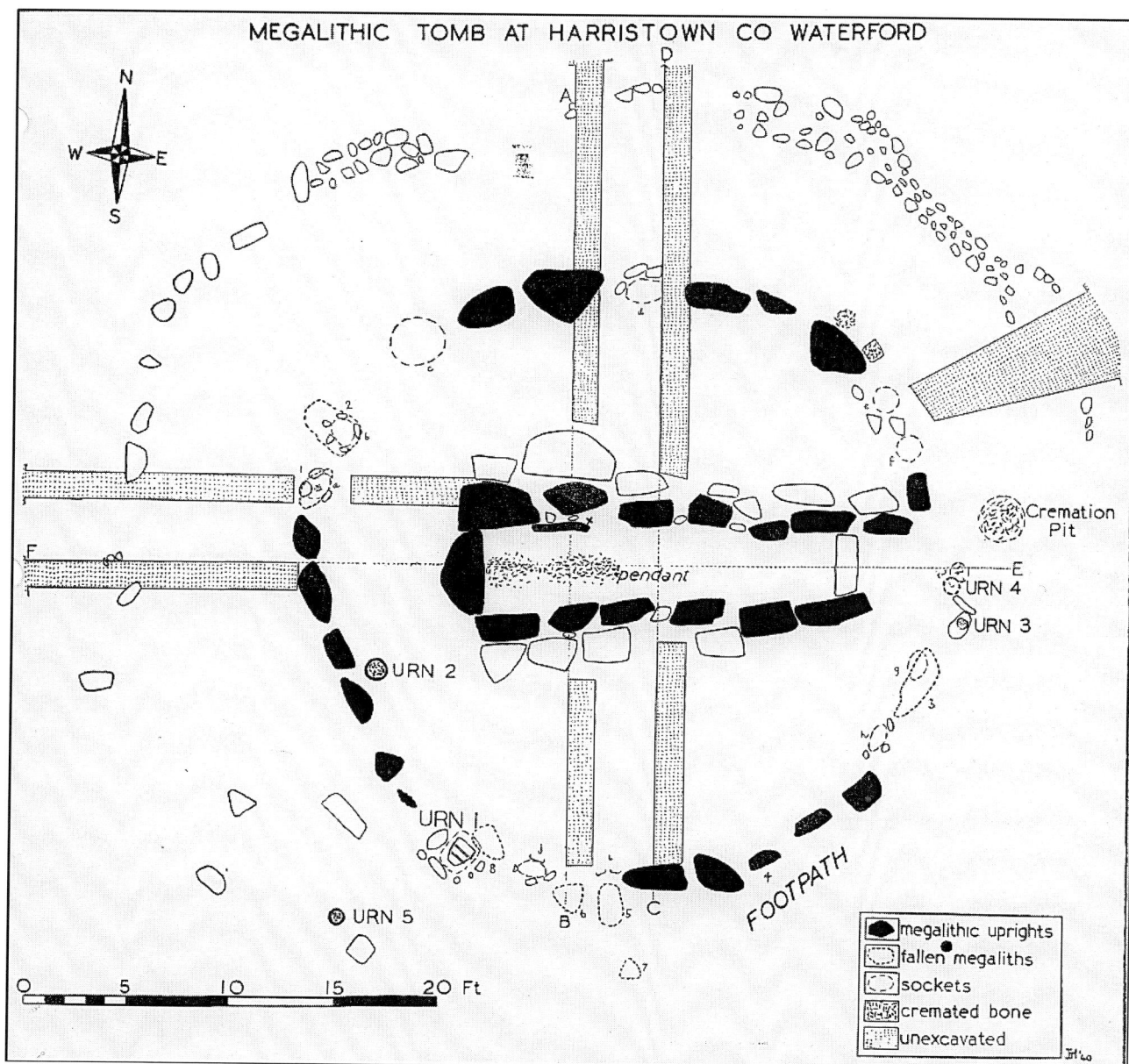

FIGURE 9.9 PLAN OF HARRISTOWN, CO WATERFORD,
FROM HAWKES (1941:FIG 1)

and probably defined a small porch. It is shown in the foreground in figure 9.10.

Although also disturbed, Harristown yielded more finds than did Carriglong. These included cremations at the back of the chamber, accompanied by a stone pendant or amulet, described by Hawkes as being in the form of a single-edged axe, and a natural pebble of similar shape (1941:137). Five urns were found in the cairn, two probably having been enclosed in cists; all contained human bones, presumably cremated, although this is specified by Hawkes in only one case (1941:141). A pit was uncovered outside the entrance to the chamber and this contained the cremated bones of a further three individuals, apparently representing two separate burial episodes. Three other deposits of cremated bone, unaccompanied by an urn or any other artefact, were found under the cairn.

Four of the urns were recovered in good condition, three of them are Cordoned Urns with panels of impressed decoration between the cordons. The fourth is a Food Vessel and is cup-shaped with horizontal bands of incised decoration. A pygmy or 'incense' cup was found in one of the urns and two bone pins were discovered, one in an urn, which also contained a bronze blade and what Hawkes described as a red sandstone bead (subsequently identified as a quoit-shaped faience bead), the other at the bottom of the cremation pit. Hawkes says that she 'is convinced that no pottery or other grave-goods had been pillaged from the tomb, and that the amulet and pebble were the only non-perishable objects to have been buried [in it].' (Hawkes 1941:137)

Hawkes, whilst acknowledging Powell's views on the Scillonian connections of the five Tramore sites, was not inclined to accept his interpretation. She suggests possible

FIGURE 9.10 TOMB AT HARRISTOWN, CO WATERFORD,
SHOWING SILLSTONE

links with the Catalan-Pyrenean area and is confident that the Tramore graves cannot be an indigenous Irish development. She does, however, note that they share the outer reinforcement of the chamber walls with Irish wedge tombs.

> Herity, having identified the sherds from Carriglong as being of Food Vessel pottery, also refers to a 'Breton barbed-and-tanged arrowhead' which he discovered with the other Harristown finds in the National Museum (1974:180). On the basis of these discoveries he dates the Tramore graves to the Early Bronze Age (c1600BC) and states that they are therefore contemporary with the similar sites in Scilly and Cornwall. He sums up their origins as follows:

> 'Their clearly local appearance would seem to stem from a long gestation in the Scilly Isles, their metallurgist builders moving at a mature phase of the Bronze Age to Cornwall and Waterford in search of extra tin and copper to support a purely local metal industry.' (Herity 1974:180)

It is hard to reconcile this statement with the absence of tin and copper as mineral deposits in Scilly and the paucity of bronze there, both in burial and settlement sites.

The only major challenge to Powell's proposition that there were five Tramore graves with links to Scilly has come from Ó Nualláin and Walsh (1986). Based on their surveys, carried out in 1983, they argued that only three of the sites (Carriglong, Harristown and Matthewstown) are 'passage-tombs' and the other two (now called Munmahoge and Carrickavrantry) are wedge tombs.

Wedge tombs are the most numerous type of megalithic tomb in Ireland with more than 500 examples identified, the majority in the west and south-west of the country; they are generally dated to the Late Neolithic and Early Bronze Age, between c2500BC and 1500BC. They typically consist of a parallel-sided or trapezoidal chamber, covered

by roof slabs, opening to the west or south-west and usually higher and wider at the entrance, hence their name.

The entrance often has a septal stone or sillstone and, in some cases, there is a small antechamber at the western (i.e. proximal) end of the main chamber. The orthostats of the chamber are generally supported by outer walling and there may be an orthostatic façade; cairns survive at some sites and are often defined by an orthostatic kerb. Finds from wedge tombs include Beaker pottery, Food Vessels and cinerary urns, worked flints and cremated human bone (O'Brien 1999:5-12).

Matthewstown, Munmahoge and Carrickavrantry have not been excavated and all three of them are in an incomplete state. The plans of these three sites are shown in figure 9.11.

At Matthewstown only the western part of a parallel-sided chamber survives, with part of an orthostatic kerb to the west of it. Ó Nualláin and Walsh refer to an Ordnance Survey report of 1841 in which it was stated that 'a row of standing stones originally surrounded it [the chamber]' (1986:25). They argue that the estimated size of the original cairn (shown as a dotted line on their plan) is closely comparable to those at Carriglong and Harristown, both of which have chambers with an east-facing opening, like Matthewstown.

Ó Nualláin and Walsh consider that the boulders between the western end of the chamber and the kerb 'appear to have been dumped here; they may once have formed part of the original tomb structure' (1986:26). Like Harristown, Matthewstown occupies a hilltop position with extensive views. It is shown in figure 9.12.

Munmahoge and Carrickavrantry are much smaller structures; Munmahoge consists of a roughly parallel-sided chamber approximately 3m in length and 0.9m wide. It has an east-west orientation but it is now not obvious at which end it originally opened. Ó Nualláin and Walsh argue that the entrance was at the western end and that there are the remains of a façade there but their plan of the site (bottom right in figure 9.11) shows that this is open to question.

These features were impossible to distinguish when the site was visited in 2010 but a tumble of stones (not shown on the plan) was noted on the eastern side of the hedge in which the structure is now located. There are no obvious signs of a cairn. Figure 9.13 shows the chamber viewed from the east.

Carrickavrantry is of a similar size, having a chamber 3m in length which is 1.1m wide at its south-western entrance, narrowing to 0.9m wide at the north-east. Ó Nualláin and Walsh suggest that the stone at the south-west end of the chamber may be the remains of a portico and those to the north may be part of the buttressing of the chamber; these are shown in their plan (bottom left in figure 9.11) but

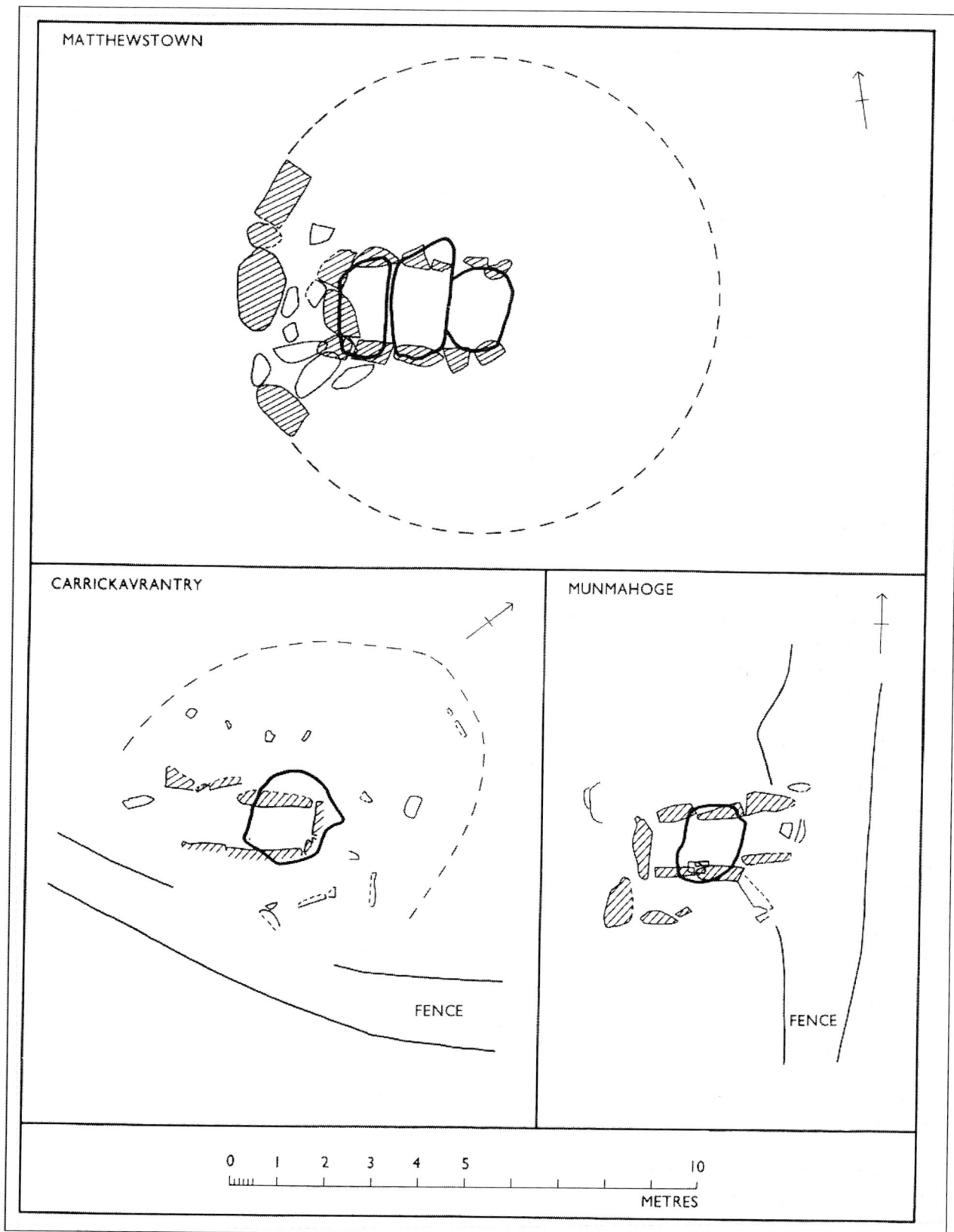

FIGURE 9.11 PLANS OF MATTHEWSTOWN, CARRICKAVRANTRY
AND MUNMAHOGE, CO WATERFORD, FROM Ó NUALLÁIN & WALSH (1986:FIG 3)

FIGURE 9.12 MATTHEWSTOWN, CO WATERFORD

FIGURE 9.13 MUNMAHOGE, CO WATERFORD

were not apparent when the site was visited in 2010. The chamber is surrounded by an oval mound and the view of it from the south-west is shown in figure 9.14.

Ó Nualláin and Walsh argue that one of the elements distinguishing Munmahoge and Carrickavrantry from the other three sites is their positioning; they suggest that these two sites are 'inconspicuously sited in more secluded locations' (1986:29). However, as can be seen from figures 9.13 and 9.14, this is due to the fact that Munmahoge is now inside a field hedge and Carrickavrantry has been planted with trees. If these recent features were removed, both would have wide-ranging views, the background in figure 9.14 bears this out.

They also draw attention to their smaller size, the western orientation of their entrances and their outer walling, façade and buttressing to make the case that they are distinct from Carriglong, Harristown and Matthewstown and are best regarded as wedge tombs. However, both Carriglong and Harristown have wedge-shaped chambers (albeit higher and wider at their distal ends) and both have clear evidence of outer walling. Matthewstown is now too badly damaged for such features, if they existed, to be apparent.

The plans of Harristown, Co Waterford and Innisidgen Carn A, St Mary's, shown below (in figure 9.15) at the same scale, suggest many apparent similarities, including the size and shape of the chamber, the proportions of the chamber to the cairn, the orientation of the chamber and the circular cairn retained by a kerb. However, they also obscure many differences. For example, the Harristown tomb, both chamber and kerb, is constructed entirely of orthostats of up to 1m in height. The chamber of Innisidgen Carn A, on the other hand, is built of large horizontal slabs with some coursed walling, originally mortared, above them. The kerb also consists of slabs laid horizontally with up to three courses of smaller stones above.

In addition, although both chambers are approximately parallel sided, Harristown widens slightly towards the distal end whereas Innisidgen Carn A is widest in the

FIGURE 9.14 CARRICKAVRANTRY, CO WATERFORD

centre and, in both cases, this is typical of other tombs in their respective locations. Innisidgen Carn A has not been excavated but at those few Scillonian sites where the exterior of the chamber walls has been examined, such as Porth Hellick Down A and Knackyboy Cairn, no trace of outer buttressing has been uncovered.

As described above, Hawkes found a sillstone across the entrance at Harristown and Powell concluded that there had been a septal stone at Carriglong but neither of these features has been recorded at any Scillonian site. Where evidence for the closing of the chamber has been identified in Scilly this has been in the form either of a jambstone, as at Porth Hellick Down A, or a blocking stone placed flush beneath the outermost capstone, as at Obadiah's Barrow. The antechamber or porch, suggested by Hawkes at Harristown, is also unknown in Scilly.

The Tramore sites, between them, share many features in common with wedge tombs. These include the use of orthostats for the construction of both the chamber and the kerb, outer walling reinforcing the chamber orthostats, chambers that have their widest point at one end, sillstones, septal stones and antechambers. The finds from the two excavated Tramore sites also show more affinities with

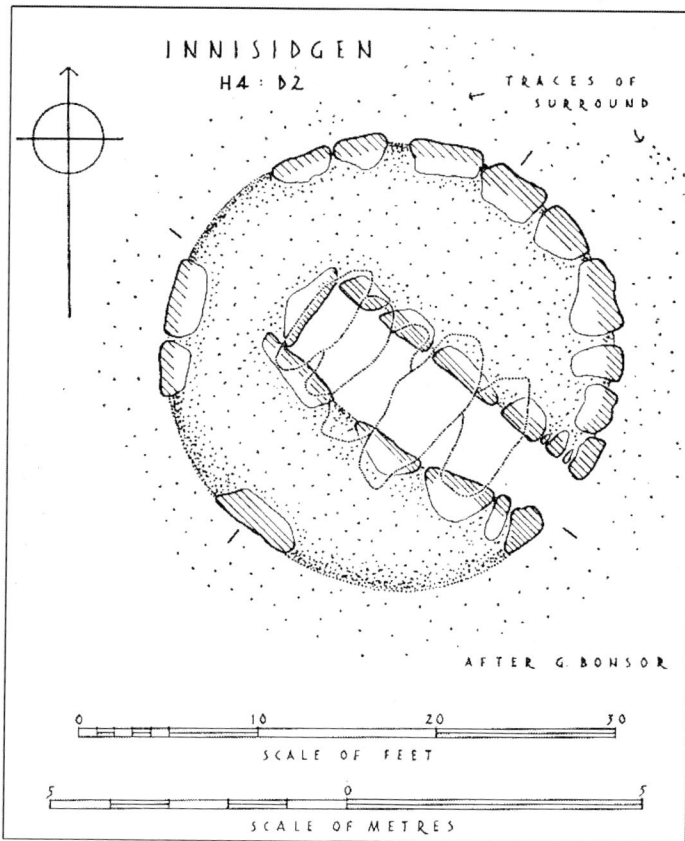

FIGURE 9.15 PLANS OF (ABOVE) HARRISTOWN, CO WATERFORD, FROM HAWKES (1941:FIG 1) AND (BELOW) INNISIDGEN CARN A, ST MARY'S, FROM ASHBEE (1974:FIG 10), BOTH SHOWN AT THE SAME SCALE

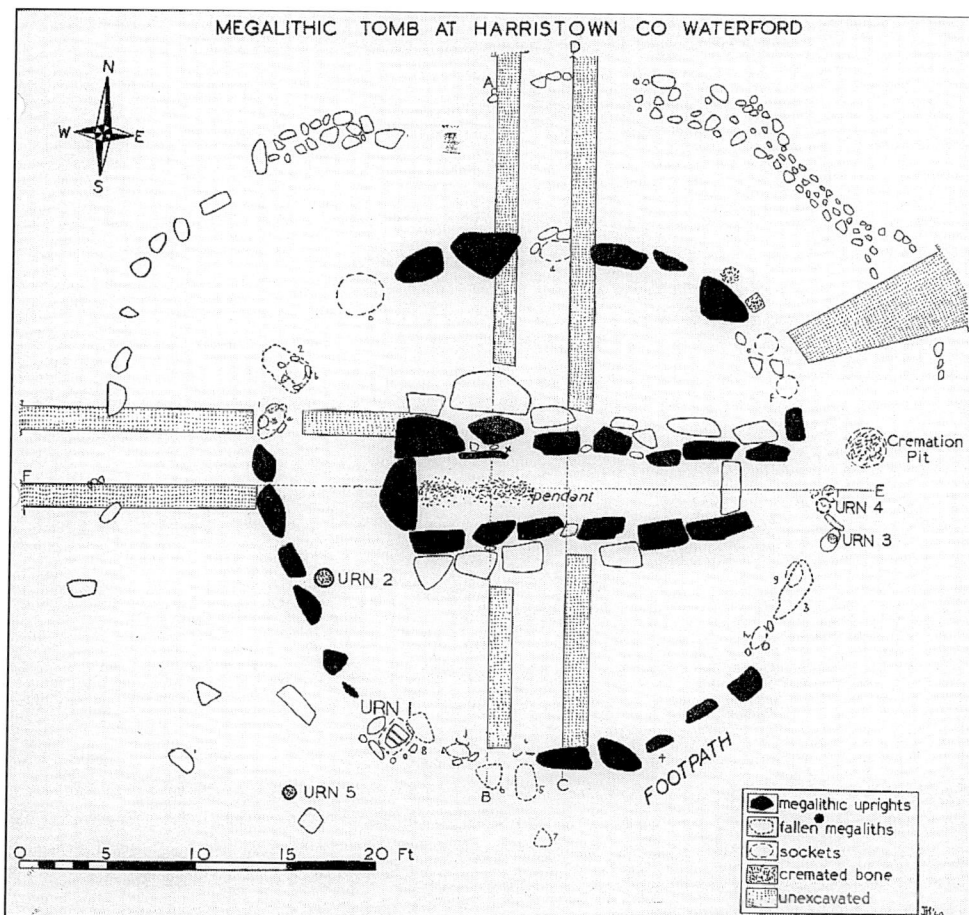

artefacts from wedge tombs than with those from the Scillonian sites.

It is suggested, therefore, that the Tramore sites do form a single group but that they are best regarded as a variant of the wedge tomb tradition, situated in an area remote from the main concentration of wedge tombs. There is no reason to believe, either from their structure or the finds associated with them, that they have any connection with the entrance graves of the Isles of Scilly.

There are no radiocarbon dates from any of the five Tramore sites although, as mentioned above, Herity suggested that Harristown dated to about 1600BC on the basis of the pottery and flint finds from it (Herity 1974). However, several determinations have been obtained from wedge tombs.

Dates from human remains indicate that burials took place in the wedge tombs at Altar, Co Cork in 2293-1781 cal BC (OxA-3289; 3670±80 BP), at Labbacallee, Co Cork beginning in 2457-2064 cal BC (OxA-2759; 3805±45 BP), at Lough Gur, Co Limerick beginning in 2481-2036 cal BC (OxA-3274; 3830±80 BP) and at Largantea, Co Derry beginning in 2467-2210 cal BC (UB-6977; 3871±37). These present a consistent picture of the use of these sites commencing shortly after 2500 cal BC and other determinations show that, in some places, burials continued until c1500 cal BC (Brindley & Lanting 1991; Schulting et al. 2008).

Sheridan argues that wedge tombs were constructed during a relatively short period between 2400 and 2100 cal BC, and that they, and the 'Tramore-Scilly V-shaped entrance tomb' may indicate maritime contact with Brittany. She suggests that there are examples of the latter group in Scilly, Penwith, the Channel Islands and Brittany. She dates the group to the late third millennium BC (Sheridan in Scarre et al. 2003).

There is a very small number of sites elsewhere in Ireland which, like Harristown and Carriglong, have been described as 'undifferentiated passage graves', as mentioned above. The most completely recorded of these is Townleyhall, Co Louth, located about 2 km north of the great passage grave at Dowth and excavated by Eogan in 1960 and 1961. Here, the coffin-shaped chamber was oriented towards the north-east and was constructed of orthostats, which had no external reinforcing. It was surrounded by a circular mound and kerb and under the mound were several concentric stone settings. The site had been badly disturbed prior to excavation and there were no significant finds.

In his review of the affinities of the site, Eogan concluded that:

> 'Outside Ireland, a comparable group of chambered tombs occurs in the Scilly Islands, and it is among these monuments ... that the plan of Townleyhall finds its closest resemblance.' (1963:71)

In fact, the Townleyhall grave is more similar in shape to the majority of the Scillonian sites than are the Tramore examples. Eogan also drew attention to the similarities between Townleyhall and two small passage graves in the Boyne valley, one at Knowth and one to the west of Newgrange, but concluded that it is unlikely that Townleyhall and its neighbouring sites were connected with either Scilly or Tramore.

9.4 Bargrennan

The comparison between the White Cairn at Bargrennan in Galloway, south-west Scotland and the sites in Scilly (and Tramore) was also initially made by Powell, who, with Piggott, had carried out an excavation of the chamber and a very small part of the cairn there over two days in the summer of 1949 (Piggott & Powell 1948-49). This excavation took place immediately after their work at the two Clyde cairns at Cairnholy, about 15 miles south-east of Bargrennan. The White Cairn differed from the Cairnholy sites in having a single undivided chamber in a circular cairn, with no façade, portals or forecourt, and it contained pottery quite unlike the Neolithic and Beaker wares from Cairnholy. The site had already been badly disturbed at the time of the excavation.

Although Piggott and Powell describe Bargrennan as a passage grave, they state that 'it is impossible to make any structural distinction between these two elements [i.e. the passage and chamber]' (1948-49:148). Together the passage and chamber measure 7.3m in length and, at the distal end, the structure is 1.2m wide, narrowing to 0.6m at the open end. The passage and chamber are oriented towards the south-east and are formed of four pairs of large orthostats with drystone walling of large blocks above. The height of the chamber is 1.4m and the roofing consists of huge capstones. The passage and chamber are shown in figure 9.16.

The circular cairn measured approximately 13.7m in diameter and up to 1.4m high and consisted of large rounded boulders. Piggott and Powell found no trace of a kerb or peristalith in the small area they excavated. Inside the chamber they uncovered a paving of flat slabs and, on these, fragments of cremated bone and pottery sherds decorated with incisions, cord impressions and impressions probably made with the edge of a cockle shell. They found it difficult to match this pottery in Scotland. Just outside the entrance to the passage and chamber they found a pit with cremated bones, charcoal and a flint tool and again commented that parallels to a pit like this were not easy to find.

Piggott and Powell believed that 'it [was] virtually impossible to parallel [the White Cairn] in the known Scottish tombs of the Passage-Grave class' but mention that there are other 'Passage-Graves of aberrant types' in south-west Scotland (1948-49:152). One of the sites they mention in this connection is a double-chambered round cairn at the Water of Deugh.

FIGURE 9.16 PASSAGE AND CHAMBER OF THE WHITE CAIRN, BARGRENNAN

This site, now generally known as the King's Cairn, was excavated in 1928 by Curle (1929-1930). In a very short report, he records that the cairn was about 21m in diameter and contained two chambers which were both set on an approximately north-south axis with their back stones about 3m apart. The chambers were both about 2m long; the southern one had a uniform width of about 0.8m, the northern one was that width at the distal end and then narrowed first to 0.6m and subsequently to less than 0.5m. The chambers were approached by passages, that to the south being at least 6.7m in length, the one to the north 5.2m long. The chambers were constructed of a combination of standing slabs and stone walling. Curle cleared both the chambers but found no artefacts or human remains.

The sites at Bargrennan and Water of Deugh were first classified as part of the same 'Bargrennan group' by Henshall (1972) who listed nine definite, two aberrant and one ruined (and so uncertain) members of the group, eight of which are located in an area of upland country measuring 22.5km by 6.5 km, with two more about 9.5 km to the south.

Subsequently Murray has examined these sites and has included eleven probable and two possible sites in the Bargrennan group (1992). Most, she says, are in a very poor condition and the majority are now in areas of forestry which makes an examination of the surroundings and an appreciation of the geographic setting of the cairns very difficult. All eleven probable sites have approximately round cairns, the majority between 16m and 20m in diameter. Six have a single chamber (although in one case it is possible that a second chamber is still obscured within the cairn), four have two chambers and one (Cairnderry) possibly has three chambers. All but one of the chambers are rectangular and they appear to have no differentiation between chamber and passage, other than an occasional sill-stone.

The techniques of chamber construction include orthostats and slabs of stone laid flat, both building styles being employed at some sites. The plans of the Bargrennan group sites show that the passages do not extend to the edge of the cairn, something noted by Piggott and Powell at the White Cairn, and Murray suggests that the entrance may have been deliberately concealed, adding that:

> 'The concept of the chamber as an inaccessible shrine rather than as a tomb for recurrent deposition of remains seems particularly appropriate in relation to the narrow Bargrennan passages' (1992:39).

Murray does not mention Piggott and Powell's suggestion that there might be a link between the Bargrennan sites and those of the 'Scilly-Tramore group'. She believes that the Bargrennan graves are a local development and there is no need to invoke concepts of intrusion from elsewhere. The Bargrennan graves, she suggests, are the product of an 'inward-looking, even isolated' society (1992:46).

Both Henshall's and Murray's work was based on survey only and there was no further excavation of a Bargrennan group site until 2002 when Cummings and Fowler started work at Cairnderry. They excavated at this site between 2002 and 2004 and also at Bargrennan White Cairn in 2004 and 2005. One of the main aims of their work was to assess the likely construction dates of the sites (Cummings & Fowler 2007).

At Cairnderry, which has two definite chambers and a further possible one, they found Early Neolithic pottery and flints below the cairn, kerbstones around part of the perimeter of the cairn and five pits (one cut into the top of another) in an arc under or immediately outside the kerb. A fragment of cremated human bone, flints and Arran pitchstone were found in the southern chamber and the pits contained charcoal, cremated human bone and, in pit 1, a Collared Urn, an accessory vessel and a stone battle axehead.

At Bargrennan White Cairn the single chamber and the pit close to its entrance, both excavated by Piggott and Powell, were re-examined. No further discoveries were made in the chamber but a small deposit of cremated bones and a fragment of burnt flint were found in the previously excavated pit 1. A cist, containing cremated human remains enclosed in a Cordoned Urn, was discovered in the cairn to the west of the south-facing chamber entrance and a pit had also been dug into the cairn on the eastern side of the entrance. This was found to contain cremated human remains and a quartz scraper.

Two further pits were found just outside the kerb, one containing a Collared Urn into which cremated human remains, a fragmented stone battle axehead and part of a bone belt hook had been placed. The other pit contained charcoal, plant remains and pottery fragments. Mesolithic flints were found in the subsoil at the site. The locations of the cist and pits are shown in the post-excavation plan of the site at figure 9.17.

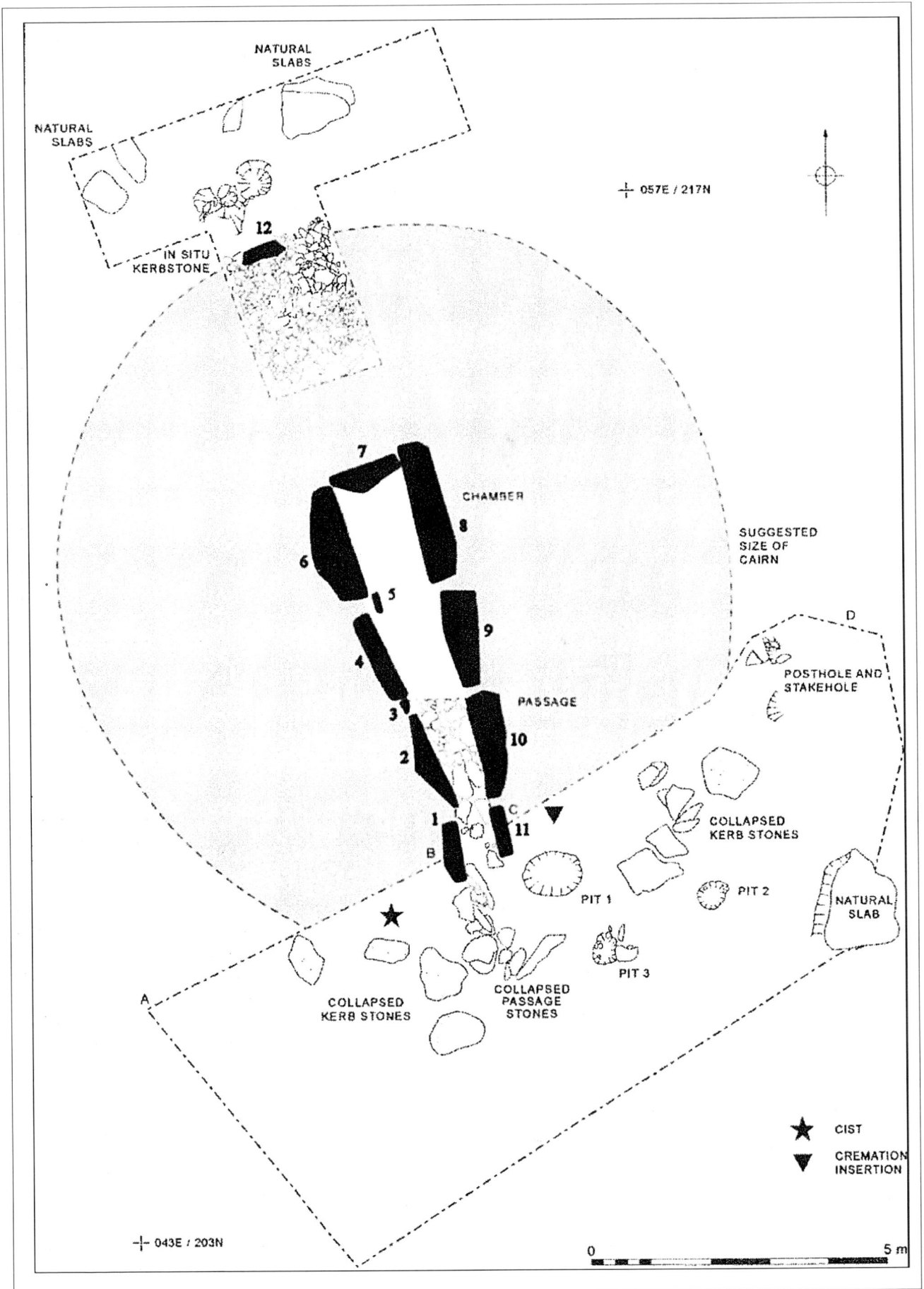

FIGURE 9.17 POST-EXCAVATION PLAN OF THE WHITE CAIRN, BARGRENNAN, FROM CUMMINGS AND FOWLER (2007:FIG 3.5)

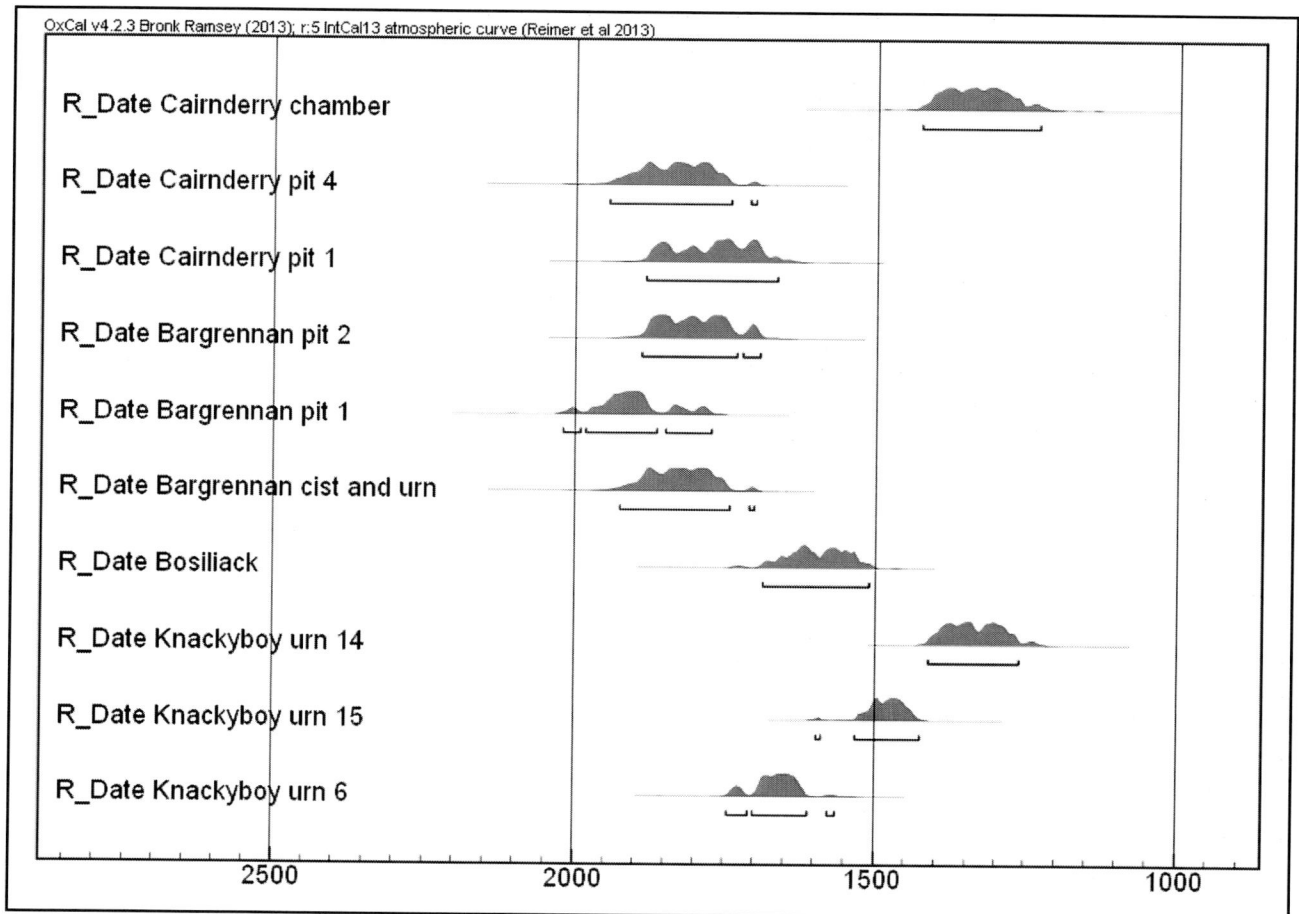

FIGURE 9.18 CALIBRATED RADIOCARBON DATES FROM BARGRENNAN GROUP, CORNISH AND SCILLONIAN SITES

Seventeen radiocarbon determinations were made, nine from Cairnderry and eight from Bargrennan. The dates from Cairnderry are all from cremated bone and range between 1946-1701 cal BC (GrA-26514; 3515±40) and 1427-1231 cal BC (GrA-26551; 3075±40 BP). At Bargrennan White Cairn, the earliest date, from charcoal found under the kerb, is calibrated to 3767-3643 cal BC (GU-14108; 4915±35 BP) but the dates from the cremated bone all fall between 2137-1930 cal BC (GU-13905; 3650±35 BP) and 1890-1693 cal BC (GU-13906; 3475±35 BP) (Cummings & Fowler 2007:166-167).

The excavators of the Bargrennan sites argue that none of the dates from cremated bone are from the period of the primary construction and use of the monuments and that all relate to subsequent Bronze Age activity. They believe that Cairnderry was constructed prior to 1900 cal BC and Bargrennan prior to 2100 cal BC and that they have their origins in the Neolithic (Cummings & Fowler 2007).

Clarke, in his review of the excavation report on Cairnderry and Bargrennan, is highly critical of this approach and points out that three of the Cairnderry dates come from material from pit 2, which lies partially under the kerb of the cairn. He argues that this is likely to indicate that the pit pre-dates the kerb and so is part of the primary phase of construction. He points out also that all the significant finds belong to the Bronze Age and regrets the fact that the excavators did not consider the possibility that the rich

assemblages might be central to an understanding of the cairns (Clarke 2008). Figure 9.18 shows recently-obtained radiocarbon dates from Bargrennan group, Cornish and Scillonian sites.

Like Murray, Cummings and Fowler do not consider the possible comparison between the graves of the Bargrennan group and those in Scilly or Tramore, put forward by Piggott and Powell. The similarities between the White Cairn and many Scillonian sites include roughly rectangular chambers, built of a combination of slabs and dry-stone walling and surrounded by circular, kerbed cairns which are not significantly larger than the chambers. However, the chambers are not strictly comparable in that the Bargrennan graves have wedge-shaped chambers, narrowing towards the entrance (similar to Carriglong and Harristown in Tramore) whereas the Scillonian chambers are typically widest in the centre.

It has been suggested that the presence of a star-shaped faience bead at Knackyboy Cairn underlines the connection between Scilly and south-west Scotland first put forward by Piggott and Powell (Ashbee 1974). A star-shaped faience bead was discovered at Glenluce, Dumfries and Galloway, some 30km from Bargrennan (Wilson 1874-1876); this, however, is a nine-rayed star and so is not directly comparable with the six-rayed example from Scilly. In addition, Newton and Renfrew's analyses of faience beads from different parts of Europe and the Near

105

East suggest differences in chemical composition between the Scottish and English examples and therefore, different places of origin (Newton & Renfrew 1970). More recent work, cited by Sheridan and Shortland (2004), also points to the use of different types of plant ash in the Scottish beads compared with those from England.

Ashbee points out that the pottery found at the White Cairn is very different from other southern Scottish wares and suggests that 'its stamped and impressed decoration distantly recalls Scillonian pottery' (1974:284). Piggott and Powell found 50 to 60 sherds of pottery during their brief excavation, of which eleven were decorated. They state that no feature of shape can be recognised but that two sherds had a 'massive cordon with finger-tip impressions', two others had a 'small raised cordon along one edge of which runs a horizontal line of fine cord impression' and another has impressions, close to its base, made with a comb or cockleshell (1948-49:151). Neither cordoned decoration nor decoration of the lower part of a vessel has been observed on pots from Scillonian graves during the course of the research reported in this volume.

During the programme of excavation at Cairnderry and the White Cairn between 2002 and 2005, Collared Urns, a Cordoned Urn and an accessory vessel were uncovered (Cummings & Fowler 2007). Sheridan (2007) identifies the sherds found by Piggott and Powell as being from up to six different vessels, including a Collared Urn, two probable or possible Collared Urns, a probable Cordoned Urn and two urns of indeterminate type; these are therefore of similar types to those discovered more recently. Collared and Cordoned Urns have not been found in any Scillonian entrance grave and stone battle axeheads and bone belt hooks are similarly unknown there.

Although the dates from the cremated bone at the Bargrennan sites are in a similar range to those from Scilly and Penwith there are no significant similarities between the material culture found in the two areas and no reason to believe that there were any links between them at the time the graves were constructed. Any similarity between the chambers and cairns in the two locations would appear to be purely fortuitous, as Thomas (1985) concluded from his analysis of possible links. The construction of small, megalithic chambers took place in widely spread locations at this time, perhaps in response to similar social or environmental factors.

9.5 Channel Isles

Comparisons have been made between the megalithic burial chambers of Scilly and those of the Channel Islands, approximately 300km to the east-south-east, in several contexts. Firstly, similarities can be drawn between the general forms of the chambered cairns in the two archipelagos (Ashbee 1982), secondly, the presence of limpet shells is attested in burial chambers in both places (Bonsor 1899-1900; 1901-1902; Johnston 1981) and, thirdly, the density of sites in Scilly can be paralleled

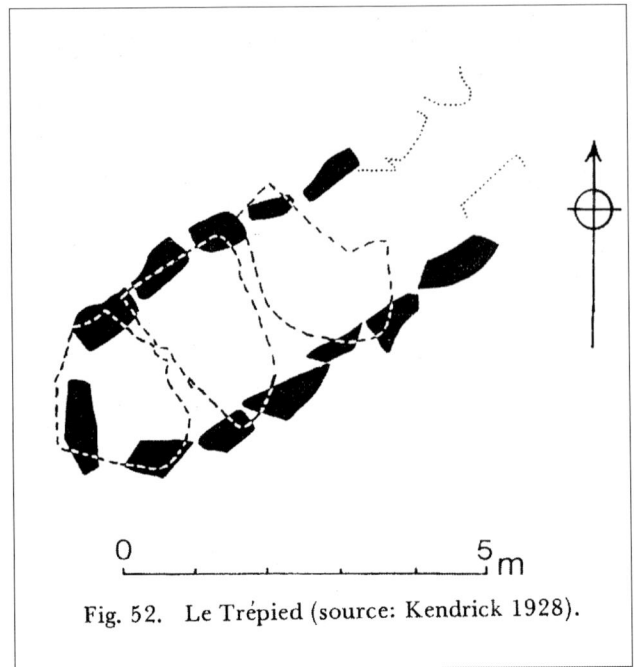

Fig. 52.   Le Trépied (source: Kendrick 1928).

FIGURE 9.19 PLAN OF LE TRÉPIED, GUERNSEY FROM JOHNSTON (1981:FIG 52)

in very few places, of which the Channel Islands and, in particular, the northern part of the island of Herm, is one (Scarre 2008; 2011c). This final aspect will be considered below in section 9.8.

In relation to the first of these, the megalithic tombs of the Channel islands fall into three groups, described by Kinnes and Grant (1983) as passage graves, long graves and cists-in-circles although, as many of the sites are in a poor state of preservation or have been extensively restored, it is not always possible to be certain about the original form of the structure (Johnston 1981). Long graves are also referred to as *allées couvertes* (Hibbs 1983) and gallery graves (Johnston 1981; Patton 1993; Sebire 2011).

The passage graves can be further divided into two types: those with a cruciform or circular chamber approached by a narrow passage, such as La Hougue Bie and La Sergenté, both in Jersey, and those, described by Johnston as 'V-shaped Passage-grave[s]', which have 'no differentiation between passage and chamber, either in plan or elevation' (1981:24). Both types of structure are typically enclosed in a circular mound or cairn. Members of the latter group, which includes sites such as the Beauport Dolmen in Jersey, Le Trépied in Guernsey and Kendrick's site number 6 on Le Grand Monceau, Herm (Kendrick 1928), are ostensibly therefore very similar in plan to the Scillonian sites. The plan of Le Trépied is shown in figure 9.19.

In practice, there is considerable variation amongst the V-shaped or undifferentiated passage graves in the Channel Islands with some monuments, such as Mont Ubé, Jersey and Le Creux ès Faïes, Guernsey, showing a distinct narrowing towards the entrance and, at sites such

FIGURE 9.20 CHAMBER AND PASSAGE OF LE CREUX ÈS FAÏES, GUERNSEY, SHOWING GRADUAL NARROWING AND REDUCTION IN HEIGHT

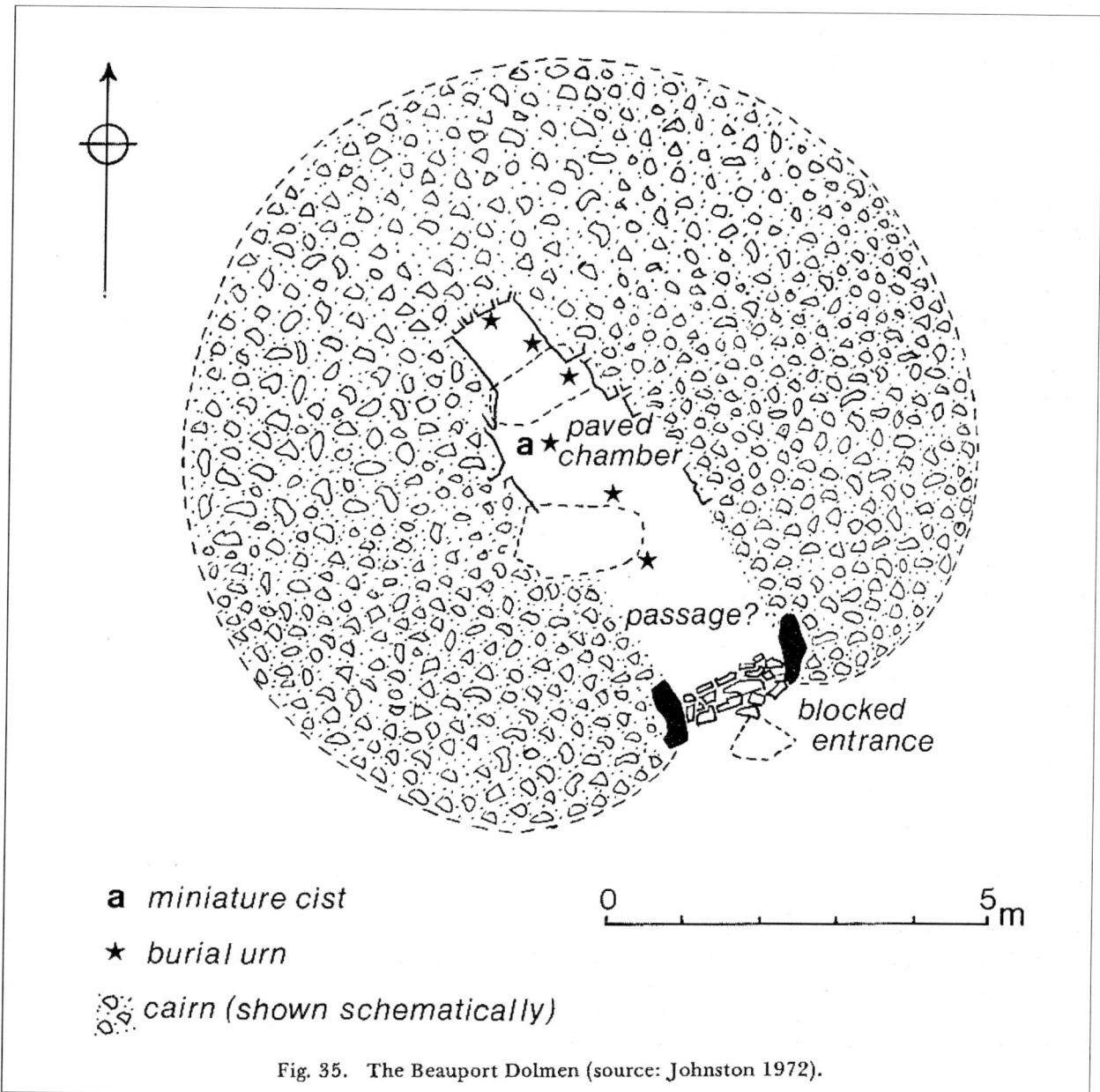

a *miniature cist*

★ *burial urn*

cairn *(shown schematically)*

Fig. 35.   The Beauport Dolmen (source: Johnston 1972).

FIGURE 9.21 PLAN OF THE BEAUPORT DOLMEN FROM JOHNSTON (1981:FIGS 35)

as the latter one where the capstones survive in place, a lowering in height as well. Johnston argues, however, that 'the monument itself [Le Creux ès Faïes], whatever the plan may suggest, shows that the builders intended no differentiation between passage and chamber' (1972:412). The gradual narrowing and reduction in height from the chamber to the passage at this site is illustrated in figure 9.20.

Even at sites such as Le Trépied which do not show this narrowing, it is clear from the plan that there is a, currently partly obscured, narrower passage leading to the chamber.

The only site in the Channel Islands where no such narrowing is apparent is the Beauport Dolmen, Jersey. This badly-damaged site was excavated in 1877 by the Société Jersiaise and was re-examined in a training excavation by the Société and the University of Southampton in 1970 (Johnston 1972). The interpretation of the site is complicated by the fact that the granite bedrock in the area naturally splits into blocks that resemble paving and orthostats.

Although much of the detail of the site is uncertain, Johnston records that the edges of the cairn turn inwards to the passage/chamber entrance which has a small upright stone on either side. Unlike the other sites in the Channel Islands where the chamber and passage walls are formed exclusively or mainly of large orthostats, the Beauport Dolmen appears to have been partly quarried into the bedrock with the resulting stones then used to build up the walls (Johnston 1972:410). Sebire describes the structure as a 'drystone gallery' (2011:78). The closest parallel to this type of construction in Scilly is South Hill C, Samson. The plan of the site is shown in figure 9.21.

Long graves are much less numerous than passage graves in the Channel Islands with only four examples being cited by Johnston: Le Couperon, Ville-ès-Nouaux and Forest Hill, all in Jersey and Robert's Cross, Herm (Johnston 1981:26, 117); all but Le Couperon are described as atypical. Sebire (2011) also mentions Porciaux North, Alderney and Delancey, Guernsey as possible members of this category.

Robert's Cross, which is shown in figure 9.22, has a parallel-sided chamber with a very narrow 'bottle-shaped' entrance. Although the shape of the chamber differs from the V-shaped passage graves in being rectilinear with a square distal end, the narrowed entrance is reminiscent of those at Mont Ubé and Le Creux ès Faïes. Johnston suggests that the outlying slabs, shown in his plan but now no longer visible, may have been part of the peristalith of a long mound. However, Scarre's excavations at the site in 2008 found no evidence for a burial mound and he concluded that 'the Robert's Cross tomb would have stood as an exposed megalithic structure' (Scarre 2008).

Although there are some broad similarities in the shape and construction of some of the megalithic burial chambers of

FIGURE 9.22 ROBERT'S CROSS, HERM

the Channel Islands and those of the Isles of Scilly, other aspects of the sites are markedly different. The burial rites at the Channel Islands sites include both cremation and inhumation with, for example, seven crouched burials and a seated skeleton being found at Les Monts Grantez, Jersey and over 30 inhumations and some cremated remains at La Varde, Guernsey (Johnston 1981; Sebire 2011). In contrast, only one site in Scilly has provided definite evidence for inhumation and that is of a single individual.

The finds from the Channel Islands sites are distinctly different from the Scillonian ones. Where artefacts have been found in the burial chambers in the Channel Islands they include pottery of local type, such as the 'Jersey bowl', as well as beakers, strap-handled urns and carinated vessels, none of which occur in the sites in Scilly. The flint industry also shows local characteristics.

There is one deposit which occurs in burial chambers in both Scilly and the Channel Islands, namely, limpet shells. As detailed in chapter 5, considerable deposits of limpet shells have been found in a small number of sites in both archipelagos, as well as elsewhere in the British Isles. However, as the sites in which they were found are all close to coasts where limpets are plentiful, no connection between the different areas is necessarily implied.

Whilst the finds from Le Déhus suggest a period of use between c3500 and 2000BC and the datable material from Le Creux ès Faïes, which is probably from the final phase of use only, is from c2000 to 1800BC (Sebire 2011) there are few radiocarbon dates from megalithic burial chambers in the Channel Islands. However, once again, the links between the sites there and those in Scilly are tenuous and there are no clear similarities in structure or material culture.

9.6 Brittany

Parallels have been drawn between the megalithic burial chambers in Scilly and those in Brittany, the closest point of which is approximately 180km to the south-east of the islands, by a number of authors. Several of the Breton sites have more than one name and, therefore, reconciling sites mentioned by different authors is not always straightforward. In the comparisons outlined below, the site name and the name of the nearest village or town as quoted by Burl (1985) are used where possible; the *département* is also given.

Both passage graves and chambered long mounds (known as *allées couvertes*) occur in Brittany. The passage graves are earlier, with some dating to before 4500 cal BC (Scarre 2011b), and they typically have a coastal distribution. Over time, the passages became shorter, for example in lateral entry passage graves. Ultimately, the V-shaped or 'undifferentiated' passage graves have only an increase in height and width to distinguish the chamber from the passage. They are succeeded by *allées couvertes* by about 3250 cal BC, although Joussaume and Laporte (2006) point out that it has not been demonstrated that V-shaped graves are transitional types. *Allées couvertes* too show variations in construction including, in some cases, an additional 'cell' accessible only from outside the tomb and the *arc-bouté* type, in which the side stones of the chamber lean inwards and there are no capstones (Hibbs 1983; Burl 1985).

In some cases, it is not clear to which category a site belongs, for example, Burl regards Ty-ar-Boudiquet, Brennilis (Finistère) as a passage grave, although accepting that it is a 'transitional form' (Burl 1985:77), whereas Patton (1993) treats it as an *allée couverte* and Joussaume and Laporte describe it as a gallery grave with a V-shaped chamber. Although it has been argued (Boujot & Cassen 1993) that there is an evolutionary sequence of funerary structures in western France, Laporte et al. (2011) have stressed the complexity of the architecture of megalithic burial structures in France and the need to consider the form and use of each, rather than attempting to fit them into a sequence from simple to complex.

Hencken considered the Scillonian tombs to be 'a provincial extension of the great megalithic cult of Brittany' and stated that they 'resemble structurally the usual Breton kind' (1932:28). In support of this, he cited Ile Longue in Brittany and Bant's Carn as both having more than one retaining wall. He also compared the occurrence of both inhumation and cremation burials and the contemporaneity of covered galleries and cists in the two places. He believed that there were close similarities in the biconical urns found in Scilly and Brittany, in particular, identifying urns from Obadiah's Barrow, Gugh and the Dolmen de Conguel, Quiberon (Morbihan), which both have several horizontal incised lines, as being comparable. He did accept, however, that much of the decoration on the Scillonian urns could not be paralleled in Brittany and that, unlike Brittany, no beakers had been found in Scilly.

In practice, the similarities between Ile Longue and Bant's Carn are very slight. Ile Longue has a passage of 11.5m in length leading to a chamber which measures 3m by 3m with a corbelled roof, originally 5m high. The enclosing cairn, which is 20m in diameter, has three concentric retaining walls. The passage has a sillstone and contains five carved stones (Burl 1985; Patton 1993). Bant's Carn has a rectangular chamber, 4.9m long, up to 1.6m wide and 1.5m high, roofed with large capstones and with a passage of 5.0m in length. In common with a number of Scillonian sites, it has two kerbs, one with a diameter of about 8.5m, the other about 13.0m. It has no corbelling, sillstone or carved stones.

O'Neil (1948-1949) also found parallels between Scilly and Brittany, again citing Conguel as, like Knackyboy Cairn, one side of its chamber is formed of natural rock. He compared some of the urns from Conguel with those from Knackyboy. Two different types of pottery were found in the passage grave at Conguel: Lower Conguel Ware consists of round-bottomed bowls and was separated in the tomb, by a 0.45m deep deposit of sterile sand, from the level containing Upper Conguel Ware. This comprises flat-bottomed, biconical pots with incised decoration around the upper part (L'Helgouach 1962; Pollès 1986). It was this latter type which O'Neil suggested was comparable with the Knackyboy urns.

Whilst there are some similarities between the pots from the two sites they are by no means identical. There are differences in their shape, in the presence of lugs only on the Knackyboy urn and in the positioning of the decoration. The Conguel vessel has a vertical incised line, crossing the horizontal ones, a typical feature of Upper Conguel Ware that does not appear on Scillonian urns.

With the exception of the use of natural rock, there are few similarities between the structures at Knackyboy and Conguel. The natural rock forms all of one side of the chamber at Conguel and the distal end and part of a side at Knackyboy. Conguel is constructed of large slabs and has a passage leading to the entrance whereas the walls of the chamber at Knackyboy are mainly of small stones set in a granite clay mortar and there is no passage. While there are some similarities between Upper Conguel Ware and one or two of the surviving urns from Knackyboy, Lower Conguel Ware bears no resemblance to any pottery found in Scilly. There seems, therefore, no reason to connect the two sites.

O'Neil also drew comparisons between the chamber shapes at Knackyboy and Kerandrèze, Moëlan-sur-Mer (Finistère) and between the pottery from Knackyboy and that from Lesconil-Plobannalec, Treffiagat (Morbihan), although stressing that the chamber shapes were different at the latter site (O'Neil 1948-1949). The exterior of Kerandrèze is shown in figure 9.23. The site is of massive construction and has a small vestibule with a low sillstone between the vestibule and the chamber, features which cannot be paralleled at Knackyboy. The artefacts recovered from the site included beaker sherds, polished stone axes and an archer's wristguard, none of which has been found in any Scillonian site.

FIGURE 9.23 EXTERIOR OF KERANDRÈZE

FIGURE 9.24 EXTERIOR OF MANÉ KERIONED I, CARNAC (MORBIHAN)

O'Neil did not specify what he believed the similarities between the two sites to be, simply saying, on a page in his notebook headed 'Breton Parallels for Knackyboy Cairn II', that Kerandrèze had a 'plan of tomb rather like Knackyboy' (O'Neil 1948-1949:159). There appears to be no obvious similarity in plan or mode of construction between the two sites but both had a paving of flat slabs in the chamber. O'Neil mentions this in relation to Conguel (1948-1949:141) but not in his comments on Kerandrèze.

Piggott considered that none of the pottery from the Scillonian tombs 'belongs or is related to' Neolithic pottery from elsewhere in the British Isles or from western France or Iberia (1954a:265). He believed that the pots from Knackyboy, for example, were Middle or Late Bronze Age in date and related to Cornish urns of that period.

Daniel (1950) suggested that there were parallels to the form of the Scillonian chambers in Iberia, Denmark, the Channel Islands and Brittany. In Brittany, he identified a passage grave at Cosquer, Plouharnel (Morbihan), where the distinction between the passage and the chamber is less well-marked, as being comparable. He also drew attention to several undifferentiated passage graves where one end of the chamber is wider than the other, such as Ty-ar-Boudiquet, Brennilis (Finistère) and Kermario, Carnac (Morbihan), as well as those where the chamber is roughly the same width throughout, as at Mané Kerioned I (the west chamber), Carnac (Morbihan) and suggested that these had parallels with Scilly.

The exterior of Mané Kerioned I is shown in figure 9.24 and it will be noted that again the mode of construction is markedly different from that of the Scillonian sites.

Daniel concluded that

'The parallels between the Breton and Scilly sites are very close indeed and the pottery found in the Scilly sites emphasizes the Breton affinities of the Scilly megalithic culture as a whole.' (Daniel 1950:149)

He later re-asserted this view, stating that 'between the Scilly-Tramore culture and the V-shaped and Entrance Graves of Brittany and the Channel Islands, … exact and direct connexions can be plausibly argued' (Daniel 1960:197).

More recent authors, however, have been less certain of these direct links. Ashbee, whilst acknowledging that there are superficial resemblances between megalithic tombs in Scilly and some in Spain, Brittany and the Channel Islands, states that 'comparisons between chamber tombs in widely separated areas … are beset with pitfalls and dangers.' He suggests that the similarities may be simply the 'homogeneity of the stone-built chamber-tomb tradition imposed by the medium.' (Ashbee 1974:285)

Mercer (1986) also believes that there are no exact parallels between Scilly and elsewhere, pointing to differences in scale or precise shape, a point re-iterated by Robinson who states that typological similarities between megalithic tombs in Scilly and Brittany 'do not withstand detailed study.' (2007:10)

Examination of a range of Breton passage graves and *allées couvertes*, during the course of this research, bears this out. As with the sites in Tramore, discussed in 9.3 above, whilst plans of selected Scillonian and Breton chambers might suggest they have much in common, in practice, the mode of construction is very different and any similarities are limited to minor aspects.

This is illustrated below in respect of the sites of Ty-ar-Boudiquet, Brennilis (Finistère) and Halangy Down, St Mary's. From the plans, the shapes of the chambers at these two sites appear to be similar but the photographs of the chamber interiors in figure 9.25 show that, in practice, the size and mode of construction differs considerably between the two. Ty-ar-Boudiquet is 13.4m in length whilst Halangy Down is only 5.0m long.

It can be seen that, at the first site, the chamber walls are constructed of huge orthostats and the chamber is covered with massive capstones whereas, at the second, the chamber walls are of drystone walling and there are much smaller capstones. There is also a large, free-standing pillar

FIGURE 9.25 CHAMBER INTERIORS AT (ABOVE) TY-AR-BOUDIQUET AND (BELOW) HALANGY DOWN

in the chamber at Ty-ar-Boudiquet, a feature which is not found in any Scillonian entrance grave. Any similarity in the shape of the chamber and passage would seem to be a minor aspect in the face of such obvious differences.

Whilst there are Breton passage graves which do include drystone walling, such as some of the passages and chambers at Barnenez, Plouézoch (Finistère), this mode of construction is associated with classic passage graves (i.e. those with a narrow passage widening to a circular, square or polygonal chamber), not with the V-shaped passage graves which have been held to be similar to the Scillonian sites. In addition, sites such as Barnenez often have corbelled chamber roofs, again something which does not occur in Scilly.

Some of the trapezoidal long mounds in Brittany and west-central France, including Barnenez, have asymmetric plans either with one straight long side and the other kinked or with the broader terminal end oblique to the central axis (Laporte et al. 2002). The chambers of Scillonian entrance graves are also sometimes asymmetrical with one straight side wall and one convex, as outlined in chapter 4. However, these aspects of asymmetry differ in that the Breton one relates to the mound and the Scillonian one to the chamber.

As with Scilly, some early attempts to date the sites in Brittany and the Channel Islands were based on the discovery of faience beads, which were believed to be imports from the eastern Mediterranean. These beads have been found at Parc Guren II, Crach (Morbihan) and Mont Ubé, Jersey as well as at Run-ar-Justicou, Kerstrobel-en-Crozon (Finistère).

The first two sites are passage graves; at Parc Guren the finds included sherds of bell beaker and fragments of a copper knife (Burl 1985) and beakers or beaker-like vessels were found at Mont Ubé (Johnston 1981). Daniel said that the faience beads at these sites were from late primary or secondary uses and he dated them to 1400 to 1200BC on the basis of comparisons with Egypt. He therefore concluded that 'the floruit of the Passage Grave culture of north-western France was well before the middle of the second millennium BC'. (Daniel 1960:202)

Taking account of the evidence from pottery as well, Daniel argued that the earliest passage graves in Brittany dated to c2300BC with their main period of use being between 2000BC and 1400BC. He dated the beginnings of the Breton allées couvertes to c1800BC (1960:211). Thirty years later, and making use of radiocarbon determinations, Patton suggested that the first passage graves dated to the Early Neolithic in Brittany at between 5100 and 4350BC (1993:71). The earliest radiocarbon date from a Breton passage grave is from Kercado, Carnac (Morbihan), where charcoal from the passage was dated to 5463-4056 cal BC (Sa-95; 5840±300 BP) (Hibbs 1983:321). However, the charcoal sample was from an early excavation and its stratigraphy, and therefore its significance, are not clear (Patton 1993:73).

Because of the acidic soil in Brittany, few bones have survived and the vast majority of radiocarbon determinations from both passage graves and allées couvertes are from charcoal. A date of 4981-4332 cal BC (Gif-1309; 5750±150 BP) has been obtained from chamber G at the multiple passage grave site of Barnenez, Plouézoc'h (Finistère) whilst the chamber at Liscuis I, Laniscat (Côtes d'Armor), described as a V-shaped passage grave by Hibbs (1983) but as an allée couverte by Burl (1985), has produced a date of 4234-3704 cal BC (Gif-3099; 5140±110 BP). Samples from the nearby allées couvertes of Liscuis II and Liscuis III have, however, yielded determinations of between 3497-2886 cal BC (Gif-3944; 4450±110 BP) and 2454-1768 cal BC (Gif-4075; 3680±110 BP) (Hibbs 1983:321-322).

The latest radiocarbon date from an allée couverte is from Kerivalan (or Kerivoelen), Plélauff (Finistère), where charcoal associated with beaker sherds and other finds is dated to 2341-1695 cal BC (Gif-3587; 3640±110BP). Some passage graves also continued in use until this time: there is a determination from chamber C of the passage grave at Kerleven, La Forêt Fouesnant (Finistère) of 2572-1915 cal BC (Gif-809; 3800±120 BP) (Hibbs 1983:323).

Even allowing for the re-assessment of some of the earliest dates with large margins of error, the origins of megalithic burial chambers in Brittany are clearly considerably earlier than those in Scilly. Some of the Breton passage graves date to before 4500 cal BC and many to around 4500 to 4200 cal BC (Scarre in Scarre et al. 2003; Scarre 2011b). The *allées couvertes* also pre-date the Scillonian sites typically having dates of 3250 to 2850 cal BC. Patton (1993) argued that both passage graves and *allées couvertes* had fallen out of use by c2250BC but there is a handful of dates that spans the late third and early second millennia BC.

In summary, therefore, it appears that the comparisons drawn by some authors between Breton and Scillonian megalithic burial chambers have been exaggerated. There are some similarities but these are in minor aspects, such as the use of natural rock to form part of the chamber or the lack of a clear distinction between passage and chamber, and overall the sites are markedly different. The radiocarbon dates from Brittany and Scilly confirm that there is no chronological link either and there seems no reason to conclude that the Scillonian sites are derived from Brittany.

9.7 Cists

As set out above, two very different types of structure are described as 'cists', one is a small slab-built box with one or more covering stones, the other is a megalithic structure, similar to an entrance grave but with a closed chamber; these latter are referred to in this work as 'megalithic cists'.

Cists occur in many parts of the British Isles, particularly in the west and north, with megalithic cists also being found in the Channel Islands and Brittany. In the latter area they are often known as *dolmens simples*, although this term is also used to describe other monument types. Although both cists and megalithic cists are quite homogenous in their size and mode of construction, there have been few suggestions in the literature that they indicate links between different parts of Britain and western Europe, in the way that has been argued for megalithic burial chambers.

In Penwith, as described above in section 9.2, cists have been found in association with entrance graves at a number of sites including Ballowall and Chapel Carn Brea. Elsewhere in south-west England, they have been found under barrows on Dartmoor, St Austell Down and Bodmin Moor, one of the best-known discoveries being the Rillaton Barrow where a gold cup was found, in a cist, with a skeleton and other artefacts in 1837 (Barnatt 1982). A recently discovered cist at Whitehorse Hill, Dartmoor contained a burial deposit accompanied by organic and other objects. The cremated human remains had been wrapped in a bear pelt. Radiocarbon dates have not yet been published in full but are between 1900 and 1600 cal BC (Jones et al. 2014).

Crawford considered that the cists in south-west England were later than the entrance graves there (which he regarded as Bronze Age in date) but he did not give any reason for this view. He also drew attention to cists, similar

FIGURE 9.26 CUP-MARKED STONE INCORPORATED IN WALL, PUNGIE'S LANE, ST MARY'S

in shape and dimensions to those in the south-west, found in Northumberland and Fife. In both these cases, the burial rite was inhumation and, in one, the skeleton was accompanied by a Beaker (Crawford 1928).

In western Scotland, a significant number of cists have been found under cairns in the Kilmartin valley, Argyll (Craw 1929-1930). Some of them were added to earlier structures including a stone circle and a henge (Butter 1999). Several of the cist slabs and covers are decorated with cup-marks and carved axe-heads. Bradley examined the decorated slab at the cist below the cairn of Nether Largie North and identified three phases of carving on it. He suggests that it may be a re-used menhir and highlights the significance of this re-working of monuments 'to conform with changing circumstances.' (1993:93)

The rich rock art of Kilmartin has recently been studied in detail by Jones et al. (2011). Their conclusion is that its production began in the Late Neolithic (c2900-2800BC) and that it is associated with early agricultural settlement in the area. They argue that it is a way of 'socialising the landscape', a process which also involved the construction of stone and timber circles, stone alignments and burial cairns (Jones et al. 2011:xviii). However, in her review of the book, Sheridan (2012) points out that none of the radiocarbon dates from Kilmartin can be unequivocally associated with the creation of the rock art.

Rock art has not been identified at any of the cist (or entrance grave) sites in Scilly although there are a few cup-marked stones in the islands, one of which is illustrated in figure 9.26, and it is possible that some or all of these were once part of, now-destroyed, burial structures. A similarity between Kilmartin and Scilly exists, however, in that nine of the cists at Kilmartin have side slabs with grooves near the ends, so that the end slabs could be inserted, like the cist excavated on Samson in 1862.

Piggott (1941) drew attention to the fact that this appears to be originally a wood-working technique and that cists may have been stone versions of wooden coffins. He suggested

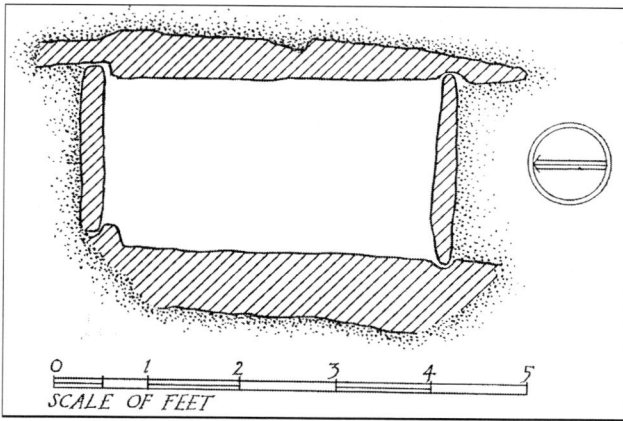

FIGURE 9.27 PLAN OF NORTH HILL H CIST, FROM PIGGOTT (1941:82)

that the occurrence of these grooved stone cists in such widely separated locations could be explained by maritime connections. Piggott's plan of the site on Samson, North Hill H, is shown in figure 9.27.

A grooved cist slab, which also has an engraved multiple lozenge design on it, was found at Badden, Kilmartin in 1960. The similarity with the Samson site was noted but the decoration on it led to links being suggested between Argyll and Wessex (where similar patterns are found on artefacts such as the gold plates from the Bush Barrow and Clandon), the carved stones at the passage grave of Barclodiad y Gawres, Anglesey and the Saale cists in Germany.

A connection between the site in Scilly (incorrectly described in the article as being on St Martin's) and the Saale valley through the tin trade was proposed as a possible explanation for the occurrence of grooved cist slabs in both places (Campbell et al. 1960-1961). If this were the case, it might be expected that grooved cist slabs would also be found in Cornwall, the source of the tin, but none has been identified there.

Jones et al. point out that the cutting of the grooves constituted a re-working of the Badden cist slab and suggest that it might have had an earlier function as a standing stone. They also stress that the grooves in the side slabs allow the cist to be architecturally stable and would also have permitted it to be dismantled (Jones et al. 2011).

Hencken, in arguing that megalithic tombs in Scilly were derived from Brittany, highlighted the example of the cist from an unknown location on St Mary's *(PRN 7246)*. This contained pottery similar to that found in the entrance graves and Hencken regarded this as a parallel with Finistère 'where such cists are contemporary with much larger tombs' (1932:28).

More recent work, however, suggests that some of the Breton cists are later than the passage graves and *allées couvertes*; assemblages from cist sites such as L'Hotié-Viviane, Brocéliande (Ille-et-Vilaine) and Lost-er-Lenn, Plumeliau (Morbihan) suggest a date of 3250 to 2850BC (Patton 1993) and the cist at Tumulus de Ligollenec,

Berien (Finistère) provided a radiocarbon date of 2278-1455 cal BC (Gif-1866; 3500±150 BP) (1971), which is not dissimilar to those from Old Town and Porth Killier in Scilly, although with a larger margin of error. Hibbs (1983) suggests that these cists may be derived from the closed chambers found under some of the Carnac mounds although some of the other *dolmens simples* may be of an earlier date.

Carnac mounds and the other, smaller, *tertres* (mounds) in southern Morbihan have been found to cover both megalithic chambers and cists, with some sites containing both types of structure. The *tertre* at Le Manio, Carnac (Morbihan) contained two larger and 37 small cists under and just outside the mound; because of the acidity of the soil no human remains were found and it is not clear whether any of the cists had been used for burial, although there were signs of burning in some and others contained pottery and flint flakes.

The larger Carnac mounds, such as Tumiac, Arzon and Tumulus de Saint-Michel, Carnac (both in Morbihan), have been found to contain rich grave assemblages including prestige objects such as polished stone axes and beads which originated at a considerable distance from Brittany. The former site had a megalithic cist, built of a combination of megalithic slabs and drystone walling, at its centre. The latter had two megalithic chambers: the central one a megalithic cist, the other a passage grave, with a cluster of cists, some too small to have contained an inhumation burial, around them (Burl 1985; Scarre 2011b). Recent radiocarbon dating of bone from the central chamber has provided a date of c4725-4650 cal BC (Schulting et al. 2009, quoted in Scarre 2011b).

In Brittany, as in Cornwall, cists and/or megalithic cists are found in combination with other megalithic structures as well as occurring independently. The dating of the Breton structures suggests that they were constructed over a period of at least 2500 years with the earlier ones usually being part of larger, composite monuments such as the Carnac mounds and the later ones occurring without other elements, other than a covering mound.

In the Channel Islands, the first phase of the *tertre* of Les Fouaillages, Guernsey covered megalithic and slab-built cists dated to c4500 to 4000BC (Kinnes & Grant 1983). As in Brittany, single burials in megalithic or slab-built cists appear to be later than the passage graves and chambered long mounds. The cists, at least some of which were covered by mounds and surrounded by stone kerbs, fall at the end of the megalithic tradition (Johnston 1981; Sebire 2011). They are often referred to as cists-in-circles and, in this precise form, appear to be unique to the Channel Islands where they are most commonly found in Guernsey and Herm. The pottery associations suggest a dating of 2500 to 1800BC.

The multi-period site at Sandy Hook, L'Islet, Guernsey includes both megalithic and slab-built cists with surrounding boulder kerbs, as well as cairns with kerbs but no cists. Although there is no parallel in Scilly for a cist site of this complexity, a few cist graves, such as the slab-built grave of Gweal Hill C and the megalithic cist of Middle Arthur B, do have boulder kerbs. In both Scilly and the Channel Islands, cist burials continued into the Iron Age.

Cists, therefore, are found widely across north-western Europe over a time range of at least 2500 years. It is likely that they are a representation in stone of wooden coffins and that their use continued particularly in areas of limited woodland and plentiful stone. In contrast to passage graves, chambered long mounds and entrance graves, the structure of both slab-built and megalithic cists implies a single burial event, and where the burial deposit survives, it is often of only one individual.

Given their wide geographical and chronological dispersion, a link between the societies which built them is unlikely. They appear to represent a widespread tradition of single burial which existed alongside that of multiple burials interred in a range of larger megalithic structures.

9.8 Island comparisons

A number of authors have speculated on the reasons for the density of Neolithic and Bronze Age megalithic burial sites on islands and archipelagos in north-western Europe. In particular, the archipelagos (or certain islands within them) of Orkney, the Hebrides, the Channel Islands and Molène, as well as Scilly, have significantly greater densities of such sites than their neighbouring mainlands (e.g. Scarre 2002b; Parker Pearson 2004; Scarre 2011c).

One reason for this may be differential preservation: many off-shore islands are still undeveloped and prehistoric sites may not have been subjected to the same levels of damage and destruction as those on the mainland. One of the major threats to ancient sites in all locations has been agriculture and burial chambers positioned on coastal headlands and other marginal positions are more likely to have survived, whether on mainlands or on islands, because of the greatly reduced likelihood of agricultural activity in such locations. The removal of stone from megalithic graves for the construction of later buildings has also caused damage to, or loss of, sites and the prevalence of this will have been reduced if the island has been sparsely populated.

Another possible argument for the large number of these monuments on islands is that their construction continued longer there than on adjacent mainlands. Daniel queried whether the community in Scilly was undisturbed 'whereas megalith builders on the mainland of Britain and France were supplanted by later invaders' (1947:118). Broodbank also has suggested that the 'curation of archaisms' was a strategy 'through which island identities were created and sustained by people who remained aware of how things were done elsewhere' (2000:20). Parker Pearson (2004) talks of island communities creating a strong sense of identity against the outside world, which becomes

something to be resisted; this leads to the maintenance of traditions on islands after they have changed elsewhere.

The distinctiveness of the Bronze Age pottery in Scilly, using local fabric rather than gabbroic clay and with different vessel forms and decoration from the contemporary Cornish wares, may be an indication of such an island identity. This, in turn, may have led to the continuation of entrance grave building in the islands long after such traditions had ended in west Cornwall.

Hencken, in speculating as to why Scilly and other islands had such a density of chambered cairns, said that early historical references suggested that 'some kind of peculiar sanctity was attached to lonely ocean islands' (1932:34). He went on to review the many Celtic myths associated with islands and concluded that 'it is quite possible that Scilly may have been among the many islands which the western Celts and possibly still earlier peoples of the Atlantic coast looked upon as the special abodes of the departed' (Hencken 1932:38).

This interpretation would appear to imply that some, at least, of the megalithic burial chambers on these islands contained the remains of people who had not lived there. It leaves open the question as to whether Hencken believed that the chambers were constructed by islanders or by those bringing the remains for burial. However, the homogeneity of the entrance graves in Scilly and their distinctiveness from those elsewhere, as outlined in the earlier sections of this chapter, would suggest that they were built by island residents. Isotope analysis of any surviving human remains might indicate whether the individuals buried in island graves originated from the island in question.

Scarre (2011b) argues that the burials on the Molène archipelago must have been mainly of members of the adjacent mainland population as the islands are too small to have had an independent community, for example, because they could not have supported separate breeding populations of domestic animals; indeed, the pottery and lithics are similar to those from the mainland. Molène is very close to the western tip of Brittany and, as Scarre acknowledges, Scilly is different, being 45km from the Cornish coast.

Two features which Molène and Scilly have in common are a location at the edge of the continent and an extensive inter-tidal zone. Much has been written about the significance of liminal areas, such as inter-tidal zones, for prehistoric communities (e.g. Cunliffe 2001; Scarre 2002b; Frieman 2008). It has been argued that, given that funerary monuments relate to the liminal area between life and death, the presence of such inter-tidal zones would have made these islands particularly appropriate places for burial. Again, this raises the question of the origin of those buried in Scilly which, unlike Molène, has no immediately adjacent mainland.

Parker Pearson compares the density of Neolithic burial tombs in Orkney (1 every 5km²) with that in the Western Isles (1 every 12km²) and suggests that, while the suitability of Orkney sandstone as a building material may be a factor, the main reason for the greater concentration in Orkney is that 'Orkney's nucleated communities, working closely together for agricultural reasons, were well organized for communal monument building' (Parker Pearson 2004:138). The boulder clay in Orkney is a much more difficult soil to work than the machair fringes of the Uists and would have required greater co-operation between communities as well as concentrated labour at key times in the agricultural cycle.

The soil in Scilly is not difficult to work so there is no reason to believe that these factors applied in Scilly. However, the scale of the islands would have meant that settlements were typically only one or two kilometres apart and that, given the small size of many of these settlements, inter-community co-operation in building not only entrance graves, but also perhaps houses, may have been the norm.

Rainbird proposes that the proliferation of ritual structures on many islands may have been an attempt to encourage visitors to them, to ensure continuing contacts with other communities (2007:72-78). He develops this argument in relation to Malta but Scarre (2011b) suggests that it could apply to the Orkney islands and Arran as well. The visibility from the sea of some, but by no means all, of the Scillonian entrance graves may indicate this as a possible interpretation for Scilly also.

The Channel Islands, which again have a considerable concentration of megalithic burial chambers, show both close links with northern France, in the form of imported stone axes, and distinctive island traits, such as the cists-in-circles described in section 9.7 above (Patton 1993; Scarre 2011b). Patton (1997) also stresses certain differences between the islands: in Guernsey and Herm the passage graves are located on the coastal plains, in the same areas as the settlements but in Jersey, in most cases, they are some distance from the coast, on the edge of the plateau. It has been argued, however, that Patton's analysis fails to take account of the destruction of sites in the last 400 years (Driscoll 2010). The later long graves and cists-in-circles are on the coastal plains in both Guernsey and Jersey.

Patton suggests that this pattern of sites indicates that in Jersey an early distinction between domestic and sacred space had broken down. A factor in this and, possibly, in the proliferation of megalithic graves, may be the impact of rising sea levels on the islands in the period from c4250 to 3250BC. Patton suggests that this may well have put pressure on social relationships as well as on the natural environment. Again, this is an argument that can be applied to Scilly, as has been set out in chapter 6, and to the Molène archipelago.

Scarre's recent work in Herm demonstrates that the majority of the burial chambers there are on the hill ridges overlooking the coastal plain, not on the plain itself. When they were built, they probably overlooked the open sea, the coastal plain having expanded, due to the deposition

of sand, since the prehistoric period. This is a similar distribution to that found on the islands of Samson and Gugh in Scilly. The present greater density of funerary sites in Herm, compared with the other Channel Islands, can probably be explained by differential preservation (Scarre 2011a).

Frieman, in discussing the Isle of Man, postulates that the construction of megalithic monuments around the edges of that island demonstrates the relationship between the liminal natures of both funerary monuments and the coastline. She also argues that 'monument building was perhaps a means of 'holding the line' against the onslaught of the Irish Sea' (Frieman 2008:146). In Scilly, a majority, but not all, of the known entrance graves were built on the coast and the same argument can be put forward in relation to the need of that archipelago to defend itself against the depredations of the Atlantic Ocean.

9.9 'Megalithic connections' – the significance of similarities

Traditionally, the similarities between megalithic burial chambers in different parts of Atlantic Europe were regarded as the result of colonisation from the Mediterranean. Because, it was argued, such a movement of people would require a motivation, Childe developed his concept of a megalithic religion (Childe 1958). Daniel, in the classic article on the subject, traced two separate movements of colonists: one bringing passage graves, the other gallery graves. He argued that burial chambers were not religious but funerary structures and that their diffusion represented the 'spread of a cult of the dead manifesting itself in a particular funerary practice'. He did not believe that this cult could have been spread through trade because there were 'established rules as to the arrangement and construction of sepulchres' that implied a folk movement (Daniel 1941:47).

This interpretation has been refined by others: Bowen (1972) argued that most travel is for economic reasons and that the pattern of trade and contact around western Europe suggested the pursuit of fish. Clark suggested specifically that the distribution of V-shaped passage graves or entrance graves in Scilly, north-east to the Land's End peninsula, north-west to Tramore, east to the Channel Islands and south to Finistère and Morbihan, pointed to a connection through fishing (Clark 1977). Ashbee (1982) developed this argument to propose that these entrance graves had their origins in the Mesolithic and that their shape might related to that of pens built to protect skin boats, a suggestion based on Piggott's observation of stone-built curragh pens on Achill Island off the west coast of Ireland (Piggott 1954b).

It is argued here that the general similarities, but differences in detail, in the construction and form of chambered cairns in different parts of western Europe are more likely to be the result of people attempting to replicate, from memory, structures they have seen elsewhere, or have had described

	Chamber built of coursed walling	Chamber built of orthostats	Chamber widest in middle	Chamber widest at one end	Reinforcing of chamber walling	No different-iation between chamber and passage	Sillstones or septal stones	Natural rock used in chamber or mound	Small round mound	Hilltop/ hillslope location
Scilly	×		×			×		×	×	×
Penwith		×	×			×			×	
Tramore		×		×	×	×	×		×	×
Bargrennan		×		×			×		×	
Channel Islands		×		×					×	×
Brittany		×		×			×	×		

TABLE 9.1 COMPARISON OF TYPICAL FEATURES OF BURIAL CHAMBERS IN THE AREAS CONSIDERED

to them, than of movements of people. Local geology will also play a part in influencing the form of structures; it is very difficult to build a corbelled roof from granite for example.

The evidence for deep sea fishing from a number of prehistoric midden sites in Scilly demonstrates that the islanders had suitable craft and the necessary knowledge to venture some distance from the archipelago (Robinson 2007). Sea-going boats dating to the Early Bronze Age have been found elsewhere in southern Britain, the best-known being the Dover boat (Clark 2004). The lack of waterlogged conditions in much of coastal south-western Britain make it unlikely that such a vessel will be found in Scilly or Cornwall.

However, there is no reason to assume that the prehistoric Scillonians did not make regular journeys to west Cornwall and perhaps further afield. Although there is doubt as to whether the Hembury Ware found in a pit at the Neolithic site at East Porth, Samson is of local manufacture or not, a sherd of Neolithic gabbroic ware found at Old Quay, St Martin's clearly is an import and demonstrates that the journey between Scilly and the mainland had been made for a considerable period of time before the construction of the entrance graves.

The presence of non-local objects, including faience, glass and bronze, in Bronze Age settlements and burial chambers in Scilly is an indicator of continuing contact with the outside world, through Scillonians travelling elsewhere, non-islanders visiting Scilly, or both. Whilst there are no records of artefacts of Scillonian origin being found outside the islands, it is possible that the items traded were perishable: marine oils have been suggested as a likely export (Evans 1983).

9.10 Conclusions

The foregoing sections of this chapter have examined the links which have been proposed between the entrance graves in Scilly and megalithic burial chambers in other parts of the British Isles and Brittany. Repeatedly, the conclusion, when the evidence is considered closely, is

that there is no exact parallel. There is only one structure – Treen South in west Penwith – which can be regarded as directly comparable with the Scillonian sites. Otherwise, the structures have only a 'superficial morphological similarity' (Mercer 1986).

Table 9.1 summarises the typical features of the chambers and mounds in the areas considered and demonstrates that no other region shares all the features typical of Scillonian entrance graves. Equally, the pottery and other objects found in the Scillonian sites cannot be directly paralleled anywhere else. Scillonian pottery of this period is distinctive and has not been found outside the islands. Unfortunately, no finds are recorded from Treen South.

The location of the Isles of Scilly in the western seaways, at the entrance to both the Irish Sea and the English Channel and within sight of Land's End, suggests that they were likely to have been used both as a navigation marker and as a refuge in bad weather for prehistoric seafarers. The likelihood of not only material objects but also ideas and stories being introduced to the islands at this time is high. It is suggested that the origins of the entrance graves in Scilly lie in links such as these rather than in any colonisation from Brittany or elsewhere.

Chapter 10

Conclusions

This final chapter will seek to summarise the key outcomes of the research, including a consideration of whether the Isles of Scilly were the 'Isles of the Dead'. It will then paint a picture of Scilly in the second millennium BC and suggest future lines of enquiry.

10.1 Key outcomes

The evaluation of early excavation reports, particularly the unpublished notebooks of George Bonsor, has significantly added to the number of entrance grave and cist sites known to have been excavated and to the information about them. It is now clear that at least thirty-six sites have been examined. Establishing the total number of entrance graves and cists in the islands is not straightforward, though, as many are too damaged or currently too overgrown for their precise structure to be determined. However, when probable and possible sites are included, there are ninety entrance graves and sixty-one cist graves in Scilly, as well as a further forty-one indeterminate sites.

Establishing a chronology for the sites has been complicated by the lack, until recently, of radiocarbon dates and by the often repeated statement that Early Neolithic pottery was found at Bant's Carn. The discovery, from Bonsor's notebooks, that the sherd, identified by Hencken as being from a round-bottomed bowl, was found at the settlement site of Halangy Porth and not at the Bant's Carn entrance grave has clarified this aspect. There is no reason to believe that any of the pottery from the entrance graves or cists is Neolithic in date.

Equally, the examination of both Bonsor and O'Neil's excavation notes has established that there is no evidence to support the suggestion that midden material was deposited in entrance graves. The black soil found at Knackyboy was made up of cremated bone and charcoal and identified by O'Neil as being almost the same as the cremations themselves. This supports the interpretation of entrance graves as places of burial by providing further data about the funerary practices which took place in them and by challenging the argument that the placing of midden material indicated a use of the chambers as shrines to ensure soil fertility.

Indeed, if the finds of greasy or coloured earth are interpreted as decomposed human remains, the number of sites with evidence for burial is significantly increased. The

recognition of the wide range of grave goods, including prestige items such as glass and faience beads, at well-preserved sites also strengthens the argument for burial being one of the primary functions of entrance graves.

It is difficult to estimate the number of individuals buried in the entrance graves as there is clear evidence from only three sites and very different numbers from each, with four burials being recorded at Bant's Carn, between twelve and twenty at Obadiah's Barrow and up to one hundred at Knackyboy Cairn. This sample is too small for any meaningful conclusions to be drawn, but the extra insights provided by the radiocarbon dates from Knackyboy suggest that, at that site, the one hundred burials took place over a period of up to 500 years. From the insular style of the urns in which the cremated remains were placed, it seems much more likely that these were residents of the islands than that Scilly was a necropolis in which the dead from the Cornish mainland, or further afield, were buried.

Whilst it appears that entrance graves were also built in inland locations in Scilly, from where many have been lost, there is a concentration of sites around the coast and on hill ridges overlooking the central area between what are now separate islands. The work of the Lyonesse Project in mapping the rate of sea level rise in Scilly has shown that a substantial and growing area of land was inundated at high spring tides in the first half of the second millennium BC. This coincides with the period of use of Knackyboy Cairn, as established by the radiocarbon dates, and suggests that there may be a link between the entrance graves and this inundation.

An interpretation of the use of entrance graves which includes a number of different functions appears to be the most satisfactory. It is suggested that they were originally built, perhaps as early as the late third millennium BC in some cases, as burial places. The evidence suggests that these may initially have been inhumation burials, but that by c1750BC cremation was the usual rite. The discovery of sherds of pottery outside the entrance at several sites tends to indicate that offerings were made there, perhaps during ceremonies to commemorate the ancestors or remember the more recent dead.

The construction of dense clusters of entrance graves and cists on prominent hilltops, however, seems likely to be linked to the inundation and could be seen as a way of 'holding the line' against the ravages of the ocean. The use of natural outcrops in the chambers and mounds may also have been seen as a way of securing the land. The coastal location of many sites may have resulted in some of them being used as navigational markers.

At this stage it is not possible to identify early and late entrance grave sites nor, indeed, to determine whether any of them were multi-phase constructions. However, on the basis of the radiocarbon dates from two cists, it seems that they may be earlier than some, at least, of the entrance graves. The cists appear from the existing evidence to have been used for individual burials. The location of some cists with substantial cairns on the highest point of the hill may indicate that they were built before the neighbouring entrance graves or that they contained the remains of high status individuals. Hilltop sites, such as North Hill H, would have been visible from many places around the islands.

A number of sites in different parts of the British Isles and Brittany have been identified in the literature as showing similarities with the Scillonian entrance graves. These and, where appropriate, their contents have been examined but no links have been identified other than with a handful of structures in Penwith, the nearest part of the mainland to Scilly. Here also, the evidence suggests that cist graves may have slightly pre-dated entrance graves. The suggestion that a group of sites in Tramore, Co Waterford are comparable with those in Scilly appears to be without foundation.

Overall, the research has clearly situated the use of the Scillonian entrance graves and cists in the second millennium BC. This is consistent with the dates for the first permanent settlement in the islands. The use, and probable construction, of small megalithic burial chambers for multiple cremation burials at this time is not something that is generally recognised in the literature. However, in addition to Scilly, there is evidence for this phenomenon in both Cornwall and south-west Scotland. In all these places, they appear to be contemporary with single cremation burials in cists and radiocarbon dates from both Scilly and Scotland suggest that their use continued until the 14th or 13th century BC.

10.2 Isles of the Dead?

There is no reason to think that Scilly was a necropolis in the Early and Middle Bronze Age. There are settlements which are contemporary with the use of the entrance graves and cists and the palaeoenvironmental evidence points to a mixed economy of agriculture and the exploitation of wild resources at the time. The construction of burial chambers appears to follow, within a few generations, the establishment of the first permanent settlements. This may indicate a concern with laying claim to the islands, honouring the founders of those settlements and with recognising an island identity distinct from that of the ancestral communities on the mainland.

The Scillonian entrance graves show considerable consistency in their dimensions, proportions and style and this points to their construction by the same community, one that was resident in the islands. The pottery styles and fabrics from the funerary structures are the same as those in the settlements, which points to their manufacture by Scillonian potters. Had human remains regularly been brought from elsewhere for burial in Scilly, it seems likely that they would have been transported and buried in urns typical of their place of origin. All the pottery found in the entrance graves and cists, with the exception of a few sherds of probable Trevisker Ware from a single site, is of local fabric and style.

This all points to an island community building burial chambers for its own dead, sometimes in locations which overlooked the settlements. These structures were built in a distinctive local style and the cremated remains were placed in the same type of vessels which were used in the settlements. This tradition continued for at least 500 years and resulted in a considerable number of burial chambers being constructed. Throughout this time people continued to live in the islands. The Isles of Scilly were not the Isles of the Dead in the second millennium BC.

10.3 Entrance graves and the early settlement of Scilly

The picture which emerges from the research reported here is of a small but resourceful community living in Scilly in the second millennium BC. It is likely that the islands were not permanently occupied until the late third millennium BC following a period of visits and short-term occupation, probably by people otherwise resident in west Cornwall. However, given the islands' location, seafarers from southern England, Brittany and the Irish Sea coasts probably visited them as well. Amongst the attractions of the islands would have been their mild maritime climate and the absence of predators.

The model set out by Woodman in relation to the Mesolithic colonisation of Ireland may well be appropriate for Scilly as well. He suggests a three stage process:

'1. Exploratory visits to an unknown landscape.
2. Pioneering visits to use and exploit the resources of a new land.
3. Based on the knowledge acquired, a movement towards long term settlement'
(Woodman 2012:14)

In Scilly, the evidence, in the form of microliths and pollen records indicating disturbance of the virgin forest, suggests that stage 1 had started by c6000BC at the latest. The appearance of cereal pollen in the record, together with a small number of stone axes, flint arrowheads and sherds of Neolithic pottery, indicate that stage 2 was well underway by c3000BC. However, evidence for stage 3, in the form of settlements with huts and middens, does not appear until shortly before 2000BC.

The burial places of these first resident Scillonians were probably the cavities and crevices of the granite carns which form such a striking part of the islands' landscape and seascape. Boulders and smaller stones were arranged around some of the carns, perhaps to mark them as graves. Propped stones – natural boulders raised at one end on a smaller stone – may also have covered early burials.

Within a few generations, more formal burial structures were being built in Scilly. The first were the cist graves, some of which were positioned on hill summits and covered with large cairns. As the granite in Scilly is very pale, these artificial carns would have formed obvious and eye-catching monuments. They contained single burials, probably of important individuals, and the cists were very similar to those found in the islanders' ancestral communities in Cornwall. However, from the beginnings of permanent settlement, the pottery in Scilly was distinctive, a way for the island potters to signify their new home and different identity.

Shortly afterwards, the construction of larger chambers for multiple burials, of all islanders, began. Like the cists, these were initially placed on hilltops and covered with cairns, creating a striking appearance particularly where they were built in lines or clusters. Although bigger than the cists, the fact that the walls of the chambers were usually of coursed drystone, rather than orthostats, meant that they could be built by a relatively small group. Only the movement and placing of the endstone and capstones would have required significant manpower resources.

The form of these entrance graves was influenced by a desire to reference the granite carns and inspired by stories of megalithic structures related by islanders who had seen them on voyages to Cornwall, Brittany and beyond. Burials, initially inhumations and later cremations in the distinctive local urns, were placed in them over several centuries. Precious objects, such as glass beads and bronze objects, brought to the islands by travellers or brought back by returning islanders, were also deposited there.

When the fragile pots disintegrated, the cremated remains they had contained were re-arranged and later burials were added. As the ocean increasingly threatened the precious sheltered agricultural land in the centre of the main island, more and more entrance graves were built on the surrounding hills as a way of harnessing the power of the ancestors to protect their homeland.

By the late second millennium BC, when it became clear that attempts to save the land would be unsuccessful, the building of entrance graves ceased and cremated remains in urns were buried in cemeteries of small cairns or with no marker at all. The entrance graves and cists, covered by their pale granite cairns, remained on the hilltops as testament to the islanders' struggle to save their land.

10.4 Future lines of enquiry

Further radiocarbon dates from entrance graves and cists would help to build a more detailed chronology for them and to ascertain whether the sites already dated are typical. There are very few other bone samples currently available for dating, although it may be possible to obtain a date from the single surviving cremation burial from Obadiah's Barrow using other fragments of bone; there is also a small amount of cremated bone from the atypical site of Middle Arthur B, which has not yet been dated. Further dating will depend on the discovery of more bone, either by locating it in museum archives or by the future excavation of entrance graves or cists. It is possible that there are also suitable charcoal samples which could be used for dating.

To date, there has been no geological study of the stones used to construct the entrance graves and cists. Whilst the bedrock in Scilly is all granite, it varies in its crystalline structure, inclusions and colour and a detailed examination might detect patterns in the use of these. This might provide evidence of stone being transported between the islands, or even from further afield.

The expression of island identity through distinctive Scillonian pottery styles has been outlined above. Specialist analysis of other elements of the prehistoric material culture, such as flint artefacts, might provide further insights into this.

There is a wealth of information in the currently unpublished notebooks of George Bonsor, documenting his archaeological recording and excavation in Scilly between 1899 and 1902, and of Bryan O'Neil, who worked in the islands between 1947 and 1954. Publication of both these archives would facilitate further research.

10.5 A final note

In the mid 20th century a number of leading scholars visited and wrote about the wide range of sites in the Isles of Scilly. Then, for several decades, less attention was paid to the islands. Now, once again, work is being carried out there and it is hoped that the research reported here will also help to foster interest in the rich archaeological heritage of this beautiful little archipelago.

Appendix 1

Catalogue of Scillonian entrance graves and cists and their contents

This Appendix summarises information about each of the sites considered in this book. The sites are listed alphabetically by island and, within each island, alphabetically and then numerically by the Permanent Record Number (PRN) from the Cornwall and Scilly Historic Environment Record (HER) entries. The information included about each site is as follows:

Site name	From HER entry	PRN	From HER entry
Site type	Categories: Entrance grave; entrance grave - probable; entrance grave – possible; cist; cist – probable; cist – possible; entrance grave or cist; entrance grave or cist – possible ; other Assessment based on visual examination (where possible) and documentary information	Grid Ref	Where site extant, measured by Garmin Etrex GPS; where site not extant or inaccessible, taken from HER entry
Dimensions	Of mound and chamber or hollow, where possible to measure. Taken from HER (or SM entry where HER entry not sufficiently detailed) and checked in field, where possible The terms 'mound' and 'chamber' are used as neutral descriptions: 'mound' includes cairn and barrow, 'chamber' includes entrance grave and cist	Orientation	Measured by compass in degrees, where possible; otherwise as compass points. For entrance graves, the orientation of the entrance end is shown first
Details	Additional information about kerbstones, capstones, location, etc		
Excavation	Excavator and date, where known	Finds	Where recorded
Condition	Categories: Extant, excellent; extant, good; extant, fair; extant, poor; extant; unknown; destroyed	Museum	Location of all or some of finds and accession number(s), where known
Hencken No	If allocated in 'The Archaeology of Cornwall and Scilly' 1932	Daniel No	If allocated in 'The Prehistoric Chamber Tombs of England and Wales' 1950

1. Bryher

Site name	Bryher	PRN	167242
Site type	Cist - possible	Grid Ref	88054 14389
Dimensions	Mound 5.5m diameter, 0.6m high Hollow 1.0m long, 0.8m wide, 0.4m deep	Orientation	
Details	In inter-tidal zone, seaweed-covered		
Excavation	None	Finds	None
Condition	Extant, fair	Museum	
Hencken No		Daniel No	

Site name	Great Bottom H	PRN	7279.08
Site type	Cist - possible	Grid Ref	87744 15940
Dimensions	Mound 6.0m diameter, 0.4m high	Orientation	
Details	Overgrown with bramble in 2012 but stones visible, under vegetation, in hollow near centre		
Excavation	None	Finds	None
Condition	Extant, poor	Museum	
Hencken No		Daniel No	

Site name	Great Bottom K		PRN	7279.10
Site type	Cist - possible		Grid Ref	87754 15839
Dimensions	Mound 6.5m by 5.0m diameter, 0.7m high Hollow 1.0m long, 0.8m wide, 0.5m deep		Orientation	NW-SE
Details	Built against outcrop of natural rock; hollow near centre			
Excavation	None	Finds	None	
Condition	Extant, poor	Museum		
Hencken No		Daniel No		

Site name	Gweal Hill A		PRN	7384.01
Site type	Entrance grave		Grid Ref	87176 14921
Dimensions	Mound 6.5m diameter, 0.3m high Chamber 2.5m long, 1.1m wide, 0.3m high		Orientation	149° or 329° SSE-NNW or NNW-SSE
Details	Chamber sides built of orthostats, no capstones or endstone, possible inner and outer kerbs			
Excavation	None	Finds	None	
Condition	Extant, poor	Museum		
Hencken No	Bryher 4	Daniel No	Bryher 3	

Site name	Gweal Hill B		PRN	7384.03
Site type	Entrance grave or cist – possible		Grid Ref	87157 14927
Dimensions	Mound 3.5m diameter, 0.3m high		Orientation	
Details	Slabs, including possible capstone, lying on mound			
Excavation	None	Finds	None	
Condition	Extant, poor	Museum		
Hencken No		Daniel No		

Site name	Gweal Hill C		PRN	7384.02
Site type	Cist		Grid Ref	87147 14917
Dimensions	Mound 8.5m diameter, 0.7m high Chamber 1.0m long, 0.5m wide, 0.4m deep		Orientation	32° NNE-SSW
Details	Inner and outer kerbs; natural rock forms one wall of cist and part of outer kerb			
Excavation	Bonsor, 1902	Finds	Pottery, charcoal	
Condition	Extant, fair	Museum	Not known	
Hencken No	Bryher 5	Daniel No	Bryher 4	

Site name	Samson Hill A		PRN	7394.01
Site type	Entrance grave or cist – possible		Grid Ref	87815 14280
Dimensions	Mound 10.5m diameter, 0.6m high Hollow 4.5m by 3.5m, 0.1m deep		Orientation	NW-SE or SE-NW
Details	Possible capstone on mound			
Excavation	None	Finds	None	
Condition	Extant, poor	Museum		
Hencken No		Daniel No		

Site name	Samson Hill B		PRN	7394.02
Site type	Entrance grave – possible		Grid Ref	87796 14270
Dimensions	Mound 4.5m by 4.0m diameter, 1.0m high Chamber 4.0m long, 1.5m wide, 0.5m high		Orientation	NW-SE
Details	Overgrown by vegetation in 2008; natural outcrop forms one side of 'chamber' which may all be natural arrangement of rocks; HER entry records kerb			
Excavation	None	Finds	None	
Condition	Extant, poor	Museum		
Hencken No		Daniel No		

Site name	Samson Hill C		PRN	7394.03
Site type	Entrance grave		Grid Ref	87938 14254
Dimensions	Mound 7.0m diameter, 0.8m high		Orientation	NW-SE or SE-NW
Details	Central hollow with 2 stones in it partly obscured by gorse in 2008; 2 probable capstones on mound; massive kerbstones			
Excavation	None	Finds	None	
Condition	Extant, poor	Museum		
Hencken No	Bryher 2	Daniel No	Bryher 7	

Site name	Samson Hill D		PRN	7394.04
Site type	Entrance grave or cist - possible		Grid Ref	87934 14243
Dimensions	Mound 8.2m by 7.3m diameter		Orientation	
Details	Possible capstone in centre; large kerbstones around natural outcrop, may be analogous to Dartmoor tor cairn			
Excavation	None	Finds	None	
Condition	Extant, poor	Museum		
Hencken No		Daniel No		

Site name	Shipman Head Down Y		PRN	7402.29
Site type	Entrance grave or cist – possible		Grid Ref	87698 15663
Dimensions	Mound 7.0m by 6.0m diameter, 0.3m high Hollow 3.0m long, 1.0m wide, 0.4m deep		Orientation	NW-SE or SE-NW
Details	Large slab on edge in hollow; close to coast			
Excavation	None	Finds	None	
Condition	Extant, poor	Museum		
Hencken No		Daniel No		

Site name	Shipman Head Down		PRN	7404.02
Site type	Cist – probable		Grid Ref	87647 15571
Dimensions	Mound 5.6m diameter, 0.6m high Chamber 1.8m long, 1.1m wide, 0.4m deep		Orientation	NW-SE
Details	Natural rock incorporated in chamber side			
Excavation	None	Finds	None	
Condition	Extant, poor	Museum		
Hencken No		Daniel No		

Site name	Shipman Head Down M		PRN	7404.04
Site type	Cist - possible		Grid Ref	87668 1547
Dimensions	Mound 9.5m diameter, 0.7m high Hollow 1.5m long, 0.8m wide, 0.2m deep		Orientation	NW-SE
Details	Large slab lying in hollow			
Excavation	None	Finds	None	
Condition	Extant, poor	Museum		
Hencken No		Daniel No		

Site name	Shipman Head Down E		PRN	7405.11
Site type	Entrance grave – probable		Grid Ref	87729 15452
Dimensions	Mound 6.0m diameter, 0.5m high Chamber at least 3.0m long, 1.1m wide, 0.5m high		Orientation	N-S
Details	Two slightly displaced capstones; kerbstones close to chamber			
Excavation	None	Finds	None	
Condition	Extant, fair	Museum		
Hencken No	Bryher 8	Daniel No	Bryher 5	

Site name	Shipman Head Down N		PRN	7405.12
Site type	Entrance grave – probable		Grid Ref	87633 15416
Dimensions	Mound 25.0m diameter, 1.6m high Hollow 3.5m long, 1.2m wide, 0.2m deep		Orientation	NW-SE or SE-NW
Details	Possible capstone on mound; several possible cists around mound perimeter			
Excavation	None	Finds	None	
Condition	Extant, poor	Museum		
Hencken No	Bryher 6	Daniel No	Bryher 2	

Site name	Shipman Head Down		PRN	7413.13
Site type	Entrance grave or cist – possible		Grid Ref	87868 15631
Dimensions	Mound 6.0m diameter, 0.8m high		Orientation	
Details	Overgrown with gorse in 2012; HER entry records irregular hollow in centre of mound; NE-SW boulder wall crosses mound			
Excavation	None	Finds	None	
Condition	Extant, poor	Museum		
Hencken No		Daniel No		

Site name	Shipman Head Down		PRN	7413.19
Site type	Cist – possible		Grid Ref	87847 15532
Dimensions	Mound 5.5m diameter, 0.5m high		Orientation	
Details	Stones in centre of mound may be remains of cist; E-W boulder wall crosses mound			
Excavation	None	Finds	None	
Condition	Extant, poor	Museum		
Hencken No		Daniel No		

Site name	Watch Hill		PRN	7380
Site type	Cist		Grid Ref	88000 15200
Dimensions	Chamber 1.2m long, 0.8m wide, 0.6m deep		Orientation	
Details	Area covered with gorse in 2010 and no trace of structure; capstones removed for building (documentary record Troutbeck, 1796)			
Excavation	None	Finds	None	
Condition	Unknown	Museum		
Hencken No		Daniel No		

Site name	Works Carn		PRN	7396
Site type	Entrance grave		Grid Ref	87828 14158
Dimensions	Mound 11.0m by 9.0m diameter, 1.0m high Chamber 6.5m long, 1.3m wide, 0.7m high		Orientation	14° NNE-SSW
Details	2 capstones in place, 4 more in chamber; double kerb in places; natural rock incorporated into kerb and mound			
Excavation	None	Finds	None	
Condition	Extant, good	Museum		
Hencken No	Bryher 1	Daniel No	Bryher 1	

2. Eastern Isles

Site name	Arthur Porth		PRN	7216
Site type	Cist – possible		Grid Ref	94080 13860
Dimensions	Not known		Orientation	
Details	HER entry states that site last reliably recorded in 1978; close to Mean High Water; no trace in 2009 or 2012			
Excavation	None	Finds	None	
Condition	Unknown	Museum		
Hencken No		Daniel No		

Site name	Great Arthur A		PRN	7221.01
Site type	Entrance grave – probable		Grid Ref	94166 13535
Dimensions	Mound 9.0m diameter, 1.5m high Hollow 3.0m diameter		Orientation	
Details	Site overgrown with grass in 2012 but several stones visible around hollow; modern cairn on NE side of mound; on highest point of ridge			
Excavation	None	Finds	None	
Condition	Extant, poor	Museum		
Hencken No		Daniel No		

Site name	Great Arthur B		PRN	7221.02
Site type	Entrance grave – probable		Grid Ref	94183 13543
Dimensions	Mound 9.0m diameter, 1.8m high Hollow 4.0m long, 3.5m wide, 1.0m deep		Orientation	NNE-SSW
Details	Site overgrown with vegetation in 2012 but at least 1 stone visible in hollow; inner kerb and possible outer kerb; boulder wall leads E to 7221.03 along ridge of hill			
Excavation	None	Finds	None	
Condition	Extant, poor	Museum		
Hencken No		Daniel No	Arthur 6	

Site name	Great Arthur C		PRN	7221.03
Site type	Entrance grave		Grid Ref	94228 13564
Dimensions	Mound 9.0m diameter, 1.7m high Chamber 3.6m long, 1.5m wide, 0.7m high		Orientation	19° NNE-SSW
Details	3 capstones in place, 2 at northern end have small stones filling gaps between them; substantial inner kerb of up to 4 courses of stone and outer kerb; boulder wall leads W to 7221.02 along ridge of hill			
Excavation	None	Finds	None	
Condition	Extant, good	Museum		
Hencken No	Arthur 1	Daniel No	Arthur 1	

Site name	**Great Ganilly A**		PRN	7210.01
Site type	**Entrance grave or cist – possible**		**Grid Ref**	**94556 14551**
Dimensions	Mound 9.0m diameter, 0.7m high Hollow 3.5m long, 2.0m wide, 0.2m deep		Orientation	
Details	Centre of mound obscured by modern cairn; 6 kerbstones visible; SM entry records that hollow exposes 2 long slabs lying side by side			
Excavation	None	Finds	None	
Condition	Extant, poor	Museum		
Hencken No		Daniel No		

Site name	**Great Ganilly C**		PRN	7210.03
Site type	Cist – possible		Grid Ref	94610 14590
Dimensions	Mound 8.6m by 7.0m diameter, 1.0m high		Orientation	
Details	Large slab exposed on flat surface of mound may be capstone; inner and outer kerbs visible			
Excavation	None	Finds	None	
Condition	Extant, poor	Museum		
Hencken No		Daniel No		

Site name	**Great Ganilly D**		PRN	7210.04
Site type	Cist – possible		Grid Ref	94630 14560
Dimensions	Chamber 3.0m long, 2.0m wide, 0.6m high		Orientation	N-S
Details	No trace of mound; 'chamber' open on one long side and may be natural rock formation			
Excavation	None	Finds	None	
Condition	Extant	Museum		
Hencken No		Daniel No		

Site name	**Little Arthur C**		PRN	7215.01
Site type	Cist - probable		Grid Ref	94140 13891
Dimensions	Mound 6.0m diameter, 0.8m high Chamber up to 2.0m long, 1.0m wide		Orientation	NE-SW
Details	Mound includes natural rock; part of kerb survives; possible capstone nearby to E			
Excavation	See 7215.02 below	Finds	See 7215.02 below	
Condition	Extant, poor	Museum	See 7215.02 below	
Hencken No	Arthur 4	Daniel No	Arthur 4	

Site name	**Little Arthur D**		PRN	7215.02
Site type	Entrance grave		Grid Ref	94142 13906
Dimensions	Mound 8.7m diameter, 1.2m high Chamber at least 2.5m long, 1.1m wide, 0.4m high		Orientation	69° ENE-WSW
Details	Two kerbs; single capstone in place at SW end			
Excavation	Pottery collected by Gibson, 1898	Finds	Pottery 'from Grave on top of Little Arthur' (PRN 7225) probably from this site	
Condition	Extant, fair	Museum	IoS: RN 1304	
Hencken No	Arthur 5	Daniel No	Arthur 5	

Site name	Little Arthur E		PRN	7215.04
Site type	Entrance grave or cist		Grid Ref	94127 13915
Dimensions	Mound 6.0m diameter, 0.8m high Chamber 2.0m long, 0.9m wide, 0.5m high		Orientation	NE-SW
Details	Several natural rocks in mound; kerb of upright stones; possible capstone on SE side of mound; very overgrown by vegetation in 2009 and 2012			
Excavation	See 7215.02 above	Finds	See 7215.02 above	
Condition	Extant, fair	Museum	See 7215.02 above	
Hencken No		Daniel No		

Site name	Little Arthur		PRN	7650
Site type	Cist – possible		Grid Ref	94050 13860
Dimensions	Chamber 1.4m long, 1.3m wide, 0.5m high		Orientation	?E-W
Details	Area overgrown in 2009 and 2012 and site not located; HER entry says it mainly consisted of natural rock			
Excavation	None	Finds	None	
Condition	Unknown	Museum		
Hencken No		Daniel No		

Site name	Middle Arthur A		PRN	7224.02
Site type	Entrance grave		Grid Ref	93991 13834
Dimensions	Mound 6.7m by 6.4m diameter, 0.9m high Chamber 3.5m long, 1.3m wide, 0.5m high		Orientation	NW-SE
Details	Four capstones in place and possible 5th one on SE side of mound; chamber earth-filled; overgrown by vegetation in 2009			
Excavation	None	Finds	None	
Condition	Extant, good	Museum		
Hencken No	Arthur 2	Daniel No	Arthur 2	

Site name	Middle Arthur B		PRN	7224.01
Site type	Entrance grave or cist		Grid Ref	93990 13807
Dimensions	Mound 4.0m by 3.4m diameter, 0.7m high Chamber 2.1m long, 1.2m wide at S end, tapering to point, 0.8m high		Orientation	NNE-SSW
Details	Triangular chamber, walled with orthostats; 1 capstone in place, slab at SSW end may be fallen capstone; kerb very close to chamber			
Excavation	O'Neil, 1953	Finds	Cremated human bone, pottery, flint	
Condition	Extant, good	Museum	RCM: 1955,38.3	
Hencken No	Arthur 3	Daniel No	Arthur 3	

3. Gugh

Site name	Carn Kimbra		PRN	7054
Site type	Entrance grave or cist – possible		Grid Ref	89157 08436
Dimensions	Mound 4.1m diameter, 0.6m high		Orientation	
Details	Overgrown by vegetation in 2008; several kerbstones; possible capstone in centre of mound			
Excavation	None	Finds	None	
Condition	Extant, poor	Museum		
Hencken No		Daniel No		

Site name	Carn of Works		PRN	7057
Site type	Entrance grave – probable		Grid Ref	89155 08028
Dimensions	Mound 22.9m (including bank of Civil War redoubt) Chamber 1.5m wide		Orientation	NE-SW or SW-NE
Details	Only short length of side walling and single probable capstone survive, incorporated into Civil War redoubt; original extent of mound not clear			
Excavation	None	Finds	Pottery	
Condition	Extant, poor	Museum	Not known	
Hencken No	Gugh 10	Daniel No	Gugh 7	

Site name	Carn Valla		PRN	7032
Site type	Entrance grave – probable		Grid Ref	88860 08470
Dimensions	Mound 7.3m diameter, 0.8m high		Orientation	
Details	Inaccessible due to gorse in 2008 and 2012; kerbstones and possible capstones recorded in HER but no sign of chamber			
Excavation	None	Finds	None	
Condition	Extant, poor	Museum		
Hencken No	Gugh 11	Daniel No	Gugh 6	

Site name	Clapper of Works M		PRN	7020.12
Site type	Entrance grave		Grid Ref	89030 07959
Dimensions	Mound 13.0m diameter Chamber 4.0m long, 1.4m wide, 0.4m high		Orientation	SE-NW
Details	Overgrown by vegetation but four capstones visible, apparently in place			
Excavation	None	Finds	None	
Condition	Extant, good	Museum		
Hencken No	Gugh 9	Daniel No	Gugh 8	

Site name	Kittern Hill A		PRN	7030.01
Site type	Entrance grave		Grid Ref	88792 08675
Dimensions	Mound 12.5m diameter, 1.5m high Chamber 5.2m long, 1.4m wide, 0.8m high		Orientation	41.5° NE-SW
Details	4 capstones in place, 1 fallen; chamber walls of drystone courses, possible sill at top			
Excavation	Pottery found in 1984	Finds	Pottery	
Condition	Extant, good	Museum	Not known	
Hencken No	Gugh 2	Daniel No	Gugh 2	

Site name	Kittern Hill B		PRN	7030.02
Site type	Cist - probable		Grid Ref	88786 08690
Dimensions	Mound 11.0m diameter, 1.4m high		Orientation	
Details	Two slabs, on edge and at right angles around trig point, may be part of earlier structure; boulder wall leads SE from mound to 7030.08			
Excavation	None	Finds	None	
Condition	Extant, poor	Museum		
Hencken No	Gugh 3	Daniel No	Gugh 3	

Site name	Kittern Hill C		PRN	7030.03
Site type	Entrance grave or cist – possible		Grid Ref	88820 08667
Dimensions	Mound 4.3m diameter, 0.2m high		Orientation	
Details	Obscured by gorse in 2009; hollow in top visible; boulder wall crosses NE edge of mound			
Excavation	None	Finds	None	
Condition	Extant, poor	Museum		
Hencken No		Daniel No		

Site name	Kittern Hill J		PRN	7030.06
Site type	Entrance grave or cist – possible		Grid Ref	88842 08660
Dimensions	Mound 4.5m diameter, 0.3m high		Orientation	
Details	Overgrown by vegetation in 2009; part of kerb visible; boulder wall crosses NE edge of mound			
Excavation	None	Finds	None	
Condition	Extant, poor	Museum		
Hencken No		Daniel No		

Site name	Kittern Hill K		PRN	7030.07
Site type	Entrance grave or cist – possible		Grid Ref	88860 08627
Dimensions	Mound 4.5m diameter, 0.1m high		Orientation	
Details	Area covered by gorse in 2009 and nothing visible; HER entry records kerb of large boulders and hollow in centre of mound			
Excavation	None	Finds	None	
Condition	Extant, poor	Museum		
Hencken No		Daniel No		

Site name	Kittern Hill L		PRN	7030.08
Site type	Entrance grave		Grid Ref	88908 08619
Dimensions	Mound 11.0m diameter, 1.7m high Chamber 4.0m long, 1.0m wide		Orientation	95.5° E-W
Details	Kerb of large stones, particularly on W side; boulder walls lead NW to 7030.02, SE to 7030.10 and SW			
Excavation	None	Finds	None	
Condition	Extant, fair	Museum		
Hencken No	Gugh 7	Daniel No	Gugh 3	

Site name	Kittern Hill N		PRN	7030.10
Site type	Entrance grave – probable		Grid Ref	88953 08607
Dimensions	Mound 13.0m diameter, 1.3m high		Orientation	
Details	Overgrown with vegetation in 2008 but evidence of 2 chambers, one on S side of mound, one on W side, both with edge-set slabs, S one with possible capstone, W one with possible kerb; possible central hollow also; boulder wall leads NW to 7030.08			
Excavation	None	Finds	None	
Condition	Extant, poor	Museum		
Hencken No	Gugh 8	Daniel No	Gugh 4	

Site name	Obadiah's Barrow		PRN	7031
Site type	Entrance grave		Grid Ref	88805 08526
Dimensions	Mound 7.0m diameter, 0.6m high Chamber 5.2m long, 1.4m wide, 1.1m high		Orientation	111.5° ESE-WNW (chamber) NE-SW (passage)
Details	Blocking stone in entrance, excavator recorded short passage (not visible now); 2 capstones in place, 2 more in chamber; walls of coursed drystone construction			
Excavation	Bonsor, 1901 Pottery collected nearby in 1965 and 2006	Finds	Cremated and inhumed human bone, pottery, animal bone and horn points, bronze awl, hammer stone, limpet shells Nearby: pottery	
Condition	Extant, good	Museum	BM: 1926,1112.10-26 IoS: RN 1078, 4249, 4679	
Hencken No	Gugh 1	Daniel No	Gugh 5	

4. Northwethel

Site name	Northwethel A		PRN	7272.01
Site type	Entrance grave		Grid Ref	89608 16284
Dimensions	Mound 6.5m diameter, 0.8m high Chamber 3.1m long, 1.2m wide in centre, tapering to 0.5m wide at entrance, 0.5m high		Orientation	E-W
Details	2 capstones in place; several kerbstones, including some on either side of entrance			
Excavation	None	Finds	None	
Condition	Extant, good	Museum		
Hencken No	Northwethel	Daniel No	Northwethel	

Site name	Northwethel		PRN	7275
Site type	Other (natural feature)		Grid Ref	89450 16310
Dimensions	N/A		Orientation	N/A
Details	Large boulder supported by two rocks with passage between them; recorded as 'chambered tomb' in HER and as 'tolmen' by Borlase in 1752, but natural feature			
Excavation	N/A	Finds	N/A	
Condition	Extant	Museum		
Hencken No		Daniel No		

5. Round Island

Site name	Round Island	PRN	7094
Site type	Entrance graves – probable (x3)	Grid Ref	90200 17700
Dimensions	'Large'	Orientation	
Details	Destroyed during building of lighthouse in 1880s (documentary record Layard,1933)		
Excavation	None	Finds	None
Condition	Destroyed	Museum	
Hencken No		Daniel No	

6. St Agnes

Site name	Burnt Island	PRN	168706
Site type	Cist – possible	Grid Ref	87411 08626
Dimensions	Mound 9.0m by 6.7m diameter, 0.3m high	Orientation	
Details	Overgrown with grass in 2008; HER entry suggests cist formed by slabs with tips exposed in turf; kerbed mound incorporates outcrops with possible kerbing, may be analogous to Dartmoor tor cairn		
Excavation	None	Finds	None
Condition	Extant, poor	Museum	
Hencken No		Daniel No	

Site name	Carn of Cove Vean G	PRN	7011.07
Site type	Cist - possible	Grid Ref	88566 07877
Dimensions	Mound 6.5m by 7.0m diameter, 0.5m high Hollow 1.0m wide, 0.15m deep	Orientation	
Details	Covered with gorse in 2009, features not obvious; HER entry records possible kerb around SE perimeter		
Excavation	None	Finds	None
Condition	Extant, poor	Museum	
Hencken No		Daniel No	

Site name	Carn of Cove Vean H	PRN	7011.08
Site type	Cist – possible	Grid Ref	88559 07868
Dimensions	Mound 8.0m by 5.0m diameter, 0.4m high	Orientation	
Details	Much natural rock incorporated into kerbed mound; central hollow with surrounding large slabs which may be natural; mound very eroded		
Excavation	None	Finds	None
Condition	Extant, poor	Museum	
Hencken No		Daniel No	

Site name	Porth Askin B	PRN	7018.02
Site type	Cist – possible	Grid Ref	88164 07278
Dimensions	Mound 5.0m diameter, 0.4m high	Orientation	
Details	Central hollow, 3 possible kerbstones on N side of mound; large stones in centre of mound may be natural		
Excavation	None	Finds	None
Condition	Extant, poor	Museum	
Hencken No		Daniel No	

Site name	Porth Askin F	PRN	7018.06
Site type	Entrance grave or cist - possible	Grid Ref	88362 07227
Dimensions	Mound 6.0m by 4.0m diameter, 0.5m high Hollow 2.0m long, 1.5m wide, 0.4m deep	Orientation	
Details	Overgrown with vegetation in 2008 but hollow visible; kerb on N and W of mound		
Excavation	None	Finds	None
Condition	Extant, poor	Museum	
Hencken No		Daniel No	

Site name	Porth Conger		PRN	7595
Site type	Cist – possible		Grid Ref	88464 08420
Dimensions	Chamber 0.8m high		Orientation	
Details	Exposed in cliff-face 3.0m above beach, access not possible, grid reference estimated			
Excavation	None	Finds	None	
Condition	Unknown	Museum		
Hencken No		Daniel No		

Site name	Porth Killier		PRN	7029
Site type	Cist – probable		Grid Ref	88100 08480
Dimensions	Mound 9.0m diameter, 0.5m high Chamber 0.8m wide, 0.4m high		Orientation	
Details	Chamber has walls formed of 3 orthostats, saddle quern on its side and boulder, no capstones; large lumps of yellow clay found in chamber; next to settlement site			
Excavation	Ratcliffe, 1996	Finds	Pottery, clay, mortar/socket stone	
Condition	Extant, good	Museum	IoS (archive not yet deposited in 2012)	
Hencken No		Daniel No		

Site name	Wingletang Down C		PRN	7015.03
Site type	Cist – possible		Grid Ref	88261 07493
Dimensions	Mound 4.0m diameter, 0.3m high Hollow 1.25m long, 0.75m wide, 0.15m deep		Orientation	
Details	Overgrown with heather in 2008, hollow not apparent; kerb includes natural outcrops			
Excavation	None	Finds	None	
Condition	Extant, poor	Museum		
Hencken No		Daniel No		

Site name	Wingletang Down D		PRN	7015.04
Site type	Cist – possible		Grid Ref	88287 07479
Dimensions	Mound 4.0m by 3.0m diameter, 0.3m high Hollow 1.5m long, 1.0m wide, 0.2m deep		Orientation	
Details	Overgrown with heather in 2008, hollow not apparent; mound incorporates natural outcrop, some kerb stones			
Excavation	None	Finds	None	
Condition	Extant, poor	Museum		
Hencken No		Daniel No		

Site name	Wingletang Down E		PRN	7016.05
Site type	Cist – possible		Grid Ref	88496 07587
Dimensions	Mound 7.0m by 6.0m diameter, 0.4m high Hollow 1.5m long, 0.8m wide, 0.2m deep		Orientation	
Details	Granite block and slabs around hollow; recent disturbance with pieces of slate present; kerb stones include quartz block on N side			
Excavation	None	Finds	None	
Condition	Extant, poor	Museum		
Hencken No		Daniel No		

Site name	Wingletang Down Q		PRN	7016.15
Site type	Cist – probable		Grid Ref	88548 07620
Dimensions	Mound 5.0m by 4.0m diameter, 0.5m high Hollow 1.0m long, 0.8m wide, 0.35m deep		Orientation	
Details	Stones visible on N and W sides of hollow; kerbed mound incorporates natural outcrops			
Excavation	None	Finds	None	
Condition	Extant, poor	Museum		
Hencken No		Daniel No		

Site name	Wingletang Down S		PRN	7016.17
Site type	Entrance grave or cist – possible		Grid Ref	88503 07636
Dimensions	Mound 8.5m by 7.5m diameter, 0.5m high		Orientation	
Details	Overgrown with vegetation in 2008 but hollow with stones and void visible in centre of mound; kerbed mound incorporates natural outcrops			
Excavation	None	Finds	None	
Condition	Extant, poor	Museum		
Hencken No		Daniel No		

7. St Helen's

Site name	St Helen's		PRN	7114.01
Site type	Cist – probable		Grid Ref	90087 16970
Dimensions	Mound 16.0m by 12.0m diameter, 1.5m high Chamber at least 0.7m long, 0.8m wide, 0.1m deep		Orientation	NW-SE
Details	Mainly obscured by vegetation in 2012 but some stones visible; possible kerb, incorporating some natural boulders on SW side of mound; recent lookout and trig point on stone platform to W of chamber			
Excavation	None	Finds	None	
Condition	Extant, poor	Museum		
Hencken No		Daniel No		

Site name	St Helen's B		PRN	7267.02
Site type	Cist – possible		Grid Ref	89964 17073
Dimensions	Mound 4.0m by 3.0m diameter, 0.1m high Hollow 1.0m long, 1.0m wide, 0.1m deep		Orientation	
Details	Overgrown with gorse, etc in 2012 and hollow not visible; two edge-set slabs and some kerbstones apparent			
Excavation	None	Finds	None	
Condition	Extant, poor	Museum		
Hencken No		Daniel No		

8. St Martin's

Site name	Barnacle Rock		PRN	7175
Site type	Entrance grave or cist – possible		Grid Ref	92623 15970
Dimensions	Hollow 0.6m deep		Orientation	
Details	Trench between two boulders of outcrop, natural rock on one side, other side possibly constructed; surrounding mound may be natural			
Excavation	Lewis, 1944	Finds	Pottery (2 sherds), flints	
Condition	Extant	Museum	Not known	
Hencken No		Daniel No		

Site name	Carrion Rock		PRN	7169
Site type	Other (misidentification)		Grid Ref	92797 15416
Dimensions	No site in this area		Orientation	
Details	Site confused with Cruther's Neck (PRN 7170)			
Excavation	N/A	Finds	N/A	
Condition	N/A	Museum		
Hencken No		Daniel No		

Site name	Chapel Brow		PRN	7127
Site type	Entrance grave – probable		Grid Ref	94219 16114
Dimensions	Mound 4.0m by 3.0m diameter, 0.5m high Hollow 1.5m long, 1.0m wide, 0.2m deep		Orientation	E-W or W-E
Details	Overgrown with bramble in 2010 but large stones visible, some around hollow			
Excavation	None	Finds	None	
Condition	Extant, poor	Museum		
Hencken No		Daniel No		

Site name	Chapel Down		PRN	7117.01
Site type	Entrance grave or cist – possible		Grid Ref	94196 16123
Dimensions	Mound 4.0m diameter, 0.6m high Hollow 1.5m long, 1.2m wide, 0.5m deep		Orientation	
Details	Overgrown and eroded in 2010, hollow not very obvious; mound incorporates some natural rock; kerb possibly recent			
Excavation	None	Finds	None	
Condition	Extant, poor	Museum		
Hencken No		Daniel No		

Site name	Chapel Down J		PRN	7117.02
Site type	Entrance grave – probable		Grid Ref	94089 16061
Dimensions	Mound 8.0m diameter, 1.0m high		Orientation	E-W or W-E
Details	Probable capstone, resting on three upright boulders, near centre of mound, all obscured by vegetation; mound incorporates natural rock; remains of kerb around mound			
Excavation	None	Finds	None	
Condition	Extant, poor	Museum		
Hencken No		Daniel No		

Site name	Chapel Down K		PRN	7117.03
Site type	Cist – possible		Grid Ref	94181 16104
Dimensions	Mound 4.5m by 4.0m diameter, 1.0m high Hollow 1.0m long, 0.5m wide, 0.3m deep		Orientation	N-S
Details	Mound incorporates some natural rock			
Excavation	None	Finds	None	
Condition	Extant, poor	Museum		
Hencken No		Daniel No		

Site name	Chapel Down A		PRN	7122.01
Site type	Cist - probable		Grid Ref	94204 15799
Dimensions	Mound 6.0m by 4.0m diameter, 0.8m high Hollow 1.0m long, 0.6m wide		Orientation	
Details	Rectangular trench, apparently recently dug, in E side of mound; edge-set stone near centre; orthostat 1.6m high set into N side of mound			
Excavation	None	Finds	None	
Condition	Extant, poor	Museum		
Hencken No		Daniel No		

Site name	Chapel Down A		PRN	7259.01
Site type	Entrance grave		Grid Ref	94388 15753
Dimensions	Mound 9.0m diameter, 1.3m high Chamber 3.5m long, 1.5m wide, 0.5m deep		Orientation	SSW-NNE or NNE-SSW
Details	Chamber constructed of edge-set slabs and very ruinous; incomplete kerb			
Excavation	None	Finds	None	
Condition	Extant, poor	Museum		
Hencken No		Daniel No		

Site name	Cruther's Hill A		PRN	7172.01
Site type	Entrance grave or cist		Grid Ref	92894 15229
Dimensions	Mound 12.0m by 8.0m diameter, 0.9m high Chamber 1.5m long, 0.7m wide, 0.5m deep		Orientation	NE-SW
Details	Boulder kerb; chamber very ruinous; 2 possible capstones on mound			
Excavation	None	Finds	None	
Condition	Extant, fair	Museum		
Hencken No		Daniel No	St Martin's 1	

Site name	Cruther's Hill B		PRN	7172.02
Site type	Entrance grave		Grid Ref	92915 15187
Dimensions	Mound 8.0m diameter, 1.7m high Chamber 4.7m long, 1.2m wide, 1.0m high		Orientation	63° ENE-WSW
Details	Boulder kerb; mound incorporates some natural rock; chamber walls of large orthostats, floor of natural rock			
Excavation	Cleared by Lewis, between 1944 and 1947	Finds	None	
Condition	Extant, good	Museum		
Hencken No	St Martin's 1	Daniel No	St Martin's 2	

Site name	Cruther's Hill C		PRN	7172.03
Site type	Entrance grave		Grid Ref	92953 15137
Dimensions	Mound 6.0m by 5.0m diameter, 0.8m high Chamber 3.0m long, 1.3m wide, 0.5m high		Orientation	E-W
Details	Overgrown with gorse in 2008 and 2012, chamber not visible; mound incorporates much natural rock; incomplete kerb with natural boulders			
Excavation	None	Finds	None	
Condition	Extant, poor	Museum		
Hencken No		Daniel No	St Martin's 3	

Site name	Cruther's Hill D		PRN	7172.04
Site type	Cist		Grid Ref	92968 15125
Dimensions	Mound 3.5m diameter, 0.7m high Chamber 1.9m long, 1.1m wide, 0.1m deep		Orientation	NE-SW
Details	Overgrown with gorse in 2008 and 2012, chamber not visible; HER records that chamber is built against natural boulder near centre of mound; incomplete kerb			
Excavation	None	Finds	None	
Condition	Extant, poor	Museum		
Hencken No		Daniel No	St Martin's 4	

Site name	Cruther's Neck		PRN	7170
Site type	Entrance grave - probable		Grid Ref	92850 15348
Dimensions	Mound 10.0m diameter, 0.7m high Hollow 5.0m long, 1.5m wide, 0.1m deep		Orientation	E-W or W-E
Details	Area cleared in 2010 and hollow visible but no sign of structure			
Excavation	Gibson, late 19th century	Finds	Cremated bone, pottery, bronze point, limpet shells	
Condition	Extant, poor	Museum	IoS: RN 1214 (bronze point)	
Hencken No		Daniel No		

Site name	Gun Hill		PRN	7146
Site type	Cist – possible		Grid Ref	93907 15392
Dimensions	Mound 13.0m by 11.0m diameter, 1.3m high		Orientation	
Details	Setting of 5 stones on top of mound around orthostat 0.7m high; incomplete kerb			
Excavation	None	Finds	None	
Condition	Extant	Museum		
Hencken No		Daniel No	St Martin's 7	

Site name	Hill Bennigates		PRN	7138.01
Site type	Cist		Grid Ref	93545 15800
Dimensions	Mound 15.5m by 13.5m diameter, 1.1m high		Orientation	E-W
Details	Large boulder in centre with signs of excavation nearby; no trace of cist now			
Excavation	O'Neil, 1952	Finds	Pottery, flints	
Condition	Extant, poor	Museum	RCM: 1955,38.5	
Hencken No		Daniel No		

Site name	John Batty's Hill		PRN	7145
Site type	Entrance grave		Grid Ref	93800 15530
Dimensions	Mound 9.0m diameter, 0.8m high Chamber 2.0m long, 1.0m wide, 0.5m high		Orientation	N-S
Details	Site inaccessible due to gorse in 2010; HER records 3 kerbstones and 1 capstone in place; mound has been dug into			
Excavation	None	Finds	None	
Condition	Extant, fair	Museum		
Hencken No		Daniel No		

Site name	Knackyboy Cairn		PRN	7162.01
Site type	Entrance grave		Grid Ref	92364 15870
Dimensions	Mound 19.0m by 16.0m diameter, 0.9m high Location of chamber now hollow 3.0m wide, 0.7m wide, 0.2m deep but chamber recorded by O'Neil as 3.7m long, 0.9m wide		Orientation	E-W
Details	Chamber built against natural outcrop, no capstones remained when excavated by O'Neil; mortar recorded between stones of chamber walls; 2 kerbs: outer one survives in part; 2 satellite burials in mound			
Excavation	Gibson, 1912 Lewis, 1944-1947 O'Neil, 1948 Mulville, 2006	Finds	Cremated human bone, pottery, flints, faience and glass beads, bronze objects, animal bone point, mortar/daub objects, ?unfinished spindle-whorl; missing: ?gold object, ?agate beads Nearby: flints	
Condition	Extant, poor	Museum	RCM: 1950,40; 1991,78c IoS: RN 882, 883, 1982, 2277, 3740, 6052, 6053	
Hencken No		Daniel No	St Martin's 8	

Site name	Little Bay		PRN	7208.01
Site type	Cist		Grid Ref	92310 16620
Dimensions	Not recorded		Orientation	Not recorded
Details	2 edge-set stones at right angles, stone-lined; found on W side of interior of building 5 (site B) of settlement site			
Excavation	Minett-Smith, 1964 Butcher, 1974 Neal, 1980	Finds	None recorded from cist: interior of hut cleared before 1974 excavation	
Condition	Unknown	Museum		
Hencken No		Daniel No		

Site name	Par Beach		PRN	Referred to in 7148
Site type	Cist		Grid Ref	93200 15300
Dimensions	Chamber 0.6m long, 0.6m wide, up to 0.4m high		Orientation	
Details	In inter-tidal zone, no trace in 1988 or 2010; constructed of 4 slabs, paving slabs on floor, joints sealed with mortar, possible capstone nearby			
Excavation	O'Neil, 1949	Finds	Mortar	
Condition	Unknown	Museum	RCM: 1955,38.10; IoS: RN 4685?	
Hencken No		Daniel No		

Site name	Pernagie Carn		PRN	7187
Site type	Entrance grave - probable		Grid Ref	91920 16821
Dimensions	Mound 10.0m diameter, 1.5m high Chamber 2.5m long, 1.5m wide		Orientation	209° SSW-NNE
Details	Chamber built against large outcrop on S side; possible capstone on SE side of mound			
Excavation	Lewis, c1947	Finds	Pottery, clay balls, charcoal	
Condition	Extant, fair	Museum	IoS: RN 3751 (items found by O'Neils in spoil left by Lewis), 6050, 6051	
Hencken No		Daniel No		

Site name	Tinkler's Hill A		PRN	7190.01
Site type	Entrance grave		Grid Ref	91704 16500
Dimensions	Mound 22.0m diameter, 1.0m high Hollow 2.0m long, 1.0m wide, 0.5m deep		Orientation	NNE-SSW
Details	Partly overgrown with gorse in 2009; part of kerb survives on N side			
Excavation	O'Neil, 1950	Finds	None	
Condition	Extant, poor	Museum		
Hencken No		Daniel No		

Site name	Tinkler's Hill E		PRN	7190.05
Site type	Entrance grave or cist – possible		Grid Ref	91677 16310
Dimensions	Mound 14.0m diameter, 0.8m high Hollow 1.5m long, 1.0m wide, 1.0m deep		Orientation	?SW-NE
Details	Overgrown with gorse in 2009; part of possible kerb of large stones (although SM entry says post-mediaeval lookout), mound extends outside kerb; area within kerb disturbed but large slab beside hollow			
Excavation	Lewis, between 1944 and 1947	Finds	'Stone with rough carving on it' (left on site but now no trace there)	
Condition	Extant, fair	Museum		
Hencken No		Daniel No		

Site name	Top Rock Hill B		PRN	7198.02
Site type	Entrance grave or cist		Grid Ref	92221 16737
Dimensions	Mound 6.0m diameter, 0.8m high Chamber 2.0m long, 1.0m wide, 0.5m high		Orientation	E-W
Details	Overgrown with gorse in 2009; HER entry records edge-set slabs on N, W and S sides of chamber; 2 possible capstones on mound; 3 possible small kerbstones			
Excavation	None	Finds	None	
Condition	Extant, fair	Museum		
Hencken No		Daniel No		

Site name	Top Rock Hill E		PRN	7198.04
Site type	Entrance grave or cist – possible		Grid Ref	92220 16684
Dimensions	Mound 6.0m diameter, 0.8m high Hollow 4.0m long, 1.0m wide		Orientation	E-W
Details	Overgrown with vegetation in 2009 and no features visible; HER entry records mound is greatly disturbed and in close proximity to lynchet			
Excavation	None	Finds	?Pot found 1890	
Condition	Extant, poor	Museum	Not known	
Hencken No		Daniel No		

Site name	Trelawney		PRN	7598
Site type	Cist		Grid Ref	92800 15800
Dimensions	Not known		Orientation	Not known
Details	Reported that ploughed up in field 8282 in 1969			
Excavation	None	Finds	None	
Condition	Destroyed	Museum		
Hencken No		Daniel No		

Site name	Turfy Hill		PRN	7128
Site type	Entrance grave or cist – possible		Grid Ref	93089 15999
Dimensions	Mound 14.0m by 12.0m diameter, 0.8m high 2 'large rectangular hollows'		Orientation	
Details	Overgrown with vegetation in 2009 and hollows not visible; large stone to SW of mound centre			
Excavation	None	Finds	None	
Condition	Extant, poor	Museum		
Hencken No		Daniel No		

Site name	Yellow Rock Carn		PRN	7163
Site type	Other (natural cleft in rock)		Grid Ref	92243 15831
Dimensions	N/A		Orientation	N/A
Details	'Funerary urn' found in cleft in rock, not clear whether cremated remains in it; carn very overgrown in 2011			
Excavation	Gibson, late 19th century	Finds	Pottery	
Condition	Extant	Museum	IoS: not located between 2006 and 2012	
Hencken No		Daniel No		

9. St Mary's

Site name	Arden Craig		PRN	7521
Site type	Other (bulb dump)		Grid Ref	91997 11698
Dimensions	Mound 20.0m by 12.0m diameter, 1.6m high		Orientation	
Details	Suggested as possible cairn by Ashbee but house-holder said in 2009 that mound is 20th century bulb dump; recorded as 'entrance grave' in HER			
Excavation	N/A	Finds	N/A	
Condition	Extant	Museum		
Hencken No		Daniel No		

Site name	Bant's Carn		PRN	7443
Site type	Entrance grave		Grid Ref	91005 12308
Dimensions	Mound 8.6m by 6.2m diameter, 2.3m high Chamber 4.9m long, 1.6m wide in centre, 1.2m at each end, 1.5m high Passage 5.0m long, 1.0m wide		Orientation	63° ENE-WSW (chamber) NE-SW (passage)
Details	All 4 capstones in place, portal stones at chamber entrance; unroofed passage now outside mound; kerb around mound is of coursed walling, outer kerb 13.2m diameter of boulders; recent field wall built over S side of mound			
Excavation	Bonsor, 1900 and 1901 Ashbee, 1970 Pumice found nearby by Gray, 1920s/1930s?	Finds	Cremated human bone, pottery, flints, quern rubber, limpet shells; Nearby: pottery, pumice bead	
Condition	Extant, excellent	Museum	Finds from excavations missing RCM: 2005,47.3 (pumice)	
Hencken No	St Mary's 2	Daniel No	St Mary's 3	

Site name	Borough Farm		PRN	7525
Site type	Entrance grave – probable		Grid Ref	91980 11980
Dimensions	'One of the largest on the island'		Orientation	
Details	Destroyed (documentary record Layard,1933 and oral record 1978)			
Excavation	None	Finds	None	
Condition	Destroyed	Museum		
Hencken No		Daniel No		

Site name	Buzza Hill A		PRN	7578.01
Site type	Entrance grave		Grid Ref	90588 10383
Dimensions	Mound 12.0m diameter, 2.5m high Chamber 2.5m long, 1.5m wide, 0.7m high		Orientation	70° ENE-WSW
Details	Closed chamber but stone at ENE end recorded as fallen capstone by Bonsor; single capstone in place; walls of coursed walling of large slabs			
Excavation	Bonsor, 1901	Finds	None	
Condition	Extant, good	Museum		
Hencken No	St Mary's 7	Daniel No	St Mary's 13	

Site name	Buzza Hill		PRN	7578.02
Site type	Entrance grave		Grid Ref	90631 10383
Dimensions	Mound 12.0m diameter? Chamber 6.7m long, 1.4m wide in centre, 0.5m wide at entrance, 1.5m high		Orientation	NE-SW
Details	Walls of chamber mortared, stones on either side of entrance; destroyed for building of windmill 1820; kerbed platform around windmill may be remains of mound			
Excavation	Borlase, 1752	Finds	'Strong unctuous earth which smelt cadaverous'	
Condition	Destroyed	Museum	Not known	
Hencken No	St Mary's 6a	Daniel No	St Mary's 16	

Site name	Buzza Hill		PRN	7578.03
Site type	Entrance grave		Grid Ref	90607 10375
Dimensions	Chamber 4.3m long, 1.2m wide in centre, 0.5m wide at entrance, 0.6m high		Orientation	ENE-WSW
Details	'Small round cell', which contained 'some earths of different colours from the natural', found in floor of chamber; mound with several large stones and one possible capstone at grid reference given, which is 13m W of 7578.02 (Borlase says site is 13m N of it), Bonsor confirms that this is location			
Excavation	Borlase, 1752	Finds	Coloured earths	
Condition	Unknown	Museum	Not known	
Hencken No	St Mary's 6b	Daniel No	St Mary's 16	

Site name	Carn Morval Down		PRN	7496
Site type	Cist		Grid Ref	91130 12030
Dimensions	'Small' mound Small, almost rectangular chamber made of 4 stones		Orientation	
Details	Site known as Klondyke field; field had flowers in 2011 and 2012, no trace of cist			
Excavation	Gibson, c1899	Finds	Ashes	
Condition	Unknown	Museum	Not known	
Hencken No		Daniel No		

Site name	Carn Morval Down A		PRN	7507.01
Site type	Entrance grave – probable		Grid Ref	90750 11990
Dimensions	Mound 12.5m diameter, 1.2m high Hollow 2.5m long, 2.5m wide, 0.3m deep		Orientation	
Details	Area overgrown with gorse in 2012; HER records possible capstone on mound			
Excavation	None	Finds	None	
Condition	Extant, poor	Museum		
Hencken No	St Mary's 18	Daniel No	St Mary's 17	

Site name	Church Point		PRN	7658
Site type	Cist – possible		Grid Ref	92240 09990
Dimensions	Not known		Orientation	
Details	No trace of cist found and not located in 1988; HER records possible slab-built cist			
Excavation	None	Finds	None	
Condition	Unknown	Museum		
Hencken No		Daniel No		

Site name	Content Farm		PRN	7519
Site type	Cist		Grid Ref	91390 11620
Dimensions	'Small' mound Chamber 0.6m long, 0.4m wide, 0.3m deep		Orientation	
Details	Area covered by vegetation in 2009 and no trace of cist; HER records that it was constructed of four boulders and covered by single flat stone			
Excavation	Treneary, 1938/1939 O'Neil and Ashbee, 1950	Finds	Pottery (Ashbee believed it was possibly a 'plant'); flints nearby	
Condition	Unknown	Museum	RCM: 1950.43	
Hencken No		Daniel No		

Site name	Giant's Grave		PRN	7472
Site type	Other (duplication)		Grid Ref	N/A
Dimensions	Chamber 4.2m long, 1.2m wide, 1.1m high		Orientation	
Details	Documentary record only (Borlase,1756); almost certainly duplication of Innisidgen Carn A (PRN 7453.01)			
Excavation	N/A	Finds	N/A	
Condition	N/A	Museum		
Hencken No	St Mary's 16	Daniel No	St Mary's 18	

Site name	Great Stitch		PRN	7451.02
Site type	Entrance grave – possible		Grid Ref	91007 12621
Dimensions	Not known		Orientation	
Details	Finds recorded as 'Associated with confused stonework … (Perhaps destroyed grave)'			
Excavation	Gray, 1920s/1930s?	Finds	Flint, pottery	
Condition	Unknown	Museum	RCM: 2005,47.3 (flint)	
Hencken No		Daniel No		

Site name	Halangy Down		PRN	7446
Site type	Entrance grave		Grid Ref	90956 12413
Dimensions	Mound 10.0m diameter, 1.3m high Chamber 5.0m long, 1.2m wide, 1.0m high		Orientation	20° NNE-SSW
Details	Overgrown by vegetation in 2008 and 2012 but chamber visible; 2 capstones in place; mound merges into apparent lynchet on uphill side; at low altitude and now close to coast			
Excavation	Gray, 1929	Finds	Pottery, flint, pig jawbone	
Condition	Extant, good	Museum	RCM: 1949,74.1	
Hencken No	St Mary's 2a	Daniel No	St Mary's 14	

Site name	Helvear Down C		PRN	7453.03
Site type	Entrance grave – possible		Grid Ref	91918 12656
Dimensions	Mound 11.5m diameter, 1.4m high		Orientation	
Details	Overgrown by dense bramble and gorse in 2010 and mound not visible; HER records traces of stone kerb and possible capstone			
Excavation	None	Finds	None	
Condition	Extant	Museum		
Hencken No		Daniel No		

Site name	Helvear Hill		PRN	7458
Site type	Entrance grave		Grid Ref	92315 12380
Dimensions	Mound 8.0m diameter, 0.3m high Chamber 3.6m long, 1.5m wide, 0.3m high		Orientation	NE-SW
Details	Only one side of chamber survives with possible capstone on mound and several kerbstones; site recorded (Layard, 1933) as one of 2 'demolished' in late 19th or early 20th century when breaking ground for pasture, adjacent site is Trenoweth PRN 7459			
Excavation	None	Finds	None	
Condition	Extant, poor	Museum		
Hencken No		Daniel No		

Site name	Inner Blue Carn A		PRN	7560.01
Site type	Entrance grave – possible		Grid Ref	91914 10104
Dimensions	Mound 9.5m diameter, 0.5m high		Orientation	
Details	Overgrown with vegetation in 2010 and not possible to see any kerb or internal structure; recorded in early 20th century as being connected by wall to 7560.02 but no trace of wall by 1950			
Excavation	None	Finds	None	
Condition	Extant, poor	Museum		
Hencken No		Daniel No		

Site name	Inner Blue Carn B		PRN	7560.02
Site type	Entrance grave – possible		Grid Ref	91910 10140
Dimensions	Not known		Orientation	
Details	Levelled during construction of airfield; recorded in HER as having large stone within the mound and as being connected by wall to 7560.01 and 7560.03			
Excavation	None	Finds	None	
Condition	Destroyed	Museum		
Hencken No		Daniel No		

Site name	Inner Blue Carn C		PRN	7560.03
Site type	Entrance grave – possible		Grid Ref	91970 10150
Dimensions	Not known		Orientation	
Details	Levelled during construction of airfield; recorded in HER as having 2 concentric kerbs and as being connected by wall to 7560.02			
Excavation	None	Finds	None	
Condition	Destroyed	Museum		
Hencken No		Daniel No		

Site name	Innisidgen Carn A		PRN	7453.01
Site type	Entrance grave		Grid Ref	92188 12656
Dimensions	Mound 9.0m by 8.0m diameter, 1.8m high Chamber 4.6m long, 1.5m wide, 1.5m high		Orientation	107° ESE-WNW
Details	All 5 capstones in place; chamber is of large slabs with some coursed walling above them; mortar recorded between stones of chamber walls; kerb around mound of up to 3 courses of walling			
Excavation	None	Finds	None	
Condition	Extant, excellent	Museum		
Hencken No	St Mary's 4	Daniel No	St Mary's 2	

Site name	King Edward's Road		PRN	7583
Site type	Entrance grave – probable		Grid Ref	90818 10276
Dimensions	Mound 10.0m diameter, 0.3m high		Orientation	
Details	3 boulders in mound, possible capstone nearby; 4 possible kerbstones around mound; documentary record (Crawford, 1920s/1930s)			
Excavation	None	Finds	None	
Condition	Extant, poor	Museum		
Hencken No		Daniel No		

Site name	Lower Innisidgen B		PRN	7453.02
Site type	Entrance grave		Grid Ref	92112 12719
Dimensions	Mound 8.5m diameter, 1.7m wide Chamber 5.4m long, 1.4m wide, 1.0m high		Orientation	195° SSW-NNE
Details	2 capstones in place, chamber of natural rock and coursed walling; kerb of large stones and natural rock; mound incorporates natural rock; dug into hillside at low altitude and now close to coast			
Excavation	None	Finds	None	
Condition	Extant, good	Museum		
Hencken No	St Mary's 17	Daniel No	St Mary's 1	

Site name	Lower Newford		PRN	7498
Site type	Cist		Grid Ref	91650 12000
Dimensions	Chamber 1.4m long, 0.7m wide, 0.4m deep		Orientation	NNE-SSW
Details	Stone-lined and had flat covering stones, natural clay base (documentary record Borlase,1758)			
Excavation	Not known, between 1753 and 1758	Finds	Human remains, pottery	
Condition	Unknown	Museum	Not known	
Hencken No		Daniel No		

Site name	Lunnon		PRN	169361
Site type	Cist		Grid Ref	92500 11100
Dimensions	Chamber 1.3m long, 1.2m wide		Orientation	
Details	Chamber walls formed of granite blocks, rounded stones and irregular slabs; probable Iron Age/ Romano-British Porthcressa-type cist grave adjacent			
Excavation	Partly uncovered and recorded in 2003 but not excavated	Finds	None	
Condition	Extant	Museum		
Hencken No		Daniel No		

Site name	Mount Todden		PRN	7436
Site type	Entrance grave – possible		Grid Ref	92877 11493
Dimensions	Mound 12.0m diameter, 0.7m high		Orientation	?NE-SW or SW-NE
Details	Mound incorporates very large natural outcrop in hilltop position; exposed tops of 3 stones suggest possible chamber, also possible capstone			
Excavation	None	Finds	None	
Condition	Extant, fair	Museum		
Hencken No	St Mary's 15a	Daniel No	St Mary's 19	

Site name	Mount Todden Down		PRN	7434.02
Site type	Entrance grave – possible		Grid Ref	92974 11559
Dimensions	N/A		Orientation	
Details	Watch house within post-mediaeval battery may be reconstructed from chamber of entrance grave; stones and banks around battery may also be associated			
Excavation	None	Finds	None	
Condition	Extant	Museum		
Hencken No		Daniel No		

Site name	Normandy Down A		PRN	7236.01
Site type	Entrance grave		Grid Ref	92976 11191
Dimensions	Mound 11.0m diameter, 1.3m high Chamber at least 4.5m long, 1.5m wide in centre, 1.2m at ends, 0.8m high		Orientation	81° E-W (or possibly 261° W-E)
Details	One capstone in place and 3 possible dislodged capstones (2 at W end, one at E end); 6 large kerbstones visible			
Excavation	Bonsor, 1902	Finds	Pottery	
Condition	Extant, good	Museum	BM: 1926,1112.27-44	
Hencken No	St Mary's 6	Daniel No	St Mary's 4	

Site name	Normandy Down B		PRN	7236.02
Site type	Entrance grave or cist		Grid Ref	93026 11175
Dimensions	Mound 22.0m diameter, 2.2m high Hollow 4.0m diameter, 0.6m deep		Orientation	E-W
Details	Several stones visible within hollow but structure not clear; trench runs from hollow to NW side of mound, kerbstones visible at NW end of this; also large pit on outer S side of mound with stones in it			
Excavation	Bonsor, 1902	Finds	None	
Condition	Extant, poor	Museum		
Hencken No	St Mary's 14	Daniel No	St Mary's 5	

Site name	Normandy Down D		PRN	7236.03
Site type	Entrance grave		Grid Ref	93077 11184
Dimensions	Mound 11.0m diameter, 0.5m high Chamber 1.9m long, 1.4m wide, 0.6m high		Orientation	288° WNW-ESE
Details	One capstone in place, probable displaced capstone at WNW end of chamber, possible one on SW side of mound; outer kerb and possible inner kerb within mound; close to coast			
Excavation	None	Finds	None	
Condition	Extant, fair	Museum		
Hencken No	St Mary's 15	Daniel No	St Mary's 6	

Site name	Old Town		PRN	7545.01
Site type	Cist		Grid Ref	91470 10240
Dimensions	Not known		Orientation	
Details	Accidentally destroyed during building work in 1964			
Excavation	None	Finds	Cremated human bone, pottery	
Condition	Destroyed	Museum	IoS: RN 904	
Hencken No		Daniel No		

Site name	Old Town		PRN	7559
Site type	Entrance grave		Grid Ref	91000 10000
Dimensions	Mound 6.7m diameter Chamber 3.4m long, 0.6m high		Orientation	E-W
Details	Excavator recorded that chamber was formed 'of large stones'; kerb around mound; circle of small stones with 'something resembling ashes' to one side of mound; location is on west side of Old Town Bay on steep hillslope above coast (10 digit grid reference is known to author); overgrown in 2009 but some stones visible			
Excavation	Gluyas, 1876	Finds	Pottery, 'greasy matter' at bottom of one urn, 'stones'	
Condition	Extant	Museum	Not known	
Hencken No		Daniel No		

Site name	Pendrathen		PRN	7485.02
Site type	Cists		Grid Ref	Approx 91260 12680
Dimensions	Not known		Orientation	
Details	Cists and urns found in the cliff; now no trace (documentary record Crawford, 1926)			
Excavation	None	Finds	Pottery	
Condition	Unknown	Museum	Not known	
Hencken No		Daniel No		

Site name	Peninnis Head B		PRN	7420.02
Site type	Entrance grave or cist – possible		Grid Ref	91007 09483
Dimensions	Mound 10.5m diameter, 0.6m high		Orientation	
Details	Covered by gorse in 2009 and not obvious; HER entry records hollows around mound, one of which exposes large boulders			
Excavation	None	Finds	None	
Condition	Extant, poor	Museum		
Hencken No		Daniel No		

Site name	Peninnis Head C		PRN	7420.03
Site type	Entrance grave or cist – possible		Grid Ref	91030 09490
Dimensions	Mound 12.5m diameter, 1.1m high		Orientation	
Details	Hollow in centre of mound and several protruding stones; stones in SW quadrant may be part of chamber or left after granite quarrying; 3 possible kerbstones			
Excavation	None	Finds	None	
Condition	Extant, poor	Museum		
Hencken No		Daniel No		

Site name	Peninnis Head		PRN	7422
Site type	Entrance grave or cist – possible		Grid Ref	91000 09500
Dimensions	Not known		Orientation	
Details	Described as 'very ancient building' (documentary record 1812)			
Excavation	Not known, 1812	Finds	Human remains, 2 bronze armlets, agate bead, spindle whorl	
Condition	Unknown	Museum	RCM:1852,13.1 (armlets)	
Hencken No		Daniel No		

Site name	Porth Hellick Down A		PRN	7528.01
Site type	Entrance grave		Grid Ref	92846 10850
Dimensions	Mound 12.2m diameter, 1.6m high Chamber 3.5m long, 1.5m wide, 1.0m high Passage 4.0m long, 0.9m wide		Orientation	326° NNW-SSE (chamber) NW-SE (passage)
Details	All 4 capstones in place, entrance restricted by portal stone; unroofed passage within mound also has portal stone at outer end; kerb around mound is of coursed walling; outer kerb has been removed			
Excavation	Bonsor, 1902	Finds	Pottery, pumice pendant	
Condition	Extant, excellent	Museum	BM:1926,1112.3-9, 1928,0604.1-2	
Hencken No	St Mary's 1	Daniel No	St Mary's 7	

Site name	Porth Hellick Down B		PRN	7528.02
Site type	Entrance grave – probable		Grid Ref	92853 10732
Dimensions	Mound 9.0m diameter, 0.9m high Hollow 3.5m long, 1.75m deep		Orientation	
Details	Overgrown with vegetation in 2009 and 2012 and little visible; HER entry records stones within hollow; 2 kerbstones on N side			
Excavation	None	Finds	None	
Condition	Extant, poor	Museum		
Hencken No		Daniel No		

Site name	Porth Hellick Down C		PRN	7528.03
Site type	Entrance grave		Grid Ref	92890 10732
Dimensions	Mound 13.0m diameter, 1.3m high Chamber 4.0m long, 1.2m wide		Orientation	N-S
Details	Overgrown by vegetation in 2009 and only capstones visible; HER entry records 2 capstones in place and that natural outcrop forms E side of chamber and much of E half of mound; 12 kerbstones recorded			
Excavation	Woodley, 1820s?	Finds	None	
Condition	Extant, good	Museum		
Hencken No	St Mary's 12	Daniel No	St Mary's 20 (E)	

Site name	Porth Hellick Down D		PRN	7528.04
Site type	Entrance grave		Grid Ref	92803 10713
Dimensions	Mound 14.0m diameter, 1.6m high Chamber 7.0m long, 1.5m wide		Orientation	75.5° ENE-WSW
Details	4 capstones in place and chamber filled with soil, chamber wider in centre than at ends; several kerbstones visible			
Excavation	None	Finds	None	
Condition	Extant, good	Museum		
Hencken No	St Mary's 5	Daniel No	St Mary's 8	

Site name	Porth Hellick Down E		PRN	7528.05
Site type	Entrance grave		Grid Ref	92850 10712
Dimensions	Mound 10.0m diameter, 1.6m high Chamber 2.8m long, 1.0m wide, 0.8m high		Orientation	352° N-S
Details	2 capstones in place at S end, E chamber wall is of drystone walling, W of slabs; short narrower section at entrance with same orientation as chamber; capstone lying outside entrance; natural rock incorporated into mound; several kerbstones visible			
Excavation	Woodley, 1820s?	Finds	None	
Condition	Extant, good	Museum		
Hencken No	St Mary's 3	Daniel No	St Mary's 9	

Site name	Porth Hellick Down G		PRN	7528.07
Site type	Entrance grave		Grid Ref	92896 10661
Dimensions	Mound 13.0m diameter, 1.7m high Chamber at least 2.0m long, 1.2m wide, 0.7m high		Orientation	328° NNW-SSE
Details	Only SSE end of chamber with 1 capstone and possible endstone survives, E wall appears to be natural rock; 4 stones of inner kerb and 2 of outer kerb visible			
Excavation	None	Finds	None	
Condition	Extant, fair	Museum		
Hencken No		Daniel No		

Site name	Porth Hellick Down H		PRN	7528.08
Site type	Entrance grave		Grid Ref	92896 10626
Dimensions	Mound 8.0m diameter, 0.7m high Hollow c2.5m long, 1.5m wide		Orientation	SW-NE
Details	Overgrown by vegetation in 2009 but 2 probable capstones visible at SW end of hollow and possible one at NE end; natural rock incorporated in mound; close to coast			
Excavation	None	Finds	None	
Condition	Extant, poor	Museum		
Hencken No		Daniel No	St Mary's 22 (G)	

Site name	Porth Hellick Down J		PRN	7528.09
Site type	Cist - possible		Grid Ref	92830 10550
Dimensions	Chamber 3.0m long, 0.5m high		Orientation	
Details	Walls of chamber probably natural arrangement of rocks but coverstone may be deliberately placed			
Excavation	None	Finds	None	
Condition	Extant, fair	Museum		
Hencken No		Daniel No	St Mary's 23 (H)	

Site name	Porth Hellick Down M		PRN	7528.12
Site type	Cist – possible		Grid Ref	92953 10798
Dimensions	Not known		Orientation	
Details	Overgrown with heather in 2012; only single slab, which may be natural, visible; small mound which may be formed of vegetation only			
Excavation	None	Finds	None	
Condition	Extant, poor	Museum		
Hencken No		Daniel No		

Site name	Porthcressa		PRN	7664
Site type	Cist – probable		Grid Ref	90645 10186
Dimensions	Not known		Orientation	
Details	In cliff face, exposed further by storm in October 2004			
Excavation	None	Finds	None	
Condition	Extant, fair	Museum		
Hencken No		Daniel No		

Site name	St Mary's		PRN	7246
Site type	Cist		Grid Ref	Not known
Dimensions	Chamber 0.9m long, 0.3m wide, 0.45m high		Orientation	Not known
Details	Location not known, recorded only as 'St Mary's'; sides and bottom of cist each formed of single slab, 5 capstones			
Excavation	Hodson, c1927	Finds	Pottery, flint	
Condition	Not known	Museum	IoS: RN 6356	
Hencken No		Daniel No		

Site name	Salakee Down A		PRN	7534.01
Site type	Entrance grave		Grid Ref	92475 10404
Dimensions	Mound 8.5m diameter, 0.8m high Chamber 3.5m long		Orientation	332° NNW-SSE (or possibly 152° SSE-NNW)
Details	Little remains of chamber except one capstone resting on single stone of side wall and possible capstone nearby; 15 stones in inner kerb and 4 in outer kerb visible			
Excavation	None	Finds	None	
Condition	Extant, fair	Museum		
Hencken No	St Mary's 10	Daniel No	St Mary's 12	

Site name	Salakee Down B		PRN	7534.02
Site type	Entrance grave		Grid Ref	92500 10414
Dimensions	Mound 6.5m diameter, 0.8m high Chamber at least 3.0m long, 1.3m wide in centre, 1.0m wide at distal end, 0.6m high		Orientation	64° ENE-WSW
Details	10 kerbstones visible			
Excavation	None	Finds	None	
Condition	Extant, fair	Museum		
Hencken No	St Mary's 9	Daniel No	St Mary's 15	

Site name	Salakee Down C		PRN	7534.03
Site type	Entrance grave or cist – possible		Grid Ref	92471 10400
Dimensions	Mound 7.0m diameter, 0.4m high		Orientation	
Details	Single large stone on top of mound; no kerbstones visible but HER entry records 6 possible stones			
Excavation	None	Finds	None	
Condition	Extant, poor	Museum		
Hencken No		Daniel No		

Site name	Salakee Down A		PRN	7537.01
Site type	Entrance grave		Grid Ref	92170 10270
Dimensions	Mound c12.0m diameter, 0.5m high Chamber up to 7.5m long (of which possible passage of 4.3m long), c1.0m wide		Orientation	E-W
Details	Kerb of upright blocks and flat slabs almost complete; wedges under stones of kerb and chamber; destroyed during construction of airfield			
Excavation	Grimes, 1942	Finds	Pottery	
Condition	Destroyed	Museum	RCM: 1956,4; 1958,6	
Hencken No		Daniel No		

Site name	Salakee Down		PRN	7539
Site type	Entrance grave - probable		Grid Ref	92180 10160
Dimensions	Mound 12.0m by 10.0m diameter, 0.8m high Chamber c3.0m long, 1.3m wide, 0.7m high		Orientation	
Details	Site now inside airport boundary and inaccessible; HER entry records drill marking from stone working			
Excavation	None	Finds	None	
Condition	Extant, poor	Museum		
Hencken No		Daniel No		

Site name	Salakee Down A		PRN	7540.01
Site type	Entrance grave or cist – possible		Grid Ref	92280 10093
Dimensions	Mound 6.0m diameter, 0.6m high Hollow 1.5m long, 1.0m wide, 0.3m deep		Orientation	
Details	Overgrown with vegetation in 2010 but outline and hollow visible; HER entry records 2 possible kerbstones			
Excavation	None	Finds	None	
Condition	Extant, poor	Museum		
Hencken No		Daniel No		

Site name	Salakee Down B		PRN	7540.02
Site type	Entrance grave or cist – possible		Grid Ref	92274 10088
Dimensions	Mound 7.3m by 4.7 diameter, 0.4m high Hollow (triangular) 2.3m by 2.2m, 0.2m deep		Orientation	
Details	Overgrown with vegetation in 2010 but outline and hollow visible; HER entry records 2 large possible kerbstones			
Excavation	None	Finds	None	
Condition	Extant, poor	Museum		
Hencken No		Daniel No		

Site name	Salakee Down C		PRN	7540.08
Site type	Entrance grave- probable		Grid Ref	92288 10039
Dimensions	Mound 5.0m diameter, 0.6m high Hollow 2.1m long, 1.2m high		Orientation	?E-W or W-E
Details	2 large probable capstones visible in hollow with cavity below them; several kerbstones apparent; at low altitude and close to coast			
Excavation	None	Finds	None	
Condition	Extant, fair	Museum		
Hencken No	St Mary's 8	Daniel No	St Mary's 25	

Site name	Salakee Farm A		PRN	7531.01
Site type	Entrance grave		Grid Ref	92351 10651
Dimensions	Mound 7.0m diameter, 0.7m high Hollow 5.7m long, 1.2m wide, 0.2m deep		Orientation	35° NE-SW (or possibly 215° SW-NE)
Details	2 stones from side of chamber visible in hollow as well as possible endstone or capstone at SW end; 15 kerbstones visible			
Excavation	None	Finds	None	
Condition	Extant, poor	Museum		
Hencken No	St Mary's 11	Daniel No	St Mary's 11	

Site name	Salakee Farm B		PRN	7531.02
Site type	Entrance grave or cist – possible		Grid Ref	92267 10756
Dimensions	Mound 16.0m by 12.0m diameter, 0.6m to 1.6m high		Orientation	
Details	Mound built against natural outcrop with modern wall crossing it, nothing visible S of wall; very overgrown in 2008 and no sign of edge-set slabs mentioned in SM record; located at low altitude on side of marshy valley			
Excavation	None	Finds	None	
Condition	Extant	Museum		
Hencken No		Daniel No		

Site name	Salakee Farm C		PRN	7531.03
Site type	Entrance grave		Grid Ref	92345 10653
Dimensions	Mound 9.0m diameter, 0.8m high Chamber 1.0m wide		Orientation	c186° S-N
Details	2 parallel rows of 3 stones each appear to be remains of chamber walls, possible capstone nearby; 12 stones of inner kerb present and gap in kerb aligns with probable chamber orientation, possible outer kerb also			
Excavation	None	Finds	None	
Condition	Extant, poor	Museum		
Hencken No		Daniel No		

Site name	Taylor's Island		PRN	168678
Site type	Entrance grave or cist		Grid Ref	90607 11490
Dimensions	Mound 10.0m diameter, 1.3m high		Orientation	?E-W or W-E
Details	Overgrown in 2008 but slabs in top of mound may be from chamber, including possible capstone; several kerbstones; now low-lying and close to coast			
Excavation	None	Finds	None	
Condition	Extant, poor	Museum		
Hencken No		Daniel No		

Site name	Toll's Island		PRN	168716
Site type	Entrance grave – possible		Grid Ref	93046 11989
Dimensions	Chamber 5.0m long, 2.3m wide		Orientation	E-W or W-E
Details	2 parallel lines of stones, some natural; no mound or kerbstones; may be ritual stone setting rather than funerary structure			
Excavation	None	Finds	None	
Condition	Extant, poor	Museum		
Hencken No		Daniel No		

Site name	Tolman Carn		PRN	7652
Site type	Cist – possible		Grid Ref	91500 10040
Dimensions	Not known		Orientation	Not known
Details	'Slab-built', recorded as doubtful in 1980; no trace found in 1988 or 2010			
Excavation	None	Finds	None	
Condition	Unknown	Museum		
Hencken No		Daniel No		

Site name	Tolman Carns		PRN	7547
Site type	Cist – possible		Grid Ref	91460 10120
Dimensions	Chamber 1.2m long, 0.8m wide, 1.0m high		Orientation	N-S
Details	Area covered with vegetation in 2009 and nothing visible; HER entry suggests 'chamber' is probably natural arrangement of rocks			
Excavation	None	Finds	None	
Condition	Extant	Museum		
Hencken No		Daniel No		

Site name	Town Lane		PRN	7517
Site type	Cist		Grid Ref	91570 11750
Dimensions	Chamber 0.9m long, 0.6m wide		Orientation	Approx NE-SW
Details	Apparently slab-built (documentary record Crawford, 1928 and photograph Gibson, c1908); now beneath tarmac of road			
Excavation	None	Finds	None	
Condition	Unknown	Museum		
Hencken No		Daniel No		

Site name	Town Lane		PRN	7518
Site type	Cist - possible		Grid Ref	Approx 91600 11800
Dimensions	Not known		Orientation	Not known
Details	Documentary reference (Crawford, 1928) that another cist said to be close to Town Lane PRN 7517 but could not be located by Gibson in c1908, could be Content Farm PRN 7519			
Excavation	None	Finds	None	
Condition	Unknown	Museum		
Hencken No		Daniel No		

Site name	Trenoweth		PRN	7459
Site type	Entrance grave – probable		Grid Ref	92295 12366
Dimensions	Not known		Orientation	Not known
Details	Possible capstone and arc of possible kerbstones revealed by tree throw; likely to be one of 2 sites recorded (Layard, 1933) as 'demolished' in late 19th or early 20th century, adjacent site is Helvear Hill PRN 7458			
Excavation	None	Finds	None	
Condition	Extant, poor	Museum		
Hencken No		Daniel No		

10. Samson

Site name	North Hill A		PRN	7068.01
Site type	Entrance grave		Grid Ref	87720 13250
Dimensions	Mound 12.0m by 10.0m diameter, 1.4m high Chamber 2.0m long, 1.2m wide, 0.3m high		Orientation	8° or 188° N-S or S-N
Details	Overgrown by vegetation in 2011; mound partly formed of natural rock; 1 capstone in chamber and another to S of it; kerbstones visible on W and N of mound			
Excavation	None	Finds	None	
Condition	Extant, fair	Museum		
Hencken No	Samson 6	Daniel No	Samson 1	

Site name	North Hill D		PRN	7068.04
Site type	Entrance grave		Grid Ref	87717 13107
Dimensions	Mound 10.5m diameter, 0.75m high Chamber 2.2m long, 1.1m wide, 0.6m high		Orientation	73° ENE-WSW
Details	Capstone on edge of mound to NE of chamber, chamber constructed of coursed walling; HER entry records kerb but obscured by heather in 2011			
Excavation	None	Finds	None	
Condition	Extant, fair	Museum		
Hencken No	Samson 7	Daniel No	Samson 2	

Site name	North Hill E		PRN	7068.05
Site type	Entrance grave		Grid Ref	87755 13101
Dimensions	Mound 11.0m diameter, 1.7m high Chamber 4.0m long, 1.4m wide, 1.0m high		Orientation	85° E-W
Details	Mound overgrown by vegetation in 2011 but excavator recorded kerb as 2 courses high on S side; 2 capstones in place, one on ground in front of entrance; chamber widest in middle as S wall straight and N wall convex; disturbed when excavated but some paving survived; boulder wall leads SSW towards 7068.11			
Excavation	Hencken, 1930	Finds	Pottery, flints, pebbles, quern rubber, hammer-stone, animal bone	
Condition	Extant, good	Museum	RCM: finds not located in 2009 or 2010	
Hencken No	Samson 1	Daniel No	Samson 5	

Site name	North Hill F		PRN	7068.07
Site type	Entrance grave		Grid Ref	87724 13090
Dimensions	Mound 8.0m diameter, 1.1m high Chamber 3.9m long, 1.4m wide, 0.4m high		Orientation	NNW-SSE
Details	Partly obscured by heather in 2011; one capstone in place at NNW end of chamber; chamber disturbed with only one course of stones remaining			
Excavation	None	Finds	None	
Condition	Extant, fair	Museum		
Hencken No	Samson 8	Daniel No	Samson 3	

Site name	North Hill G		PRN	7068.08
Site type	Entrance grave – probable		Grid Ref	87729 13088
Dimensions	Mound 10.0m diameter, 1.4m high		Orientation	?NE-SW or SW-NE
Details	Large stones forming kerb; probable capstone on top of mound, several stones protruding from soil			
Excavation	None	Finds	None	
Condition	Extant, poor	Museum		
Hencken No	Samson 9	Daniel No	Samson 4	

Site name	North Hill H		PRN	7068.09
Site type	Cist		Grid Ref	87729 13079
Dimensions	Mound 21.5m by 17.5m diameter, 2.2m high Chamber 1.6m long, 1.2m wide, 0.5m deep		Orientation	0°/180° N-S
Details	Many small stones visible in sides of trench cut into mound; base of chamber paved, side slabs have grooves for end slabs; covering slab adjacent; mortar recorded between paving slabs, wall slabs and capstone; 2 large kerbstones on W side of mound and smaller ones on NW and SW and at SE end of trench; on highest point of hill			
Excavation	Smith, 1862	Finds	Cremated bone (described by excavator as male aged about 50), flint flake	
Condition	Extant, excellent	Museum	RCM: finds not located in 2009 or 2010	
Hencken No		Daniel No	Samson 17	

Site name	North Hill J		PRN	7068.11
Site type	Entrance grave		Grid Ref	87740 13052
Dimensions	Mound 10.5m diameter, 1.3m high Chamber 4.2m long, 1.3m wide, 0.4m high		Orientation	192° SSW-NNE (or possibly 12° NNE-SSW)
Details	Many stones visible in mound; kerbstones on NW, NE, E and S sides, probably inner and outer kerbs; possible capstone at N end of chamber; boulder wall leads NNE towards 7068.05			
Excavation	None	Finds	None	
Condition	Extant, fair	Museum		
Hencken No	Samson 10	Daniel No	Samson 6	

Site name	North Hill K		PRN	7068.12
Site type	Entrance grave or cist – possible		Grid Ref	87737 13044
Dimensions	Mound 4.5m diameter, 0.5m high		Orientation	
Details	Only W half of mound extant; some large stones in mound and hollow in centre			
Excavation	Bonsor, 1902	Finds	2 flints, 1 worked	
Condition	Extant, poor	Museum	BM: 1926, 1112.1-2	
Hencken No		Daniel No	Samson 15	

Site name	North Hill L		PRN	7068.13
Site type	Entrance grave - probable		Grid Ref	87732 13032
Dimensions	Mound 13.5m by 8.5m diameter, 1.3m high Chamber 2.4m wide, 1.5m wide, 0.7m high		Orientation	?SE-NW
Details	2 kerbs of large boulders; polygonal chamber, entrance not obvious; possible large capstone on SE side of mound; excavator interpreted site as hut			
Excavation	Bonsor, 1902	Finds	None	
Condition	Extant, fair	Museum		
Hencken No	Samson 11	Daniel No	Samson 7	

Site name	North Hill M		PRN	7068.14
Site type	Entrance grave		Grid Ref	87744 13014
Dimensions	Mound 13.0m by 11.0m diameter, 1.6m high Chamber 3.5m long, 1.0m wide, 1.2m high		Orientation	342° NNW-SSE
Details	Smaller stones of outer kerb survive on E side, larger stones of inner kerb on S side; only W half of mound extant; W wall of chamber is convex, possible capstone at NNW end of chamber; boulder wall leads NNW			
Excavation	None	Finds	None	
Condition	Extant, fair	Museum		
Hencken No	Samson 12	Daniel No	Samson 8	

Site name	North Hill P		PRN	7068.16
Site type	Entrance grave or cist – possible		Grid Ref	87763 12964
Dimensions	Mound 12.5m diameter, 0.7m high Hollow 0.5m deep		Orientation	
Details	Area overgrown with heather in 2012 and little visible; HER entry suggests it is kerbed cairn with antiquarian damage in centre			
Excavation	None	Finds	None	
Condition	Extant, poor	Museum		
Hencken No		Daniel No		

Site name	North Hill R		PRN	7068.18
Site type	Entrance grave		Grid Ref	87772 12936
Dimensions	Mound 8.0m diameter, 1.1m high Chamber 2.7m long, 1.7m wide, 0.6m high		Orientation	E-W
Details	No sign of chamber in 2012 but area on E side of mound covered by deep growth of honeysuckle; irregular kerb of large granite blocks			
Excavation	None	Finds	None	
Condition	Extant, fair	Museum		
Hencken No		Daniel No		

Site name	North Hill T		PRN	7068.20
Site type	Cist – possible		Grid Ref	87810 12880
Dimensions	Mound 8.0m diameter, 1.0m high		Orientation	
Details	Area overgrown by vegetation and inaccessible in 2012			
Excavation	None	Finds	None	
Condition	Extant, poor	Museum		
Hencken No		Daniel No		

Site name	North Hill U		PRN	7068.21
Site type	Cist – probable		Grid Ref	87794 12923
Dimensions	No mound Chamber 1.3m long, 0.8m wide, 0.4m deep		Orientation	NW-SE
Details	Single large capstone, partially dislodged; no trace of mound			
Excavation	None	Finds	None	
Condition	Extant, good	Museum		
Hencken No		Daniel No		

Site name	North Hill W		PRN	7068.23
Site type	Cist – probable		Grid Ref	87720 13000
Dimensions	No mound Chamber 2.0m long, 1.8m wide, 0.2m deep		Orientation	NW-SE
Details	Area overgrown with heather in 2012, some stones visible but cist not obvious; HER records polygonal chamber with 2 capstones but not found in 1988			
Excavation	None	Finds	None	
Condition	Unknown	Museum		
Hencken No		Daniel No		

Site name	South Hill A		PRN	7081.01
Site type	Entrance grave		Grid Ref	87858 12413
Dimensions	Mound 12.0m by 8.0m diameter, 1.1m high Chamber 4.5m long, 1.8m wide, 0.5m high		Orientation	149.5° SSE-NNW
Details	On rock platform, chamber of slab construction, possible capstone inside chamber at NW end; Bonsor recorded kerb, now obscured by vegetation			
Excavation	Bonsor, 1901 Pottery found in rabbit scrape, 1978	Finds	None from excavation Pottery (single sherd)	
Condition	Extant, fair	Museum	IoS: not located between 2006 and 2012	
Hencken No	Samson 5	Daniel No	Samson 9	

Site name	South Hill B		PRN	7081.02B
Site type	Entrance grave		Grid Ref	87866 12384
Dimensions	Mound 15.0m by 13.0m diameter, 1.7m high (also covers South Hill C and E) Chamber 4.7m long, 1.5m wide, 0.5m high		Orientation	S-N
Details	Obscured by vegetation between 2006 and 2012 and difficult to assess; Hencken and Daniel suggested that single kerbed mound encompassed 3 chambers but Ashbee believed this was natural configuration of rock; chamber has own circular kerb also; single capstone nearby			
Excavation	None	Finds	None	
Condition	Extant, fair	Museum		
Hencken No	Samson 4	Daniel No	Samson 10	

Site name	South Hill C		PRN	7081.02C
Site type	Entrance grave		Grid Ref	87867 12382
Dimensions	Mound 15.0m by 13.0m diameter, 1.7m high (also covers South Hill B and E) Chamber 5.0m long, 2.0m wide, 1.1m high		Orientation	149.5° SSE-NNW
Details	Surroundings obscured by vegetation between 2006 and 2012 but chamber clear; 2 capstones in place; W wall of chamber formed of natural rock; chamber has own circular kerb			
Excavation	Bonsor, 1901	Finds	None	
Condition	Extant, good	Museum		
Hencken No	Samson 2	Daniel No	Samson 12	

Site name	South Hill D		PRN	7081.03
Site type	Entrance grave		Grid Ref	87950 12360
Dimensions	Mound 6.0m diameter, 1.0m high Chamber 2.8m long, 1.5m wide		Orientation	NW-SE
Details	Inaccessible due to vegetation between 2006 and 2012; HER entry records kerb of slabs, missing on E side, and that site is abutted by boulder walling			
Excavation	None	Finds	None	
Condition	Extant, good	Museum		
Hencken No		Daniel No		

Site name	South Hill E		PRN	7081.04
Site type	Cist - possible		Grid Ref	87867 12383
Dimensions	Mound 15.0m by 13.0m diameter, 1.7m high (also covers South Hill B and C) Chamber 2.0m long, 1.0m wide, 0.3m high		Orientation	N-S
Details	Obscured by vegetation between 2006 and 2012; between South Hill B and C; HER entry suggests that it may be formed by elements of B and C rather than being a separate chamber			
Excavation	None	Finds	None	
Condition	Extant, fair	Museum		
Hencken No	Samson 3	Daniel No	Samson 11	

Site name	South Hill G		PRN	7081.05
Site type	Entrance grave		Grid Ref	87870 12370
Dimensions	Mound 7.0m by 5.0m diameter, 1.5m high Chamber 3.0m long, 2.0m wide, 0.7m high		Orientation	N-S
Details	Obscured by vegetation between 2006 and 2012; HER entry says it is built against face of rock outcrop, with large capstone at N end and boulder wall abutting NE side			
Excavation	None	Finds	None	
Condition	Extant, fair	Museum		
Hencken No		Daniel No		

Site name	South Hill A		PRN	7083.01
Site type	Entrance grave or cist - possible		Grid Ref	87715 12509
Dimensions	Mound 10.0m by 12.0m diameter, 1.4m high		Orientation	
Details	Overgrown with vegetation in 2012; orthostat on top of mound visible but other stones recorded in HER not clear			
Excavation	None	Finds	None	
Condition	Extant, poor	Museum		
Hencken No		Daniel No		

Site name	South Hill B	PRN	7083.02
Site type	Entrance grave – possible	Grid Ref	87752 12498
Dimensions	Mound 8.0m by 9.5m diameter, 1.0m high	Orientation	
Details	Partially overgrown with vegetation in 2012 and kerb recorded in HER not visible; top of mound clear and possible capstones visible in turf		
Excavation	None	Finds	None
Condition	Extant, fair	Museum	
Hencken No		Daniel No	

11. Teän

Site name	Great Hill A	PRN	7110.01
Site type	Entrance grave	Grid Ref	90988 16555
Dimensions	Mound 6.5m diameter, 1.4m high Chamber 3.4m long, 1.1m wide	Orientation	SW-NE
Details	Chamber formed of edge-set slabs; several large kerbstones visible; on hilltop next to natural outcrop and mound and kerb incorporate natural rock		
Excavation	None	Finds	None
Condition	Extant, fair	Museum	
Hencken No		Daniel No	

Site name	Great Hill B	PRN	7110.02
Site type	Entrance grave	Grid Ref	91019 16518
Dimensions	Mound 7.5m diameter, 0.5m high Chamber 2.8m long, 1.5m wide, 0.5m high	Orientation	SW-NE
Details	Covered by bramble and gorse between 2006 and 2012; HER entry records chamber constructed of slabs and coursed stones with NW wall curving out in centre; one capstone in place, another possible leaning against outside of chamber; kerb of large slabs		
Excavation	Pottery found by O'Neil, 1953	Finds	Pottery (3 sherds)
Condition	Extant, fair	Museum	RCM: 1955,38.10
Hencken No		Daniel No	

Site name	Old Man	PRN	7103
Site type	Entrance grave or cist	Grid Ref	90474 16319
Dimensions	Mound 5.0m diameter Chamber 3.0m long, 1.4m wide, 0.5m high	Orientation	NE-SW
Details	Covered by bramble and gorse between 2006 and 2012; HER entry records that chamber incorporates natural rock, has walls of slabs and coursed stones and paved floor; one capstone in place; on highest point of islet		
Excavation	None	Finds	None
Condition	Extant, fair	Museum	
Hencken No	Old Man	Daniel No	Old Man

12. Tresco

Site name	Borough Farm	PRN	7599
Site type	Cist	Grid Ref	89990 14990
Dimensions	Chamber 1.0m long	Orientation	
Details	Chamber consisted of 4 upright stones and 1 capstone, orange clay below; found and possibly destroyed during excavation of mooring, 1985		
Excavation	None	Finds	None
Condition	Unknown	Museum	
Hencken No		Daniel No	

Site name	Castle Down J		PRN	7281.09
Site type	Cist – possible		Grid Ref	88407 16245
Dimensions	Mound 6.0m diameter, 0.6m high Hollow 1.0m diameter, 0.1m deep		Orientation	
Details	Overgrown with heather in 2010 but 2 stones in hollow and 3 possible kerbstones in arc visible			
Excavation	None	Finds	None	
Condition	Extant, poor	Museum		
Hencken No		Daniel No		

Site name	Castle Down Y		PRN	7281.23
Site type	Cist – possible		Grid Ref	88673 16444
Dimensions	Mound 5.1m diameter, 0.4m high		Orientation	
Details	Overgrown with heather in 2012 but shallow depression in centre visible; in corner of enclosure but appears to pre-date walls; at low altitude and close to coast			
Excavation	None	Finds	None	
Condition	Extant, poor	Museum		
Hencken No		Daniel No		

Site name	Castle Down HH		PRN	7281.32
Site type	Cist – possible		Grid Ref	88257 16347
Dimensions	Mound 6.5m diameter, 0.4m high		Orientation	
Details	Overgrown with heather in 2010 but at least 8 kerbstones visible; HER entry records hollow in centre			
Excavation	None	Finds	None	
Condition	Extant, poor	Museum		
Hencken No		Daniel No		

Site name	Castle Down D		PRN	7300.04
Site type	Entrance grave – possible		Grid Ref	88469 16182
Dimensions	Mound 7.0m diameter, 0.8m high Hollow 4.0m long, 2.8m wide, 0.9m deep		Orientation	?NE-SW or SW-NE
Details	Several large stones visible in mound and in hollow, also possible kerbstone			
Excavation	None	Finds	None	
Condition	Extant, poor	Museum		
Hencken No		Daniel No		

Site name	Castle Down P		PRN	7300.21
Site type	Cist – possible		Grid Ref	88547 16006
Dimensions	Mound 6.4m diameter, 0.3m high		Orientation	
Details	Single edge-set slab visible in mound			
Excavation	None	Finds	None	
Condition	Extant, poor	Museum		
Hencken No		Daniel No		

Site name	Castle Down U		PRN	7300.24
Site type	Entrance grave		Grid Ref	88755 15921
Dimensions	Mound 14.0m by 6.0m diameter, 1.5m high Chamber at least 3.5m long, 0.8m wide, 0.5m high		Orientation	SW-NE
Details	Obscured by rhododendron and gorse in 2009, only single capstone visible; HER entry says mound incorporates several natural rocks and has inner and outer kerbs, chamber has coursed stones in SE wall, single stones elsewhere			
Excavation	None	Finds	None	
Condition	Extant, good	Museum		
Hencken No		Daniel No		

Site name	Castle Down C		PRN	7356.03
Site type	Entrance grave or cist – possible		Grid Ref	88664 15716
Dimensions	Mound 6.2m diameter, 0.75m high		Orientation	
Details	Possible capstone protruding from mound, no other stones visible or found by probing			
Excavation	None	Finds	None	
Condition	Extant, poor	Museum		
Hencken No		Daniel No		

Site name	Dolphin Town		PRN	7791
Site type	Cist – probable		Grid Ref	89370 15390
Dimensions	Mound 4.0m diameter		Orientation	
Details	Uncovered during watching brief but not fully excavated; kerbstones around most of perimeter; flat slabs and smaller stones in centre; next to settlement site			
Excavation	Taylor, 2003	Finds	None (BA pottery, burnt clay and flint found in over-lying layer)	
Condition	Extant	Museum	IoS: RN 6041 (finds from settlement site)	
Hencken No		Daniel No		

Site name	King Charles' Castle		PRN	7295
Site type	Entrance grave – possible		Grid Ref	88275 16095
Dimensions	Chamber 2.6m long, 1.4m wide, 0.7m high		Orientation	Approx W-E
Details	'Chamber' consists of cavity below natural slabs, open at both ends; entirely enclosed by natural rocks and no evidence of additions or alterations			
Excavation	None	Finds	None	
Condition	Extant	Museum		
Hencken No		Daniel No		

Site name	Oliver's Battery		PRN	7348.03
Site type	Entrance grave or cist – possible		Grid Ref	89030 13490
Dimensions	Not known		Orientation	Not known
Details	Finds from inside and outside rampart			
Excavation	None	Finds	Pottery, flint, burnt bone (?human or animal)	
Condition	Destroyed	Museum	RCM: 1955,38.10 (pottery found by O'Neil, 1954)	
Hencken No		Daniel No		

Site.name	Tregarthen Hill A		PRN	7283.03
Site type	Entrance grave or cist – possible		Grid Ref	88625 16350
Dimensions	Mound 10.0m by 8.0m diameter, 1.0m high Chamber 3.0m long, 0.4m wide, 0.5m high		Orientation	NW-SE
Details	'Chamber' appears to be natural arrangement of rocks; kerbstones around natural outcrop, may be analogous to Dartmoor tor cairn			
Excavation	None	Finds	None	
Condition	Extant	Museum		
Hencken No		Daniel No		

Site name	Tregarthen Hill B		PRN	7283.04
Site type	Entrance grave or cist – possible		Grid Ref	88643 16314
Dimensions	Mound 11.5m diameter, 1.6m high Hollow 3.0m long, 1.2m wide, 0.3m deep		Orientation	NE-SW
Details	Overgrown with heather in 2012; built around natural outcrop, may be analogous to Dartmoor tor cairn; HER entry records 4 kerbstones			
Excavation	None	Finds	None	
Condition	Extant, poor	Museum		
Hencken No		Daniel No		

Site name	Tregarthen Hill C		PRN	7283.05
Site type	Entrance grave or cist – possible		Grid Ref	88655 16282
Dimensions	Mound 12.0m diameter, 1.0m high Hollow 4.0m long, 2.0m wide, 0.3m deep		Orientation	NE-SW
Details	Overgrown with heather in 2012, single kerbstone apparent			
Excavation	None	Finds	None	
Condition	Extant, poor	Museum		
Hencken No		Daniel No		

Site name	Tregarthen Hill D		PRN	7283.01
Site type	Entrance grave		Grid Ref	88655 16272
Dimensions	Mound 12.5m diameter, 1.2m high Chamber 2.4m long, 1.6m wide, 0.7m high		Orientation	78° ENE-WSW
Details	2 capstones in place, chamber walls of coursing and single stones; inner and outer kerbs			
Excavation	None	Finds	None	
Condition	Extant, good	Museum		
Hencken No	Tresco	Daniel No	Tresco 1	

Site name	Tregarthen Hill E		PRN	7283.02
Site type	Entrance grave – possible		Grid Ref	88664 16216
Dimensions	Mound 12.5m diameter, 1.1m high Hollow 2.8m long, 1.0m wide, 0.3m deep		Orientation	NW-SE or SE-NW
Details	Single stone visible in hollow and other large stones in mound			
Excavation	None	Finds	None	
Condition	Extant, poor	Museum		
Hencken No		Daniel No	Tresco 2	

Site name	Vane Hill A		PRN	7373.01
Site type	Entrance grave or cist – possible		Grid Ref	89083 15242
Dimensions	Mound 14.0m diameter, 1.0m high Hollow 4.0m long, 0.5m deep		Orientation	
Details	Overgrown with gorse and bramble in 2009 and no features visible; HER entry records possible kerbstone			
Excavation	None	Finds	None	
Condition	Extant, poor	Museum		
Hencken No		Daniel No		

Site name	Vane Hill B		PRN	7373.02
Site type	Cist – possible		Grid Ref	89097 15212
Dimensions	Mound 14.0m diameter, 1.0m high Hollow 2.0m long, 1.0m wide, 0.3m deep		Orientation	NE-SW
Details	Overgrown with gorse and bramble in 2009 but some recent stonework visible; HER entry records coastguard lookout station cut into side of cairn			
Excavation	None	Finds	None	
Condition	Extant, poor	Museum		
Hencken No		Daniel No		

Site name	Vane Hill C		PRN	7373.03
Site type	Cist – possible		Grid Ref	89061 15189
Dimensions	Mound 11.5m diameter, 1.0m high Hollow 2.0m long, 0.8m wide, 0.25m deep		Orientation	E-W
Details	Overgrown with gorse and bramble in 2009 and no features visible; HER entry records large stones flanking hollow and one on S edge of mound			
Excavation	None	Finds	None	
Condition	Extant, poor	Museum		
Hencken No		Daniel No		

13. White Island

Site name	Stony Porth		PRN	7096
Site type	Entrance grave		Grid Ref	92246 17620
Dimensions	Mound 7.0m diameter, 1.0m high Chamber 4.0m long, 1.0m wide, 0.5m high		Orientation	147° SSE-NNW
Details	Obscured by vegetation in 2010; 2 capstones, 1 at N end, 1 over entrance probably not in original position, also possible capstone to S of entrance; coursed walling at N end of chamber; kerb around edge of mound			
Excavation	None	Finds	None	
Condition	Extant, good	Museum		
Hencken No	White Island	Daniel No	White Island	

Appendix 2

Concordance of sites

Site Name	Island	PRN	Page No (Appendix 1)
Arden Craig	St Mary's	7521	135
Arthur Porth	Eastern Isles	7216	123
Bant's Carn	St Mary's	7443	135
Barnacle Rock	St Martin's	7175	130
Borough Farm	St Mary's	7525	135
Borough Farm	Tresco	7599	150
Bryher	Bryher	167242	120
Burnt Island	St Agnes	168706	128
Buzza Hill	St Mary's	7578.02	136
Buzza Hill	St Mary's	7578.03	136
Buzza Hill A	St Mary's	7578.01	135
Carn Kimbra	Gugh	7054	125
Carn Morval Down	St Mary's	7496	136
Carn Morval Down A	St Mary's	7507.01	136
Carn of Cove Vean G	St Agnes	7011.07	128
Carn of Cove Vean H	St Agnes	7011.08	128
Carn of Works	Gugh	7057	125
Carn Valla	Gugh	7032	126
Carrion Rock	St Martin's	7169	130
Castle Down C	Tresco	7356.03	151
Castle Down D	Tresco	7300.04	151
Castle Down HH	Tresco	7281.32	151
Castle Down J	Tresco	7281.09	151
Castle Down P	Tresco	7300.21	151
Castle Down U	Tresco	7300.24	151
Castle Down Y	Tresco	7281.23	151
Chapel Brow	St Martin's	7127	130
Chapel Down	St Martin's	7117.01	131
Chapel Down A	St Martin's	7122.01	131
Chapel Down A	St Martin's	7259.01	131
Chapel Down J	St Martin's	7117.02	131
Chapel Down K	St Martin's	7117.03	131
Church Point	St Mary's	7658	136
Clapper of Works M	Gugh	7020.12	126
Content Farm	St Mary's	7519	136
Cruther's Hill A	St Martin's	7172.01	131
Cruther's Hill B	St Martin's	7172.02	132
Cruther's Hill C	St Martin's	7172.03	132
Cruther's Hill D	St Martin's	7172.04	132
Cruther's Neck	St Martin's	7170	132
Dolphin Town	Tresco	7791	152
Giant's Grave	St Mary's	7472	137
Great Arthur A	Eastern Isles	7221.01	123
Great Arthur B	Eastern Isles	7221.02	123
Great Arthur C	Eastern Isles	7221.03	124

Site Name	Island	PRN	Page No (Appendix 1)
Great Bottom H	Bryher	7279.08	120
Great Bottom K	Bryher	7279.10	121
Great Ganilly A	Eastern Isles	7210.01	124
Great Ganilly C	Eastern Isles	7210.03	124
Great Ganilly D	Eastern Isles	7210.04	124
Great Hill A	Tean	7110.01	150
Great Hill B	Tean	7110.02	150
Great Stitch	St Mary's	7451.02	137
Gun Hill	St Martin's	7146	132
Gweal Hill A	Bryher	7384.01	121
Gweal Hill B	Bryher	7384.03	121
Gweal Hill C	Bryher	7384.02	121
Halangy Down	St Mary's	7446	137
Helvear Down C	St Mary's	7453.03	137
Helvear Hill	St Mary's	7458	137
Hill Bennigates	St Martin's	7138.01	132
Inner Blue Carn A	St Mary's	7560.01	137
Inner Blue Carn B	St Mary's	7560.02	138
Inner Blue Carn C	St Mary's	7560.03	138
Innisidgen Carn A	St Mary's	7453.01	138
John Batty's Hill	St Martin's	7145	133
King Charles Castle	Tresco	7295	152
King Edward's Road	St Mary's	7583	132
Kittern Hill A	Gugh	7030.01	126
Kittern Hill B	Gugh	7030.02	126
Kittern Hill C	Gugh	7030.03	126
Kittern Hill J	Gugh	7030.06	126
Kittern Hill K	Gugh	7030.07	126
Kittern Hill L	Gugh	7030.08	127
Kittern Hill N	Gugh	7030.10	127
Knackyboy Cairn	St Martin's	7162.01	133
Little Arthur	Eastern Isles	7650	125
Little Arthur C	Eastern Isles	7215.01	124
Little Arthur D	Eastern Isles	7215.02	124
Little Arthur E	Eastern Isles	7215.04	125
Little Bay	St Martin's	7208.01	133
Lower Innisidgen B	St Mary's	7453.02	138
Lower Newford	St Mary's	7498	138
Lunnon	St Mary's	169361	139
Middle Arthur A	Eastern Isles	7224.02	125
Middle Arthur B	Eastern Isles	7224.01	125
Mount Todden	St Mary's	7436	139
Mount Todden Down	St Mary's	7434.02	139
Normandy Down A	St Mary's	7236.01	139
Normandy Down B	St Mary's	7236.02	139
Normandy Down D	St Mary's	7236.03	139
North Hill A	Samson	7068.01	146
North Hill D	Samson	7068.04	146
North Hill E	Samson	7068.05	146
North Hill F	Samson	7068.07	146
North Hill G	Samson	7068.08	146
North Hill H	Samson	7068.09	147
North Hill J	Samson	7068.11	147
North Hill K	Samson	7068.12	147
North Hill L	Samson	7068.13	147
North Hill M	Samson	7068.14	147

Site Name	Island	PRN	Page No (Appendix 1)
North Hill P	Samson	7068.16	148
North Hill R	Samson	7068.18	148
North Hill T	Samson	7068.20	148
North Hill U	Samson	7068.21	148
North Hill W	Samson	7068.23	148
Northwethel	Northwethel	7275	127
Northwethel A	Northwethel	7272.01	127
Obadiah's Barrow	Gugh	7031	127
Old Man	Tean	7103	150
Old Town	St Mary's	7545.01	140
Old Town	St Mary's	7559	140
Oliver's Battery	Tresco	7348.03	152
Par Beach	St Martin's	7148	133
Pendrathen	St Mary's	7485.02	140
Peninnis Head	St Mary's	7422	140
Peninnis Head B	St Mary's	7420.02	140
Peninnis Head C	St Mary's	7420.03	140
Pernagie Carn	St Martin's	7187	133
Porth Askin B	St Agnes	7018.02	128
Porth Askin F	St Agnes	7018.06	128
Porth Conger	St Agnes	7595	129
Porth Hellick Down A	St Mary's	7528.01	141
Porth Hellick Down B	St Mary's	7528.02	141
Porth Hellick Down C	St Mary's	7528.03	141
Porth Hellick Down D	St Mary's	7528.04	141
Porth Hellick Down E	St Mary's	7528.05	141
Porth Hellick Down G	St Mary's	7528.07	142
Porth Hellick Down H	St Mary's	7528.08	142
Porth Hellick Down J	St Mary's	7528.09	142
Porth Hellick Down M	St Mary's	7528.12	142
Porth Killier	St Agnes	7029	129
Porthcressa	St Mary's	7664	142
Round Island	Round Island	7094	128
St Helen's	St Helen's	7114.01	130
St Helen's B	St Helen's	7267.02	130
St Mary's	St Mary's	7246	142
Salakee Down	St Mary's	7539	143
Salakee Down A	St Mary's	7534.01	143
Salakee Down A	St Mary's	7537.01	143
Salakee Down A	St Mary's	7540.01	143
Salakee Down B	St Mary's	7534.02	143
Salakee Down B	St Mary's	7540.02	144
Salakee Down C	St Mary's	7534.03	143
Salakee Down C	St Mary's	7540.08	144
Salakee Farm A	St Mary's	7531.01	144
Salakee Farm B	St Mary's	7531.02	144
Salakee Farm C	St Mary's	7531.03	144
Samson Hill A	Bryher	7394.01	121
Samson Hill B	Bryher	7394.02	121
Samson Hill C	Bryher	7394.03	121
Samson Hill D	Bryher	7394.04	122
Shipman Head Down	Bryher	7404.02	122
Shipman Head Down	Bryher	7413.13	122
Shipman Head Down	Bryher	7413.19	123
Shipman Head Down E	Bryher	7405.11	122
Shipman Head Down M	Bryher	7404.04	122

Site Name	Island	PRN	Page No (Appendix 1)
Shipman Head Down N	Bryher	7405.12	122
Shipman Head Down Y	Bryher	7402.29	122
South Hill A	Samson	7081.01	148
South Hill A	Samson	7083.01	149
South Hill B	Samson	7081.02B	149
South Hill B	Samson	7083.02	150
South Hill C	Samson	7081.02C	149
South Hill D	Samson	7081.03	149
South Hill E	Samson	7081.04	149
South Hill G	Samson	7081.05	149
Stony Porth	White Island	7096	153
Taylor's Island	St Mary's	168678	144
Tinkler's Hill A	St Martin's	7190.01	134
Tinkler's Hill E	St Martin's	7190.05	134
Toll's Island	St Mary's	168716	145
Tolman Carn	St Mary's	7652	145
Tolman Carns	St Mary's	7547	145
Top Rock Hill B	St Martin's	7198.02	134
Top Rock Hill E	St Martin's	7198.04	134
Town Lane	St Mary's	7517	145
Town Lane	St Mary's	7518	145
Tregarthen Hill A	Tresco	7283.03	152
Tregarthen Hill B	Tresco	7283.04	152
Tregarthen Hill C	Tresco	7283.05	152
Tregarthen Hill D	Tresco	7283.01	153
Tregarthen Hill E	Tresco	7283.02	153
Trelawney	St Martin's	7598	134
Trenoweth	St Mary's	7459	145
Turfy Hill	St Martin's	7128	134
Vane Hill A	Tresco	7373.01	153
Vane Hill B	Tresco	7373.02	153
Vane Hill C	Tresco	7373.03	153
Watch Hill	Bryher	7380	123
Wingletang Down C	St Agnes	7015.03	129
Wingletang Down D	St Agnes	7015.04	129
Wingletang Down E	St Agnes	7016.05	129
Wingletang Down Q	St Agnes	7016.15	129
Wingletang Down S	St Agnes	7016.17	130
Works Carn	Bryher	7396	123
Yellow Rock Carn	St Martin's	7163	135

Appendix 3

Extracts from the notebooks of George Bonsor

FIGURE A3.1 GEORGE BONSOR AT THE 'GREAT TOMB' (PORTH HELLICK DOWN A),
ST MARY'S; PHOTOGRAPH BY C J KING, 1902

George Bonsor (1855-1930) was born in Lille, France to an English father and a French mother. His mother died when he was a few months old and, as a small child, he spent much of his time with his uncle and aunt at Seaborough Court, near Crewkerne. His father was an industrial engineer who travelled a great deal and, when he was older, George often accompanied him and so had the opportunity of studying in a number of European cities. He had a particular interest in fine arts and studied technical drawing at the Royal Academy of Fine Arts in Brussels, where he won a prize for archaeological illustration.

Once qualified, he travelled to Spain to visit museums and monuments. On this trip he first started keeping a diary of his travels with notes of his expenses. After touring Spain and north Africa he settled in Carmona, near Seville. His growing interest in antiquities led him to begin excavating at the Alcázar de Sevilla gate there, followed by the necropolis and the amphitheatre. He later worked at a number of sites in Los Alcores, at the Roman town of Baelo Claudia in Cadiz and elsewhere in Andalucía. In 1902 he bought the mediaeval castle of Mairena del Alcor which he excavated and then restored as his home. Although he had British nationality he usually spoke and wrote either in French or Spanish.

Bonsor visited Scilly, for about a month, in September and October each year from 1899 to 1902. His work in the islands has been outlined in chapter 3. During the course of the research reported in this work, his notebooks about the islands were located in the Archivo General de Andalucía in Seville and scanned copies obtained.

The first notebook, which covers Bonsor's visits in 1899 and 1900, is 154 pages long; the second, for 1901 and 1902, runs to 294 pages. They are handwritten, mainly in

French, and for the most part are in diary form. However, they also include newspaper cuttings as well as notes and extracts from other books about Scilly.

In addition to recording details about his archaeological surveys and excavations, the notebooks report on the weather, the correspondence he sent and received (with copies of some, usually in English), the sailings of the ferry to and from Penzance, his meetings with local antiquarians and many other aspects of island life. There are numerous illustrations, including detailed surveys of sites and drawings of pottery and other finds, as well as sketches of island views.

Throughout the journals, place and island names have been written in red crayon. These would appear to be reference headings, put in as later annotations, probably in preparation for publication, which never took place.

This appendix contains translations of parts of the notebooks, in particular those concerned with Bonsor's excavations, most of which have not been published in English. The page references given are Bonsor's original numbering.

Bonsor normally uses the spelling 'Hallangy' rather than the usual 'Halangy' in his notebooks, although his letters in English generally use 'Halangy'. The site he refers to as 'Hallangy Tomb' or 'Hallangy Dolmen' is now called Bant's Carn. The entrance grave on Gugh excavated by Bonsor in 1901 is now known as Obadiah's Barrow after Obadiah Hicks, who worked there with him.

The entry [...] indicates that words have been omitted from the translation because they could not be deciphered.

An Archaeological Exploration
of the Scilly Isles 1899-1900

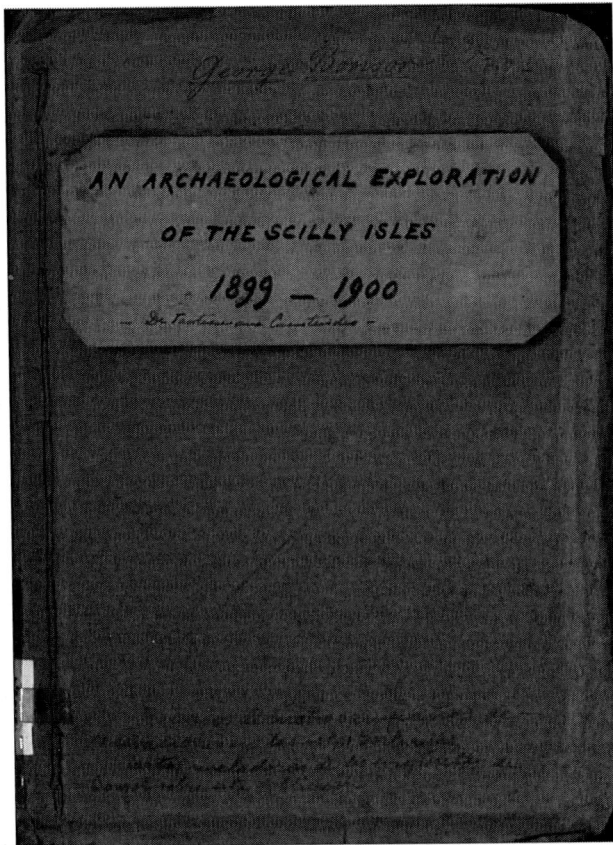

(p 129)

Monday 24 September 1900

This morning T Williams went to work at Hallangy Down to remove the brambles and bushes which are covering the dolmen.

I went to watch the Penzance steamer leave.

Today the weather changed completely and the west wind is very strong. The equinoxes are beginning and may last for several days. I went with Mr King to the new fort on the Garrison Hill to see some stones.

In the afternoon I wrote home – towards the evening before dinner I went for a walk as far as Hallangy Down

Tuesday 25 September 1900

This morning [...] I went to Hallangy. I met Williams who was not working today. I took him with me to the sites to show him what to do tomorrow. Then he showed me a place by the edge of the sea to the north of the dolmen where someone told him yesterday that they had seen some fragments of pottery and

some bones in the section of earth by the sea. Going down in this direction, I first of all noticed roughly 20 metres north of the dolmen and at a lower level some big stones had been laid out that seemed to me to be prehistoric circular dwellings etc - we shall have to study these ruins.

In the section of earth by the sea, I found first of all a big stone, worn or polished by rubbing. It is quite certainly a stone which was used to mill grain.

(p 132)

Wednesday 26 September 1900

Then I went to the place where Williams was working (Hallangy Dolmen). He has cleared a good part of the exterior construction on the north side. Together we put back in place several stones which had fallen into the interior of the funerary chamber.

(p 136)

Friday 28 September 1900

This morning I wrote to Mr Knowles, Ballymena, Ireland. I took my lunch with me and went to Hallangy Down where I helped Williams to put some of the barrow stones back into their original place - around 11 o'clock I left for Innisidgen Carn.

The tumulus indicated on the map to the north-west of Innisidgen, on the little hill, is quite certainly a destroyed tomb from which the big stones have all been removed to leave just a stone circle (p 137) or rather a stone tumulus in which one can see in the middle the space left by the burial chamber. Near this last tomb I also noticed traces of lines of stones. At the base of the tumulus to the north-east there is another of the capstones of the tomb.

Having made some further notes on the Innisidgen tomb, I went along to examine the 'blockhouse' – there is nothing but the ruins of the fort of earth and stones. Then I went up on to the tomb on Helvear Hill opposite, where, at the site of a stone circle on the map, I recognised a tomb like the ruined one at Innisidgen and which must have been very important. I then went to Toll's Hill, where I marked the spot of a probable tomb (in ruins) and another one further along indicated on the map by a circle.

...

Back to the Hallangy Down excavations – I received a visit from Mr Allen Bluett and his son. I showed them the tomb which has been mostly cleared today, and then we went down to the edge of the sea where I showed them the rubbish pits from the huts and the two querns for milling grain. Williams has done a good job today. I came back to the hotel quite tired after my day.

I can explain to myself the existence of a village on this part of the island near Bant's Carn. It is because from Bar Point close by one could quite certainly at that time cross at low tide by the sand banks as far as St Martin's and perhaps to Tresco - nowadays the depth is not more than 4 feet. One can see the direction of the sand bank by the emerald green colour of the sea, whereas in the deep parts it is a darker green or blue.

(p 139)

Saturday 29 September 1900

This morning, wonderful weather - at 10 o'clock I went to Hallangy where Williams was working – this morning we began to empty the interior of the burial chamber. There is a lot of soil. Around 11 o'clock I received a visit from Mr Bluett and his sister-in-law – they arrived by sea. At noon we stopped work – Williams tells me that in Scilly it is customary on Saturday only to work until 3 pm. Therefore he won't be going home for lunch. Meanwhile I go and have my (p 140) lunch on the beach at Hallangy Porth and at the same time draw the section of earth where the quern was found as well as the rubbish from the huts.

Around 1 o'clock I went back to work on emptying the tomb – several men and ladies came to visit – in the soil at the bottom of the tomb we have so far found numerous sherds of a primitive pottery, which resembles that in the rubbish from the huts, some limpets and a small fragment of unburnt bone. At 3 o'clock Williams and I went back to town – he must come this evening so that I can pay him for his week's work. From today the steamer *Lyonesse* will no longer come to the Scillies. It is the turn of the little steamer *Lady of the Isles*, which is quite a lot smaller.

...

I paid Williams for the week of excavations at Hallangy Down. 6 days at 3/0 = 18/0. This evening I received two letters from Guadelupe de Carmona, one of them gives news of the little town and the other is from my brother William.

(page 142)

Sunday 30 September 1900

I had arranged to go to the island of Samson this morning: but it was raining at 8.00 – and later it was violently windy – the sea was very rough – complete contrast with yesterday's weather – moreover the Plymouth newspaper had forecast this bad weather. I stay quietly at home reading and writing.

Monday 1st October 1900

This morning the weather has changed a little, there is not so much wind. At 8.30am I took Williams to Buzza Hill to investigate the tomb there. I was mistaken: the funerary chamber is not closed on all sides as I had previously drawn it, but it is a chamber with an entrance on the side of the mill. I must get it partially cleared.

After lunch I went to work at Hallangy – I stayed there all day where I received several visits: the Town Clerk and Mr Trevellick of Rocky Hill, a long-winded old man who is very interested in island antiquities and who invited me to go to see his lovely gardens on Sunday at 2 o'clock. I gave him a present of a nice piece of primitive pottery which came from the Hallangy tomb. He was very happy with it.

(p144)

Tuesday 2 October 1900

This morning after breakfast, I went to see Mr King who showed me proofs of some photographs taken at Hallangy. Then I left for Hallangy – Williams is working today to clear the tomb entrance, which faces east. As for me, I worked on the interior, at the back of the tomb on the west side where I found on the ground the contents of [...] cinerary urns which were desecrated there. The ashes are composed of a yellowish earth, no doubt burnt, containing charcoal and calcined bones. I have also collected many fragments of urns (p145) decorated with dotted lines impressed in the fresh clay. On the inner surface of several fragments, I recognised ashes and bones sticking to them.

- I went back to the hotel at midday.

First day of rain, that is to say, showers. However, we did not work.

I returned to Hallangy at 2.30.

2 clergymen came to see me, as well as an acquaintance from the hotel. I cleaned a part of the tomb interior, going into all the crevices to see if, by chance, there had been an interment or some sort of object left behind by these primitive people. Nothing.

The *Lady of the Isles* arrived today. I received a postcard from Agnes, asking me when I am thinking of returning to Seaborough.

Wednesday 3 October 1900

This morning I went to watch the boat leave at 10 o'clock. The weather is lovely today. I was told that around 3 or 4 o'clock the young ladies from the Abbey would come over to visit Hallangy and the tomb we have uncovered.

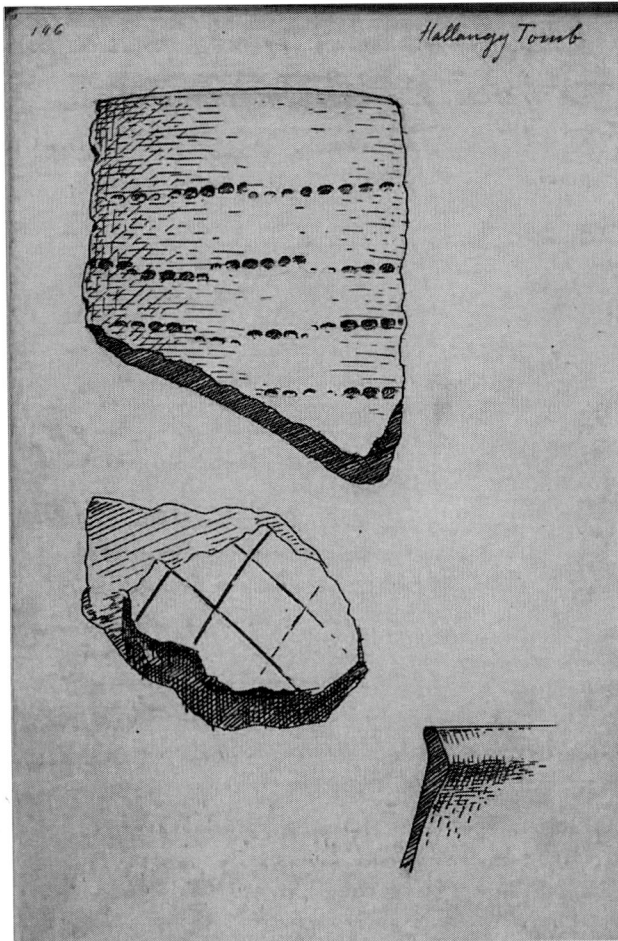

FIGURE A3.3 PAGE 146 OF THE FIRST NOTEBOOK, SHOWING
BONSOR'S DRAWINGS OF POTTERY FROM BANT'S CARN

This morning I washed all the pieces of pottery found in the Hallangy tomb, several of them were decorated with patterns.

I took a photograph of the harbour, seen from the gallery in front of my window.

In the afternoon, I went to Hallangy and the young ladies, the sister, a friend and the governess, arrived by boat to see my excavations.

I went back to the hotel at 5.30 pm. We have had glorious weather all day. The sea very calm.

(p149)

Thursday 4 October 1900

This morning it rained hard and towards midday a storm blew up from the west. Moreover, it had been forecast. I stayed at the hotel to draw. I went to see Mr. King. The weather was so bad today that the boat *Lady of the Isles* could not leave Penzance.

(p150)

Today, Williams has cleared the entrance of the funerary chamber – outside, the ground was covered with pottery debris; the remainder of the pieces that had been found inside. This indicates that the people who raided the tomb broke the urns that they found there in order to tip the contents on to the ground. The rim of these urns is slightly out-turned, (p151) the base is flat and the body is decorated with zones of lines of hollows, impressed with the aid of a punch approximately 4cm in length. This explains how each line of this length is more or less broken – it would have been different if these impressions had been produced by means of a little wheel.

Mr. Cowling – an engineer in charge of the work on the forts on the Hugh, St Mary's, has sent me a packet of a clay that exists on the island and which is used to make chimneys and hearths, 'Fire Clay'. I think that, this clay being found on the island, the primitive people would have used it to make their urns and various pots - 'Porth Clay'.

Friday 5 October 1900

This afternoon I was at Hallangy measuring the tomb. It was fiendishly windy. Mr Trevellick of Rocky Hill came – at Hallangy Porth he found a large fragment of cooking pot pierced with a flint, just as I have found in Spain.

(p153)

Sunday 7 October 1900

Whilst the islanders are at church, I decided to seize the opportunity of taking some (p154) measurements at Hallangy - but from a distance I saw that the tomb was covered with people, there were more than 50 there and others arriving by all the paths, so I turned my steps in another direction.

(p156)

Monday 8 October 1900

Later, towards 11 o'clock, I went to Hallangy to take some measurements.

...

In the afternoon I drew at home and at 3 o'clock I returned to Halangy to take some more measurements for the plan of the tomb which I am in the process of doing. I will not be able to finish it this year.

**An Archaeological Exploration
of the Scilly Isles 1901-1902**

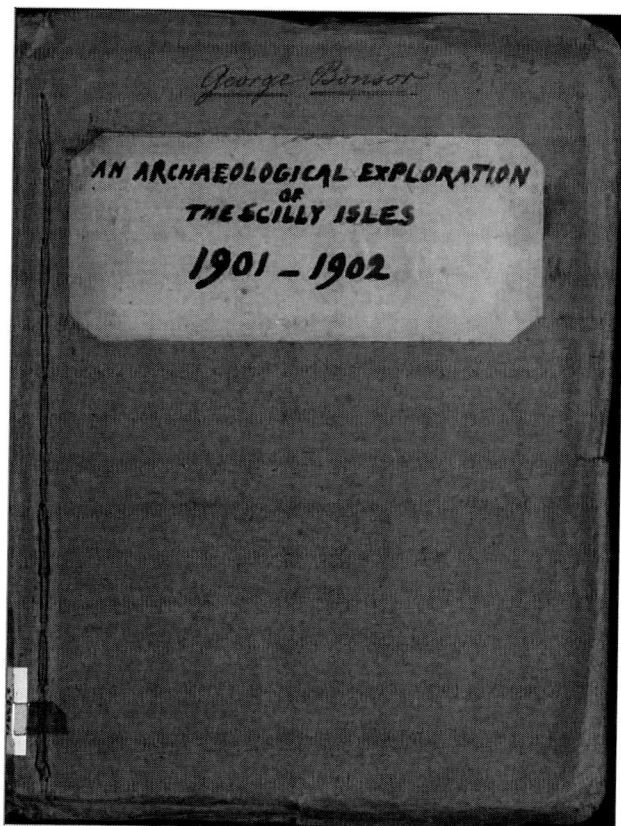

An Archaeological Exploration
of
The Scilly Isles
1901 - 1902

FIGURE A3.4 FRONT COVER OF THE SECOND NOTEBOOK

Seaborough Court,
Crewkerne
28th Oct 1900
Dear Mr Dorrien Smith:

Not having had the opportunity, before I left Scilly, of communicating to you the results of my researches, I am writing to give you a few informations on the subject, hoping you will find them interesting.

I have only had time this year to explore the North-East part of St Mary's. I emptied the funeral chamber or kistvaen on Hallangy down, where I found in the earth numerous fragments of the cinerary urns; some of which were ornamented with a series of parallel indented lines; like several urns, which have been discovered in Cornwall. The human ashes were found in small heaps on the floor of the chamber, when the urns had been emptied, many centuries ago.

The Hallangy tomb is, I think, the most interesting monument of its kind in England. You will see that one of the 4 large covering stones had been overturned and had fallen on the entrance. I should like next year when I return to Scilly, to put this stones [sic] and several others, back again in their original places, to restore this tomb as far as it is possible to do so.

There was a cluster of ancient huts, forming an important village, half way between the Halangy tomb and Bant's Carn. By the seaside, to the West of Bant's Carn, I discovered some foundations of huts and their ashpits. I extracted from the ashpits several concaved stones which had been used for grinding corn. Underneath a layer of limpet shells was found. Limpets must have been, at that period, the principal food of the people; Although they occasionally had meat, many bones of animals having been found among the shells. I have collected these bones to send them to a specialist, so as to give him the opportunity of studying the fauna of Scilly in prehistoric times.

In other layers composed of burnt earth and charcoal, I found some broken pots, of the same kind of earthenware which appeared in the kistvaen above, indicating that the Halangy tomb and the huts […] belonged to the same people. The discovery of a primitive village on this part of the coast of St. Mary's Island seems to indicate the existence at that time of a passage at low tide with St. Martin's and Tresco.

The islands of Great Arthur and Ganilly could also probably be reached from St Martin's or also Tresco to Bryher and Samson - the Island of St. Agnes seems to have been at that period the only inhabited land completely isolated from the rest.

It is my intention to return to Scilly early in August next year to explore two or three kistvaens – on Samson and on the Gugh of St. Agnes, which I believe not to have been opened before.

I shall leave for Spain about the 15th of […]

I wish kind remembrances to yourself and your family - Believe me yours very sincerely

(p172)

Friday 6 Sept 1901

This morning looking out early from my window (Room No 21) I saw that the sea was calm, it was raining a little. I decided to leave. The boat was to leave at 08.30. so I breakfasted hurriedly and settled my hotel bill - £2.3.0. 2/0. – The return fare to Scilly, valid a month, 10/6, 1/0. – When we passed Land's End, the sea was not calm at all and I suffered horribly. The *Lyonnesse* arrived at St Mary's at noon. I went to the hotel, Holgate's. And I went to lie down for a while having had a cup of tea. Around 5 o'clock I went to see the pharmacist Mr King to catch up on the news. I learned that Mr Dorrien Smith was at home on Tresco and that the agent Mr Allen was absent.

After dinner I entered into conversation with one of the visitors.

I received a letter from Fernandez [the co-director of his excavations in Spain] and a journal '*La Andalucia Moderna*'. The catalogue from Pollard in Penzance.

Saturday 7 Sept 1901

This morning the sea opposite the hotel is very calm; no or little wind. I wrote to Agnes at Seaborough. After breakfast I went to Gibson's the photographer. He was away on the island of Tresco. But I was assured that he was coming back today.

(p173)

Then I went up to Star Castle, where I saw Mrs Allen, the wife of the Steward who is away. I asked her to let the Governor know by telephone that I had arrived and that I wished to see him. She told me that he should get to St Mary's around 9.00 when the ferry arrives. I therefore decided to go down to the quay at that time to see him. Mrs Allen gave me the latest news; they had just received a telegram to the effect that the United States president, Mr McKinley had been the victim of a Polish anarchist. I do not yet know the details of this attack. (Postcards 0/6d – 0/1d).

General Smith Dorrien did not come to Tresco. He leaves for India in October. Both of Mr Dorrien Smith's sons are still in the Transvaal, the eldest (Arthur) will probably come back soon.

I saw Mr King. Then I went for a walk to see the Halangy Down tumulus and kistvaen. I had the satisfaction of seeing that nothing had been touched since last year.

...

I went back to the hotel for lunch. Then I received a letter from Mr Dorrien Smith inviting me to Tresco on Monday for 2 days. I wrote back to accept. Then I went to see Mr Trevellick at Rocky Hill. I got some information about people available for excavation work. In a few days' time, he should help me with good labourers for my work. A labourer might work here from 8 in the morning until 5 in the afternoon. – 9 hours (including I think 1 hour for rest) at 4d per hour – 36 - 3/0.

(p174)

As I write these words, I can see from my window a veritable flotilla of French fishing boats (crab-fishing I am told). I have counted 17 so far. They agreed to meet in Scilly. They appear light, painted black, red sails. Here we have many boats which are no bigger than the ancient Phoenician ships and which, like them, travel from Cape Finistère or from Ushant to the Scillies quite easily with favourable winds.

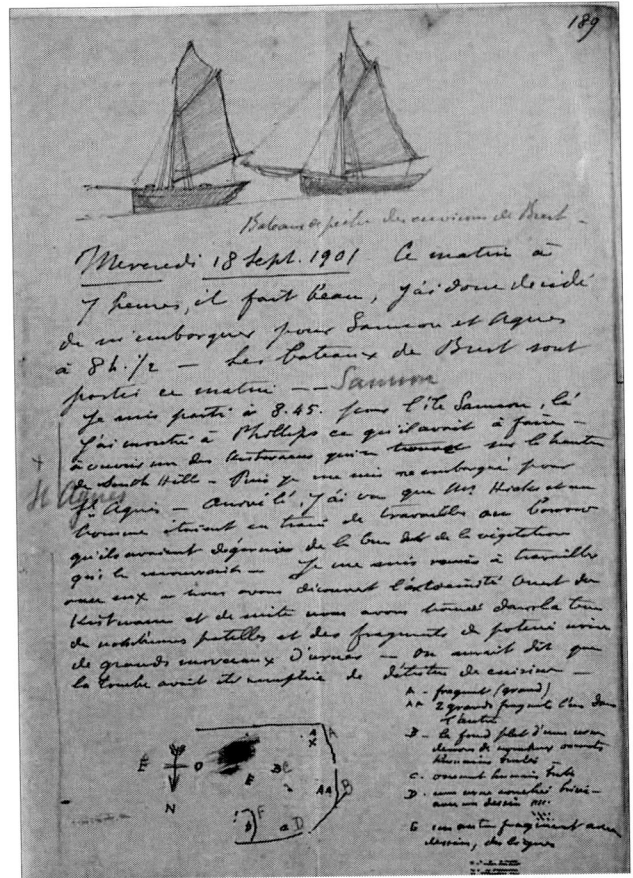

FIGURE A3.5 PAGE 189 OF THE SECOND NOTEBOOK, WITH SKETCH OF BRETON FISHING BOATS AND PLAN OF PART OF CHAMBER OF OBADIAH'S BARROW

(p181)

Friday 13 Sept 1901

After lunch, I went to Hallangy Down to continue the study of the tomb discovered last year. I drew the section of its length from East to West. Close to the door, I found a few pottery fragments. There must be a lot still to come. There is no saying. The tomb was in perfect condition when it was desecrated. The urns were carried to the exterior, into the passage and there they were destroyed.

(p189)

Wednesday 18 Sept 1901

This morning at 7 o'clock, beautiful weather, I therefore decided to take a boat to Samson and Agnes at 8.30. The Brest boats left this morning. I left at 8.45 for Samson. There I showed Phillips what he had to do to open one of the kistvaens which is located on the top of South Hill. Then I got on a boat for St Agnes. Once there, I saw that Mr Hicks and a man were working on the barrow, which they had cleared of the vegetation that had covered it. I began to work with them. We uncovered the western side of the kistvaen and thereafter we found numerous limpets in the earth and some fragments of pottery from large pieces of urns. One would have said that the grave had been filled with kitchen rubbish.

A fragment (large)
AA2 large fragments – one inside the other
B the flat base of an urn, under many
burnt human bones
C burnt human bone
D a broken urn on its side with decoration
E another fragment with a decoration, of lines

(p190)

There was a layer of limpets that was over 30cm in thickness, with black and reddish pottery fragments. One bone point and other objects to study. Some pottery fragments to draw. I must go to St Agnes for a few days to Mr Hicks' house to continue the excavation and to draw the tomb, which is very interesting.

Towards 4.35 we went back to Samson. I saw the burial chamber opened by Phillips, who had done a good job. The tomb has not yet got a very clear entrance. It is dug down in a stone circle. I will have to go back to Samson for a whole day with Phillips to finish the work, to draw the tomb and to explore the island.

At 5.10 we left for St Mary's - arrived at 6.10.

I brought back from the tomb on St Agnes on the Gugh a basket full of 1st fragments of pottery - 2nd human ashes - 3rd uncremated human bones - 4th bone awls.

I had a good day's work today. Expenses:

1 man and his boat	- 8 shillings
2 men to excavate	- 6 shillings
Tools, etc	- 1 shilling
2 lunches	- 2 shillings
My hotel board	- 9 shillings 6d
Total	-26s 6d

(p191)

I arrived tired at the hotel and I will go to bed early. A visitor here at the hotel, Mr Barwell of Birmingham, accompanied by his two sisters, is holding, at the little St Mary's Town Hall, a dance this evening for his friends and acquaintances. Apparently he does this every year. He loves dancing! My new labourer Phillips is a Scillonian back from Australia after an absence of 15 years. He claims there is nothing to do in Australia.

Thursday 19 Sept 1901

As everyone went to the dance yesterday evening, there is no-one to reply to the archaeologist's call at 07.30. I arranged to meet Phillips this morning at 8 o'clock at Hallangy Down.

This morning I see that the 'Gun boat' is back. It is not very good weather.

I got to Hallangy at 9 o'clock. Phillips was there. I put him to work at 65 paces to the north of Hallangy Tomb, where there is an important group of huts contemporary with the tomb. These huts appear to have a circular shape but having to take advantage of the big rocks which occurred there naturally, they are of all kinds of shapes. This grouping of rooms communicating by little entrances in the walls – a cluster of habitation like the Chysauster huts in Cornwall. There used to be stone and earthen walls around this village of which one can still find traces. The tomb at the top was situated exactly at an angle from the wall of the enclosure. The tilled part of the ground was between the village (on the hill-slope) and the sea. More than half [...] would have (p192) disappeared into the sea.

(p225)

Seaborough Court   Scilly 2nd Oct 1901
Crewkerne
Somersetshire

Dear Mr Dorrien-Smith

I am sending you a drawing of the Urn I discovered last Friday, on the Gugh – the Tomb, as you know, is about 60 paces N.W. of Carn Valla; it is of the kind described by Lukis (Prehistoric Stone Monuments – Cornwall p.13 – pl.XXIX) (p226) as a chambered Cairn or barrow. I believe it must have contained more than 20 Urns, all broken but one which I found against the North side wall of the Chamber, it was reversed on the ground and covering the ashes which I collected back again into the Urn.

In the middle of the Tomb and under the layer of ashes from the broken urns, I discovered the skeleton of a man, partly buried in the earth and clay forming the original floor of the chamber. I think this discovery is exceedingly important, it seems at least to indicate that the custom of burial was practised here before cremation.

I am also sending you a photograph of the site, on the shore, near Halangy Point, where Bones of Animals were found together with primitive pottery, a granite flat mill (which you will notice in the foreground of the photograph) and numerous limpet shells; (p227) the detritus from a village of Huts above and to which corresponds the Halangy Tomb (also a chambered Cairn).

It would be desirable to find a specialist, sufficiently interested in the above discoveries, to examine these bones and, if possible, to give us from them a note on the Fauna of the Islands at that early Age. I have collected all the bones in a parcel. It is ready to be forwarded to you if you wish it. I am sending the parcel together with a basket full of broken urns to Star Castle.

I shall leave Scilly on Friday. It is my intention before returning Home to visit Harlyn Bay.

With kind regards
Yours sincerely
GB

(p232)

Monday 7 Oct 1901

I then went to see the photographer Mr Gibson senior where I bought 7 photographs 7/0 – and I had the opportunity to talk for quite a while with the old man, who gave me some good information about the antiquities of St Martin's particularly. He told me, with enthusiasm details about the discovery of a kistvaen, in the place called on the map Cruther's Neck, on (p233) the left of the path as you go up … This kistvaen is destroyed now - it comprised a funerary chamber covered with large stones.

(p234)

Tuesday 8 Oct 1901

This morning I saw that the weather had not changed – same wind, same sea state. At 10 o'clock I went with Phillips to Buzza Hill, to open Borlase's kistvaen. There were 3 tombs on Buzza Hill, one is now under the windmill, the two others are to the north-west of the mill. So I emptied tomb C of Buzza Hill. The stone at the east end is a capstone which has fallen into this position. All of the chamber which was to the east of this stone has been destroyed, someone has removed all the stones and not long ago.

(p286)

Friday 26 Sept 1902

(p288)

We then went to Gweal Hill where I excavated the cist.

A – cist composed of rocks – circle around it

B – little mound – hut or sepulchre or pyre

C – destroyed tomb – direction of chamber from north to south.

We removed the earth from the cist. At the bottom we found pottery.

Gweal Hill, Bryher

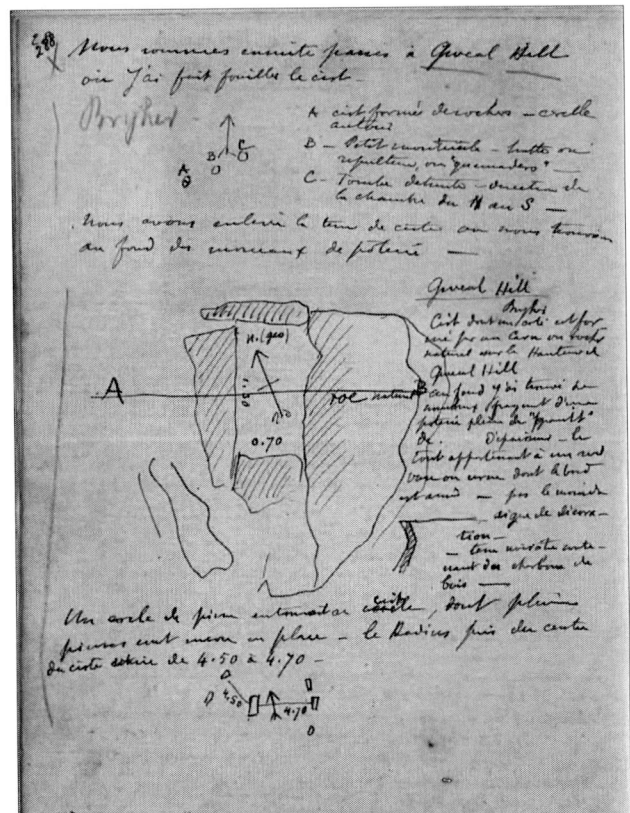

FIGURE A3.6 PAGE 288 OF THE SECOND NOTEBOOK, WITH PLANS OF SITES ON GWEAL HILL AND EXCAVATED CIST

Cist of which one side is formed by a carn, a natural rock on the top of Gweal Hill. At the bottom I found many fragments of pottery full of quartz.

As regards thickness, everything belongs to a single vase or urn of which the rim is rounded - not the slightest sign of decoration - blackish earth containing charcoal.

A circle of stones went round the cist, of which several stones are still in place. The radius taken from the centre of the cist varies from 4.50 to 4.70.

(p289)

This tomb belongs to the same period as the one explored by Mr Augustus Smith on the island of Samson.

It was 4.30 – we went towards our boat. The wind being against us, we arrived late at St Mary's. I received a letter from the Baron of Pontalba and a postcard from Gilchrist Clark-Maxwell.

Bibliography

1971. Chronique des Datations Radiocarbone Armoricaines. *Annales de Bretagne,* 78(1), 169-172.

ApSimon, A. M., 1972. Tregiffian Barrow, St Buryan. *Cornish Archaeology,* 11, 56.

Arbery, G., 2004. A Heritage and Cultural Strategy for the Isles of Scilly, St Mary's, Isles of Scilly: Council of the Isles of Scilly.

Ashbee, P., 1953. Two Stone Cists on St Mary's. *Proceedings of the West Cornwall Field Club,* One(1), 28-31.

Ashbee, P., 1955. An Urn from Par Beach, St Martin's, Isles of Scilly. *Proceedings of the West Cornwall Field Club,* One(3), 123-124.

Ashbee, P., 1960. *The Bronze Age Round Barrow in Britain,* London: Phoenix House.

Ashbee, P., 1974. *Ancient Scilly,* Newton Abbot: David and Charles.

Ashbee, P., 1976. Bant's Carn, St Mary's, Isles of Scilly: An Entrance Grave Restored and Reconsidered. *Cornish Archaeology,* 15, 11-26.

Ashbee, P., 1980. George Bonsor: An Archaeological Pioneer from Spain on Scilly. *Cornish Studies,* 8, 53-62.

Ashbee, P., 1982. Mesolithic Megaliths? The Scillonian Entrance-Graves: A New View. *Cornish Archaeology,* 21, 3-22.

Ashbee, P., 1996. Halangy Down, St Mary's, Isles of Scilly, Excavations 1964-1977. *Cornish Archaeology,* 35, 1-201.

Ashmore, P., 2002. *Calanais: The Standing Stones,* Edinburgh: Historic Scotland.

Ashmore, P. J., 1999. Radiocarbon dating: avoiding errors by avoiding mixed samples. *Antiquity,* 73, 124-130.

Aspinall, A., S. E. Warren, J. G. Crummett & R. G. Newton, 1972. Neutron Activation Analysis of Faience Beads. *Archaeometry,* 14, 27-40.

Barber, J., 2000. Death in Orkney: a Rare Event, in *Neolithic Orkney in its European context,* ed. A. Ritchie Cambridge: McDonald Institute for Archaeological Research, 185-187.

Barnatt, J., 1982. *Prehistoric Cornwall: The Ceremonial Monuments,* Wellingborough: Turnstone Press.

Beagrie, N., 1989. Excavations by Bryan and Helen O'Neil on the Isles of Scilly, in *From Cornwall to Caithness: Some Aspects of British Field Archaeology. Papers presented to Norman V Quinnell,* eds. M. Bowden, D. Mackay & P. Topping Oxford: British Archaeological Reports, 49-54.

Beck, H. C. & J. F. S. Stone, 1935. Faience Beads of the British Bronze Age. *Archaeologia,* 85, 203-252.

Bender, B., S. Hamilton & C. Tilley, 1997. Leskernick: Stone Worlds; Alternative Narratives; Nested Landscapes. *Proceedings of the Prehistoric Society,* 63, 147-178.

Bennett, M., R. Bushell, C. T. Mumford, S. Pritchard & S. Watt, 1991. *One Hundred Years of the Council of the Isles of Scilly,* St Mary's, Isles of Scilly: Council of the Isles of Scilly.

Berridge, P. & A. Roberts, 1986. The Mesolithic Period in Cornwall. *Cornish Archaeology,* 25, 7-35.

Binns, R. E., 1967. Drift Pumice in Northern Europe. *Antiquity,* 41, 311-312.

Blight, J. T., 1870. *The Cromlechs of Cornwall,* Penzance: Morrab Library.

Bonsor, G., 1899-1900. *An Archaeological Exploration of the Scilly Isles 1899-1900,* Seville: Archivo General de Andalucia.

Bonsor, G., 1900. *Letter to Mr Dorrien-Smith 28 October 1900,* Seville: Archivo General de Andalucia.

Bonsor, G., 1901. *Letter to Mr Dorrien-Smith 2 October 1901,* St Mary's: Isles of Scilly Museum.

Bonsor, G., 1901-1902. *An Archaeological Exploration of the Scilly Isles 1901-1902,* Seville: Archivo General de Andalucia.

Bonsor, G., 1928. From Tarshish to the Isles of Tin. *Art and Archaeology,* XXV(1), 10-17.

Bonsor, G., nd c1904. *Letter to unknown recipient,* St Mary's: Isles of Scilly Museum.

Borlase, W., 1753. An Account of the great Alterations which the Islands of Sylley have undergone since the Time of the Antients... *Philosophical Transactions of the Royal Society,* XLVIII(1), 55-67.

Borlase, W., 1756. *Observations on the Ancient and Present State of the Islands of Scilly,* Oxford.

Borlase, W., 1758. *The Natural History of Cornwall,* Oxford.

Borlase, W., 1769. *Antiquities Historical and Monumental of the County of Cornwall,* London.

Borlase, W. C., 1872. *Naenia Cornubiae,* London: Longmans, Green, Reader and Dyer.

Boujot, C. & S. Cassen, 1993. A pattern of evolution for the Neolithic funerary structures of the west of France. *Antiquity,* 67, 477-474.

Bowen, E. G., 1972. *Britain and the Western Seaways,* London: Thames and Hudson.

Bowley, R. L., 1990. *The Fortunate Islands,* Isles of Scilly: Bowley Publications.

Bradley, R., 1989. Darkness and Light in the Design of Megalithic Tombs. *Oxford Journal of Archaeology,* 8(3), 251-259.

Bradley, R., 1993. *Altering the Earth,* Edinburgh: Society of Antiquaries of Scotland Monograph Series No 8.

Bradley, R., 2000. *The Good Stones: a new investigation of the Clava Cairns,* Edinburgh: Society of Antiquaries of Scotland.

Bradley, R., 2007. *The Prehistory of Britain and Ireland,* Cambridge: Cambridge University Press.

Bradley, S. L., G. A. Milne, F. N. Teferle, R. M. Bingley & E. J. Orliac, 2009. Glacial isostatic adjustment of the British Isles: new constraints from GPS measurements of crustal motion. *Geophysical Journal International,* 178, 14-22.

Breen, E., 2006. Constructing Meanings from the Architecture of Landscape on the Isles of Scilly. *Journal of Iberian Archaeology,* 8, 265-280.

Breen, E., 2008. Encounters with place in prehistory: writing a case study for Shipman Head Down, Isles of Scilly, in *Recent Approaches to the Archaeology of Land Allotment,* ed. A. M. Chadwick, Oxford: Archaeopress, 97-109.

Brindley, A. L. & J. N. Lanting, 1991. Radiocarbon Dates from Wedge Tombs. *The Journal of Irish Archaeology,* 6, 19-26.

Bronk Ramsey, C., 2013. OxCal 4.2. https://c14.arch.ox.ac.uk/oxcal/OxCal.html.

Broodbank, C., 2000. *An Island Archaeology of the Early Cyclades,* Cambridge: Cambridge University Press.

Brophy, K., 2005. Not my type: discourses in monumentality, in *Set in Stone: New Approaches to Neolithic Monuments in Scotland,* eds. V. Cummings & A. Pannett, Oxford: Oxbow Books, 1-13.

Brück, J., 2001. Monuments, power and personhood in the British Neolithic. *The Journal of the Royal Anthropological Institute,* 7(4), 649-667.

Brück, J., 2005. Experiencing the past? The development of a phenomenological archaeology in British prehistory. *Archaeological Dialogues,* 12(1), 45-72.

Burl, A., 1985. *Megalithic Brittany,* London: Thames and Hudson.

Butcher, S., 1978. Excavations at Nornour, Isles of Scilly, 1969-73: the Pre-Roman Settlement. *Cornish Archaeology,* 17, 29-112.

Butcher, S., 2000-2001. Roman Nornour, Isles of Scilly: a reconsideration. *Cornish Archaeology,* 39-40, 5-44.

Butter, R., 1999. *Kilmartin: Scotland's richest prehistoric landscape,* Kilmartin: Kilmartin House Trust.

Callaghan, R. & C. Scarre, 2009. Simulating the Western Seaways. *Oxford Journal of Archaeology,* 28(4), 357-372.

Camidge, K., D. Charman, C. Johns, J. Meadows, S. Mills, J. Mulville, H. M. Roberts & T. Stevens, 2010. The Lyonesse Project: Evolution of the coastal and marine environment of Scilly, Year 1 Report, Truro: Historic Environment, Cornwall Council.

Campbell, M., J. G. Scott & S. Piggott, 1960-1961. The Badden Cist Slab. *Proceedings of the Society of Antiquaries of Scotland,* 94, 46-61.

Case, H., 1969. Neolithic Explanations. *Antiquity,* 43, 176-186.

Chapman, H. P., 2003. Rudston 'Cursus A' - Engaging with a Neolithic Monument in its Landscape Setting Using GIS. *Oxford Journal of Archaeology,* 22(4), 345-356.

Charman, D., P. Dudley, R. Fyfe, M. Gehrels, R. Gehrels, J. Hatton, M. Perez & B. Tapper, 2012a. Sea-level change on the Isles of Scilly, in *The Lyonesse Project: A Study of the Evolution of the Coastal and Marine Environment of the Isles of Scilly; Draft Final Report,* ed. C. Johns, Truro: Historic Environment, Cornwall Council, 169-179.

Charman, D., R. Fyfe, M. Gehrels, R. Gehrels, J. Hatton & M. Perez, 2012b. Palaeoenvironmental analysis, in *The Lyonesse Project: A Study of the Evolution of the Coastal and Marine Environment of the Isles of Scilly; Draft Final Report,* ed. C. Johns, Truro: Cornwall Council, 134-168.

Cherry, J. F., 1981. Pattern and Process in the Earliest Colonization of the Mediterranean Islands. *Proceedings of the Prehistoric Society,* 47, 41-68.

Childe, V. G., 1940. *Prehistoric Communities of the British Isles,* London: Chambers.

Childe, V. G., 1958. *The Prehistory of European Society,* Harmondsworth: Penguin Books.

Clark, A. J., 1978. Radiocarbon and Magnetic Dating in Butcher, S A Excavations at Nornour, Isles of Scilly, 1969-73: the Pre-Roman Settlement. *Cornish Archaeology,* 17, 66-67.

Clark, G., 1977. The Economic Context of Dolmens and Passage-Graves in Sweden, in *Ancient Europe and the Mediterranean: Studies presented in honour of Hugh Hencken,* ed. V. Markotic, Warminster: Aris and Phillips, 35-49.

Clark, P. (ed.) 2004. *The Dover Bronze Age Boat in Context: Society and water transport in prehistoric Europe,* Oxford: Oxbow Books.

Clarke, D., 2008. Book Review: From Cairn to Cemetery: An Archaeological Investigation of the Chambered Cairns and Early Bronze Age Mortuary Deposits at Cairnderry and Bargrennan White Cairn, South West Scotland by Vicki Cummings and Chris Fowler, in *http://www.le.ac.uk/has/ps/reviews/08_06_cairnderry. htm* Accessed 17 April 2010.

Clarke, D. V., T. G. Cowie & A. Foxon, 1985. *Symbols of Power at the Time of Stonehenge,* Edinburgh: National Museum of Antiquities of Scotland.

Cornish, T., 1878. The Conversazione. *Annual Report of the Royal Institution of Cornwall,* 60, 67-69.

Craw, J. H., 1929-1930. Excavations at Dunadd and at other Sites on the Poltalloch Estates, Argyll. *Proceedings of the Society of Antiquaries of Scotland,* 64, 111-146.

Crawford, O. G. S., 1927. Lyonesse. *Antiquity,* 1, 5-14.

Crawford, O. G. S., 1928. Stone Cists. *Antiquity,* 2, 418-422.

Cummings, V., 2002. Between mountains and sea. A reconsideration of the Neolithic monuments of south-west Scotland. *Proceedings of the Prehistoric Society,* 68, 125-146.

Cummings, V., 2004. Connecting the mountains and sea: the monuments of the eastern Irish Sea zone, in *The Neolithic of the Irish Sea: Materiality and traditions of practice,* eds. V. Cummings & C. Fowler, Oxford: Oxbow Books, 29-36.

Cummings, V. & C. Fowler, 2007. *From Cairn to Cemetery: An archaeological investigation of the chambered cairns and early Bronze Age mortuary deposits at Cairnderry and Bargrennan White Cairn, south-west Scotland,* Oxford: Archaeopress.

Cummings, V., C. Henley & N. Sharples, 2005. The chambered cairns of South Uist, in *Set in Stone: New Approaches to Neolithic Monuments in Scotland,* eds. V. Cummings & C. Fowler, Oxford: Oxbow Books.

Cummings, V. & A. Pannett, 2005. Island views: the settings of the chambered cairns of southern Orkney, in *Set in Stone: New Approaches to the Neolithic Monuments in Scotland,* eds. V. Cummings & A. Pannett, Oxford: Oxbow Books, 14-24.

Cummings, V. & A. Whittle, 2003. Tombs with a view: landscape, monuments and trees. *Antiquity,* 77, 255-266.

Cummings, V. & A. Whittle, 2004. *Places of special virtue: megaliths in the Neolithic landscapes of Wales,* Oxford: Oxbow Books.

Cunliffe, B., 2001. *Facing the Ocean: The Atlantic and its Peoples,* Oxford: Oxford University Press.

Curle, A. O., 1929-1930. Examination of a Chambered Cairn by the Water of Deuch, Stewartry of Kickcudbright. *Proceedings of the Society of Antiquaries of Scotland,* 64, 272-275.

Daniel, G. E., 1941. The Dual Nature of Megalithic Colonisation of Western Europe. *Proceedings of the Prehistoric Society,* VII, 1-49.

Daniel, G. E., 1947. The Megalithic Tombs of the Scillies, in *The Scillonian,* 116-118.

Daniel, G. E., 1950. *The Prehistoric Chamber Tombs of England and Wales,* Cambridge: Cambridge University Press.

Daniel, G. E., 1960. *The Prehistoric Chamber Tombs of France,* London: Thames and Hudson.

Daniel, G. E., 1963. *The Megalith Builders of Western Europe,* Harmondsworth: Penguin Books.

Daniel, G. E., 1969. Editorial. *Antiquity,* XLIII(171), 169-175.

Daniel, G. E., 1970. Megalithic Answers. *Antiquity,* 44, 260-269.

Daniel, G. E., 1982. Editorial. *Antiquity,* 56, 1-9.

Darvill, T., 2000. Neolithic Mann in Context, in *Neolithic Orkney in its European context,* ed. A. Ritchie, Cambridge: McDonald Institute for Archaeological Research.

Darvill, T., 2002. White on Blonde: Quartz Pebbles and the Use of Quartz at Neolithic Monuments in the Isle of Man and Beyond, in *Colouring the Past: The Significance of Colour in Archaeological Research,* eds. A. Jones & G. MacGregor, Oxford: Berg, 73-91.

Davidson, J. L. & A. S. Henshall, 1989. *The Chambered Cairns of Orkney,* Edinburgh: Edinburgh University Press.

Davies, M., 1946. The diffusion and distribution pattern of the megalithic monuments of the Irish Sea and North Channel coastlands. *Antiquaries Journal,* 26, 38-60.

Douch, H. L., 1962. Archaeological Discoveries recorded in Cornish Newspapers before 1855. *Cornish Archaeology,* 1, 92-98.

Driscoll, P., 2010. The Past in the Prehistoric Channel Islands. *Shima: The International Journal of Research into Island Cultures,* 4(1), 65-81.

Dudley, D., 1968a. Excavations on Nor'nour in the Isles of Scilly, 1962-6. *Archaeological Journal,* CXXIV, 1-64.

Dudley, D., 1968b. Tregiffian, St Buryan. *Cornish Archaeology,* 7, 80.

Edmonds, M., 1999. *Ancestral Geographies of the Neolithic,* London: Routledge.

English Heritage, 1996. Record of Scheduled Monuments: Kittern Hill, Gugh, Monument No.15445.

English Heritage, nd. National Monuments Record Monument Type Thesaurus, http://thesaurus.english-heritage.org.uk/thesaurus.asp?thes_no=1: Accessed 26 October 2011.

Eogan, G., 1963. A Neolithic Habitation-Site and Megalithic Tomb in Townleyhall Townland, Co. Louth. *Journal of the Royal Society of Antiquaries of Ireland,* 93, 37-81.

Evans, J. D., 1973. Islands as laboratories for the study of culture process, in *The Explanation of Culture Change: Models in Prehistory,* ed. C. Renfrew, London: Duckworth, 517-520.

Evans, J. G., 1983. The Examination of Residues upon Sherds of Pottery from Halangy Porth. *Cornish Archaeology,* 22, 37.

Fleming, A., 1999. Phenomenology and the Megaliths of Wales: A Dreaming Too Far? *Oxford Journal of Archaeology,* 18(2), 119-125.

Fleming, A., 2005a. Megaliths and post-modernism: the case of Wales. *Antiquity,* 79, 921-932.

Fleming, A., 2005b. *St Kilda and the Wider World: Tales of an Iconic Island,* Macclesfield: Windgather Press.

Fleming, A., 2006. Post-processual Landscape Archaeology: a Critique. *Cambridge Archaeological Journal,* 16(3), 267-280.

Fowler, P. & C. Thomas, 1979. Lyonesse revisited: the early walls of Scilly. *Antiquity,* 53, 175-189.

Frieman, C., 2008. Islandscapes and «Islandness»: The Prehistoric Isle of Man in the Irish Seascape. *Oxford Journal of Archaeology,* 27(2), 135-151.

Garrow, D. & F. Sturt, 2011. Grey waters bright with Neolithic argonauts? Maritime connections and the Mesolithic-Neolithic transition within the «western seaways» of Britain, c5000-3500BC. *Antiquity,* 85, 59-72.

Garrow, D. & F. Sturt, 2014. Neolithic Stepping Stones: Excavations at Old Quay, St Martin's, September 2013 and September 2014 http://www.neolithicsteppingstones.org/_/Isles_of_Scilly_Excavations.html Accessed 21 October 2014

Gibson, A., 1986. *Neolithic and Early Bronze Age Pottery,* Princes Risborough: Shire.

Gillings, M., 2009. Visual Affordance, Landscape, and the Megaliths of Alderney. *Oxford Journal of Archaeology,* 28(4), 335-356.

Giot, P.-R., 1987. *Barnenez, Carn, Guennoc,* Rennes: Travaux du Laboratoire d'Anthropologie, Préhistoire, Protohistoire et Quaternaire Armoricains.

Gray, A., 1972. Prehistoric Habitation Sites on the Isles of Scilly. *Cornish Archaeology,* 11, 19-49.

Grimes, W. F., 1960. *Excavations on Defence Sites 1939-1945, I Mainly Neolithic - Bronze Age,* London: HMSO.

Guido, M., J. Henderson, M. Cable, J. Bayley & L. Biek, 1984. A Bronze Age glass bead from Wilsford, Wiltshire: Barrow G42 in the Lake group. *Proceedings of the Prehistoric Society,* 50, 245-254.

Hamilton, S., R. Whitehouse, w. K. Brown, P. Combes, E. Herring & M. Seager Thomas, 2006. Phenomenology in Practice: Towards a Methodology for a 'Subjective' Approach. *European Journal of Archaeology,* 9(1), 31-71.

Harding, A., 1971. The earliest glass in Europe. *Archeologicke Rozhledy,* XXIII(2), 188-200.

Harding, A. & S. E. Warren, 1973. Early Bronze Age faience beads from Central Europe. *Antiquity,* 46, 64-66.

Harvey, J. (ed.) 1965. *William Worcestre; Itineraries, edited from the unique MS. Corpus Christi College Cambridge 210,* Oxford: Clarendon Press.

Hawkes, J., 1941. Excavation of a Megalithic Tomb at Harristown, Co. Waterford. *Journal of the Royal Society of Antiquaries of Ireland,* 71(4), 130-147.

Heath, R., 1750. *A Natural and Historical Account of the Islands of Scilly,* London.

Hencken, H. O. N., 1929. The Bronze and Iron Ages in Devon and Cornwall, Unpublished PhD thesis, University of Cambridge.

Hencken, H. O. N., 1932. *The Archaeology of Cornwall and Scilly,* London: Methuen & Co Ltd.

Hencken, H. O. N., 1933. Notes on the Megalithic Monuments in the Isles of Scilly. *Antiquaries Journal,* XIII, 13-29.

Henderson, C. G., 1917. Notebooks of Parochial Antiquities Volume II, Truro: Courtney Library, Royal Cornwall Museum.

Henderson, J., 1978. Glass, and the Manufacture of Prehistoric and Other Early Glass Beads. Part I: Technical Background and Theory. *Irish Archaeological Research Forum,* 5, 55-62.

Henderson, J., 1988. Glass production and Bronze Age Europe. *Antiquity,* 62, 435-451.

Henderson, J., 1989. The earliest glass in Britain and Ireland, in *Le verre préromain en Europe occidentale,* ed. M. Feugère, Montagnac: Eds Monique Mergoil, 19-28.

Henshall, A. S., 1972. *The Chambered Tombs of Scotland Volume 2,* Edinburgh: Edinburgh University Press.

Herity, M., 1974. *Irish Passage Graves,* Dublin: Irish University Press.

HES, 1987-2005. Cornwall and Scilly Historic Environment Record, Cornwall County Council.

HES, 2004. Sites, Monuments and Buildings Record, Cornwall County Council.

Hibbs, J., 1983. The Neolithic of Brittany and Normandy, in *Ancient France: Neolithic Societies and their Landscapes 6000-2000bc,* ed. C. Scarre, Edinburgh: Edinburgh University Press, 271-323.

Johns, C., 2002-03. An Iron Age sword and mirror cist burial from Bryher, Isles of Scilly. *Cornish Archaeology,* 41-42, 1-79.

Johns, C. (ed.) 2011. *Scilly Historic Environment Research Framework (SHERF): Resource Assessment,* Truro: Historic Environment Projects, Cornwall Council.

Johns, C. (ed.) 2012. *The Lyonesse Project: A Study of the Evolution of the Coastal and Marine Environment of the Isles of Scilly; Draft Final Report,* Truro: Historic Environment, Cornwall Council.

Johns, C., w. c. from, J. Allan, E. Breen, A. Brodie, A. M. Jones, T. Kirk, A. Martin, J. Marley, J. Mulville, P. Rainbird, K. Sawyer, F. Sturt & A. Tyacke, 2011. Introduction to the Project and the Islands, in *Scilly Historic Environment Research Framework (SHERF): Resource Assessment,* ed. C. Johns, Truro: Historic Environment Projects, Cornwall Council.

Johns, C. & J. Mulville, 2012. Discussion, in *The Lyonesse Project: A Study of the Evolution of the Coastal and Marine Environment of the Isles of Scilly; Draft Final Report,* ed. C. Johns, Truro: Historic Environment, Cornwall Council, 180-193.

Johnson, M., 1999. *Archaeological Theory,* Oxford: Blackwell

Johnston, D. E., 1972. The Re-Excavation of the Beauport Dolmen. *Annual Bulletin of the Societe Jersiaise,* 20, 405-417.

Johnston, D. E., 1981. *The Channel Islands: An Archaeological Guide,* London: Phillimore.

Jones, A. M., 1999. Local Colour: Megalithic Architecture and Colour Symbolism in Neolithic Arran. *Oxford Journal of Archaeology,* 18(4), 339-350.

Jones, A. M., 2002. A Biography of Colour: Colour, Material Histories and Personhood in the Early Bronze Age of Britain and Ireland, in *Colouring the Past: The Significance of Colour in Archaeological Research,* eds. A. Jones & G. MacGregor, Oxford: Berg, 159-174.

Jones, A. M., 2005. *Cornish Bronze Age Ceremonial Landscapes c.2500-1500BC,* Oxford: Archaeopress.

Jones, A. M., D. Freedman, B. O'Connor, H. Lamdin-Whymark, R. Tipping & A. Watson, 2011. *An Animate Landscape: Rock Art and the Prehistory of Kilmartin, Argyll, Scotland,* Oxford: Windgather Press.

Jones, A. M., J. Marchand, A. Sheridan & V. Straker, 2014. Dartmoor cist burial, in *British Archaeology*, 139, 16-23.

Jones, A. M. & H. Quinnell, 2011. The Neolithic and Bronze Age in Cornwall, c4000 cal BC to c1000 cal BC: an overview of recent developments. *Cornish Archaeology,* 50, 197-229.

Jones, A. M. & A. C. Thomas, 2010. Bosiliack and a Reconsideration of Entrance Graves. *Proceedings of the Prehistoric Society,* 76, 271-296.

Joussaume, R. & L. Laporte, 2006. Monuments funéraires néolithiques dans l'ouest de la France, in *Origine et développement du mégalithisme de l'ouest de l'Europe, Actes du colloque international de Bougon, 26-30 oct.2002,* eds. R. Joussaume, L. Laporte & C. Scarre, Bougon: Musée des tumulus de Bougon, 319-344.

Kendrick, T. D., 1928. *The Archaeology of the Channel Islands Volume 1: The Bailiwick of Guernsey,* London: Methuen.

Kinnes, I. & J. A. Grant, 1983. *Les Fouaillages and the Megalithic Monuments of Guernsey,* Alderney: Ampersand Press.

Kirch, P. V., 1986. Introduction: the archaeology of island societies, in *Island Societies: Archaeological Approaches to Evolution and Transformation,* ed. P. V. Kirch, Cambridge: Cambridge University Press.

Kirk, T., 2004. Memory, tradition and materiality: the Isles of Scilly in context, in *The Neolithic of the Irish Sea: Materiality and traditions of practice,* eds. V. Cummings & C. Fowler, Oxford: Oxbow Books, 233-244.

L'Helgouach, J., 1962. Le dolmen de Conguel en Quiberon (Morbihan). *Bulletin de la Societe Prehistorique Francaise,* 59(5-6), 371-381.

Laporte, L., L. Jallot & M. Sohn, 2011. Mégalithismes en France: Nouveaux acquis et nouvelles perspectives de recherche. *Gallia Prehistoire,* 53, 289-338.

Laporte, L., R. Joussaume & C. Scarre, 2002. The perception of space and geometry: Megalithic monuments of west-central France in their relationship to the landscape, in *Monuments and Landscape in Atlantic Europe,* ed. C. Scarre, London: Routledge, 73-83.

Larsen, G., A. J. Newton, A. J. Dugmore & E. G. Vilmundardottir, 2001. Geochemistry, dispersal, volumes and chronology of Holocene silicic tephra layers from the Katla volcanic system, Iceland. *Journal of Quaternary Science,* 16(2), 119-132.

Layard, J., 1933. The Prehistoric Heritage of Scilly, in *The Scillonian,* 119-135.

Leland, J., 1745. *The Itinerary of John Leland the Antiquary,* Oxford.

Lewis, H. A., 1945. St Martin's, St Helen's and Tean, in *The Scillonian,* 44-56.

Lewis, H. A., 1948. *St Martin's, St Helen's and Tean (Isles of Scilly) in Legend and History*: Privately published.

Lewis, H. A., 1949. Knackyboy Break-In - circa 1905-8, St Mary's: Isles of Scilly Museum.

Lewis, H. A., nd-a. Archaeological Examinanda, St Mary's: Isles of Scilly Museum.

Lewis, H. A., nd-b. Knackyboy Barrow, Past History (From older inhabitants of St Martin's), St Mary's: Isles of Scilly Museum.

Lynch, F., 1998. Colour in Prehistoric Architecture, in *Prehistoric Ritual and Religion,* eds. A. Gibson & D. Simpson, Stroud: Sutton.

Lynch, F., 2004. *Megalithic Tombs and Long Barrows in Britain,* Princes Risborough: Shire.

MacArthur, R. H. & E. O. Wilson, 1967. *The Theory of Island Biogeography,* Princeton: Princeton University Press.

Mackenzie, M., 1965. Isles of Scilly Museum Association, in *The Scillonian,* 123-124.

MacWhite, E., 1956. On the Interpretation of Archeological Evidence in Historical and Sociological Terms. *American Anthropologist,* 58(1), 3-25.

Maier, J., 1999. *Jorge Bonsor (1855-1930): Un Academico Correspondiente de la Real Academia de la Historia y la Arqueologia Espanola,* Madrid: Real Academia de la Historia.

Manske, K., M. A. Owoc, M. Greek, J. Illingworth & J. M. Adovasio, 2004. Island Threads: Bronze Age Textile Production and Identity on the Isles of Scilly, UK, Erie, Pennsylvania: Mercyhurst Archaeological Institute.

Mens, E., 2008. Refitting megaliths in western France. *Antiquity,* 82, 25-36.

Mens, E., 2011. Choices and intentions of the standing-stone builders: comparisons between France and the British Isles, paper given at the «Hands Across the Water» Conference Bournemouth.

Mercer, R., 1986. The Neolithic in Cornwall. *Cornish Archaeology,* 25, 35-80.

Mulville, J., 2007. *Islands in a Common Sea; Archaeological fieldwork in the Isles of Scilly 2006,* Cardiff: Cardiff University.

Murray, J., 1992. The Bargrennan Group of Chambered Cairns: Circumstance and Context, in *Vessels for the Ancestors,* eds. N. Sharples & A. Sheridan, Edinburgh: Edinburgh University Press, 33-48.

Neal, D. S., 1983. Excavations on a Settlement at Little Bay, Isles of Scilly. *Cornish Archaeology,* 22, 47-80.

Neal, D. S., forthcoming. The 1970/1 excavations at East Porth, Samson. *Cornish Archaeology.*

Newton, A. J., 2004. Pumice, in *Camas Daraich: a Mesolithic site at the Point of Sleat, Skye,* eds. C. R. Wickham-Jones & K. Hardy, Edinburgh: Society of Antiquaries of Scotland, 47-48.

Newton, R. G. & C. Renfrew, 1970. British Faience Beads Reconsidered. *Antiquity,* 44, 199-206.

O'Brien, W., 1999. *Sacred Ground: Megalithic Tombs in Coastal South-West Ireland,* Galway: Department of Archaeology, National University of Ireland.

O'Neil, B. H. St. J., 1948-1949. Knackyboy Cairn, in *O'Neil Archive Notebook II* St Mary's: Isles of Scilly Museum.

O'Neil, B. H. St. J., 1949a. *Ancient Monuments of the Isles of Scilly,* London: HMSO.

O'Neil, B. H. St. J., 1949b. Plan of Par Beach, St Martin's, Scilly, Cist II, in the O'Neil archive, St Mary's: Isles of Scilly Museum.

O'Neil, B. H. St. J., 1949c. A Romano-British Hut in Scilly, in *The Scillonian*, 163-164.

O'Neil, B. H. St. J., 1952. The Excavation of Knackyboy Cairn, St Martin's, Isles of Scilly, 1948. *Antiquaries Journal,* 32, 21-34.

O'Neil, B. H. St. J., 1954. A triangular cist in the Isles of Scilly. *Antiquaries Journal*, XXXIV, 235-237.

Ó Nualláin, S. & P. Walsh, 1986. A Reconsideration of the Tramore Passage-Tombs. *Proceedings of the Prehistoric Society,* 52, 25-29.

Owoc, M. A., 2002. Munselling the Mound: The Use of Soil Colour as Metaphor in British Bronze Age Funerary Ritual, in *Colouring the Past: The Significance of Colour in Archaeological Research*, eds. A. Jones & G. MacGregor, Oxford: Berg, 127-140.

Parker Pearson, M., 1990. The Production and Distribution of Bronze Age Pottery in South-Western Britain. *Cornish Archaeology*, 29, 5-32.

Parker Pearson, M., 1995. Southwestern Bronze Age pottery, in «*Unbaked Urns of Rudely Shape*»: *Essays on British and Irish Pottery for Ian Longworth*, eds. I. Kinnes & G. Varndell, Oxford: Oxbow Books, 89-100.

Parker Pearson, M., 2004. Island Prehistories: a View of Orkney from South Uist, in *Explaining social change: studies in honour of Colin Renfrew*, eds. J. F. Cherry, C. Scarre & S. Shennan, Cambridge: McDonald Institute for Archaeological Research, 127-140.

Patchett, F. M., 1944. Cornish Bronze Age Pottery. *Archaeological Journal*, CI, 17-49.

Patton, M., 1993. *Statements in Stone: Monuments and Society in Neolithic Brittany,* London: Routledge.

Patton, M., 1997. The social construction of the Neolithic landscape of the Channel Islands, in *Neolithic Landscapes*, ed. P. Topping, Oxford: Oxbow Books, 41-53.

Penrose, G., 1942. Notes on Peninnis Head artefacts, Truro: Royal Cornwall Museum.

Perry, C. M. & D. A. Davidson, 1987. A Spatial Analysis of Neolithic Chambered Cairns on the Island of Arran, Scotland. *Geoarchaeology: An International Journal*, 2(2), 121-130.

Piggott, S., 1941. Grooved Stone Cists, Scotland and the Scillies. *Antiquity*, 57, 81-83.

Piggott, S., 1954a. *The Neolithic Cultures of the British Isles,* Cambridge: Cambridge University Press.

Piggott, S., 1954b. Some Primitive Structures in Achill Island. *Antiquity*, 28, 19-24.

Piggott, S. & T. G. E. Powell, 1948-49. The excavation of three Neolithic chambered tombs in Galloway, 1949. *Proceedings of the Society of Antiquaries of Scotland,* 83, 103-161.

Pollard, T., 1999. The drowned and the saved: archaeological perspectives on the sea as grave, in *The Loved Body's Corruption*, eds. J. Downes & T. Pollard, Glasgow: Cruithne Press, 30-51.

Pollès, R., 1986. Le style de Conguel: nouveaux elements. *Bulletin de la Societe Prehistorique Francaise*, 452-469.

Pool, P. A. S., 1964. Tolcreeg Barrow, Gulval. *Cornish Archaeology*, 3, 105-107.

Pool, P. A. S., 1986. *William Borlase,* Truro: Royal Institution of Cornwall.

Powell, T. G. E., 1941a. Excavation of a Megalithic Tomb at Carriglong, Co. Waterford. *Journal of the Cork Historical and Archaeological Society*, 46, 55-62.

Powell, T. G. E., 1941b. A New Passage Grave in South Eastern Ireland. *Proceedings of the Prehistoric Society,* 7, 142-143.

Powell, T. G. E. & G. E. Daniel, 1956. *Barclodiad y Gawres: The Excavation of a Megalithic Chamber Tomb in Anglesey,* Liverpool: Liverpool University Press.

Pumphrey, R. J., 1956. Contents of the Hearth Sample, in *Barclodiad y Gawres: The Excavation of a Megalithic Chamber Tomb in Anglesey*, eds. T. G. E. Powell & G. E. Daniel, Liverpool: Liverpool University Press.

Quinnell, H., 2010. Pottery in Jones, A M and Thomas, A C Bosiliack and a Reconsideration of Entrance Graves. *Proceedings of the Prehistoric Society*, 76, 277-282.

Quinnell, H., forthcoming. The pottery in Ratcliffe, J, C Johns and A Young, Results of archaeological recording during the 1996 Coast Protection Scheme at Porth Killier and Porth Coose, St Agnes, Isles of Scilly. *Cornish Archaeology*.

Rainbird, P., 1999. Islands Out of Time: Towards a Critique of Island Archaeology. *Journal of Mediterranean Archaeology*, 12(2), 216-234.

Rainbird, P., 2002. A Message for Our Future? The Rapa Nui (Easter Island) Ecodisaster and Pacific Island Environments. *World Archaeology*, 33(3), 436-451.

Rainbird, P., 2007. *The Archaeology of Islands,* Cambridge: Cambridge University Press.

Ratcliffe, J., 1989. *The Archaeology of Scilly,* Truro: Cornwall Archaeological Unit.

Ratcliffe, J., 1991. *Lighting up the Past in Scilly,* Truro: Cornwall Archaeological Unit.

Ratcliffe, J., 1993. Fieldwork in Scilly 1991 and 1992, Truro: Cornwall Archaeological Unit.

Ratcliffe, J., 1997. British Telecom Trenching on St Martin's, Isles of Scilly, Summer 1992, Truro: Cornwall Archaeological Unit.

Ratcliffe, J. & C. Johns, 2003. *Scilly's Archaeological Heritage,* Truro: Twelveheads Press.

Ratcliffe, J., C. Johns & A. Young, forthcoming. Results of archaeological recording during the 1996 Coast Protection Scheme at Porth Killier and Porth Coose, St Agnes, Isles of Scilly. *Cornish Archaeology*.

Ratcliffe, J. & A. Sharpe, 1990a. Archaeological Evaluation for the St Mary's Airport Runway Extension, Truro: Cornwall Archaeological Unit.

Ratcliffe, J. & A. Sharpe, 1990b. Fieldwork in Scilly Autumn 1990, Truro: Cornwall Archaeological Unit.

Ratcliffe, J. & V. Straker, 1996. *The Early Environment of Scilly,* Truro: Cornwall Archaeological Unit.

Reimer, P. J., E. Bard, A. Bayliss, J. W. Beck, P. G. Blackwell, C. Bronk Ramsey, C. E. Buck, H. Cheng, R. L. Edwards, M. Friedrich, P. M. Grootes, T. P. Guilderson, H. Haflidason, I. Hajdas, C. Hatté, T. J. Heaton, D. L. Hoffman, A. G. Hogg, K. A. Hughen, K. F. Kaiser, B. Kromer, S. W. Manning, M. Nu, R. W. Reimer, D. A. Richards, E. M. Scott, J. R. Southon, R. A. Staff, C. S. M. Turney & J. van der Plicht, 2013. IntCal13 and Marine13 Radiocarbon Age Calibration Curves, 0-50,000 Years cal BP. *Radiocarbon,* 55(4), 1869-1887.

Renfrew, C., 1973a. *Before Civilisation,* London: Jonathan Cape.

Renfrew, C., 1973b. Monuments, mobilization and organization in neolithic Wessex, in *The Explanation of Culture Change: Models in Prehistory*, ed. C. Renfrew London: Duckworth, 539-558.

Renfrew, C., 1976. Megaliths, Territories and Populations, in *Acculturation and Continuity in Atlantic Europe: Papers presented at the IV Atlantic Colloquium, Ghent 1975*, ed. S. J. De Laet, Brugge: De Tempel, 198-220.

Renfrew, C., 1979. *Investigations in Orkney,* London: Society of Antiquaries.

Richards, C., 1996. Monuments as Landscape: Creating the Centre of the World in Neolithic Orkney. *World Archaeology,* 28(2), 190-208.

Richardson, A., 2005. Kent - 58F468 A Bronze Age Armlet, Portable Antiquities Scheme: http://finds.org.uk/database/artefacts/record/id/88747, Accessed 3 September 2011.

Robinson, G., 2005. The Prehistoric Island Landscape of Scilly, Unpublished PhD thesis, University College London.

Robinson, G., 2007. *The Prehistoric Island Landscape of Scilly,* Oxford: Archaeopress.

Rowe, T.-m., 2005. *Cornwall in Prehistory,* Stroud: Tempus.

Russell, V., 1971. *West Penwith Survey,* St Austell: Cornwall Archaeological Society.

Russell, V., 1980. *Isles of Scilly Survey*: Isles of Scilly Museum and Institute of Cornish Studies.

Sahlins, M., 1961. The Segmentary Lineage: An Organization of Predatory Expansion. *American Anthropologist,* 63(2:1), 322-345.

Samuels, J. R., 1975. A Coarse Storage Vessel in a Clay-Lined Pit, Pendrathen, St Mary's, Isles of Scilly. *Cornish Archaeology,* 14, 117.

Sawyer, K., 2011a. Multi-Use Games Area (MUGA), South'ard, Bryher, Isles of Scilly: Archaeological recording, St Mary's, Isles of Scilly.

Sawyer, K., 2011b. Sandy Lane Chalet, Middle Town, St Martin's, Isles of Scilly: Archaeological recording, St Mary's, Isles of Scilly.

Scaife, R. G., 1984. A History of Flandrian Vegetation in the Isles of Scilly: Palynological Investigations of High Moors and Lower Moors Peat Mires, St Mary's. *Cornish Studies,* 11, 33-47.

Scarre, C., 2002a. Epilogue: Colour and Materiality in Prehistoric Society, in *Colouring the Past: The Significance of Colour in Archaeological Research,* eds. A. Jones & G. MacGregor, Oxford: Berg, 227-242.

Scarre, C., 2002b. A pattern of islands: the Neolithic monuments of north-west Brittany. *European Journal of Archaeology,* 5(1), 24-41.

Scarre, C., 2007. *The Megalithic Monuments of Britain and Ireland,* London: Thames and Hudson.

Scarre, C., 2008. Herm: Island of the dead? The buried Neolithic landscape of Herm, www.dur.ac.uk/herm.project/: Accessed 8 April 2010.

Scarre, C., 2011a. All at Sea? The island archaeology of Herm (Channel Islands) in its broader regional setting, paper given at the «Hands Across the Water» Conference Bournemouth.

Scarre, C., 2011b. *Landscapes of Neolithic Brittany,* Oxford: Oxford University Press.

Scarre, C., 2011c. Recherches récentes sur L'Île de Herm (Îles anglo-normandes). Note préliminaire *Bulletin de l'Association Manche-Atlantique pour la Recherche Archeologique dans les Iles (on Durham Research Online http://dro.dur.ac.uk/9371/),* 23, 37-46.

Scarre, C., 2011d. Stone people: monuments and identities in the Channel Islands, in *Megaliths and Identities: Early Monuments and Neolithic Societies from the Atlantic to the Baltic,* eds. M. Furholt, F. Lüth & J. Müller, Bonn: Dr. Rudolf Habelt GmbH, 95-104.

Scarre, C., P. Arias, G. Burenhult, M. Fano, L. Oosterbeck, R. Schulting, A. Sheridan & A. Whittle, 2003. Megalithic Chronologies, in *Stones and Bones: Formal disposal of the dead in Atlantic Europe during the Mesolithic-Neolithic interface 6000-3000 BC*, eds. G. Burenhult & S. Westergaard, Oxford: Archaeopress, 65-111.

Schulting, R., A. Sheridan, S. Clarke & C. Bronk Ramsey, 2008. Largantea and the Dating of Irish Wedge Tombs. *The Journal of Irish Archaeology,* 17, 1-17.

Schulting, R., A. Tresset & C. Dupont, 2004. From Harvesting the Sea to Stock Rearing Along the Atlantic Façade of North-West Europe. *Environmental Archaeology,* 9(2), 143-154.

Schulting, R. J., J. Lanting & P. Reimer, 2009. New dates from Tumulus Saint-Michel, Carnac, in *Autour de la Table. Explorations archeologiques et discours savants sur les architectures neolithiques a Locmariaquer, Morbihan (Table des Marchands et Grand Menhir)*, ed. S. Cassen, Nantes: Universite de Nantes, 769-773.

Scourse, J. D., 2006a. Preface, in *The Isles of Scilly Field Guide*, ed. J. D. Scourse, London: Quaternary Research Association, 3-9.

Scourse, J. D., 2006b. Solid geology, in *The Isles of Scilly Field Guide*, ed. J. D. Scourse, London: Quaternary Research Association, 10-12.

Scourse, J. D. (ed.) 2006c. *The Isles of Scilly Field Guide,* London: Quaternary Research Association.

Sebire, H., 2011. *The Archaeology and Early History of the Channel Islands,* Stroud: The History Press.

Shanks, M. & C. Tilley, 1982. Ideology, symbolic power and ritual communication: a reinterpretation of Neolithic mortuary practices, in *Symbolic and structural archaeology*, ed. I. Hodder, Cambridge: Cambridge University Press, 129-154.

Sheridan, A., 2007. Appendix One: The pottery from Cairnderry and Bargrennan, in *From Cairn to Cemetery: An archaeological investigation of the chambered cairns and early Bronze Age mortuary deposits at Cairnderry and Bargrennan White Cairn, south-west Scotland*, eds. V. Cummings & C. Fowler, Oxford: Archaeopress.

Sheridan, A., 2008. Towards a fuller, more nuanced narrative of Chalcolithic and Early Bronze Age Britain 2500–1500 BC. *Bronze Age Review*, 1, 57-78.

Sheridan, A., 2012. Book Review: An Animate Landscape: Rock Art and the Prehistory of Kilmartin, Argyll, Scotland by Andrew Meirion Jones, Davina Freedman, Blaze O'Connor, Hugo Lamdin-Whymark, Richard Tipping and Aaron Watson, in *www.prehistoricsociety. org/files/reviews/An_Animate_Landscape_final_ review.pdf* Accessed 8 April 2013.

Sheridan, A. & A. Shortland, 2004. «... beads which have given rise to so much dogmatism, controversy and rash speculation»: faience in Early Bronze Age Britain and Ireland, in *Scotland in Ancient Europe: The Neolithic and Early Bronze Age of Scotland in their European Context*, eds. I. A. G. Shepherd & G. J. Barclay, Edinburgh: Society of Antiquaries of Scotland, 263-279.

Smith, A., 1863. Narration of the Discovery and Opening of a Kist-vean on the Island of Samson, at Scilly, 3rd September, 1862. *Report of the Royal Institution of Cornwall*, 45, 50-53.

Smith, R. A., 1872. Descriptive list of antiquities near Loch Etive. *Proceedings of the Society of Antiquaries of Scotland*, 9, 396-418.

Spriggs, M., 1985. Prehistoric man-induced landscape enhancement in the Pacific: examples and implications, in *Prehistoric Intensive Agriculture in the Tropics (Part I)*, ed. I. S. Farrington, Oxford: British Archaeological Reports S232, 409-434.

Sprockhoff, E., 1938. *Die nordische Megalithkultur*, Berlin & Leipzig: Walter de Gruyter.

Stone, J. F. S., 1952. Report on Beads from Knackyboy Cairn, St Martin's, Isles of Scilly in O'Neil, B H St J The Excavation of Knackyboy Cairn, St Martin's, Isles of Scilly, 1948. *Antiquaries Journal*, XXXII, 30-34.

Stone, J. F. S. & L. C. Thomas, 1956. The Use and Distribution of Faience in the Ancient East and Prehistoric Europe. *Proceedings of the Prehistoric Society*, XXII, 37-84.

Taylor, S. R. & C. Johns, 2009-2010. Archaeological recording of a multi-period site at Dolphin Town, Tresco, Isles of Scilly. *Cornish Archaeology*, 48-49, 99-125.

Teague Cowan, Z., 1991. *The Story of Samson*, Cirencester: Englang.

Thomas, A. C., 1965. Letter about «Urn sherds from between Old Town and Airport», St Mary's: Isles of Scilly Museum RN 904.

Thomas, A. C., 1984. *Preliminary Report on the Excavation of a Chambered Cairn, Huts and Field-system at Bosiliack, Madron, West Cornwall*, Exeter: Institute of Cornish Studies.

Thomas, A. C., 1985. *Exploration of a Drowned Landscape*, London: Batsford.

Thomas, J., 1988. The Social Significance of Cotswold-Severn Burial Practices. *Man*, 23(3), 540-559.

Thomas, J., 1999. *Understanding the Neolithic*, London: Routledge.

Tilley, C., 1984. Ideology and the legitimation of power in the middle neolithic of southern Sweden, in *Ideology, power and prehistory*, eds. D. Miller & C. Tilley, Cambridge: Cambridge University Press, 111-146.

Tilley, C., 1994. *A Phenomenology of Landscape* Oxford: Berg.

Tilley, C., 1995. Rocks as resources: landscapes and power. *Cornish Archaeology*, 34, 5-57.

Tilley, C., 1996. The Powers of Rocks: Topography and Monument Construction on Bodmin Moor. *World Archaeology*, 28(2), 161-176.

Tilley, C. & W. Bennett, 2001. An Archaeology of Supernatural Places: The Case of West Penwith. *Journal of the Royal Anthropological Institute*, 7, 335-362.

Troutbeck, J., 1796. *A Survey of the Ancient and Present State of the Scilly Islands*, Sherborne.

Tyacke, A., 2010. Corn - C5CCB7 A Post Medieval Bead, Portable Antiquities Scheme: http://finds.org. uk/database/artefacts/record/id/289980, Accessed 3 September 2011.

Ulguim, P. F., 2011. Skeletal Assessment Report: The Analyses of Human Cremated Remains from four archaeological sites of the Bronze Age period, Unpublished MSc dissertation, University of Exeter.

Van de Noort, R., 2003. An ancient seascape: the social context of seafaring in the early Bronze Age. *World Archaeology*, 35(3), 404-415.

Wailes, B., 1976. Review: Ancient Scilly by Paul Ashbee. *Antiquity*, 50, 242-243.

Watson, A. & D. Keating, 1999. Architecture and sound: an acoustic analysis of megalithic monuments in prehistoric Britain. *Antiquity*, 73, 325-336.

Watson, A. & D. Keating, 2000. The Architecture of Sound in Neolithic Orkney, in *Neolithic Orkney in its European context*, ed. A. Ritchie, Cambridge: McDonald Institute for Archaeological Research, 259-263.

Weatherhill, C., 1981. *Belerion, Ancient Sites of Land's End*, Tiverton: Cornwall Books.

Wickham-Jones, C. R., 2004. The worked pumice, in *Camas Daraich: a Mesolithic site at the Point of Sleat, Skye*, eds. C. R. Wickham-Jones & K. Hardy, Edinburgh: Society of Antiquaries of Scotland, 48-49.

Wilson, G., 1874-1876. Notes on a Collection of Stone Implements and Other Antiquities, from Glenluce, Wigtownshire, now presented to the Museum. *Proceedings of the Society of Antiquaries of Scotland,* 11, 580-587.

Woodley, G., 1822. *A View of the Present State of the Scilly Islands,* London.

Woodley, G., 1833. *Appendix to a View of the Present State of the Scilly Islands,* London.

Woodman, P. C., 1992. Filling in the spaces in Irish prehistory. *Antiquity,* 66, 295-314.

Woodman, P. C., 2012. Making Yourself at Home on an Island: The First 1000 Years (+?) of the Irish Mesolithic. *Proceedings of the Prehistoric Society,* 78, 1-34.